LET'S GO
www.letsgo.com

ROME, VENICE & FLORENCE

researcher-writers
Julia Rooney
Alex Tomko
Elizabeth Weinbloom

staff writers
Sophie Arlow
Juan Cantu
Rachel Granetz
Mark Warren

research manager
Chris Kingston

editor
Bronwen Beseda O'Herin

managing editor
Marykate Jasper

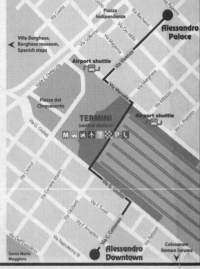

CONTENTS

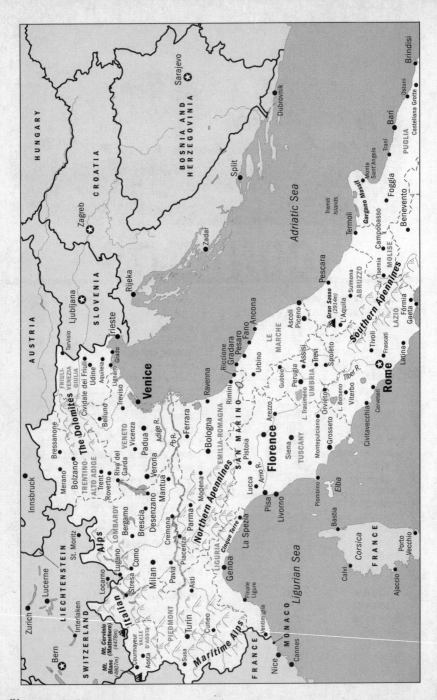

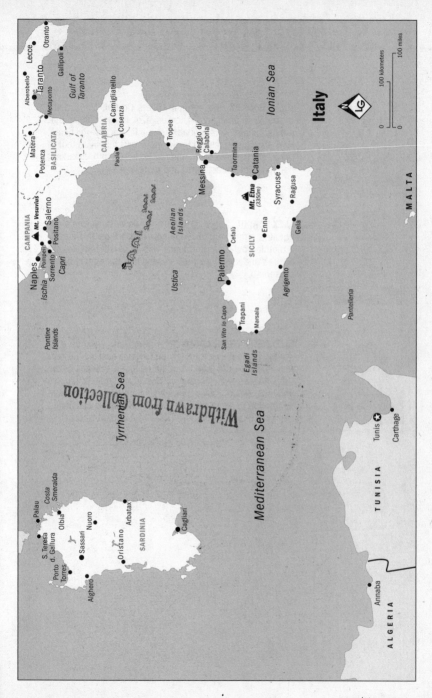

Italy

Ionian Sea

Tyrrhenian Sea

Mediterranean Sea

MALTA

TUNISIA

ALGERIA

Lecce
Otranto
Alberobello
Taranto
Gallipoli
Metaponto
Gulf of Taranto
Matera
BASILICATA
Potenza
Camigliatello
Cosenza
CALABRIA
Tropea
Paola
Reggio di Calabria
Taormina
Messina
Catania
Mt. Etna (3350m)
Syracuse
Ragusa
Cefalù
Enna
SICILY
Gela
Palermo
Agrigento
Ustica
Aeolian Islands
CAMPANIA
Naples
Mt. Vesuvius
Salerno
Pompeii
Positano
Sorrento
Capri
Ischia
San Vito lo Capo
Trapani
Marsala
Egadi Islands
Pontine Islands
Pantelleria
Palau
Costa Smeralda
Olbia
S. Teresa di Gallura
Arbatax
Nuoro
Sassari
Oristano
SARDINIA
Cagliari
Porto d. Torres
Alghero
Annaba
Tunis
Carthage

0   100 kilometers
0   100 miles

RESEARCHER-WRITERS

JULIA ROONEY. This veteran of *Let's Go Italy 2009* demonstrated a prodigious knowledge of Italian culture that put her editors—and probably even a few locals—to shame. From trying (and failing) to sketch Marcus Aurelius's foot to devouring dangerous amounts of Roman gelato, Julia kept her cool with perfect prose and *perfetto italiano*.

ALEX TOMKO. Refusing to be worn down by Venice's antiquated structure, Alex somehow found time to train for a triathlon between afternoons visiting palatial hotels and nights wandering the streets in search of the perfect bar in Dorsoduro.

ELiZABETH WEINBLOOM. After the Dark Ages of grad school, Elizabeth went to Italy for *Let's Go* seeking her own Renaissance—and found it in the hallowed galleries of the Uffizi. After stressful encounters with Tuscan train schedules and angry San Gimignano nuns, Elizabeth resisted the temptation to settle down in Lucca and instead completed her route like a champ.

DISCOVER

ROME, VENICE & FLORENCE

Congratulations! If you're reading this, you've likely made the wise (if not entirely original) decision to spend some time in three of the world's greatest cities: Rome, Venice, and Florence. Yes, these are the destinations everyone hopes to visit, but they've got their must-see reputations for a reason. People come here to live out the romance of moonlit gondola rides in Venetian canals, melting gelato in the sun-baked Piazza della Signoria, and sunset at the Colosseum; to revel in the spine-tingling, larger-than-life testaments to the human spirit that fill the Sistine Chapel and Uffizi. All three cities are ready to reward you with as many magical moments as you can handle—so long as you're ready to embrace them. Some travelers find Italy's quirks (supermarkets closed on Sunday, spotty air-conditioning, etc.) frustrating and let that get in the way of their experience abroad. As a student traveler, however, you are uniquely situated to experience Rome, Venice, and Florence in all their ridiculousness *and* sublimity. Striking out on your own, likely on a budget, you'll open yourself up to what someone who stays at the swankiest hotel and eats at all the five-star restaurants misses: making connections with the people and way of life in these metropolises. *Let's Go* researchers have reported being given copious amounts of free food, receiving unsolicited assistance from disinterested passersby, and sharing drinks with complete strangers. It's not like they wear neon orange *Let's Go* T-shirts while they're covering the region—they were treated this way because as they navigated the caprices of cities in which things we take for granted ("the customer is always right," street signs, etc.) are conspicuously absent, they reached out to locals and adapted themselves to their new surroundings. You too can learn to see the beauty of Italy's sometimes befuddling customs, as getting to know the people of these cities becomes as much a priority as taking in all the Renaissance art, Roman grandeur, and religious relics. Who knows? Maybe by the time you're ready to leave, some of those Italian oddities won't seem so ridiculous after all.

when to go

The number-one reason to study abroad in Rome, Venice, or Florence is the opportunity to visit these cities in the spring or fall, when the weather is mild and the tourist hordes have dwindled. However, if you can't figure out a good excuse to spend a semester in Italy and have already booked your tickets to Cabo for spring break, be prepared to deal with summer crowds and heat: in Rome and Florence, temperatures climb into the mid-90s. Unlike Rome and Florence, Venice is also plagued by humidity during the summer months. Most Italians go on vacation in August, so follow their lead and find somewhere else to be during this month (Winnipeg, perhaps?).

You can expect cooler temperatures during the winter (in the 40s and 50s, slightly colder in Venice) as well as rain in Venice and Florence. Many sights keep shorter winter hours, and some hotels and restaurants even take vacation during this part of the year. When your wait to enter the Vatican Museum is only 10min. and doesn't involve heatstroke, you'll be glad you chose to take on these minor inconveniences.

top 5 places to dine alfresco

5. PALATINE HILL: Have your slave serve you up a gourmet picnic and live like a modern-day emperor in the place that was once home to rulers of a more ancient Roman variety.

4. PONTE VECCHIO: It may not be Tiffany's, but breakfast while gazing through the windows of the jewelry shops along this Florentine bridge will put a smile on any diva's face.

3. PIAZZA NAVONA: Chow down on pizza *alla Romana* while enjoying Rome's Baroque jewel.

2. VENICE'S CAMPANILE: See if you can make it to the top of the city's iconic 325 ft. bell tower without letting your gelato melt.

1. DAVID: Eat a juicy fig at the foot of Michelangelo's famous statue in Florence...and don't forget a leaf to cover him up.

what to do

EATING IN THE MOTHERLAND OF THE CARBO-LOAD

Yes, this is the land of pizza, pasta, risotto, and polenta, but it's also where fresh, quality ingredients reign supreme. In this way, Italy is totally on-trend—indeed, pre-trend—as it anticipated the whole locavore thing before it even began. Focusing your travels on just three cities, you can conduct your own informal study of three of the country's regional cuisines. In Rome, delight in the fresh produce of the fertile Lazio region and home-style cooking that wastes nothing (tripe, anyone?). In Venice, indulge in the fruits of the Adriatic as well as the wild game and mushrooms of the northern Italian mainland. And in Florence, revel in Tuscan specialties like *panzanella* (a summer bread salad), *ribollita* (a soup made with seasonal veggies, beans, and bread), and *bistecca alla fiorentina*. Even if you can't splurge on a multi-course feast every night, you can still eat like royalty in any of these cities if you know where to look. Hit up grocers for gourmet picnics, *fornaio*s for sinfully affordable pizza, and *aperitivo* happy hours for assorted *antipasti* and the house wine: the local sensibility shines through whatever you order. Is Treviso radicchio in season? You can bet you'll find it in the pasta dish you order in Venice, but don't count on finding it on the pizza you scarf down in Rome. So make like a cow and graze your way through these cities—you'll probably wish you had four stomachs, too.

- **GUSTO:** Stop by this combination *ristorante*, pizzeria, and *enoteca* during happy hour to fill up on a buffet of gourmet *antipasti* before a night out in the Piazza di Spagna. (Rome; p. 70.)

- **NAVE DE ORO:** This Venetian *enoteca* with multiple outposts invites you to fill up your empty bottles with any of the regional wines sold by the liter. (Venice; p. 156.)

- **ANTICA GELATERIA FIORENTINA:** Sample off-beat flavors like rosewater, cheesecake, and green tea—no need to limit yourself, as a scoop of one variety costs only €1. (Florence; p. 218.)

- **CACIO E PEPE:** Take your obligatory trip to Vatican City as an excuse to eat this friendly trattoria's heaping plate of fresh egg pasta topped with oil, grated cheese, and black pepper. (Rome; p. 74.)

- **DA VINATTIERI:** This hole-in-the-wall sandwich joint will make your delectable panini to order on classic Tuscan bread for a lunch that'll set you back no more than €3.50. (Florence; p. 216.)

WHERE REBIRTH WAS BORN

If this book were titled *Let's Go: Rome, Venice, Florence, and the Louvre*, we'd be covering practically every must-see work of art in the western hemisphere. As it is, we're covering quite a lot. Plan your time wisely to avoid lines and crowds as best you can, and then get ready to marvel at the wonders of humanity. Men like Leonardo and Michelangelo, who ushered in the humanistic spirit of the Renaissance, created the art that fills these cities with you in mind: they stretched the bounds of human expression to prove what we were capable of doing, and the sense of excitement in their accomplishment that radiates from their work is contagious. Sure, Florence can start feeling like the Medici's giant Renaissance storage facility, but when it seems as if you just can't handle even one more Madonna and Child, take a minute to dig a little deeper into what makes these artistic wonders so special. Escape the crowd in the Sistine Chapel as you imagine what it would be like to lie on your back, paint dripping down on your face, as you attempt to depict something as epic as the creation of the world. Ponder what Venus might be thinking and feeling as she pulls tendrils of windswept hair about her in Botticelli's famous painting. Blow on the Bernini sculptures in the Galleria Borghese and see if they come to life. Take pleasure in all the vitality of these eternally captivating works of art.

- **UFFIZI GALLERY:** This is where you'll find Botticelli's biggies: *Birth of Venus, Allegory of Spring, Adoration of the Magi,* and *Slander.* Even if you don't get why these are touchstones of art history, you've got to admit that Venus is pretty damn sexy. (Florence; p. 197.)

- **VATICAN MUSEUMS:** All the goodies the Catholic church hauled in for itself during its succession of the Roman Empire as the arbiter of culture in the Western world. Resist the urge to race through these museums in order to reach the Sistine Chapel. (Rome; p. 52.)

- **GALLERIA DELL'ACCADEMIA:** Even more hot Florentine nudity, this time in male form. Spend some time in this home of Michelangelo's *David* and a surprisingly informative musical instruments exhibit. (Florence; p. 206.)

- **PALAZZO DUCALE:** Get a feel for Venetian-style Renaissance opulence at this complex that once served as residence to the city's mayor. Don't miss hometown hero Tintoretto's *Paradise.* (Venice; p. 128.)

LIVING AT NIGHT

Get ready to forget what "staying in" means as you explore the nighttime scene in Rome, Venice, and Florence. While you'll be able to find an ample supply of clubs, bars, and lounges in Rome, a fair number in Florence, and a good handful in Venice, you'll also want to take advantage of these cities' hot summer nights, cheap local wine, and picturesque *piazze* to make your own nightlife, a kind that might not fly in the puritanical US of A. Be sure to start your night at an *aperitivo* happy hour for a dinner of buffet-style *antipasti* that won't break the bank. Don't forget to take in all the sights you've visited during the daytime after the sun sets. Floodlit after dusk, places like Campo de' Fiori and the Ponte Vecchio become even more romantic when some wine and the darkness of the witching hours bring the spirits of the historic cobbled streets to life.

Please avoid being the ugly American who drinks simply to get wasted. Take a tip from the natives and let a few glasses of good wine or Vin Santo work their

student superlatives

- **MOST PROMISING FIXER-UPPER:** All that's needed is a few tons of marble and roughly 40,000 Christian slaves to bring the Baths of Diocletian (p. 57) back to their former glory.

- **MOST LIKELY TO SUCCEED:** The enterprising Piazzale Michelangelo (p. 214) somehow managed to transcend its primary purpose as a parking lot, becoming a destination for millions of camera-toting tourists. If you've seen a photo of Florence, it was probably taken here.

- **MOST GLAMOROUS:** Each year, the Venice Film Festival (p. 174) brings stars to the city's beach resort on the island of Lido.

- **MOST BLING:** The pope's crib (a.k.a. Vatican City, p. 22), where you'll find Swiss guards donning tricked out colorful uniforms and the sickest frescoes ever, yo.

- **MOST ONE-OF-A-KIND:** Club Piccolo Mondo (p. 167) is Venice's only club, quite the rebel among all of the city's conformist canals and *palazzi*.

enlightening effect, allowing you to appreciate your city of choice with a renewed, slightly intoxicated enjoyment. Don't chug a bottle of the cheapest stuff you can find in order to have a crazy night that ends with you passed out on David's shoulders— he probably won't appreciate it, and you'll be missing all the magic of Florence at night.

- **PIAZZA COLONNA:** After taking in a moonlit Pantheon, head to this square midweek for some low-key Italian-style drinking and mingling. Enjoy observing the people strolling up V. del Corso. (Rome; p. 83.)

- **LAS PALMAS:** Soak up the block-party feel of this happening bar that fills up a blacktop-like *piazza* with an ample *aperitivo* buffet, summer film screenings, and plenty of welcoming conviviality. (Florence; p. 229.)

- **CAMPO SAN MARGHERITA:** This is the place to go for Venetian nightlife. Start the evening entertainment before sunset at your choice of dance or jazz club, Irish pub, or relaxed bar and lounge. (Venice; p. 167.)

- **AKAB:** A *Let's Go* favorite of Rome's Monte Testaccio club scene, Akab offers live music and dancing in a hip setting. (Rome; p. 94.)

- **PONTE VECCHIO:** The ultimate nighttime stop for a romantic smooch or two after hours. (Florence; p. 202.)

BEYOND TOURISM

Hate tourists? Then don't be one. Instead, travel to Rome, Venice, or Florence as a student, volunteer, or salaried employee. It's hard to dread the first day of school when Rome is your campus and heaping bowls of pasta *al dente* and creamy gelato *alla fragola* make up your meal plan. Those with especial interests in art and architecture, archaeology and ancient civilizations, fashion design, or food and wine will find a wealth of study-abroad programs that take advantage of these cities' particular resources in such areas. The Indiana Jones wannabes among you can volunteer in archaeology work camps. Resumé-padders ought to consider interning in a Florentine architecture firm. Hippies might check out the World Wide Organization of Organic Farming (WWOOF) to find out about opportunities to get down-and-dirty on organic farms in the land outside the city, and those with magical, bottomless carpetbags and umbrellas with talking-parrot handles should look into au pairing adorable Italian *bambini*.

Living as a non-tourist in Italy, you'll gain an interesting perspective on local culture as well as undeniable street cred. Plus, it's super-cool when you begin to blend in so well that American tourists bust out their broken Italian to ask you for directions. Not many people can call Venice their home-away-from-home, but as a student, volunteer, or worker in the city, you'll earn that privilege.

- **UNIVERSITÀ DEGLI STUDI DI ROMA SAPIENZA:** Party a semester away at this university conveniently located near Rome's Termini train station. (Rome; p. 270.)

- **STUDIO ART CENTERS INTERNATIONAL:** Enroll in a year-long program to receive a Post-Baccalaureate Certificate in art, art history, or art conservation—or just futz around the beautiful city during the summer. (Florence; p. 272.)

- **ARCHAEOSPAIN:** When you aren't clubbing at Monte Testaccio, come dig up the ruins of the "ancient pottery dump" left here by people of the first few centuries. (Rome; p. 272.)

- **PEGGY GUGGENHEIM COLLECTION:** Intern at this first-rate museum that boasts works by artistic superstars like Miró, Picasso, Dalí, and Magritte and calls a gorgeous *palazzo* its home. (Venice; p. 275.)

- **APICIUS INTERNATIONAL SCHOOL OF HOSPITALITY:** Train to be a chef, sommelier, baker, or just someone who really appreciates food and wine at this hospitality school with a culinary wing. (Florence; p. 272.)

suggested itineraries

BEST OF ROME, VENICE, AND FLORENCE IN 15 DAYS
Have fun exploring this holy trinity of Italian cities.

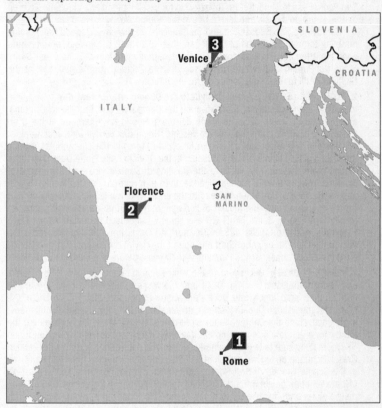

1. ROME (7 DAYS): Start out strong, hitting the Colosseum, Roman Forum, and Velabrum in the morning, then moving on to Trastevere through the Isola Tiberina to check out Gianicolo Hill and the lovely Chiesa Di Santa Maria. End your **first day** with dinner at one of the neighborhood's homey trattorias and then soak up its vibrant nightlife. Make Vatican City your destination for **day two,** giving yourself enough time to thoroughly explore the Musei Vaticani and St. Peter's Basilica as well as the Sistine Chapel. For a comparatively low-key chaser, head to Castel Sant'Angelo before grabbing dinner. Cool off with some jazz at Fonclea and icy goodness at Old Bridge Gelateria to complete the evening. Begin your **third day** at the Galleria Borghese (remember to reserve your ticket in advance) and then eat a picnic brunch in the gardens that surround the museum. Follow V. Veneto to Capuchin Crypt and Piazza

Barberini. Try to erase the crypt's reminder of your mortality from your memory as you spend the rest of the day shopping and eating your way through the area around the Fontana di Trevi, Piazza di Spagna, and Piazza del Popolo. Make **day four** one of pilgrimage to Rome's best churches. Start with San Giovanni in Laterano, San Clemente, Santa Maria Maggiore, and San Pietro in Vincoli. Take a siesta, then head to Centro Storico for San Luigi dei Francesi and the Pantheon, an equally inspiring religious structure. Spend your **fifth day** in southern Rome, diving back into ancient history with a visit to the Circus Maximus. If you're ready for a walk, head to the Centrale Montemartini, or take the metro to get there and to reach the Basilica di San Paolo Fuori le Mura. Return to Testaccio for excellent food and clubbing. Go even deeper south on **day six** and take a bus to the Appian Way, where you can investigate the Catacombo San Sebastiano and San Callisto. On **day seven,** spend the morning rambling through the Baths of Diocletian, then head to P. del Popolo for lunch and pass the afternoon strolling down V. del Corso, making detours to check out Santa Maria del Popolo church and the Museo dell'Ara Pacis at your leisure. End at the Capitoline Hill for one final survey of the eternal city.

2. FLORENCE (5 DAYS): Head straight to the Duomo on your **first day,** taking time to explore the Baptistery of San Giovanni, the Campanile and Brunelleschi's dome, and the Museo Opera di Santa Maria del Fiore. Spend the afternoon at the Uffizi (reserve in advance) and the Palazzo Vecchio. Begin **day two** viewing sculptures at the Bargello and Accademia. Get your fill of San Marco in the afternoon by visiting the Museo di San Marco and the Museum of the Opificio Delle Pietre Dure. **Day three** means more religion, with visits to the Basilica di Santa Croce and Synagogue of Florence. Wander around P. della Signoria, then turn north to Palazzo Medici Ricardi and the Basilica di San Lorenzo. Head to the environs of Santa Maria Novella on your **fourth day.** Don't miss the Museo di Ferragamo, then hit up other small sights like the Palazzo Strozzi, Santa Maria Novella church, the Museo Nazionale Alinari Della Fotografia, and the Chiesa di San Salvatore Ad Ognissanti. On **day five,** cross the river to the Oltrarno neighborhood and spend the day at the Palazzo Pitti and Boboli Gardens. Catch sunset at the Piazzale Michelangelo before you move on to Venice.

3. VENICE (4 DAYS): Begin your visit in Venice's most famous square, P. San Marco, and tour its majestic basilica. Duck into the Museo Correr to escape the tourist hordes, then grab lunch and do a little window shopping along Calle Larga XXII Marzo. Hit the Palazzo Ducale for hardcore Venetian history. If you want the full tourist experience, climb the Campanile for a pre-dinner stretch of the legs or shell out the money for a gondola ride to complete **day one.** Start your **second day** around Rialto Bridge, making sure to take in its market scene and considering a stop in the Palazzo Grassi. Continue on to Frari church in San Polo and check out the Tintoretto canvases in the Scuola Grande di San Rocco. After lunch, move on to Dorsoduro, *Let's Go's* favorite Venetian neighborhood. Tour the Peggy Guggenheim Collection, Santa Maria della Salute, and, if you're up to it, the Accademia. Consider rounding out your day with a vaporetto ride down the Grand Canal. On **day three,** explore the lagoon by vaporetto, stopping at Lido and Burano. Head to Santa Croce and fill your afternoon with Venice's Museum of Natural History. Eat an affordable meal in the neighborhood and wander back to see P. San Marco at night. Hit the Ca' d'Oro on **day four** and stroll through the Jewish Ghetto midday. Do any last-minute shopping or return to a museum you missed or of which you'd like to see more. Then party it up around the Campo Santa Margherita as you say goodbye to *Venezia.*

THAT'S AMORE

Celebrate life and love in the places where *la dolce vita* was invented.

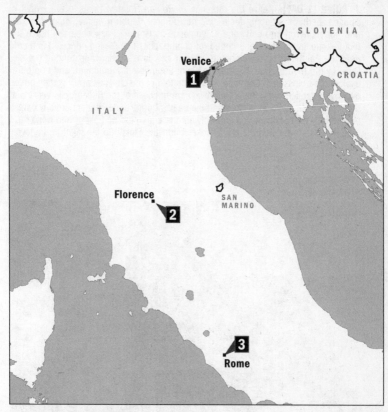

1. VENICE (2 DAYS): Spend your first few hours on a cruise of the grand canal and get those thoughts of love going as you're inspired by the city's beauty. At lunchtime, head to the market at Rialto Bridge and pick up something for your honey. Then traipse on over to P. San Marco and take in the sights. At sunset, don't forget to take a gondola ride so that you can kiss your sweetcakes under the Bridge of Sighs, thereby ensuring your eternal love and happiness together. **Next morning,** take to the high seas of Venice's lagoon, stopping at Burano to buy some wedding-appropriate lace. Lunch in Dorsoduro and spend the afternoon at one of its museums. Have dinner at a romantic canal-side restaurant and then meander toward P. San Marco to enjoy drinks or dessert.

2. FLORENCE (2 DAYS): Get to the Ponte Vecchio to buy a little sumthin'-sumthin' for your poopsie, then head to the Duomo. Try climbing the dome or tower of the famous church. Your head will be swimming before you even have a chance to land a wet one on the apple of your eye, and you'll be rewarded with an equally swoon-inducing view. Dine in the romantic setting of Osteria dell Porcellino's alleyway space and head to P. della Signoria for a lovely (and hopefully love-filled) evening. Start **day two** at the Uffizi, where the beauty of Botticelli's paintings should get you in the mood to cuddle. In the afternoon, romp through the Boboli gardens with your loved one. At nightfall, head to Ponte Santa Trinita for some scenic canoodling.

3. ROME (1 DAY): Relive the romance of *Roman Holiday*. Head to the Piazza di Spagna, perhaps stopping for a chic new Aubrey Hepburn haircut along the way, and hopefully run into someone as gorgeous as Gregory Peck when you reach the picturesque steps. Stop for a coffee (or champagne, if you're the princess) in a cafe near the Pantheon before hopping on your new love's Vespa and touring the city. Drive by the Theater of Marcellus, the Victor Emanuele II monument, and hop off to explore the Colosseum. Continue your Vespa tour of the city; just avoid getting pulled over by the police. Now check your lover's truthfulness at the Bocca della Verita and then head to Castel Sant'Angelo and the nearby bridge to see if there are any barges parked for a party. Luckily, you probably are not a princess on holiday and won't have to leave your lover when the clock strikes midnight. Finish up the night in the lovely Piazza Navona.

THE DARK SIDE

You really don't want to spend too much time wallowing in all the dark stuff, but Rome, Venice, and Florence aren't all Renaissance beauty and light. If you're feeling morbid, here's a quick tour that should satisfy your mood.

1. ROME (1 DAY): Delight in your mortality at the Cappucin Crypt, be reminded of the history of human suffering at Mamertine Prison, and take in all the catacombs you can handle along the Appian Way.

2. VENICE (1 DAY): Buy yourself a creepy plague-doctor mask (you know, the ones with the spooky beak-like nose) and don it as you explore a city that was ravaged by the epidemic back in the day. Make sure to wander through the labyrinth of cells in the dungeon prison of the Palazzo Ducale and remember that the Bridge of Sighs is named as such due to the final outtake of breath prisoners awaiting execution would give as they saw it before they died.

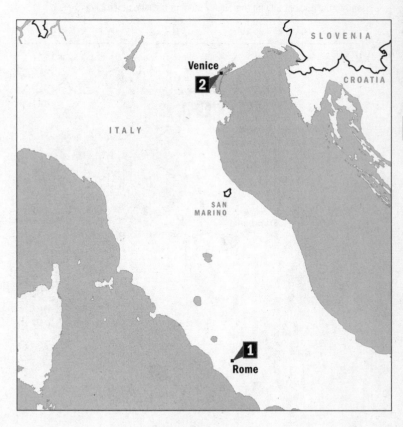

BACK TO THE FUTURE

As much as these cities are all about their past, they've also got a ⚓**boat**load of contemporary stuff going for them.

1. VENICE (2 DAYS): Take in the wonderful modern art museums found in this city, including the Palazzo Grassi, Punta della Dogana, and Guggenheim collection. If you can, come when the Biennale, a contemporary arts event, is in session (in 2011, June 4-Nov 27). Eat at a restaurant less rooted in tradition like San Marco's Trattoria Pizzeria Ai Fabbri.

2. FLORENCE (1 DAY): See what's new in footwear at the Museo di Ferragamo, and turn to Palazzo Strozzi for contemporary exhibits. Immerse yourself in the modern soccer phenomenon with a visit to Stadio Artemio Franchi, the home of Florence's team.

3. ROME (2 DAYS): For a taste of Rome's modern art scene, take in the exhibits at Palazzo della Esposizione, Fondazione Roma Museo, and Galleria d'Arte Moderna. Head to the Ancient City for thoroughly modern nightlife at Ice Club.

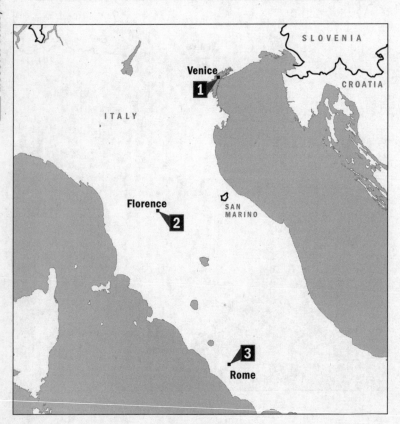

how to use this book

CHAPTERS

In the next few pages, the travel coverage chapters—the meat of any *Let's Go* book—will begin. They proceed in the order of this book's title: Rome, Venice, then Florence.

But that's not all, folks. We also have a few extra chapters for you to peruse:

CHAPTER	DESCRIPTION
Discover Rome, Venice & Florence	Discover tells you what to do, when to do it, and where to go for it. The absolute coolest things about any destination get highlighted in this chapter at the front of all *Let's Go* books.
Essentials	Essentials contains the practical info you need before, during, and after your trip–visas, regional transportation, health and safety, phrasebooks, and more.
Rome, Venice & Florence 101	Rome, Venice and Florence 101 is just what it sounds like–a crash course in where you're traveling. This short chapter on the history and culture of these cities makes great reading on a long plane ride.
Beyond Tourism	As students ourselves, we at *Let's Go* encourage studying abroad, or going beyond tourism more generally, every chance we get. This chapter lists ideas for how to study, volunteer, or work abroad with other young travelers in Rome, Venice, and Florence to get more out of your trip.

LISTINGS

Listings—a.k.a. reviews of individual establishments—constitute a majority of Let's Go coverage. Our Researcher-Writers list establishments in order from **best to worst value**—not necessarily quality. (Obviously a five-star hotel is nicer than a hostel, but it would probably be ranked lower because it's not as good a value.) Listings pack in a lot of information, but it's easy to digest if you know how they're constructed:

ESTABLISHMENT NAME 💳🚫💳♿🚫♿📶🍸❄⛅▼ type of establishment ❶
Address ☎phone number 🖥website
Editorial review goes here.
✥ Directions to the establishment. ℹ Other practical information about the establishment, like age restrictions at a club or whether breakfast is included at a hostel. $ Prices for goods or services. ⏰ Hours or schedules.

ICONS

First things first: places and things that we absolutely love, sappily cherish, generally obsess over, and wholeheartedly endorse are denoted by the all-empowering 👍**Let's Go thumbs-up.** In addition, the icons scattered throughout a listing (as you saw in the sample above) can tell you a lot about an establishment. The following icons answer a series of yes-no questions about a place:

💳	Credit cards accepted	🚫💳	Cash only	♿	Wheelchair-accessible
🚫♿	Not wheelchair-accessible	📶	Internet access available	🍸	Alcohol served
❄	Air-conditioned	⛅	Outdoor seating available	▼	GLBT or GLBT-friendly

The rest are visual cues to help you navigate each listing:

☎	Phone numbers	🖥	Websites	✥	Directions
ℹ	Other hard info	$	Prices	⏰	Hours

OTHER USEFUL STUFF

Area codes for each destination appear in the orientation section for that city, in a box helpfully titled, "Call me!" Finally, in order to pack the book with as much information as possible, we have used a few **standard abbreviations.** You'll see these generally in addresses or directions, where Via becomes V., Viale becomes Vle., Piazza becomes P., and Corso becomes C. In Venice, if the directions begin "V:," it indicates a vaporetto stop.

PRICE DIVERSITY

A final set of icons corresponds to what we call our "price diversity" scale, which approximates how much money you can expect to spend at a given establishment. For **accommodations,** we base our range on the cheapest price for which a single traveler can stay for one night. For **food,** we estimate the average amount one traveler will spend in one sitting. The table below tells you what you'll *typically* find in these three cities at the corresponding price range, but keep in mind that no system can allow for the quirks of individual establishments.

ACCOMMODATIONS	RANGE	WHAT YOU'RE LIKELY TO FIND
❶	under €20	Generally a bed in a hostel dorm room or a campsite. Expect bunk beds and a shared bath. You may have to provide or rent towels and sheets.
❷	€20-30	Upper-end hostels or decidedly lower-end hotels. If you get a private room in this range, chances are it will be decidedly tiny. It's unlikely you'll have a private bathroom, either.
❸	€31-45	A small room with a private bath. Should have decent amenities, such as phone and TV.
❹	€46-65	Should have bigger rooms than a ❸, with more amenities or in a more convenient location. Breakfast probably included.
❺	over €65	Large hotels or upscale chains. If it's a ❺ and it doesn't have the perks you want (and more), you've paid too much.

FOOD	RANGE	WHAT YOU'RE LIKELY TO FIND
❶	under €7	A wide variety of establishments, most commonly bakeries or *gelaterie*. Some of the cheapest pizzerias or cafes may squeeze into here. A ❶ is unlikely to have table seating.
❷	€7-15	Cheap restaurants or expensive cafes. Most ethnic eateries are a ❷. You should generally be able to sit down.
❸	€16-25	A good-quality restaurant. Since you'll have the luxury of a waiter, tip will set you back a little extra.
❹	€26-33	A fancy restaurant. Entrees tend to be heartier or more elaborate, but you're really paying for decor and ambience. Few restaurants in this range have a dress code, but some may look down on T-shirts and sandals.
❺	over €33	We list very few ❺s, so if when we do, there's a reason—it's something fabulous, famous, or both. Slacks and dress shirts may be expected. Offers foreign-sounding food and a decent wine list. Don't order a PB and J.

ROME

Rome: the epitome of Italy, and its biggest enigma. It condenses every stereotype that plagues the country into one sprawling metropolis...and then rambles on another few kilometers and centuries to reverse them all. With neighborhoods off the map and streets too small to be mapped, this is a city as expansive as it is walkable, as global as it is local. And here's the biggest paradox of all: it's as young as it is old. And that doesn't mean Rome averages out to some middle-aged soccer mom. This city will blow your ears out with teenage gusto and shake its finger at you in codgerly reproval. Within its confines, crumbling bricks fight for space with candy-colored hotels, and centuries-old cobblestones shake to their bones as rubber tires roll over their weathered surface.

Good food, great art, and grand people—it's all here. But you could get these things in any Italian city (and honestly, Rome wouldn't win the prize in any of these categories). Instead, for every "quintessentially Italian" item you check off your list while here, Rome, challenging the tourists who come simply to make the rounds, will hit you with five more experiences that truly define the Italian character—and bend your preconceptions about what exactly that is. Don't expect to conquer Rome, especially not with a list. (Carthage tried to do it with an entire army and failed.)

Don't be fooled by the hundreds of postcards simplifying Rome's streets: the Eternal City is anything but picture perfect. Dirtier than Naples, bigger than Naples, and rougher than Florence, this is a city to be reckoned with. Rather than bowing to its tourists, it nods it head in recognition of them and marches on its way. Sometimes, like the speeding Vespas that only stop when you walk in front of them, Rome requires that you stand up to it. Are you ready for the challenge?

greatest hits

- **BUY ONE COUNTRY, GET ONE FREE.** Fed up with Italy? The Vatican City, small but magnificent, is still doing pretty well for itself (p. 22).
- **HOSTEL HEAVEN.** Rolling into Termini station, you're on the brink of one of Europe's biggest concentrations of cheap beds (p. 31).
- **ANCIENT ANTIQUES.** The Colosseum is just the beginning of Ancient Rome's gifts to the modern city (p. 35).

student life

It's not only archaeology students who'll find something of interest in Rome. For a destination with such a prominent Ancient City, Rome is shockingly young, with a culture that's strongly influenced by its students and 20-something residents. The 147,000 students of Rome's **Sapienza University** give the city one of Europe's largest student bodies. Sapienza is based in the San Lorenzo neighborhood a little to the east of Termini Station. By a convenient coincidence, that puts it right next to tourists' main entrance point and the city's highest concentration of budget accommodations. If you're wondering where the young people stay, this area is the answer. In a remarkably unsurprising development, the combination of students and student travelers in Termini has transformed this area into one of the city's biggest nighttime destinations, with bars and clubs crowding the streets. Be aware that students aren't the only people around after dark: pickpockets love to operate here.

As much as Termini and San Lorenzo are the central student destinations, they're just the beginning in this diverse city. The **Centro Storico** may be full of Roman *piazze* and grand temples to the dead, but it also features extremely accessible bars that serve great *aperitivo* buffets each night. Try Drunken Ship if you've been away from a beer pong table for a little too long. To find international students, head across the Tiber to **Trastevere,** home of an American liberal arts college, John Cabot University. This is a favorite haunt of study abroad students, so come here and relax in Cafe Friends anytime between 7am and 2am. The southern neighborhoods of **Testaccio and Ostiense** are other great options. Or just chill at the Colosseum. Just because we're students doesn't mean we don't care about history, right? In Rome, though, with so much going on in the present, you just might forget to appreciate what the city is most famous for: its past.

orientation

call me!

The phone code for Rome is ☎06.

Rome is easily navigable on foot: every time you think you might be lost, another monument pops up and you're back on track. And when it's not a monument, it's a river, park, or ruin. Geographically (and perhaps metaphorically, as well), the best way to think of Rome is as a body: a few major arteries (some with significant blockage problems) will take you from region to region, while countless capillaries branch off into compact neighborhoods.

Starting from the ground up, **Termini** is definitely the foot: it gets trampled and does the trampling. As Rome's main intra- and intercity transportation hub, it is, not surprisingly, home to the highest number of budget accommodations in the city. The slightly quieter **San Lorenzo,** a few blocks east, teems with the students of Rome's largest university and the cheap food and clothing dives to match. With grid-like streets, this part of town is easy to navigate, though—like most feet—not too fun to look at. Sleep here and move on.

Two main streets, **Via Cavour** and **Via Nazionale**, are the legs leading in a straight shot up to the **Ancient City**, Rome's (once bloody) gut. Here, you'll find a lot of dirt (the **Fori Imperiali**), a traffic-light-less rotunda of zooming cars **(Piazza Venezia)**, and unabashed Italian pride crowned in green horses (the gleaming white **Vittorio Emanuele II Monument)**. This last landmark can be seen from virtually every elevated sight in Rome, making it a helpful edifice to recognize. From this busy center, the best way back out (and better out than in, we always say) is to take **Via del Quirinale**, which becomes **Via XX Settembre** as you head toward Termini: these wide boulevards are less trafficked and will lead you to the quieter region of **Via Nomentana** and its villas.

If you stay in the *centro*, **Via dei Fori Imperiali**, heading southeast, will take you past the **Roman Forum** and the **Colosseum**, where gladiators still reside, wearing plastic armor, feathered hats, and sandals. If you're more of a fashionista than those burly men, head northwest up **Via del Corso**, Rome's commerical mecca. Narrow and overcrowded with shopping bags, cars, and the owners of each, this is the city's busiest artery. It heads directly to **Piazza del Popolo** and is bordered on each side by those capillaries we spoke of earlier—Rome's most intricate web of tiny streets. Rather than trying to pinpoint your exact location on the map, orient yourself according to the major monuments: the **Trevi Fountain, Campo dei Fiori, Piazza Navona,** and the **Pantheon.** As might be expected, you can think of this cluster as Rome's heart, the **Centro Storico.** A more direct route through these flows up **Corso Vittorio Emanuele,** an artery that's slightly less clogged. If you do indulge Rome's heart condition and continue up V. del Corso, you'll hit the **Piazza di Spagna** region, a mini-Milan of clothing and commercialism.

At this point, it's time to mention the **Tiber River (Fiume Tevere),** the neck that separates Rome's body from its slightly less crazy head. Heading southwest on **Via Arenula** from C. Vittorio Emanuele, you'll pass through the **Jewish Ghetto** and cross either **Ponte Garibaldi** or **Isola Tiberina** into the residential **Trastevere.** The major destination across the river is (drumroll, please) **Vatican City.** From Trastevere, you'll have a pleasant walk up the river or through **Giancolo Hill** to reach the tiny city-state, which lies directly northeast of them. However, most people visiting the Vatican from Rome's center will take **Via Cola di Rienzo** from P. del Popolo. A grid of quiet streets leading to the Vatican offsets the crowds inside.

If you want to veer off Rome's central map, the areas south of the Roman Forum and Palatine Hill are worth exploring: **Aventine, Testaccio,** and **Ostiense** offer lots of good nightlife, food, residential streets, and a spattering of less-trafficked basilicas and museums. North of Piazza del Popolo, the refined and residential **Villa Borghese** and **Flaminio** await. Both are best attacked with a picnic basket and pair of shades.

ANCIENT CITY

With one of the highest camera-to-square-inch-of-sidewalk ratios in Rome, the Ancient City doesn't exactly feel "ancient" anymore. This vast stretch of tourist heaven, whose sights are the single reason many people come to Italy, is a stunning mix of old and new. For every ruin you'll see (and there are plenty), there's a plastic replica to match; for every nude statue, an overpriced sweatshirt to cover you up. And while you might have pecs rivaling those of the "gladiators" wandering around the Colosseum, you'll definitely need to put something on over those babies if you intend to enter any of the region's renowned churches. With so many sights worth seeing, it is all right for once to abandon your pride and surrender yourself to tourism in its full glory—photos with costumed gladiators, lines that only seem short compared to the 190m frieze on Trajan's column, and enough overpriced gelato to make even Augustus's purse feel a little empty. Throw away your flip-flops and don a pair of walking shoes to "hike" up the Palatine Hill, pick your way through the Roman Forum, or just get from one end of the City to the other—unlike most neighborhoods, which actually have an epicenter, the Ancient City is as scattered as some of its ruins.

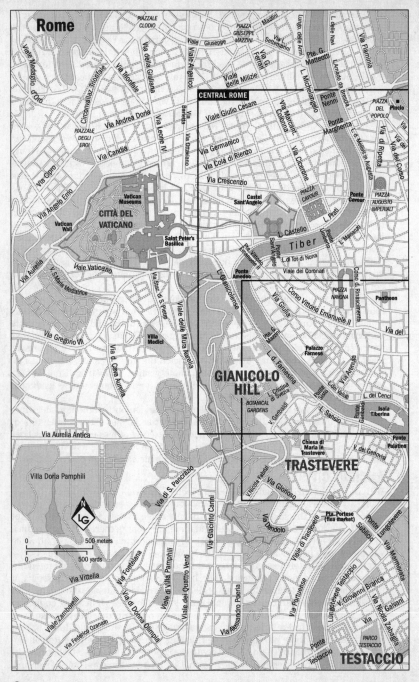

Rome

PIAZZALE CLODIO

PIAZZA GIUSEPPE MAZZINI

Mazzini

Lungo. delle Armi

L. delle Navi

L. d. Sassia

Pte. G. Matteotti

Via Flaminia

PIAZZA DEL POPOLO

Pincio

Viale Medaglie d'Oro

Viale Giuseppe

Via delle Giuliana

Via Trionfale

Via Angelico

Viale delle Milizie

Via G. Ferrari

Via Settembrini

Ponte Nenni

L. Michelangelo

PIAZZA DEGLI EROI

Circonvallaz. Trionfale

Via Andrea Doria

Via Leone IV

Via Barletta

Viale Giulio Cesare

Via Germanico

Via Cola di Rienzo

Via Ottaviano

Via Marcantonio Colonna

Via Cicerone

Via Michelangelo

Ponte Margherita

CENTRAL ROME

L. Amedeo da Bressa

Ponte Cavour

Via di Ripetta

Via del Corso

Via Cipro

Via Angelo Emo

Vatican Museums

Via Crescenzio

PIAZZA CAVOUR

L. d. Mellini in Augusta

PIAZZA AUGUSTO IMPERIALE

Vatican Wall

CITTÀ DEL VATICANO

Saint Peter's Basilica

Castel Sant'Angelo

L. Prati

Ponte Cavour

Via Aurelia

V. S Maria Mediatrice

Viale Vaticano

Via Staz di S. Pietro

Ponte Vittorio Emanuele

Ponte Sant'Angelo

L. Castello

Tiber

L. di Tor di Nona

L. Marianio

Via Gregorio VII

Villa Medici

Viale delle Mura Aurelia

Ponte Amedeo

Viale dei Coronari

Via d. Cava Aurelia

Via Giulia

Corso Vittorio Emanuele II

PIAZZA NAVONA

Corso d. Rinascimento

Pantheon

Via del

GIANICOLO HILL

Pte. di Mazzini

Palazzo Farnese

Via Arenula

L. d. Farnesina

L. de Vallati

L. dei Cenci

BOTANICAL GARDENS

L. Cristina di Svezia

Ponte Sisto

L. Sansio

Isola Tiberina

V. Garibaldi

Via Aurelia Antica

Chiesa di Maria in Trastevere

V. dei Genovisi

Ponte Palatino

Villa Doria Pamphili

V.Nicola Fabrizi

Via Glorioso

TRASTEVERE

Via di S. Pancrazio

Via Giacinto Carini

Pta. Portese (flea market)

Ponte Sublicio

0 500 meters
0 500 yards

Via Dandolo

Via di Trastevere

Lungotevere

L. Mermorata

Via Fonteiana

Viale di Villa Pamphili

Viale dei Quattro Venti

Via Nessandro Poerio

Via Fortunese

Lungotevere Testaccio

v. Giovanni Branca

Via Nicola Zabaglia

Via Vittelia

Via di Donna Olimpia

PARCO TESTACCIO

Viale Zambarelli

Via Federico Oznam

Ponte Testaccio

TESTACCIO

rome

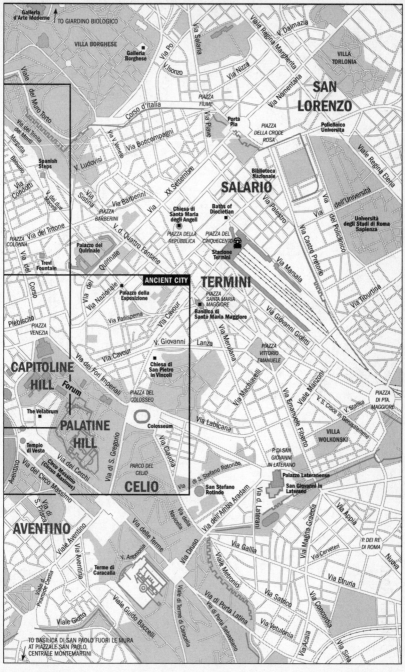

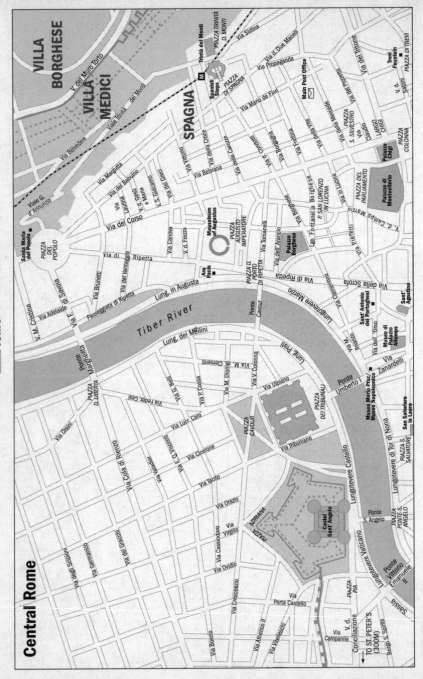

Central Rome

VILLA BORGHESE

VILLA MEDICI

SPAGNA

Tiber River

rome

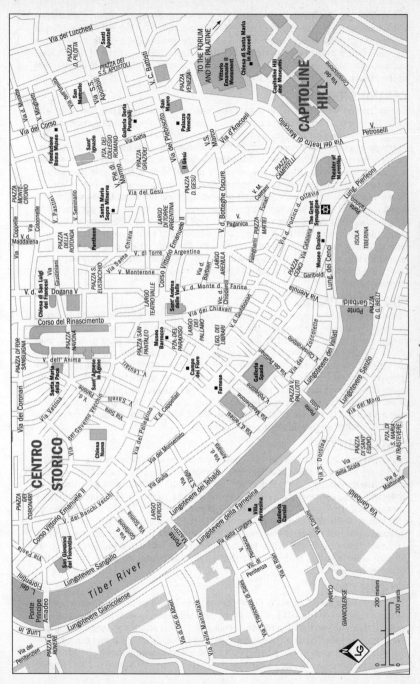

But don't worry, by the time you reach your destination—be it ruin or restaurant—you'll have forgotten the crowds and costs you endured to get there. Perhaps it's that feeling of traveling through time as you survey the remains of a civilization extinct for more than a millennium, or maybe it's the mouth-watering aroma of fresh-baked pizza dough that does it, but, whatever the cause, tourist travails pale in comparison to the pleasures of the Ancient City.

CENTRO STORICO

To the traveler who has paid one too many euro after waiting in one too many 4hr. lines, the Centro Storico offers a reprieve: nearly all of the churches, monuments, and *piazze* in this part of town are free of charge, and the only lines you'll be waiting in are the ones for overpriced gelato or food. With most of the main attractions compactly clustered on either side of **Corso Vittorio Emanuele,** this tangled web of streets is manageable in size, though not as easily navigable as a more grid-like pattern might be. Expect to get lost as *vias* suddenly split into numerous *vicolos*, so use the Corso as a departure point and the vibrant urban living rooms of **Campo de Fiori** and **Piazza Navona** on either side as your major landmarks. Letting yourself get lost in the neighborhood's little alleyways might be the best way to approach the area, though; you'll find yourself effortlessly arriving at unassuming churches and monuments, only to realize that they're famous landmarks. The entire region seems to be in a constant state of entropy, with tourists bumping into each other as they dart from one photo opp to another in a part of town that is already high-energy even into the late-night hours.

PIAZZA DI SPAGNA

Rome has a 5th Avenue too, and this is it. Bordered by the overbearing **Via del Corso,** the grid-like streets surrounding the Spanish Steps are full of people shopping and goggling in front of windows at Rome's highest end stores. It's hard to find a well-priced meal or a respite from the congestion unless you make a return to nature along the Tiber River or in the Villa Borghese park, both of which cushion the tourist enclave. Also redeeming the area are some of the best sights in the city. As in the **Centro Storico,** many landmarks are outside and free to the public, so the only obstacle to an enjoyable experience will be the crowds. To avoid the capitalist onslaught, take a stroll on the elevated **Viale di Trinita dei Monti,** which offers the best view of P. di Spagna's madhouse as well as its artistic marvels.

JEWISH GHETTO

You could pass through the Jewish Ghetto and notice nothing more than a surprisingly quiet Friday evening and Saturday morning and slightly more ethnic cuisine than Rome's majority. Now occupying little more than a few streets near the Tiber River, this compact neighborhood was actually home to the first real community of Jews in Western Europe. Originally a true ghetto blocked off from the city proper with sturdy walls and plagued by an unfortunate tendency to flood, today it is a pleasant stretch of residential houses and excellent restaurants that dish up some of the best artichokes around. A low-key and less touristed area to meander through on the way to the nearby Centro Storico, the Jewish Ghetto may be small, but it is rich in history and flavor.

VATICAN CITY

The people-to-square-foot ratio is significantly cockeyed in this tiny state: an expected madhouse of crowds in the Vatican contrasts sharply with the mostly empty boulevards in the surrounding region of **Prati,** making any attempt to measure population density a joke. That's actually a good thing though—after forging through the crowds to pay a visit to the pope, you'll be able to wander effortlessly down the region's tree-lined streets, frequented by dog-walkers and the occasional lost tourist

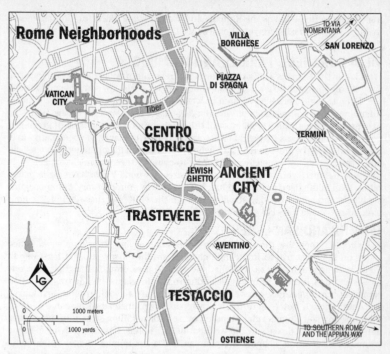

Rome Neighborhoods

TO VIA NOMENTANA

VILLA BORGHESE

SAN LORENZO

PIAZZA DI SPAGNA

VATICAN CITY

Tiber

CENTRO STORICO

TERMINI

JEWISH GHETTO

ANCIENT CITY

TRASTEVERE

AVENTINO

TESTACCIO

N LG

0   1000 meters
0   1000 yards

TO SOUTHERN ROME AND THE APPIAN WAY

OSTIENSE

looking for a big dome (a.k.a. **St. Peter's**). If the concentration of plastic souvenirs, bright flags, and English menus isn't enough to indicate which of the two regions you're in, then the brick wall which physically separates Vatican City from Prati should give you a clue. Walk around outside its boundary on the Prati side, and you'll find surprisingly affordable hotels and casual trattorias scattered throughout fairly modern residential buildings colored in pastel greens and pinks. And for all this talk of the crowds in Vatican City, even when you make your way back into the pope's digs, the throng of people is more manageable than what you'll find in Central Rome. Maybe it's the gargantuan size of St. Peter's and its *piazza*, or perhaps peoples' religious consciences that check them, but somehow the tourist crush west of the Tiber and north of Trastevere is more diluted than you'd expect.

TRASTEVERE

Trastevere is to Rome what Brooklyn is to New York—overlooked by tourists, loved by locals, and removed from the metropolitan center while still being in the thick of things. Just across the Tiber River, this enclave of cobblestone streets and small *piazze* boasts some of the best nightlife Rome has to offer; it's as popular with international students at the nearby university as it is with neighborhood residents whose families have called Trastevere home for generations. Although you likely won't spend the night here, as there are few budget-friendly accommodations, dinner in Trastevere won't break the bank. Restaurants that have managed to escape the tourist bubble abound—just throw away your map, get a little lost, and make your way into one of the tasty and unpretentious homegrown establishments that fill the neighborhood. If you've had enough of monuments and ruins, take a walk in the lush gardens leading into Monteverde (which has "green" in its name for a reason). You knew you weren't going to get through this book without reading that old saying, "When in Rome, do as the Romans do." Well, if living like a true Roman means making friendly Trastevere your home as well, following that well-worn adage can't do you wrong.

VILLA BORGHESE, PARIOLI, AND FLAMINIO

Who knew the Romans had a thing for palm trees and pastel-colored curlicues? In this city of cities, maybe it's a sign of a subconscious desire for some leisurely beach life. Even though there isn't a patch of water for miles around (save a few famous fountains), the cool residents of Villa Borghese have done well for themselves—the expansive gardens which span most of the neighborhood are an oasis of green gardens and shady streets that will make you wonder, "Who needs the beach anyway?" It's a good thing the grass inspires thoughts of picnics and light lunches, though—sit-down restaurants are expensive and harder to come by then you might expect. Even the business men who frequent the serene streets around **Via Po** have made panini rather than full-fledged *piatti* their lunch. Throw away your itinerary, lather on some sunblock, and spend the day strolling through the chill "Borghese bubble," whose pink houses make it feel like summer all year round.

TERMINI AND SAN LORENZO

Ask people if they saw the Vatican, the Colosseum, or any other number of famed sights on their last trip to Rome, and chances are they'll say no to at least one of them: with so much to take in, something's got to give. Ironic, then, that *everyone* passes through Termini, as mundane and unromantic as it is. It's the transportation capital of the capital city, after all. Too bad there isn't a beach around the block— there are enough hotels here to rival a resort town. Instead of a scenic vista or even a renowned Roman ruin, prepare yourself for a stifling stream of merchants, hotels, restaurants, dives, and, did we mention? . . . hotels. If you're arriving in Rome without a reservation, chances are you can find a last-minute budget option here, but even those who plan ahead often pick this bustling spot as their residence of choice. With prime access to the Metro, all major bus lines, some great nightlife (read: international student mania), and even a few sights of its own, no other part of Rome matches Termini in convenience. Our only advice: try to arrive by daylight. With a backpack, an unwieldy suitcase, and a long plane ride behind you, trekking around at night through the maze of people and advertisements that populate the area can provide not only a disheartening first impression of Rome, but a somewhat dangerous one as well.

TESTACCIO AND OSTIENSE

Located south of the Colosseum, Testaccio and Ostiense are left off most tourist itineraries and are literally left off of Rome's central map. Take advantage of this relative anonymity and get lost in their quiet streets by day, making sure to save energy for their pulsing clubs at night. Comprised of newer, residential housing and paved streets, these uncongested neighborhoods let you put away the guidebook for an afternoon (though studies have shown that copies of *Let's Go* double their lifespan if exposed to ample sunlight, so consider keeping yours out) and just wander a bit. The only lines in which you'll be waiting are those for Testaccio's clubs, some of the city's best despite their removed location. If, after a few nights, you've had enough of the good food and party scene, wander down and around the long **Via Ostiense** for sights that might not have brought you to Rome but which rival the Vatican in beauty and size. You might not come here with high expectations, but this will make the culinary, cultural, and clubbing surprises of these neighborhoods even more charming.

SOUTHERN ROME AND THE APPIAN WAY

Just because they're off the tourist map doesn't mean these parts of the city aren't worth at least a day of exploring—and we really do mean exploring—without an itinerary. The stretch of city below everything in your sightseeing schedule consists of quiet residential streets, enough churches to convert you to Catholicism, and, yes, more ruins of sorts. Though it takes a while to reach the more serene stretch of the Appian Way, once you do, you'll feel miles away from bustling Rome. The catacombs, though secluded (duh...they're underground), might remind you more of the city than you would expect—they can fill your guided-tour, hefty-entrance-fee, and historical-fact fixes. In the end, though, you'll want to meander through this region of Rome, popping into churches when you reach them and strolling along the Appian Way until your legs give out.

VIA NOMENTANA

V. Nomentana and the area surrounding it may be close to Termini, but they feel miles away. Good restaurants, scenic and serene streets, great nightlife, and a truly residential feel make this a worthwhile area to explore on the way to Villa Borghese—or perhaps on a day of its own. Just outside the city center but still only a step away from the bustle of Termini, this lively strip of land deserves a place in the itinerary of anyone who wants to hit something a bit less touristy and a bit truer to Roman life.

accommodations

Finding lodging in Rome is not as daunting as it may seem, even though the tourist offices do not provide as extensive listings as those in other cities. Options range from cheap hostels to four-star hotels and a slew of places in between. Low season starts around November and goes until early March, with the lowest rates coming at the Christmas holiday. High season starts mid-March, peaks during April and May, and doesn't let up until October.

At bigger hotel chains and hostels, the best way to book is generally online, where you can get specific prices and sometimes promotional deals. If you ask in person, these types of establishments will usually refer you to their website (and are reluctant even to give price ranges) unless you're talking exact dates. Expect the most standard and comprehensive services at hotels, with a price to match. Better hostels have kitchens, no curfew, and services geared to students such as maps, internet access, tours, and even bars. Smaller *pensione*, bed and breakfasts, and *alberghi* (the Italian word for hotels) are often located within a larger building of apartments and thus may be harder to find without advance knowledge. Such establishments often offer fewer rooms and services but more availability during high season, even at the last minute. Disregard the rule for hotels and hostels at these lodging houses and make reservations in person. These are often more convenient for the proprietors and may get you a lower rate. Discounts are often given for longer stays and for payments made in cash.

Convents are another great option for female travelers who can deal with the early curfew and usually bare-minimum facilities. They are often more willing to accommodate longer-term stays. Men and those not eager to deal with the particular oddities of convent life can find apartment agencies scattered throughout the city. Be aware, however, that they are usually only helpful for buying or renting in the very long term (one year or more). For periods of one to six months, consult **Porta Portese** newspaper, sold at all *tabaccherie* for €1 (also available online at www.portaportese.it) Other good online databases are **Easystanza** (www.easystanza.it) and www.expatriates.com, an online community for foreigners in Rome. Also check out public places such as libraries, universities (John Cabot, American University in Rome and St. John's University), and even local cafes, which often post paper fliers advertising short-term rooms in shared apartments. In terms of convenience, residential feel, and cost, **Trastevere** (across the river), **Testaccio/Ostiense,** and **San Giovanni** (south of Termini) are ideal places to find your home-away-from-home.

Termini is the best place, especially for travelers arriving by train, to find last-minute and conveniently-located accommodations. If you have not booked in advance, however, be wary of hotel scouts who will jump at the opportunity to advertise overpriced rooms late in the evening. Before booking, be sure to ask about services offered: some places charge for breakfast, A/C, internet, or, even worse, all three.

prego

Prego. The word is like pizza: Italians have somehow found a way to top or dress it with anything; to have it in any context, at any time of day; and to make it hot, cold, or even lukewarm to match the occasion. Whatever the situation, it all flies:

- **"PREGO?"** The first thing you'll hear as you walk into a *pasticceria.* Translation: "How can I help you?" or "What do you want?" And they expect you to know, immediately. (Standing around asking prices doesn't fly too well.)

- **"PREGO!"** A favorite of the Sistine Chapel guards. Amid the clamor of docents shushing people and telling them not to take pictures, you hear the word muttered sternly, more like a reprimand than anything else. Translation: "Geez...thanks for being quiet after the 15th time I've told you to turn off your camera and shut your trap!"

- **"PREGO."** The sweetest version of them all, when it's just a simple statement, often following *"grazie."* After you buy a gelato or compliment someone, the recipient of your cash or flattery will often acknowledge his or her thanks by calmly uttering the word. Translation: "You're welcome" or "I'm honored."

- **"PREGO" (WITH OPTIONAL "!")** Actually used as the verb it is, this *prego* can mean "I pray." Now, Italians pray for all kinds of things—in religious contexts, in which case the exclamation mark probably isn't necessary, but also in more mundane or demanding contexts. It's often a favorite of cleaning ladies. Walking into a room full of strewn backpack contents, you might catch a despairing *"Pre-e-g-o-ooooo."*

ANCIENT CITY

Home to some of the biggest monuments in Rome, the Ancient City is not the cheapest place to plant yourself during a visit to Italy's capital, though if you're willing to shell out at least €100 a night, you'll have more than enough four-star options to choose from. Never fear, however; plenty of bed and breakfasts and *pensioni* offer decent services at a much lower cost.

CASA SANTA PUDENZIANA   CONVENT ❷
V. Urbana 158   ☎06 48 80 056

If you're of the female persuasion and don't mind a 10:30pm curfew (12:30am on Sa), the quiet and spacious grounds of Casa Santa Pudenziana might just provide a welcome relief from the more crowded (and somewhat pricier) hostels nearby. This convent's six-bed dorm, double, and single make for a small community of guests—and that's if there are no vacancies. Guests here often run into each other at breakfast, dinner, or throughout the day in the peaceful central garden.

Library and chapel upstairs as well as clean common spaces with television, refrigerator, and microwave. Wi-Fi from nearby hotels floats through some parts of the convent, but *Let's Go* does not recommend relying on stolen Wi-Fi. No lockers or keys, so get ready to greet the friendly staff every time you buzz to get in.

⚵ ⓂA: Cavour. From V. Cavour, turn onto V. Urbana. *i* Women only. Breakfast included 7-9am; dinner 8pm, €10. ⓢ Dorms €22; singles €40; doubles €52. Inquire about discounts for longer stays. Ⓩ Strict curfew M-F 10:30pm, Sa 12:30am, Su 10:30pm.

STUDENT HOUSE
⬤⊗⁽ᵠ⁾ HOSTEL ❶

V. Merulana 117 ☎No phone—reserve online. ◼www.hostelworld.com

This small hostel does indeed feel like a house—the central reception area is more like a living room complete with bookshelves, photos, TV, and colorful furniture than a place to check in and out. Student House's rooms consist of two six-bed co-ed dorms, so don't plan on making it your private getaway. The living spaces are sunny and equipped with bunks and mirrors. The hall bathrooms might not be convenient, but the small communal kitchen and free Wi-Fi are. Brush up on your Italian before you get here—the owner speaks no English.

⚵ ⓂA: Manzoni. From V. Emanuele Filberto, walk straight on V. Manzoni and make a right onto V. Merulana. *i* Reserve your space at hostelworld.com. Set up check-in time in advance to avoid arriving when the owner is out. Towel rental €1. ⓢ Dorms €20.

HOTEL SAN DANIELE BUNDÌ
⬤⊗⁽ᵠ⁾❄ HOTEL ❹

V. Cavour 295 ☎06 48 75 295 ◼www.hotelsandanielebundi.it

Neighboring establishments recommend Hotel Bundì for its simple rooms and accommodating staff. Although the hotel is small, its central location, competitive prices, and surprising tranquility make it a good bet. Rooms have Wi-Fi, air-conditioning, private bathrooms and TVs. Complimentary breakfast is an added perk.

⚵ ⓂA: Colosseum. From V. dei Fori Imperiali, make a right onto V. Cavour. Buzz at the doors and take Scale B to the 3rd fl. ⓢ Singles €65; doubles €85. Ⓩ Reception closes at 8pm.

PENSIONE ROSETTA
⬤⊗⁽ᵠ⁾❄ PENSIONE ❹

V. Cavour 295 ☎06 47 82 30 69 ◼www.rosettahotel.com

A friendly staff and clean, though spartan, rooms make Pensione Rosetta a convenient option for those who hope to roll out of bed and check out the Colosseum in their pajamas. Each of Rosetta's 20 rooms have a private bathroom, a telephone, a TV, and air-conditioning; free Wi-Fi is available in public areas. The central courtyard provides a welcome respite from the busy V. Cavour.

⚵ ⓂA: Colosseum. From V. dei Fori Imperiali, make a right onto V. Cavour. Buzz at the doors and take Scala B to the 1st fl. ⓢ Singles €65; doubles €90; triples €105; quads €120.

CESARE BALBO INN
⬤⊗⁽ᵠ⁾❄ HOTEL ❹

V. Cesare Balbo 43 ☎06 98 38 60 81

Conveniently located entirely on the first floor, Cesare Balbo Inn is the perfect choice for those too lazy to climb a flight of stairs or walk more than a mile to Rome's ancient sights. Rooms here are big, colorful, and sunny. The staff is friendly, but they might get a little confused if you ask questions about topics as complicated as how much a room costs. Free internet, private bathrooms, in-room breakfast, and air-conditioning round out this small establishment.

⚵ ⓂA: Cavour. From V. Cavour, make a right on V. Panisperna; walk 2 blocks and make a right on V. Cesare Balbo. ⓢ Doubles €90; triples €100; quads €110. Ⓩ Reception 24hr.

CENTRO STORICO

The Centro Storico is not the cheapest place to stay, but hotels here often have a lot more character and offer better services than those found elsewhere. Reserve rooms well in advance and don't expect them to be cheap.

👍 ALBERGO DEL SOLE
🚫💳🚫♿📶❄ HOTEL ❺

V. del Biscione 76 ☎06 68 80 68 73 🖥www.solealbiscione.it

Especially well-furnished rooms with antique furniture, paintings, and curtains make this place feel more like a home than a hotel. Great common spaces, including a garden terrace and sitting rooms on each floor, give Alberge del Sole a lived-in quality. Knowledgeable staff are welcoming and straight-forward.

➡ Exit P. di Fiori onto V. del Biscione. ℹ Most rooms with A/C, otherwise with fan. Wi-Fi €1.50 per hr. $ Singles €70, with bath €110-125; doubles €100-105/€120-160. ⏰ Reception 24hr.

HOTEL SMERALDO
💳🚫♿📶❄ HOTEL ❺

Vicolo dei Chiodaroli 9 ☎06 68 75 929 🖥www.hotelsmeraldoroma.com

Somewhat tight rooms are clean and bright, sporting well-coordinated decor. The gracious reception staff inspires confidence in guests by happily giving advice to travelers. There are no surprises here—rooms are well-equipped and neatly kept.

➡ From Campo dei Fiori, walk down V. dei Giubbonari, turn left onto V. dei Chiavari and right onto Vicolo dei Chiodaroli. ℹ Breakfast included. All rooms have private bath. Wi-Fi €5 per hr. in common areas; public computer available. $ Singles €70-110; doubles €90-145. ⏰ Reception 24hr.

ALBERGO POMEZIO
💳♿📶❄ HOTEL ❺

V. dei Chiavari 13 ☎06 68 61 371

This hotel's fast-paced and assertive owner offers large and nicely decorated rooms with curtains and matching trimmings. Good services, including free Wi-Fi, for the location and price. The large breakfast room is one of the few common spaces for guests.

➡ From Campo dei Fiori, walk down V. dei Giubbonari and turn left onto V. dei Chiavari. ℹ All rooms have private bath. Free Wi-Fi. $ Singles €70-100; doubles €100-140. Weekends tend to be more expensive.

CASA BANZO
💳♿📶❄ B AND B ❺

P. del Monte di Pieta 30 ☎06 68 33 909 🖥www.casabanzo.it

Frescoed walls, potted plants, and stained-glass windows at the reception desk give a hint of the beauty to be found in the rooms and mini-apartments of this converted 15th-century *palazzo*. Some rooms have kitchens and balconies overlooking the plant-covered central courtyard. All are fully furnished and epitomize comfort—some nearly palatial. Accommodating and attentive staff.

➡ From Campo dei Fiori, walk down V. dei Giubbonari, turn left onto V. Pieta, and walk into P. Monte di Pieta. ℹ Breakfast €6. All rooms have private bath. Free Wi-Fi. $ Standard rooms €120; apartments €120-160. ⏰ Reception 8:30am-1pm and 4pm-midnight; call about arrival time. Guests get key to enter.

PIAZZA DI SPAGNA

Staying in the Piazza di Spagna area is a pricey affair, and though you might be getting newer accommodations and slightly better services, you'll be surrounded by more crowds than are present in the Ancient City or Centro Storico. Boasting little nightlife to boot, this neighborhood is a better bet for older folks who want reliable services than for youth seeking value and fun.

👍 HOTEL PANDA
💳🚫♿📶❄ HOTEL ❹

V. della Croce 35 ☎06 67 80 179 🖥www.hotelpanda.it

Luckily (or not), there are no panda bears around, but you'll feel as warm and fuzzy as one of these bamboo-chomping cuties while staying at this small, family-run hotel. Simply decorated rooms come with A/C, Wi-Fi, and TV at a better price than the spiffier hotels down the street. Opt for a bigger room if you can, as the small ones really are small. Though there isn't much common space (read: narrow hallways and no breakfast room), the rooms are enough of a retreat for this shortfall to be inconsequential.

➡ Ⓜ A: Spagna. From the Spanish Steps, take V. Condotti, turn right onto V. Belsiana and right onto V. della Croce. Hotel is on the 2nd fl. ℹ Breakfast €5 at downstairs bar. A/C €6. Free Wi-Fi. $ Singles €55-68, with bath €65-80; doubles €68-78/€85-108; triples €120-140. ⏰ Reception 24hr.

DEPENDANCE ANAHI
💳🚭📶❄ HOTEL [5]

V. della Penna 22 ☎06 36 10 841 💻hotellocarno.com

Though Dependance Anahi is an offshoot of the grander and more expensive Hotel Locarno, it still boasts a prime location and stellar services, if less history and pomp than its sister across the street. Mostly double rooms and two singles all have TV, A/C, private bath, minibar, and free Wi-Fi, and Art Nouveau detailing gives the place more flavor than your standard rooming house. Head across the street to enjoy a buffet breakfast in the quiet, vine-covered patio or relax in the palatial lounge rooms.

➡ Ⓜ A: Flaminio. From P. del Popolo, exit near V. di Ripetta and immediately turn right onto V. Penna d'Oca. Across the street from Hotel Locarno; reception at V. della Penna 22. ℹ Breakfast included. Bath, minibar, and safe ensuite. Free bike rental. Free Wi-Fi. $ Singles €90-120; doubles €110-190. ⏰ Reception 24hr.

HOTEL DE PRETIS
💳🚭📶❄ HOTEL [5]

V. Rasella 142 ☎06 48 19 626 💻www.hoteldepetris.com

Not only are rooms equipped with all the basics—TV, A/C, free Wi-Fi, and minibar—but they're especially elegant. Superior rooms have hardwood floors and modern furniture, while the standards are less luxe, though bigger than average. Expect no surprises from the reliable rooms and staff.

➡ Ⓜ A: Barberini. From P. Barberini, take V. del Tritone, turn left onto V. Boccaccio and left onto V. Rasella. ℹ Breakfast included. All rooms have ensuite bath. Free Wi-Fi. $ Singles €94-136; doubles €113-171. Extra bed €46. ⏰ Reception 24hr.

DOMUS JULIA
💳🚭📶❄ HOTEL [4]

V. Rasella 32 ☎06 47 45 765 💻www.domusjulia.it

The friendly dog at Domus Julia makes up for the reception staff who can be a bit short of temper at times. The hotel's 18th-century building retains its historic look but brings itself up to the 21st century with all the expected comforts, including free internet. If you've gotten a bit bored of seeing Roman ruins, rent one of their bikes for free or even earn an extra euro by walking the dog. The breakfast room is a nice hang-out even in the evening.

➡ Ⓜ A: Barberini. From P. Barberini, take V. del Tritone, turn left onto V. Boccaccio and left onto V. Rasella. ℹ Breakfast included. All rooms have minibar and ensuite bath. Free Wi-Fi. $ Singles €60-100; doubles €78-180; triples €89-210. ⏰ Reception 24hr.

HOTEL ELITE
💳🚭📶❄ HOTEL [5]

V. Francesco Crispi 49 ☎06 67 83 083 💻www.elitehotel.eu

It will be well worth your extra euro to opt for a superior room at this half-renovated, half-old hotel. Potpourri and clean, white decor in the reception lounge are a precursor to the sparkling superior rooms with glass shower doors, modern, office-like furnishings, and free Wi-Fi. Standard rooms are much smaller and contain older, less cared-for furnishings.

➡ Ⓜ A: Barberini. From P. Barberini, take V. del Tritone and turn right onto V. Francesco Crispi. ℹ Breakfast included. All rooms have TV and ensuite bath, superior rooms have A/C and free Wi-Fi. Wi-Fi in lounge €3 per hr., €7 for 3hr. $ Standard singles €90; doubles €110-120; superior singles €115; superior doubles €140. ⏰ Reception 24hr.

VATICAN CITY

When it comes to hotels, the area immediately around the Vatican is as overpriced as the pizza and souvenirs. However, the quieter streets nearer the river and Prati offer many affordable options, mostly small hotels within residential buildings. A nice area in which to stay due to its proximity to the sights and distance from the *centro*'s chaos, it may only be lacking in nightlife, which is (expectedly) quiet.

COLORS 💳🚭📶❄ HOTEL, HOSTEL ❶

V. Boezio 31 ☎06 68 74 030 💻www.colorshotel.com

The rooms smell fresh like wood and look bright, as colors should. The boldly pigmented adornments of their 23 rooms help keep guests' stays comfortable, while the free Wi-Fi is simply convenient (and rare for this neighborhood). If the rainbow inside has you wanting some straight-up green, head to the rooftop terrace. One dormitory with five beds gives this hotel a hostel spirit. The room has A/C though, putting it miles beyond most hostels.

➥ [M]A: Ottaviano. Walk down V. Ottaviano; turn left onto V. Cola di Rienzo and right onto V. Terenzio; at the intersection with V. Boezio. ℹ *Breakfast included at hotel; €7 in dorm. Common terrace, TV room, and mini-kitchen. Free Wi-Fi.* $ *Dorms €15-30; singles €30, with bath €50-80; doubles €70-100.* ⏰ *Reception 24hr.*

HOTEL AL SAN PIETRO 💳🚭📶❄ HOTEL ❸

V. Giovanni Bettolo 43 ☎06 37 00 132 💻www.sanpietrino.it

Small green frogs (don't worry, they're ceramic) and the smell of flowers greet guests at this small hotel, located only 5min. from the Vatican museums. Though the rooms aren't particularly large, free Wi-Fi and staff that matches the upbeat decor make it a better deal than hotels advertised nearby. No breakfast, but there's an organic grocery store down the street.

➥ [M]A: Ottaviano. Exit onto V. Barletta and turn left onto V. Bettolo. ℹ *Singles without bath. Free Wi-Fi.* $ *Singles €40-50; doubles €70-89; triples €115.* ⏰ *Reception 24hr.*

HOTEL GIUGGIOLI 💳🚭📶❄ HOTEL ❺

V. Germanico 198, 2nd fl. ☎06 36 00 53 89 💻www.hotelgiuggioli.it

The silver accents and geometric furniture give this top-notch hotel a distinctly modern feel. Carpeted rooms are very clean and generously sized, though a bit dimly lit. If long lines at the Vatican aren't your thing, bike rental gives you another reason to travel elsewhere in the city. The lovely bar and kitchen area *(open 1-9pm)* feels more like an upscale restaurant then a hotel add-on.

➥ [M]A: Lepanto. Walk down V. Ezio and turn right onto V. Germanico. ℹ *Breakfast included. All rooms have bath and minibar ensuite. Wi-Fi €1 per hr.* $ *Singles €70-110; doubles €80-130. Bike rental €12 per hr.* ⏰ *Reception 24hr.*

HOTEL LADY 💳🚭📶 PENSIONE ❹

V. Germanico 198, 4th fl. ☎06 32 42 112 💻www.hotelladyroma.it

Aesthetics trump amenities here: the old-fashioned charm of this former monastery is unfortunately accompanied by a lack of A/C and Wi-Fi. Still, the original wood-beamed ceilings and amber stained-glass windows create a comforting feel that most modern hotels can't replicate. Fans and antique wooden furniture that looks like it's been here for a century add to Hotel Lady's appeal. Rooms without bathrooms may be less convenient but are significantly bigger.

➥ [M]A: Lepanto. Walk down V. Ezio and turn right onto V. Germanico. ℹ *Singles and triples with shared bath only. Internet room available.* $ *Singles €60; doubles €75, with bath €90; triples €120.* ⏰ *Reception 24hr., but call about arrival time.*

A ROMA SAN PIETRO B AND B 💳🚭📶❄ B AND B ❸

V. Crescenzio 85 ☎06 68 78 205 💻www.ftraldi.it

Though it may not be quirkier than a hotel, this small bed and breakfast offers brightly colored (though somewhat blandly furnished) rooms with excellent perks: A/C, free Wi-Fi, and complimentary breakfast make it better than some hotels. Reserve in advance and schedule arrival time, as there are only five rooms and the owner might be out. Watch out for the dripping water in the courtyard.

➥ [M]A: Ottaviano. Walk down V. Ottaviano and turn left onto V. Crescenzio. ℹ *Breakfast included.*

Free Wi-Fi. Ⓢ Singles €40-50; doubles €60-110; triples €70-140. Extra bed €10-25. ⏰ Call to schedule arrival time.

PENSIONE PARADISE
💳🚭📶 PENSIONE ❹

Vle. Giulio Cesare 47, 3rd fl. ☎06 36 00 43 31 💻www.pensioneparadise.com

The rooms at Pensione Paradise come at good prices but with less charm than older establishments and fewer amenities than newer ones. Narrow halls match small rooms, though both are welcoming with their warm lighting and old stone floors. Rooms without bathrooms have sinks. Free Wi-Fi in public areas wins it major brownie points, but you're on your own for breakfast.

➡ⓂA: Lepanto. Walk down Vle. Giulio Cesare toward the river. i Fans ensuite. Free Wi-Fi in public areas. Ⓢ Singles €55, with bath €65; doubles with bath €75. ⏰ Reception 24hr.

HOTEL NAUTILUS
🍳🚭 PENSIONE ❷

V. Germanico 198, 3rd fl. ☎06 32 42 118 💻www.hotelnautilusroma.it

Except for old drawings of Rome, there's not much in the way of decoration or even amenities here. If the Vatican has inspired you, turn your stay here into a monastic experiment: no TV or internet access means it'll be easy to devote yourself to a life of reflection. Though lacking many modern amenities, rooms are especially big, and those without toilets still contain private showers. A comfortable place to stay if you don't need much and want some quiet.

➡ ⓂA: Lepanto. Walk down V. Ezio and turn right onto V. Germanico. i Breakfast included. Ⓢ Singles €30-40, with bath €50; doubles €50-75/€60-90; quads €130. ⏰ Reception 24hr., but call about arrival time.

HOTEL LA ROVERE
💳♿🍸❄ HOTEL ❺

Vicolo San Onofrio 4/5 ☎06 68 80 67 39 💻www.hotellarovere.com

This large and elaborately styled establishment provides the typical hotel experience, which is why it comes at a slightly higher price. Superior rooms on the top floor have slanted, wood-beamed ceilings and big windows with great views of the city. Lower floors are less carefully accoutered, but a public lounge and bar make up for the blandness with their mix of Chinese urns and Roman sculptures.

➡ ⓂTermini. Take bus #40 or 64 to Saint Peter. From Ponte Vittorio Emanuele II, walk down Lungotevere in Sassia until it becomes Lungotevere Gianicolense. Turn right onto V. di S. Onofrio and right onto the vicolo. i Breakfast included. All rooms have private bath and minibar ensuite. Free Wi-Fi. Ⓢ Singles €118-190; doubles €126-190; triples €146-210. ⏰ Reception 24hr.

TERMINI AND SAN LORENZO

Termini abounds with hotels, hostels, bed and breakfasts, and *pensioni*. There's a roughly one-to-one ratio of extremely cheap to extremely overpriced options, so do research beforehand and try to book at least one week in advance, especially for summer stays. Although the proximity to Termini station makes living here convenient, the area is not the safest place at night. Be wary of pickpockets and, if possible, avoid walking about in the late hours.

👍 M AND J PLACE HOSTEL
🍳🚭📶❄ HOSTEL ❷

V. Solferino 9 ☎06 44 62 802 💻www.mejplacehostel.com

A prime location, helpful staff, and clean rooms grace this wonderful hostel. M and J Place boasts great common spaces (kitchen, balcony, and TV lounge) as well as a calm feel enhanced by rooms that are neat and not too crowded. Private rooms are more reminiscent of a hotel with A/C, computers, TV, and towels ensuite. The reception desk posts weekly events in the city, provides laptop rentals, lends books, offers printing and photocopying services, and has public computers in case you need to get organized. If you'd rather relax, the downstairs restaurant, bar, and club provide food all day, an *aperitivo* hour at 6pm, and a chance to dance at 11pm.

⚐ Ⓜ*Termini. Walk down V. Marsala away from the station, and turn right onto V. Solferino.* ⓘ *Breakfast included in some reservations; book online and choose (€3 otherwise). Lockers outside room. Free luggage storage until 9pm. Towels €2. 1hr. free internet with booking; €2 per hr. or €5 per 4hr. thereafter. All-female dorms available.* Ⓢ *10-bed dorms €25; 8-bed €26; 6-bed €32-35; 4-bed €35-37.50. Singles €75; doubles €80-120; triples €150; quads €180.* ⚃ *Reception 24hr. Restaurant/bar open daily 7am-late. Kitchen open 3-10pm.*

🏠 ALESSANDRO DOWNTOWN
💨⊗((·)) HOSTEL ❶

V. C. Cattaneo, 23   ☎06 44 34 01 47 🖳www.hostelsalessandro.com

This conveniently located hostel is a bit less party-hardy than its sister, the **Palace**, but offers great services to backpackers and students. Large common spaces, communal kitchen, and dorms make it less cramped than nearby hostels, although bunk beds can take down the comfort level of the largest dorms. Other than the midday cleaning which prevents you from resting in your room until after 3pm, Alessandro Downtown is ready to take care of you after a long day in the city.

⚐ Ⓜ*Termini. Take V. Giovanni Giolitti and turn left onto V. C. Cattaneo.* ⓘ *Breakfast included. Free pasta dinners M-F 7pm. 30min. Lockers ensuite; free luggage storage before 2pm. Towel rental. Book online 1 week in advance Apr-Aug. 30 min. free Wi-Fi daily; €2 per hr. thereafter.* Ⓢ *8-bed dorms €14-29; 6-bed €15-30; 4-bed (co-ed) with bath €19-40; doubles €50-53, with bath €55-110.* ⚃ *Reception 24hr. Rooms must be evacuated 10am-3pm for cleaning.*

🏠 ALESSANDRO PALACE
💨⊗((·))𝖸 HOSTEL ❶

V. Vicenza 42   ☎06 44 61 958 🖳www.hostelsalessando.com

A historically decorated bar (check out the "frescoed" ceiling) turned modern (check out the speakers and TV!) makes this one of the most social hostels around. While the nightly pizza giveaway *(8:30pm)* goes fast, great happy hours and drink specials keep guests around all evening. A/C keeps the rooms bearable in the mid-July Roman heat, though big dorm size can make restful sleep difficult. Still, this is as close as a hostel gets to being a palace.

⚐ Ⓜ*Termini. Walk up V. Marsala away from the station and turn right onto V. Vicenza.* ⓘ *Breakfast included; free pizza daily Apr-July 8:30pm. Lockers ensuite. Fridges in some doubles. Reserve online at least 1 week in advance during high season. 30min. free Wi-Fi daily. all dorms have private bathroom.* Ⓢ *8-bed dorms €15-30; 6-bed €16-36; 4-bed €18-38, with bath €21-42. Doubles €55-115, with bath €65-130; triples €75-135/€81-147.* ⚃ *Reception 24hr. Free luggage storage before 3pm. Bar open daily 6pm-2am.*

🏠 THE YELLOW
💨⊗((·))𝖸❄ HOSTEL ❶

V. Palestro 44   ☎06 49 38 26 82 🖳www.the-yellow.com

This hostel isn't called "yellow" because it's scared, but because it's so darn happy. The perfect place for social butterflies, this establishment boasts a full bar (customers will likely spend more time here than in their somewhat small rooms) and over five floors of dorms as well as colored lights and funky posters in the hallways. Skype headsets, locks, and even laptops are conveniently available to rent or purchase at the reception desk. Come here for fun times . . . not to wake up at 6am for a hike to the Vatican.

⚐ Ⓜ*Termini. Take V. Milazzo away from the station and turn left onto V. Palestro.* ⓘ *Breakfast €2-10 at the bar next door. Lockers ensuite; free luggage storage before 1:30pm. €10 towel deposit. 30min. free internet per day on public computers. No Wi-Fi.* Ⓢ *12-bed dorms €18-24; 7-bed €20-26; 6-bed €22-34; 4-bed €24-35.* ⚃ *Reception 24hr.*

LEGENDS HOSTEL
💨⊗((·)) HOSTEL ❷

V. Curtatone 12   ☎06 44 70 32 17 🖳www.legendshostel.com

This cramped but well-equipped hostel close to Termini brings in a mixed crowd of backpackers and older folk. There's little common space, and rooms are fairly distant from one other (some in a separate building). However, the small kitchen gives the place a sense of community, especially during delicious breakfasts and pasta dinners. The friendly and low-key staff is ready to assist you during your stay in Rome. Shared bathrooms can be a bit messy, but at least they come with soap.

☀ ⓂTermini. Walk up V. Marsala away from the station; turn right onto V. Gaeta and right onto V. Curtatone. Buzz and walk to 1st fl. *i* Breakfast included; free pasta offered M-F 7pm. Lockers ensuite. 5hr. free Wi-Fi; €1 per hr. thereafter. Public computers at reception desk. Fans in rooms. Ⓢ 8-bed dorms €23-33; 6-bed €25-37; 5-bed €28-41; 4-bed €30-44. Triples €48-51; doubles €41-71. ☼ Reception 24hr.

FREEDOM TRAVELLER
💨⊗⟨ŗ⟩❄ HOSTEL ❶

V. Gaeta 23 ☎06 48 91 29 10 🖳www.freedom-traveller.it

Freedom Traveller is a friendly and slightly less crowded hostel with the same great perks as nearby spots. Its sunny reception area and common spaces (TV room, backyard, and kitchen) immediately make you feel welcome. The first-floor location and proximity to Termini make it especially convenient for weary travelers. Free Wi-Fi is luxurious compared to most hostels that charge by the hour.

☀ ⓂTermini. Take V. Marsala away from the station and turn right onto V. Gaeta. *i* Free pizza and beer party Tu evenings. Free luggage storage until 2.30pm. All-female dorms available. Free Wi-Fi in common spaces and some rooms. Ⓢ 6- and 4-bed dorms €17-32; doubles €60-110; triples €75-135; quads €80-160. ☼ Reception 24hr. Lockout 10:30am-2pm (except for private rooms). Quiet hours 11pm-8am. Communal kitchen open until 10:30pm.

MOSAIC HOSTEL
💨⊗⟨ŗ⟩⟳ HOSTEL ❷

V. Carlo Cattaneo ☎06 44 70 45 92 🖳www.hostelmosaic.com

Right below the busier **Alessandro**, this similar hostel's reception boasts a comfy leather couch, warmly painted walls, and a helpful staff that immediately fosters a sense of home. Rooms that feel less utilitarian than those of your typical hostel (despite the requisite bunks) provide everything you need for a comfortable stay in Rome.

☀ ⓂTermini. Take V. Giovanni Giolitti and turn left onto V. C. Cattaneo. On the 2nd fl. *i* Breakfast included; free pasta dinner M-F. Lockers ensuite; free luggage storage upon arrival. Towels €2. Kitchen access M-F. Female-only dorms available. Reserve online at least a week in advance. 30min. free Wi-Fi daily; €1 per hr. thereafter. Ⓢ 8-bed dorms €22; 6-bed €24; 5-bed €25; 4-bed €27. ☼ Reception 24hr.

CASA OLMATA
🖥⊗⟨ŗ⟩ HOSTEL ❶

V. dell'Olmata 36 ☎06 48 30 19 🖳www.casaolmata.com

This quiet, well-kept, and cheerfully run hostel finds itself in a nicer region than most. Mixed 6-bed dorms, triples, doubles, and singles are a bit cramped, but wooden bunks and homey decorations (check out the old clocks and lace curtains in some rooms) provide a comfy, lived-in feel. Many rooms come with fully-equipped ensuite kitchens, TV, fans, and private bath; others have access to a communal kitchen down the hall with microwave and fridge. Definitely not a party hostel (quiet hours after midnight), but all the better for it.

☀ ⓂTermini. Walk toward P. Santa Maggiore and down V. Paolina. Turn left onto W. Quattro Cantoni and left onto V. Olmata. *i* Breakfast included. Lockers in hallway and ensuite. 15min. free internet per day at public computer. Roof terrace. Free Wi-Fi. Ⓢ Dorms €18-20; singles €38; doubles €56-58. Inquire about discounts for longer stays. ☼ Reception 8am-2pm and 4pm-midnight.

HOTEL PAPA GERMANO
💨⊗⟨ŗ⟩❄ HOTEL ❷

V. Calatafimi 14/A ☎06 48 69 19 🖳www.hotelpapagermano.com

Hopefully, Hotel Papa Germano's tacky decor will make you smile rather than judge, for if you write this place off too swiftly, you'll be missing out on its many great services. If the wallpaper doesn't make you grin, maybe the especially friendly reception or free Wi-Fi will. The modest rooms' TV, A/C, and telephone make them good deals. If you're not looking for a private room, the dormitory is an economical alternative that remains slightly nicer than hostel options.

✈ Ⓜ*Termini. Take V. Marsala away from the train station, proceed straight as it becomes V. Volturno, and turn right onto the small V. Calatafimi.* ⓘ *Breakfast included. 3 public computers available.* Ⓢ *Dorms €15-30; singles €30-60; doubles €40-95, with bath €50-120; triples €50-100/€60-140; quads €70-130/€80-150.* Ⓚ *Reception 7am-midnight.*

BED AND BREAKFAST A CASA DI ZIA SERAFINA
⊛ⓧ(ºⁱ⁾❄ B AND B ❹

V. Filippo Turati 107 ☎06 44 66 458 ▣www.casaserafina.it

A gracious host welcomes you to her four furnished and immaculately kept rooms off the bright central hallway of her apartment at this intimate bed and breakfast. A great deal amid most of Termini's less-than-charming accommodations, Signora Serafina's rooms are equipped with Wi-Fi, TVs, A/C, and cheerful decor. Chambers without bathrooms have access to a sparkling clean one in the hallway. Homemade breakfast cooked each morning by the signora herself.

✈ Ⓜ*Termini. Walk down V. Ratazzi and turn left onto V. Filippo Turati. Buzz and proceed to 3rd fl. Call in advance to set up arrival time; key given to enter building and room.* Ⓢ *Doubles €70, with bath €80; triples €110.*

AFFITTACAMERE ARIES
✦ⓧ(ºⁱ⁾❄ HOTEL ❹

V. XX Settembre 58/A ☎06 42 02 71 61 ▣www.affittacamerearies.com

The lovely owner might be reason enough to stay here—she'll be happy to offer you coffee upon arrival. A bit removed from the Termini cluster, this charming hotel decorated with flowers and frescoes offers six simple but spacious rooms. The stone floors and metal-framed beds might not be the warmest and fuzziest things around, but the accommodating service, friendly dog (which sometimes follows the owner around), and great amenities make up for it.

✈ Ⓜ*Termini. Veer left toward P. della Repubblica, proceed onto V.V.E. Orlando, and turn right onto V. XX Settembre. Buzz and take Scala B to the 2nd fl.* ⓘ *Breakfast included. Free Wi-Fi.* Ⓢ *Singles €50; doubles €80; triples €105. Ask about a discount for longer stays.* Ⓚ *Guests are given a key to enter, but reception essentially 24hr.*

HOSTEL IVANHOE
✦ⓧ(ºⁱ⁾ HOSTEL ❶

V. Urbana 50 ▣www.hostelworld.com

A bit removed from Termini, this small hostel is a real find. Free Wi-Fi and a communal kitchen are particularly convenient and will save you a few euro (which you can spend on breakfast since it's not included). Modern and brightly decorated hallways lead to eight comfortably sized dorms with big windows. The midday lockout, though, means you better stay busy in Rome through siestatime.

✈ Ⓜ*B: Cavour. Head down the stairs and walk up V. Urbana. (Or, a 15min. walk from Termini.) Don't confuse the Hotel Ivanhoe across the street with this hostel.* ⓘ *Breakfast €2. Ages 18-35 only. Book online. Free Wi-Fi.* Ⓢ *12-bed dorms €12-24; 8-bed (co-ed) €13-26, 8-bed (women-only) €13-28; 6-bed €13-26, with bath €15-27. Doubles with bath €26-36.* Ⓚ *Reception 24hr. Lockout 11am-4pm.*

HOTEL SCOTT HOUSE
✦ⓧ(ºⁱ⁾❄ HOTEL ❺

V. Gioberti 30 ☎06 44 65 379 ▣www.scotthouse.com

On the fourth floor of a building full of hotels, Scott House is more welcoming than the rest. Warm orange hallways, attentive staff, and clean facilities engender confidence and comfort in the tired traveler, despite the hotel's proximity to a particularly busy street. Private bathrooms, free Wi-Fi, flatscreen TVs, and big windows in every room vault Scott House over and above the other tenants of 30 V. Gioberti.

✈ Ⓜ*Termini. Walk down V. Giovanni Giolitti and make a right onto V. Gioberti. Hotel is on the 4th fl.* ⓘ *Breakfast included. Free Wi-Fi.* Ⓢ *Singles €70; doubles €98. €5 discount if you pay with cash.* Ⓚ *Reception 24hr.*

HOTEL POSITANO

V. Palestro 49

✈🖢❄ HOTEL, HOSTEL ❶

☎06 49 03 60 📧www.hotelpositano.it

This is a decent option for both hotel- and hostel-seekers even though it's probably not on most students' radar and is less suped-up than the average hotel. Private rooms will get you A/C, a TV, a bathroom, and even a fridge. Five- and six-bed dorms are simple and share a common bathroom.

🚇 Ⓜ*Termini. Take V. Milazzo away from the station and turn left onto V. Palestro.* *i* *Breakfast €6 across the street. Email or fax to reserve.* Ⓢ *Dorms €15-25; singles €40-60; doubles €60-90.* 🕐 *Reception 24hr.*

HOTEL PENSIONE DI RIENZO

V. Principe Amedeo 79/A

✈🖢 HOTEL ❸

☎06 44 67 131

No-nonsense and chipper owner Signor Rienzo offers 15 sparse but clean rooms. The metal bedframes may not inspire a sense of home, but the big windows overlooking a central courtyard make the rooms sunny and quiet. Ceiling fans help offset the lack of air-conditioning, but with no TV or internet, there's not much to do here except sleep.

🚇 Ⓜ*Termini. Take V. Cavour and turn left onto V. Principe Amedeo. Buzz, walk to the right in the courtyard, and take stairs or elevator to 1st fl.* Ⓢ *Singles with bath €40; doubles €50, with bath €70.* 🕐 *Reception 24hr.*

HOTEL CERVIA/RESTIVO

V. Palestro 55

✈⊗❄ HOTEL ❸

☎06 44 62 172 📧www.hotelrestivo.com

Hotel Cervia/Restivo's friendly owner keeps the place clean, with small, cheerful, high-ceilinged rooms. A/C and TV make it better than a hostel, but the lack of internet is inconvenient. Still, this hotel's central location and generally pleasant aura are definite pluses. Call the owner to set up an arrival time.

🚇 Ⓜ*Termini. Take V. Milazzo away from the station and turn left onto V. Palestro.* *i* *Free luggage storage.* Ⓢ *Singles €40, with bath and breakfast €65; doubles €70/90.* 🕐 *Reception 24hr.*

sights

Do the sights of Rome even require an introduction? Like the extrovert who will shake your hand before you take your coat off, Rome's famous destinations have no trouble making themselves known: interrupting, side-tracking, and dragging out your itinerary before you even get started, they seem to beckon from every street corner and *piazza*. Don't worry—that's a good thing. If they were anything less than spectacular, the gargantuan number of must-sees in Rome would feel burdensome. Luckily, they *are* spectacular and, luckily again, fairly concentrated within the city. You'll run into about half of them by default. On your way to get gelato, for example, you'll come across a fountain that looks, to put it mildly, vaguely familiar. The sights you won't stumble upon while hunting for a good pizzeria can be tackled with a good pair of walking shoes, a whole lot of ambition, and an espresso to keep you going. Our suggestion: take at least one day without the guidebook or map and simply see where you end up. Chances are you'll hit a lot of those "must-sees" without even trying.

ANCIENT CITY

🏛 COLOSSEUM

ANCIENT ROME

Bordered by V. di San Gregorio, V. Cello Vibenna, and V. N. Salvi ☎06 39 96 77 00 for information and booking 📧www.pierreci.it

A walk through the Colosseum provides an interesting mix of old and new—crumbling bricks and empty "cells" evoking the unfortunate ancients who once occupied them are juxtaposed against the vision of dozens of modern-day tourists who eagerly peer into the Colosseum's arena, a formerly sandy pit in which bloody (and sometimes not so bloody) combat took place. Perhaps the first thing you'll notice is the mix of architectural elements—admittedly, some of the more modern additions are attempts to keep this ancient structure from crumbling altogether. (You'll run into several construction workers assembling metal reinforcements on the ground level.) Contemporary alterations aside, the four types of architecture used to construct Rome's massive amphitheater are still evident, particularly on its northern side (the south side has been subjected to the looters of the city, who have been snatching the Colosseum's marble siding for themselves since the sixth century CE). The amphitheater's bottom tier, made of massive blocks of Travertine, was built the thickest. Its levels become lighter in both weight and appearance as you move upward. This visual "ranking" matched the organization of Roman spectators, who although given free admission, were assigned to seats in accordance with their social class. The emperor not only got VIP seating but also had the privilege of entering through the secret, "Passage of Commodus," an underground tunnel which protected him from the public. It would seem that gladiators and wild beasts were also granted this immunity (though likely for different reasons), as they too entered the Colosseum via winding corridors beneath the arena. Today, disintegrating walls and vaults covered in wooden planks are all that remain of the 15 original underground pathways. Of the 80 porticos dotting the arena's circumference, four were reserved for the emperor and the games' performers.

For the ◎**best view** of the arena, climb to the upper tiers, where you can see the structure in its entirety—a massive 188m by 156m oval. Looking down, you'll get a feel for what it was like to witness the combats that took place in this arena. Most famously, this was the place where **gladiators**, men who could be anything from slaves to convicts to prisoners, to emperors (actually, the only one on record is Commodus, the emperor after whom the Colosseum is named) met for battle in the frenzy of the Roman games. Trained from the age of 17 and given rankings based on the number of fights they won, these combatants were seldom actually killed as they usually begged for mercy when defeat seemed imminent. It wasn't until the Middle Ages that massacre became the norm. Ranking had its own taxonomy, complete with scientific-sounding names (Retiarius, Oplomachus and Cruppellarius to name a few) and armor specific to the fighter's status. Check out the detailed costume and weaponry exhibits in display cases on the upper level. If you want to see the gladiator armor on something other than a stuffed mannequin, consider getting your picture taken with one of the costumed dudes accosting middle-aged women around the concession stands out front (usually €5). Probably bloodier than fights between the gladiators were those between wild animals, since back in ancient Rome there was no ASPCA watching out for the beasts used in executions and staged combat. Bones from some of the biggest animals, including the Libyan bears and giant ostriches, are also on display beside the armor.

While the arena takes center stage for most visitors, peer around the back side for a great view of the Arch of Constantine, the tree-lined V. San Gregorio, and the Roman Forum just across the way. ⊞Tickets to the Colosseum can be purchased at the Palatine Hill/Roman Forum entrance on V. San Gregorio. Head there midday, after the early morning frenzy, to avoid waiting in a 2hr. line at the Colosseum.

✠ Ⓜ B: Colosseo or Ⓜ Termini, then bus #75. *i* Ⓢ Tickets are purchased for entrance to the Colosseum, Palatine Hill, and the Roman Forum, 1 entrance per sight, used over the course of 2 days. €12, EU students ages 18-24 €7.50, EU citizens under 18 and over 65 free. Guided tour €4; audio tour €4.50; video guide €5.50. All available in English. ◔ Open daily 8:30am until 1hr. before sunset.

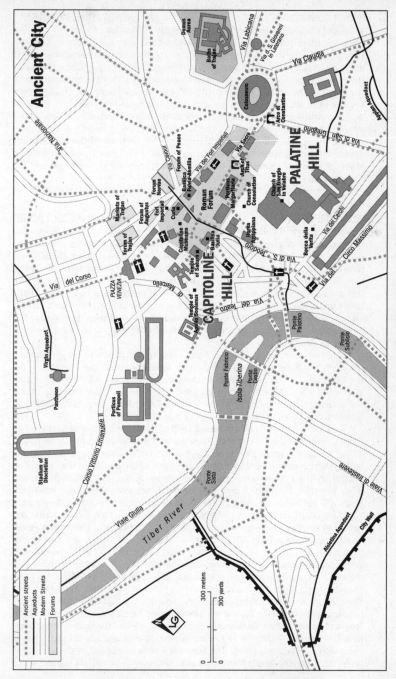

Ancient City

Baths of Trajan
Domus Aurea
Via Labicana
Via d. S. Giovanni in Laterano
Via Claudia
Colosseum
Arco di Constantine
PALATINE HILL
Via di San Gregorio
Appian Aqueduct
Via Cavour
Forum of Peace
Via dei Fori Imperiali
Via Sacra
Forum of Nerva
Basilica di Paola-Aemilia
Roman Forum
Arch of Titus
Forum of Augustus
Foro Imperiali
Portico Margaritaria
Church of San Giorgio in Velabro
Curia
Markets of Trajan
Capitoline Museums
Basilica Julia
Horrea Agrippiana
Via del Teatro
Forum of Trajan
Temple of Saturn
CAPITOLINE HILL
Church of Consolation
Via di S. Teodoro
Via del Cerchi
Bocca della Verità
Via del Corso
Via di
Via del
PIAZZA VENEZIA
di Marcello
Temple of Apollo Sosianus
Ponte Palatino
Virgin Aqueduct
Ponte Subliclo
Ponte Fabricio
Ponte Cestio
Isola Tiberina
Portico of Pompeii
Pantheon
Stadium of Diocletian
Corso Vittorio Emanuele II
Ponte Sisto
Viale Giulia
Viale di Trastevere
Tiber River
Abdeloa Aqueduct
City Wall

sights • ancient city

Ancient streets
Aqueducts
Modern Streets
Forums

300 meters
300 yards

LG

N

0

0

◪ ARCO DI CONSTANTINE   ⴟ ANCIENT ROME, MONUMENT

V. San Gregorio, South of the Colosseum near the Palatine Hill entrance.

Although most people only pass the Arch of Constantine on the way to the Colosseum or the Roman Forum across the street, its size and beauty are reason enough to seek it out. Towering an impressive 70 ft. over the V. San Gregorio, the arch stands in commemoration of Constantine's victory over Maxentius at the Battle of the Milvian Bridge in 312 CE. Despite the metal gates that prevent visitors from walking through the arch, those interested can take a closer look at the beautiful engravings and inscriptions depicting Constantine's battles and victories that etch the structure. The Romans, who seem awfully good at "borrowing" things (check out the torn-away marble sections of the Colosseum), continued the tradition here, decorating the side of the arch with medallions stolen from other monuments nearby. Guess there's something to be said for kleptomania after all.

✱ Ⓜ️B: Colosseo or Ⓜ️Termini, then bus #75. Walk down V. San Gregorio from the Colosseum. Ⓢ Free.

ROMAN FORUM   ⊛⊗ ANCIENT ROME

A walk through the Roman Forum provides a pleasant (though somewhat bumpy) one-hour respite from the busy city just outside its gates, even if you don't know a bit of its history or read a single plaque. Chances are, though, you didn't pay €12 for a walk in the park. For that, try the **Domus Aurea**. To justify spending cash on ruins instead of gelato, consider picking up an audio tour that will at least clue you in to the history of a few of the sections you'll pass. There aren't many informational plaques along the way, so unless you're enough of a Latin scholar to understand the original inscriptions, your map (provided at the ticket office) and audio tour are the only things helping you tell your Tempios from your Basilicas.

Your route through the Roman Forum depends on the entrance you choose. Although the lines at this site tend to be significantly shorter than those for the Colosseum, you can make them even shorter by coming in the mid- to late afternoon, when the early-morning crowds have died off. The free map of the Forum suggests that its main entrance is at V. Largo Ricci, though the lines may be shorter at V. San Gregorio.

Walking in, you will see a stunning view of the Forum, a plot of land used as a marketplace by the Greeks and Etruscans of the seventh and eighth centuries. Today, the area consists mostly of grassy and gravelly paths, crumbling temples, and a few reconstructed sites that contain most of the history of the place. The central area is lowest to the ground; as you move out, the pathways become more elevated. Because of this topographical fact, even those who don't purchase a ticket inside can get great views of the Forum's layout from the street.

Walk down **Via Sacra**, the oldest street in Rome, which runs through the center of the Forum. To the right, you'll find the remains of the **Basilica Fulvia-Aemilia**, originally built in 179 BCE by two Marcuses—Fulvia and Aemilia—but then renovated by the Aemilia family, perhaps as a mode of self-promotion. If you're having trouble finding the basilica, that's because it no longer exists—just the skeleton of a floor plan and some remains housed under a roof are still here. Step inside the **Curia**, originally the meeting place of the Senate, for a museum-like display of coins, columns, and recovered friezes that once decorated the basilica, including ◪**The Rape of the Sabine Women.** Outside again, you'll find the **Temple of Saturn** and the **Basilica Julia** flanking the sides of the central area. Duck into the tiny hut dedicated to Caesar, where flowers and photos add a bit of color to the dirt-covered area. The **Tempio di Romolo** on the left, with its massive green door, and the **Tempio di Antoninus and Faustina,** with beautiful pink and white columns guarding the entrance, are straight ahead. While the **Arco di Constantine** might have been free, you'll be glad you paid to see the **Arch of Titus,** built in 81 CE by Emperor Domitian to commemorate the victory over Jerusalem by his brother Titus. Although smaller than Constantine's, Titus' arch boasts a coffered archway and beautiful interior frieze depicting a hoard of horses, a menorah, and crowds of people after the victory that make it especially stunning. Further on, walk down the dirt paths of the **Severan Horrea** which are bordered by brick cell enclosures and excavation areas.

✚ Ⓜ*B: Colosseo or* Ⓜ*Termini, then bus #75. Enter at V. San Gregorio (near the Arch of Constantine), V. dei Fori Imperiali (halfway between Trajan's column and the Colosseum), or directly opposite the Colosseum. Entrance to the Forum is joint with that to the Palatine Hill, a neighboring site.* ***i*** *Tickets are purchased for entrance to the Colosseum, Palatine Hill, and the Roman Forum, 1 entrance per sight, used over the course of 2 days. €12, EU students ages 18-24 €7.50, EU citizens under 18 and over 65 free. Audio tour to the Forum €4, combined with the Palatine €6; available in English.* ✷ *Open daily 8:30am until 1hr. before sunset.*

PALATINE HILL

ⓂⓈ ANCIENT ROME

The Palatine Hill, occupying the stretch of elevated land between V. dei Cerchi, V. di San Gregorio, and V. di San Teodoro, was once *the* place to live (even Cicero and Mark Antony had their homes here). Today, it consists mostly of grassy patches and ruined temples, though it still provides some of the best views of the city and the adjacent Roman Forum. At the very least, bring a camera, some water, and maybe a sandwich for a pleasant stroll through its grounds.

Entering at V. San Gregorio, you can either head right (which will lead you into the Roman Forum) or left (which will lead you to the Palatine Hill). The ascent up the hill is a bit steep and winding, but some convenient steps make getting to the top much easier and faster. On the left, you'll find the **Stadium and Severan Complex** whose huge territory was once used as a riding school. Immediately onward is the **Domus Augusatana**. (Its lower floor is on the left, the upper on the right.) Cushioned between the domus's remnants is the **Palatine Museum,** which houses a small collection of statues, tiles, busts, and other archaeological items from wealthy Roman households. *(Open daily 8am-4pm, 30 people per fl., 20min. at a time. Free.)* Next along your walk is the start of the **Domus Flavia,** a huge region which includes reception rooms, a peristyle, and the Nymphaeum, a space which houses an octagonal fountain that once covered the entire area and symbolized power but today is dried up. The **Casa di Livia**, sectioned between, was property of the Roman aristocracy during the first century BCE and today provides a welcome escape from the sun. Play a little "Theseus and the Minotaur" (a classic game for children circa 200 BCE), and walk through the surrounding labyrinth of dank tunnels containing placards that describe the area. The **Casa di Augustus** and the **Casa di Romolo** are immediately on the left, surrounded by tiny Romulean Huts. Most scenic of all are the ▪**Farnese Gardens**, which offer an unparalleled vista of the Roman Forum, the Colosseum, and Capitoline Hill. They're also a good place to stop for a picnic (which some travelers supplement with oranges from one of the nearby trees). Descend the stairs to check out the **Nymphaeum of the Rain**, a small cave with running water.

✚ Ⓜ*B: Colosseo or* Ⓜ*Termini, then bus #75. Enter at V. San Gregorio (near the Arch of Constantine), V. dei Fori Imperiali (halfway between Trajan's column and the Colosseum), or directly opposite the Colosseum. Next to the Roman Forum.* ***i*** *Tickets are purchased for entrance to the Colosseum, Palatine Hill, and the Roman Forum, 1 entrance per sight, used over the course of 2 days. €12, EU students ages 18-24 €7.50, EU citizens under 18 and over 65 free. Audio tour to the Palatine Hill €4, combined with the Forum €6, available in English.* ✷ *Open daily 8:30am until 1hr. before sunset.*

sights · ancient city

FORI IMPERIALI
                                                               ✝ ANCIENT ROME

V. dei Fori Imperiali   ☎06 67 97 702

Walking down V. dei Fori Imperiali, it's impossible to miss—you guessed it—the Imperial Fora. Built in the 150 years after Caesar's reign, the four fora located here marked a new period of Roman dominance that ushered in a return to Hellenistic architecture. The open area enclosed by a colonnade to sequester the center from the surrounding, urban activity was the place where the business of the forum took place. This central region used for government affairs was topped off by a small temple decorated with friezes and paintings commissioned by the day's ruler to display his financial and political power. The first two fora were constructed by Caesar and Augustus, the next (christened the "Forum of Peace" to mark a calmer period in the empire's history) by Vespasian, and the last (called the Forum of Nerva) by Domitian. Down the way, you'll find the biggest forum of all, the **Forum of Trajan,** built between 107 and 113 CE.

In 1924, some of the land that once held the fora was paved over to make way for V. dei Fori's modern-day, less-than-regal central thoroughfare. Although the grounds themselves have been closed to the public for years, you can still admire them from the sidewalk, pick up a map of them at the tourist office and give yourself a tour, or explore them on a guided tour.

✣ *From the Colosseum, walk down V. dei Fori Imperiali. Ruins are on the right.* ⚹ *Call the tourist office for more information.* Ⓢ *Free.* ☖ *Exhibition and info center open daily 9:30am-6:30pm.*

DOMUS AUREA
                                          ✝ ANCIENT ROME, PARK

Vle. della Domus Auerea 1 (Colle Oppio Gardens)   ☎06 39 96 7700

The expansive grounds of Domus Aurea sit between the Colosseum and busy V. Merulana. Shallow hills, patches of grass, and small children's playgrounds make a walk through this park a refreshing change of pace from the tourist crowds just next door. In the morning and early evening, the park is especially populated with dog walkers and joggers. Although you probably aren't here to see any monuments (by now, you might be eager to escape them), make sure to check out the **Trajan Baths,** which lie near the V. delle Terme di Traiano.

✣ *From the Colosseum, walk down V. Terme di Tito. Park is on the right and continues until V. Merulana* Ⓢ *Free.* ☖ *Open daily 7am-9pm.*

CHIESA DI SAN PIETRO IN VINCOLI
                                         ⊛ CHURCH

P. di San Pietro in Vincoli, 4/a   ☎06 97 844 950

Sitting atop a small hill just off V. Cavour, this fourth-century church houses Michelangelo's famous statue of Moses. After gazing at the bigger-than-life sculpture, take some time to admire the brightly-colored fresco ceilings and meander through the clean, white colonnade.

✣ *From V. Cavour turn onto V. S. Francis di Pacia and walk down V. Eudossiana. The church is on the left.* ⚹ *Fully covered legs and shoulders required.* Ⓢ *Free.* ☖ *Open daily 8am-12:30pm, 3-6pm.*

CIRCUS MAXIMUS
                                               ✝ ANCIENT ROME

It's only logical to pay a visit to the Circus Maximus after a long tour of the Colosseum and the Palatine Hill. While only a shadow of what it used to be (since it no longer exists and therefore actually can't cast a shadow), the Circus Maximus rounds out the key sights of your tour through Ancient Rome. At the end of V. di San Gregorio (near the P. di Porta Capena), this grassy plot of land was once Rome's largest stadium, home to more than 300,000 screaming Romans who came to watch the chariot races. Now, the fields only reach similar volumes during summer concerts and city celebrations, scheduled on a monthly basis. The best view of the long track is either from within the elevated Palatine Hill (where Emperor Augustus used to sit) or from the V. del Circo Massimo, which has fewer cars and is also slightly elevated (unlike the V. dei Cerchi). Other than tourists hoping to enjoy the view from these vantage points, dog walkers, joggers, and even some sunbathers come here to get away from the city congestion.

✦ ⓂB: Circo Massimo or bus #118. ⓈFree.

THE VELABRUM
                                                                ♿ ANCIENT ROME

Amidst all the nearby monuments boasting elevated views of the city, the Velabrum may feel a bit subterranean, but don't let that turn you off. The ruins in this valley blend into the surrounding neighborhood in a way that would be simply impossible for a structure the size of the Colosseum. You can approach the Velabrum from the waterfront (Ponte Palatino practically leads straight into it) or on V. Petroselli coming from the **Teatro di Marcello**, a round structure that looks remarkably like the Colosseum... perhaps because it was the model for Rome's most famous ruin. The **Portico d'Ottavia**, now only a skeleton of columns, sits at the corner of V. del Portico d'Ottavia, but the real star of the square is the **Chiesa di Santa Maria in Cosmedin**, a medieval church whose facade holds the famous **Bocca della Verità**. According to legend (and Gregory Peck in *Roman Holiday*), he who places his hand in the stone mouth will have it bitten off if he is a liar. Watch as dozens of people line up to prove their honesty or perhaps just have their picture taken.

✦ From the Circo Massimo, walk down V. dei Cerchi until you reach P. S. Anastasia. The Velabrum and its sights are in the flat region at the base of the hill. Ⓢ Free. ☑ Church open daily 9:30am-5:50pm.

CAPITOLINE HILL
                                                 ⊗ PIAZZA, MUSEUM

Rome's small but magnificent capital sits nestled between the **Vittorio Emanuele II Monument** and the Roman Forum. From both these sites, views of the little Capitoline Hill are hard to miss. Coming up V. Arco di Settimio at the backside of the hill, you'll arrive at the **Piazza di Campidoglio,** designed by Michelangelo in 1536. At the center of the piazza sits an equestrian statue of **Marcus Aurelius**. It's actually a replica of the original, which you can view in a weatherproof chamber located in the Palazzo Nuovo. Still, this oft-photographed bronze statue is an impressive monument to one of Rome's more philosophically-inclined emperors. Piazza di Campidoglio is ringed by the **Capitoline Museums**. which hold a treasure trove of Roman and Greek sculpture as well as the oldest public collection of ancient art in the world. If you instead arrive at the piazza from V. del Teatro Marcello, you will be forced to climb a somewhat awkwardly slanted staircase. But get ready to be greeted by two symmetrical (and seductive) stone statues of a nude dude and his horse.

✦ From V. dei Fori Imperiali, veer left towards the Monumento a Vittorio Emanuele II. Turn onto V. Teatro Marcello and head uphill Ⓢ Capitoline Museums €6.50, EU students 18-25 €4.50, EU citizens under 18 and over 65 free. Audio tour €5. Available in English. ☑ Capitoline Museums open Tu-Su 9am-8pm. Ticket office closes 1hr. before museums close.

CHIESA DI SANTA MARIA IN ARACOELI
                                                      ⊗ CHURCH

While its exterior boasts nothing more than a dull wall of bricks, Chiesa di Santa Maria in Aracoeli's stunning pink-and-gold interior will reward those hardy enough to climb all 124 steps leading to its entrance. Built in the seventh century, this small church houses the **Bufalini Chapel** (to the right of the altar), decorated with Renaissance–era frescoes by Pinturicchio, and the even more entrancing **Cappella del San Bambino** (to the left of the altar), wallpapered with letters from sick children. Even if you don't spend much time in the church, take more than a minute to admire the exceptional view of the city from this vantage point. Five prominent domes dot the city's skyline, including the Dome of St. Peter's and, closest of all, the Cupola della Chiesa del Gesù. For an even better view of the city, consider taking the **Roma dal Cielo** elevator ride which takes you up to the **Terrace of the Quadrigas.**

From Teatro Marcello, climb 124 steps to reach the church's perch. i Fully covered shoulders and legs required. $ €7, ages 10-18 and over 65 €3.50. Open M-Th 9:30am-6:30pm, F-Su 9:30am-7:30pm. Last ticket sold 45min. before close.

CENTRO STORICO

The Centro Storico abounds with sights that are as quintessentially Roman as pasta is Italian. Luckily, you won't have to pay or wait in line to see many of them, and their close proximity to one another makes it possible to visit all these sights in one rewarding afternoon.

PANTHEON — ♿ ANCIENT ROME

P. della Rotunda ☎06 68 30 02 30

Even without looking at your map, you're bound to stumble upon the Pantheon as you wander through the Centro Storico: signs pointing the way and crowds hovering outside will indicate that something great is coming. Corinthian columns and the large pediment atop give the edifice, which is currently under construction, the look of a Greek temple. An impressive 20 tons each, the bronze doors (originally plated in gold) leading into the Pantheon are enough to make visitors feel miniscule. Inside, the building's circular forum is full of people craning their necks to admire the perfect hemispherical dome (142 ft. in diameter and height) which, until Brunelleschi's Duomo in Florence, was the largest in the world. If you ever thought concrete was a poor man's material, think again. A mix of pumice, ash, sand, water, and chemical solidifiers, this material made the dome's casting possible by providing a viable alternative to the heavier stone blocks typically used. The coffered ceiling looks almost modern in form—a true geometrical abstraction—especially in contrast to the more traditional frescoes around it. Consider that the Pantheon's only source of light is the 27 ft. oculus at its center: over the course of the day, the beam of sun shining through it slowly moves along the temple's beautiful marble floor. (The best time to come, nevertheless, is on a rainy day, when water droplets flow directly through the central ring.) Notable for the architectural accomplishment of its design alone, the Pantheon is also a significant reflection of religious tolerance, dedicated to every god (of Ancient Rome, that is).

From P. Navona, follow signs for the Pantheon toward V. della Dogana Vecchia. $ Free. Open M-Sa 8:30am-7:30pm, Su 9am-6pm.

CAMPO DEI FIORI — ♿ PIAZZA

Between P. Farnese and C. Vittorio Emmanuele

Cushioned between stately Palazzo Farnese one block away and the busy C. Vittorio Emanuele, Campo dei Fiori is an enclosed world of its own where students, merchants, nighttime revelers, and performers make it their home. At its center, the somewhat ominous statue of a cloaked Giordano Bruno towers above the crowds. Aside from his imposing figure, street mimes clad in ridiculous garb are the only other even remotely statuesque shapes around. During the day, check out the market where merchants sell everything from **fish** to fresh produce to **alcohol** to clothes *(M-Sa 7am-2:30pm)*. At night, the Campo is literally abuzz with the chatter of diners, while the clink of wine glasses and the thumping of a few disco-like clubs add to the jocular clatter of this happening center for city life.

From P. Navona, head towards C. Vittorio Emanuele and cut straight across to Campo dei Fiori. i Watch your valuables at night. $ Free.

PIAZZA NAVONA — ♿ PIAZZA

Surrounded by V. di Santa Maria dell'Anima and C. del Rinascimento.

One of Rome's most picturesque *piazze*, Navona is right up there with the Colos-

rome

seum and the Vatican in tourist popularity. Luckily for visitors, there's neither a 4hr. line nor a hefty admission price. Rather, the oval arena, originally a stadium built by Domitian in 86 CE, is full of tourists snapping pretty pictures, mimes performing at either end, artists selling trite watercolors, and musicians playing what sounds like the soundtrack of a Frank Sinatra film. This scene makes everything you heard about "classic Italy" seem true. Weave your way through the crowds—even grab a seat if you can—to take a closer look at Bernini's magnificent **Fontana dei Quattro Fiumi,** a massive stone sculpture that depicts four river gods, each representing a continent. The mix of masterfully cut rock and unadulterated, raw stone makes the figures and their "natural" environment especially convincing. The obelisk at the fountain's center may seem a bit out of place, but it actually mirrors many others scattered throughout the city. This one bears the mark of Pope Innocent X. Flanking the Fontana dei Quattro Fiumi, the less spectacular **Fontana di Nettuno** and **Fontana del Moro** draw significantly smaller crowds but provide good spots to take a seat and view the scene from afar.

⇟ Entrances into P. Navona at Palazzo Braschi, V. Agonale, V. di Sant'Agnese di Agone, and Corsia Agonale.

CHIESA DI SAN LUIGI DEI FRANCESI — [⊗] CHURCH

P. San Luigi dei Francesi 5 — ☎06 68 82 71

From the exterior, this 16th-century church could easily be overlooked by pedestrians: its French facade is pretty unimpressive by Roman standards. Consequently, the surprise inside is even sweeter than it might have been. Three of Caravaggio's most impressive works, **[✓]The Calling of St. Matthew, St. Matthew and the Angel,** and **The Crucifixion,** grace the Contarelli Chapels in back. (If you're having difficulty finding them, it might be because they are not illuminated. Deposit €1 to light them up, or wait for someone else to step up.) Because they occupy the inner wall, it is slightly hard to get enough distance to view the paintings properly. However, these three works rival the private collection of Caravaggio's work held by the Galleria Borghese, so make sure to take them in as best you can. Their intense *chiaroscuro*, characterized by high contrast between light and dark, is characteristic of the religious and emotional meaning Caravaggio is famed for bringing out in his subjects.

⇟ From P. Navona, exit onto Corsia Agonale, turn left onto C. del Rinascimento and right onto V. Santa Giovanna d'Arco. $ Free. ⏰ Open M-W 10am-12:30pm and 4-7pm, Th 10am-12:30pm, F-Su 10am-12:30pm and 4-7pm.

VITTORIO EMANUELE II MONUMENT — [⊗] MONUMENT, MUSEUM

In P. Venezia — ☎06 67 80 664; museum ☎06 67 93 526 💻www.risorgimento.it

The stunning Vittorio Emanuele II Monument towers—grandiose, theatrical, and triumphant—above P. Venezia. In fact, this flamboyant building remains a captivating presence. Even in far-away P. del Popolo, it towers in the distance down V. del Corso. The monument is affectionately (and a bit mockingly) referred to as "The Wedding Cake"—and justly so: its multiple tiers and pristine white facade look good enough to eat and garish enough to flaunt. Out front, huge Italian flags wave majestically as gladiators—or rather plump men in metal garb—pose alongside confused tourists. Designed in 1884 and finally finished in 1927 by Mussolini, the huge building is as close as you can get to a giant megaphone that constantly yells out, "We are Italy! We are great!" The monument is best seen from P. Venezia or even from a few blocks away, but if you venture up its mighty steps, you'll find the **Museo del Risorgimento,** a slightly dull (and extremely dark) collection of artifacts tracing the course of Italian unification, inside. Though the museum is free, the view from outside is lighter, brighter, and more worth your time.

⇟ In P. Venezia. $ Free. ⏰ Monument open M-Th 9:30am-6:30pm, F-Su 9:30am-7:30pm. Museum open daily 9:30am-6:30pm.

PALAZZO VENEZIA ♿ PALAZZO

V. del Plebiscito 118 ☎06 69 99 41; info and booking ☎06 32 810 💻www.galleriaborghese.it

In the northwest corner of P. Venezia, the Palazzo stands out as a result of its simple, brick facade rather than any particularly beautiful or ornate characteristic. As one of Rome's first Renaissance buildings, it certainly reflects an air of stateliness and grace, though it seems like a shy, quiet wallflower in comparison to the Vittorio Emanuele II Monument across the way. Though today it is not a site of governmental power, Mussolini once used it as his headquarters. The museum inside the Palazzo holds an impressive collection of documents, tapestries, paintings from the early Renaissance, and sculptures.

🚏 Across the way from Vittorio Emanuele II Monument, in P. Venezia. $ €4, EU citizens 18-25 €2, EU citizens under 18 and over 65 free. ⏰ Open Tu-Su 8:30am-7:30pm. Ticket office closes at 6:30pm.

PIAZZA DELLA ROTUNDA ♿ PIAZZA

P. della Rotunda, right outside the Pantheon

The P. della Rotunda is either the *antipasto* or the *dolce* to your exploratory entree (which is the 🏛**Pantheon,** in case you haven't guessed). Before or after strolling under the beautiful dome of Rome's stately temple, crowds throng around the Egyptian obelisk crowning the center of this *piazza.* An 18th-century monument was created out of this obelisk when Clement XI "de-paganized" it by sticking a cross on top. The somewhat whimsical fountain in the square sports serpents and sharp-toothed heads that spew water out of their mouths. The *piazze* surrounding this central spot are noticeably less crowded but contain some monuments of their own worth checking out. **Piazza della Minerva** features yet another obelisk sitting atop Bernini's elephant statues, whose figures supposedly represent the powerful "mind" needed to support the obelisks' wisdom. **P. di Sant'Eustachio** is full of small cafes and bars, including the famous **Sant'Eustachio Il Caffe** coffee den.

🚏 Outside the Pantheon. $ Free.

FONDAZIONE ROMA MUSEO ♿ MUSEUM

V. del Corso 320 ☎06 67 86 209 💻www.fondazioneromamuseo.it

Founded in 1999, this small museum is a place to remember due to its excellent selection of temporary art exhibits, lectures, and performances devoted to specific artists and periods in art history. Since the museum's opening, its curators have hosted approximately 30 shows in collaboration with other international museums, most recently a show devoted to Edward Hopper. The exhibitions here tend to present a retrospective of the artist's work alongside more interactive components as well as excellent commentary. Check their website for a full program of upcoming events.

🚏 From Palazzo Venezia, walk up V. del Corso for 7min. ℹ Rotating exhibits usually last at least 1 month; check online for updated information. Hours may vary according to each exhibition and its demand. $ €10; groups, under 26, and over 65 €8; under 6 free. ⏰ Open M 10am-6pm, Tu-Th 10am-8pm, F-Sa 10am-10pm, Su 10am-8pm. Ticket office closes 1hr. before museum.

PALAZZO DELLA ESPOSIZIONE ♿ EXHIBITION SPACE

V. Nazionale 194 💻www.palazzoesposizioni.it

The Palazzo della Esposizione is a cultural center devoted to curating art shows as well as housing performances, lectures, and events on a monthly basis. Its huge exhibition space is an excellent venue for the diversity of programs it offers. Most recently, it held a Giorgio De Chirico retrospective, tracing the origins and development of the 20th-century Italian artist in addition to his impact on modern art and Italy. Shows usually run for at least one month and are accompanied by supplementary lectures. Check online for a more detailed program of events.

✚ *From the Fori Imperiali, walk up V. Nazionale 7min.* ℹ *Check online for a program of upcoming shows; each usually lasts around 1 month.* Ⓢ *€12.50, under 25 and over 65 €10, disabled persons and under 6 free. Students €4 Tu-F. Free 1st W of the month 2-7pm.* 🕐 *Open Tu-Th 10am-8pm, F-Sa 10am-10:30pm, Su 10am-8pm. Last entry 1hr. before closing.*

PIAZZA DI SPAGNA

▨ PIAZZA DEL POPOLO
                                                            ♿ PIAZZA

At the end of V. del Corso

From the center of P. del Popolo, you can see the magnificent **Vittorio Emanuele II Monument** glowing (yes, it's so white, it glows) in the distance. Likewise, from the monument, a straight shot up V. del Corso has you gazing at this gigantic *piazza*, the "people's square," no ▧**Communist connotation** intended. Despite the Corso's noise and crowds, this street is probably the best way to arrive at and appreciate the openness of the *piazza* which, for being so famous, is surprisingly uncongested. Perhaps it merely appears so thanks to its size and an oblong shape which makes its edges feel wider. At the center, the **Obelisk of Pharaoh Ramses II** stands triumphantly, attracting a few tourists to sit at its base. The ▧**Santa Maria del Popolo** church is worth a visit, as it contains two Caravaggio masterpieces in the Capella Cerasi: *The Conversion of St. Paul* and *Crucifixion of St. Peter*, both of which are stunning examples of the artist's attention to *chiaroscuro* and the religious import this stylistic technique carried.

✚ Ⓜ*A: Flaminio.* Ⓢ *Church is free.* 🕐 *Church open M-Sa 7am-noon and 4-7pm, Su 8am-1:30pm and 4:30-7:30pm.*

▨ MUSEO DELL'ARA PACIS
                                                         ♿ MUSEUM

At intersection of Lungotevere in Augusta and P. Porto di Ripetta ☎06 06 08 🖳www.arapacis.it

This truly serene museum is a fitting space for its central monument, the **Ara Pacis.** The bare white walls and huge windows of the space reflect the peace of the monument, a frieze-covered enclosure constructed in 13 BCE to commemorate Augustus's victories throughout Spain and Gaul. Visitors can walk inside the structure to get a closer look at the 40m string of acanthus plant carved in the marble to represent renewal and unity under Augustus's Golden Age. On the outside, a mostly intact frieze of the ruler and his family reflects the tranquility of the period—the figures seem at ease, carved with an eye towards realism. Ironically, Augustus's body is chipped off in the procession and only his head remains. In the front of the museum, a row of busts including the head of Ottavia lie across from a reconstructed family tree. Check out the small model and accompanying map which shows the monument's original location in the context of Rome's current street layout. The area, now occupied by stores, restaurants, hotels, and, above all, tourists, was originally an open field where youth and soldiers used to compete in races and other athletic events. It's a shame that the only exercise going on now is the rush from shop to shop.

✚ Ⓜ*A: Spagna. Take V. del Carrozze towards V. del Corso and proceed into P. Augusto Imperiale.* ℹ *Audio tour available in English €3.50.* Ⓢ *€6.50, EU students 18-25 €4.50, EU citizens under 18 and over 65 free.* 🕐 *Open Tu-Su 9am-7pm. Last entry 1hr. before close.*

TREVI FOUNTAIN
                                                            ♿ FOUNTAIN

Right beyond P. Acc. S. Luca

The best time to see the fountain is at 4:30am, because it's probably the only hour where you'll be able to sit on one of the stone ledges without hearing the sounds of vendors selling overpriced trinkets and tourists snapping picture-perfect shots in the background. That's certainly the hour that Anita Ekberg, actress of Fellini's *La Dolce Vita*, came by when she took a dip in the fountain's gushing waters. (While you can make a late-night visit, don't follow her lead or

could you spare a million bucks?

If you've been to the Trevi fountain, then it's more than likely you've thrown a few coins in for good luck. What you probably don't know is that someone is making a living off of your spare change. **Roberto Cercelletta** has been taking money from the bottom of the fountain for the past 30 years, making upwards of US$150,000 a year in the process. The Roman and Italian courts have ruled that he is not stealing public money, and his activities are thus deemed legal. Almost every day, Cercelletta and his two minions slip on neon vests and enter the fountain in the early hours for 20-30min. to collect coins. The only day that he and his crew take a break is Sunday, when a local charity, Caritas, takes over the job, donating their findings to the poor. Caritas and other such organizations recently began protesting against Cercelletta's fishing. In counter-protest (warning: this story is about to get very real), Cercelletta climbed into the fountain numerous times and slashed his body with a knife, just to show that he is serious about his revenue stream, although apparently less so when it comes to his bloodstream. This all goes to show that, if you can't find a job back home, you should go to Italy. Even the criminally insane can make a living in Rome.

you risk a steep fine.) Even if you don't make it during this empty hour, Nicolo Salvi's mix of masterfully cut rock and stone in the raw is phenomenal. Neptune, surrounded by the goddesses of abundance and good health as well as two brawny horsemen, is carved with exacting detail, while the environment in which he sits is realistic merely because it has been left untouched. As good as gelato might be, save your coins for the fountain: one will ensure a prompt return to Rome, two will bring you love in the Eternal City, and three will bring about your wedding.

✠ ⓜA: Barberini. Proceed down V. del Tritone and turn left onto V. Stamperia.

PIAZZA DI SPAGNA AND THE SPANISH STEPS   ⊗ MONUMENT, PIAZZA
P. di Spagna

In every sense, the P. di Spagna is a conglomeration of international roots—not only does it draw a global tourist crowd to its sandy-colored steps, but its history encompasses the Italians (who designed it), the British (who occupied it), the French (who financed it), and, oh yeah, the Spaniards (you've got this one). Built in 1723 as a way to connect the Piazza with the new **Trinita dei Monti** church above it, the magnificent steps now seem to be more of a hangout spot for tired shoppers, gelato eaters, and youth looking to avoid the expensive bar scene of this commercial neighborhood. The best view of the steps and Piazza is actually from the church's steps directly above—from there, you can get a better sense of their size while avoiding the cluster of people below. When you do make your way down, check out the **Fontana della Barcaccia** built by Bernini the Elder before the steps were even constructed. The absurdly pink house and its two palm trees might remind you of leisurely beach life, but they actually commemorate the death of John Keats, who died there in 1821.

✠ ⓜA: Spagna.

TRINITA DEI MONTI   ⊗ CHURCH
At the top of the Spanish Steps, at the intersection of V. Sistina and P. Trinita dei Monti

If you don't want to climb the steps just for the view, then this small church can give you an incentive. Built in 1502 and pillaged dozens of times, poor Trinita dei Monti has lost all of its original pieces but the transept above the highest altar. Check out the hand-drawn floor plan at the entrance to seek out some of the more famed frescoes gracing the chapels. Daniele da Volterra's *Descent from the Cross* was especially lauded by Poussin and justly so—despite having undergone several restorations, it still brings a lot of color to the building's otherwise bleak walls.

➜ [M]A: Spagna. Walk up the steps. $ Free. 🕐 Open daily 7am-noon and 4-7pm.

JEWISH GHETTO

The Jewish Ghetto consists of a few blocks just off Isola Tiberina. Come here for great food and a look back at one of the first Jewish communities in Western Europe.

👍 THE GREAT SYNAGOGUE ♿ SYNAGOGUE

Corner of Lungotevere dei Cenci and V. Catalana ☎06 68 40 06 61 💻www.museoebraico.roma.it

From afar, the Synagogue occupies a place in the Roman skyline right up there with many of the city's other, more famous cupolas. The Synagogue's beautiful, palm-tree-surrounded roof is distinct from the architecture and ruins which surround it, so stroll by to glimpse a different element of Rome's urban design. Construction of the Synagogue began in 1904 as part of an effort to revitalize and rebuild the Jewish Ghetto, which had for many decades suffered from flooding and unsanitary conditions. By 1904, the Synagogue, designed with a curious mix of Persian and Babylonian influences, had been completed. Its unique design was intended to make it stand apart from the city's many Catholic churches. Inside, highlights include a stunning mix of painted floral patterns by Annibale Brugnoli and Domenico Bruschi and an upper section of stained glass. Look up top for the small portion of clear glass commemorating a child who was killed in a 1982 plane crash.

➜ At the corner of Lungotevere dei Cenci and V. Catalana. i Open for services. $ Free.

PIAZZA MATTEI ♿ PIAZZA

Between V. dei Falegnami and V. dei Funari

The tiny P. Mattei is the center of the Jewish Ghetto, though today most of the neighborhood's culinary and social activity occurs on V. del Ottavio. Visit this *piazza* for a look at the **Fontana delle Tartarughe,** a 16th-century monument by Taddeo Landini that depicts four figures bearing tortoises and a strange basin atop their heads. The rest of the Piazza is comprised of merchants and residential houses, save the **Chiesa di Sant'Angelo** in Pescheria, an unimposing eighth-century church named for its proximity to the fish market that once operated near Porta Ottavia. Though technically the center of the ghetto, this square feels more like a quiet respite from the busier streets nearby.

➜ From the Area Sacra, walk down V. Arenula and turn left onto V. dei Falegnami; P. Mattei is on the right. i The church cannot be entered due to repairs.

MUSEO EBRAICO ♿ MUSEUM

Corner of Lungotevere dei Cenci and V. Catalana ☎06 68 40 06 61 💻www.museoebraico.roma.it

The Jewish Museum, located within the Synagogue, displays a comprehensive collection of Jewish artifacts tracing the history of Jews in Rome as far back as the 16th century. The collection, which includes textiles, silver pieces, ancient writings, and stone engravings, has been growing since 1960, the year of the museum's opening. Touring the museum is an informative supplement to a stroll through the nearby ghetto, which today retains most of its authenticity through its cuisine and residents.

➜ From Ponte Garibaldi, turn right onto Lungotevere de Cenci and veer left toward the synagogue. $ €7, EU students €4, under 10 and handicapped persons free. Free guided tours of the Great Synagogue and the Spanish Synagogue available in English every hr. 🕐 Open June 16-Sept 15 M-Th 10am-6:15pm, F 10am-3:15pm, Su 10am-6:15pm; Sept 16-June 15 M-Th 10am-4:15pm, F 9am-1:15pm, Su 10am-4:15pm.

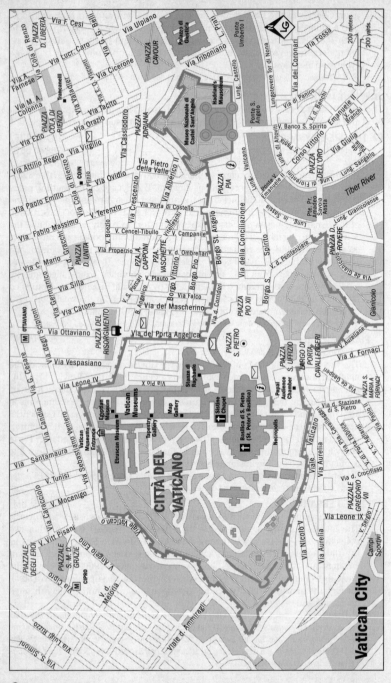

Vatican City

VATICAN CITY

More so than any other region of Rome, Vatican City fuses Roman history, artistic mastery, and Catholic ideology. As the administrative and spiritual headquarters of the Catholic Church, it has historically remained relatively independent from the rest of Rome, minting its own currency (the Italian *lire*), using colorfully-clad Swiss guards at its entrance, and running its own postal system. Expect some of the longest lines in the city but the greatest art to match, contained most notably in **St. Peter's Basilica** *(Basilica di San Pietro)* and the **Vatican Museums.**

St. Peter's Basilica and Environs

PIAZZA DI SAN PIETRO ♿ PIAZZA

At the end of V. della Concializione ☎06 69 81 662 🖳www.vaticanstate.va

There is no way to escape the arms of St. Peter—from the start of V. della Conciliazione they beckon pedestrians into the *piazza*, and once you've made your way inside, their embrace is enough to silence even the chattiest tourist in your group. If Bernini had seen this effect more than 400 years after the square's construction, he would have smiled. He intended the colonnade enclosing the *piazza*'s ovular area to symbolize the welcoming arms of the Catholic Church and greet tired pilgrims after a circuitous trek through the city. To enhance the vortex-like feel drawing people in, he designed the *piazza* in the form of an oval kissing a trapezoid. When standing at the square's center, you'll notice that this layout creates a perspective that makes the Basilica appear closer than it actually is. The row of 140 saints crowning the colonnade adds to the sense that the Basilica is pulling you inward. Stand at one of the round disks, and the quadruple rows of colonnades will seem to align themselves perfectly. Though it doesn't exactly compete with St. Peter's dome, the central obelisk (only 84 ft. tall) is at least a favorite with the pigeons, who often cluster at its base before perching on the saints' heads.

🚏 Bus #23, 34, 40, 271, or 982 to P. Pia or bus #62 down V. della Conciliazione. i The Pilgrim Tourist Office, to the left of the Basilica, has a multilingual staff, a gift shop, free bathrooms, a first-aid station, brochures, maps, currency exchange, and Vatican post boxes inside or nearby. Call the number or visit the website above for more info. $ Free. ⏰ Piazza open 24hr. Tourist Office open M-Sa 8:30am-6:15pm.

ST. PETER'S BASILICA ♿ CHURCH

At the end of V. della Concializione ☎06 69 81 662 🖳www.saintpetersbasilica.org

If the Vatican's special post boxes aren't enough to remind you that you've entered another jurisdiction, then perhaps the airport-like security required before entering the Basilica will be. Though lines here don't get nearly as long as those for the **Vatican Museums** (see below), people are required to pass through scanned security before entering the church during visiting hours. Once you've cleared the metal detectors, head through any one of the colossal doors. You won't be able to use the **Porta Sancta** (last door on the right of the entrance porch) though: it's only opened during Holy Years.

Depending on the time of day, the church's interior appears in incredibly varied degrees of illumination—the ceilings are so high that on dark days the small windows near the Basilica's top do little to illuminate the nave. Immediately to the right, find Michelangelo's **Pieta,** one of the most moving renderings of Mary and Jesus ever created. Since 1972, when a vandal attacked it with an axe, breaking Jesus's nose and Mary's hand, it has sat behind the bulletproof glass that slightly obscures the view even while it protects the precious piece of art. As you proceed onward, notice the strip of gold mosaics studded with Latin letters lining the perimeter of the nave and adding to the incredibly dogmatic and somewhat overbearing feel of the church.

Though it's hard to pinpoint the church's crowning element, Michelangelo's dome at least wins in size—at a spectacular 138m in height and 42m in width, it remains the largest in the world. Directly below it, the somewhat ridiculous *baldacchino* (note the sculpted bumblebees buzzing around its twisting columns) marks the altar place used by the pope. The supposed tomb of St. Peter sits immediately below the altar. For a more complete story, visit the **Scavi Office** (see **St. Peter's Grave** listing), where you can sign up for an exclusive tour of the burial site.

Despite the hordes of people who frequent the Basilica each day, its size is enough to dwarf even the biggest crowds (60,000 and counting). Though most people come to the church as tourists, and the flash of cameras is nearly constant, consider participating in Mass, which is conducted before Bernini's bronze **Cathedra Petri** and lit from behind by glowing alabaster windows. If you're feeling really ambitious, it's even possible to hold your wedding in the Basilica, though the wait and price for the most famous church in the world could leave you eternally single. Only Catholics need apply.

i Free guided tours in English leave from the Pilgrim Tourist Information Center. No shorts, miniskirts or tank tops. For information on weddings visit 💻www.saintpetersbasilica.org $ Free. ⏰ Basilica open daily Apr-Sept 7am-7pm; Oct-Mar 7am-6:30pm. Tours in English Tu at 9:45am, Th-F at 9:45am. Mass M-F 8:30am, 10am, 11am, noon, and 5pm; Su and holidays 9am, 10:30am, 11:30am, 12:15pm, 1pm, 4pm, and 5:45pm. Vespers daily 5pm.

ST. PETER'S GRAVE (PRE-CONSTANTINIAN NECROPOLIS) ⊕⊗ TOMB

Office to the left of St. Peter's, tombs below Scavi Office ☎06 69 88 53 18

The beauty of St. Peter's Basilica draws crowds flocking to its doors, but the mystery of the saint and first pope's tomb has people flocking to the internet: the only way to pay his alleged remains a visit is to book a tour online well in advance of your desired day. If you finally get a spot, expect a claustrophobic walk through the tombs accompanied by explanations of the sight's historical and religious significance. The story goes that in about 330 CE, Roman Emperor Constantine constructed his first basilica directly over St. Peter's tomb. Over 1000 years later, the Renaissance basilica we see today was built in its place. The discovery of ancient ruins and a number of bones in 1939 had the Pope claiming that St. Peter's remains did in fact exist under the original altar. Though successive popes have affirmed the presence of the holy remains, many believe that the bones were removed during the Saracen pillaging of Rome in 849 CE. Don't expect to play Sherlock during the tour—just enjoy the sarcophagi, mosaics, and funerary inscriptions along the way.

✣ In the piazza. Instead of entering the Basilica, veer left and look for Swiss Guards dressed in stripes who will grant you access to the courtyard. The Scavi Office is on the courtyard's right side. i The Necropolis can only be seen via a guided tour organized by the Scavi Office. Reservations must be made at least 1 day prior (but should be made as far in advance as possible, as much as 90 days). Pick up a reservation form at the office and hand deliver it or email. Do not call. Tours last 90min. and are available in English. Fully covered attire required. No backpacks or bulky items. Must be at least 15 years old. $ €12. ⏰ Scavi Office open M-Sa 9am-5pm.

CUPOLA AND GROTTE VATICANE ⊕⊗ CHURCH

To the right of the Basilica 💻www.vaticanstate.va/EN/Monuments/Saint_Peters_Basilica

If you haven't seen enough of Rome's sky or soil, consider the ascent up to St. Peter's Cupola or the descent into its *grotte* (underground caves). If you head skyward, get ready to be swept away: lose your breath climbing the 551 steps to the top (320 with the elevator), then have it stolen by the gasp-inducing view—one of the city's most spectacular panoramas and the only one in which St. Peter's doesn't steal the show as the biggest dome. A walk through the low-ceilinged tombs is eerie rather than breathtaking, as what feels like an endless

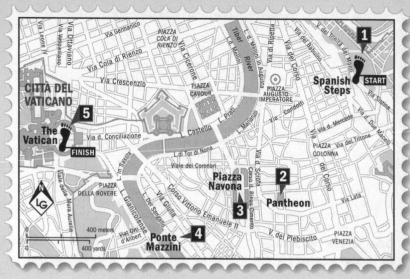

border hopping

1. SPANISH STEPS. In the cosmopolitan city of Rome, a brief walk from one neighborhood to another can in fact feel like moving from one country to another. And if that walk takes you to the Vatican City, then that's not just a feeling—it's fact. For this tour, start at the top of the Spanish Steps. Admire the view over the city, particularly of St. Peter's Basilica, which is where you're headed after all. Then proceed down the steps into the P. di Spagna and proceed along the V. di Condotti for what may be to many people a foreign experience: the glitz and high prices of the area's designer stores. Turning left onto V. del Corso, then right, will get you to the next stop: the Pantheon.

2. THE PANTHEON. This majestic relic from Ancient Rome remains in superb condition (sadly, the same cannot be said for the Colosseum and *definitely* not for the Circus Maximus). Appreciate its Classical design and the huge dome, which would remain as the largest in the world for more than a millennium.

3. PIAZZA NAVONA. Having experienced the glitz of the P. di Spagna and the history of the Pantheon, you can head to P. Navona to see modern Rome at its greatest. The place still has a ton of history, of course—where in Rome doesn't?—but with a huge crowd at all times of day performing, watching, or just hanging out, it's a lively and fascinating place to spend time.

4. PONTE MAZZINI. From P. Navona, continue heading west until you reach the Tiber River, an oft-forgotten feature of this city. Crossing over the Ponte Mazzini, you'll get the chance to experience Project "Tevereterno," which aims to elevate the visibility and importance of the Tiber to the city.

5. THE VATICAN. Turn right after the river and head north and then west to reach P. di San Pietro, admiring the majesty of St Peter's Basilica as you do so. Having started in Spain (OK, only by a very loose definition), you've proceeded through a whole series of flavors of Italian culture. Now, soak in the piety of the Vatican City State.

WALKING TOUR

collection of sarcophagi (including those of the last four popes) lines the stone passageways. Petri Apostoli's *sepolcro*, guarded by stone lions and protected behind glass, attracts the most attention, but don't miss the gold mosaics crowning Pius XI's final resting place.

➔ Walk to the last door on the right of the Basilica. In the courtyard, entrance to the Cupola is on the right, the Treasury on the left. ℹ Be prepared for at least 320 steps of climbing to the cupola, and a slightly claustrophobic setting in the Grotte. $ Cupola €5, with elevator €7. Grotte free. 🕐 Cupola and Grotte open daily Apr-Sept 8am-6pm; Oct-Mar 8am-5pm.

TREASURY ⊗ MUSEUM

In St. Peter's Basilica, to the left 🖥www.vaticanstate.va/EN/Monuments/Saint_Peters_Basilica

If St. Peter's Basilica's gold decorations aren't enough to dazzle you, then pay a visit to the Treasury, a small museum containing gifts bestowed upon the great pope's tomb. Goggle at the gold-and-silver-plated, gem-encrusted papal tiara, the intricate gold and silver embroidery on the Dalmatic of Charlemagne, and the several diamond, emerald, and ruby rings that are placed on St. Peter—his statue, that is—to commemorate Saints Peter and Paul Day every June 29th.

➔ Inside St. Peter's Basilica toward the left; look for the multilingual sign. ℹ No photography. $ €6, under 12 €4. 🕐 Treasury open daily Apr-Sept 8am-6:50pm; Oct-Mar 8am-5:50pm.

Other Vatican City Sights

👍 VATICAN MUSEUMS ⊗♿ MUSEUM

Entrance at Vle. Vaticano ☎06 69 88 38 60 🖥www.museivaticani.va

After waiting in a 4hr. line, we hope you spend at least half as much time in the galleries themselves. Unfortunately, the lure of the Sistine Chapel (and frequent arrows pointing the way) pull people onward, creating a human stream with a very strong current. But you're not a 🐟**fish!** Jump out and admire some of the more obscure treasures which are not only on display but comprise the building itself: stunning wall frescoes, floor mosaics, and even a **bronze double-helix ramp.** Check it out upon entering, as the intricate metal work on the side is harder to see while on the stairs.

Maps, guidebooks, and audio tours will be for sale at the airport-like entrance where, yes, you are required to pass through scanned security. If this is your first time through these museums, forget the itinerary and just wander a bit, stopping at whatever piques your fancy. If you try to read and see everything in a guidebook, you will tire before getting even halfway through. Part of the pleasure is arriving at masterpieces unexpectedly.

After entering the complex, most people start in the **Museo Pio-Clemetino,** which contains the world's greatest collection of antique sculptures, including the famous **Laocoon** in an octagonal courtyard. The sculpture, depicting a violent struggle between Laocoon and sea serpents as his sons try to rescue him, is a Greek masterpiece which awed even Michelangelo. Don't miss the **Stanza degli Animali,** filled with statues of roaring lions and more sedate donkeys. Look to your feet for an impressive mosaic floor of fruits, more animals, and abstract designs. The (relatively) small **Egyptian Museum** to the side generally attracts a smaller crowd if you need a spot to recuperate. Before heading upstairs, make sure to circumnavigate the 👍**Sala Rotonda,** a small room with unbelievable mosaics on the floor and a domed roof recalling the **Pantheon's** coffered ceiling and oculus.

Head directly upstairs to find the **Etruscan Museum,** which contains a daunting 18 rooms' worth of Etruscan artifacts, sarcophagi, and vases that offer a glimpse into Italy's earliest civilization. The **Candelabra Gallery** and dimly lit **Tapestry Gallery** are often treated as thoroughfares, but the **Map Gallery** is worth a stop. Huge frescoed maps of Italy line the walls and provide an eye into the country's diverse geographical regions. You can carry on via a shortcut to the Sistine Chapel from here, but if you can wait, meander through the **Stanza Sobieski,** with its strange mix of religious and military work, and then the **Stanze di Rafaele.** These four rooms, originally Julius II's apartments, were decorated by the great Rafaele, and include the 👍**School of Athens** fresco on one large wall.

In no other collection would all the aforementioned works possibly be considered a *precursor* to the main show. But you're in the Vatican Museum, and it's time for the main course. The 👍**Sistine Chapel** is undoubtedly the most sought out, crowded, and monumental part of the museum. Every few minutes, the guards shush the mass of people, reminding them not to take photos and ushering them onward. Minutes later, the chatter recommences, and a flash goes off. Expect an unpleasant experience in the way of people but a remarkable one in the way of art. If craning your neck to see the ceiling hurts after a few minutes, imagine Michelangelo actually making the work—he painted the frescoes on a platform while bending backward and never recovered from the strain. Even those not versed in art history will recognize the famous **Creation of Adam,** one of nine panels depicting scenes from the story of Genesis. Occupying the entirety of the altar wall, the **Last Judgment** can be viewed with much less physical contortion. This huge fresco is, in a way, free of composition—it is a massive conglomeration of muscular figures, clouds, and land masses—but this adds to its uncontainable and inconceivable force. Though it can be difficult to focus on one area, look for the flayed human skin that hangs between heaven and hell, a self-portrait included by Michelangelo.

➔ Ⓜ A: Ottaviano. Head down V. Ottaviano, turn right onto V. dei Bastioni di Michelangelo, and follow the wall until you see the end of the line to the museums. Entrance is on Vle. Vaticano. ℹ A wheelchair-accessible itinerary is available as well as wheelchairs for rent. Call ☎06 698 81589 for info. $ €15, EU citizens ages 18-26 and 6-18 €8; under 6 free. Last Su of every month all enter free. Entrance with guided and audio tours €31/€25. ⏰ Galleries open M-Sa and last Su of each month 9am-6pm. Last entry 2 hr. before close. Open Apr-July F 7-11pm for special viewing only; online reservation required, €4.

MUSEO NAZIONALE DI CASTEL SANT'ANGELO — 🚫♿ CASTLE, MUSEUM

Lungotevere Castello 50 ☎06 68 19 111 💻www.castelsantangelo.com

If you thought all of Rome was basilicas and ruins, think again: that circular, brick structure on the river is a castle, complete with moat (okay, it's dried up) and torches (fine, they're electric). Originally built in the first century CE as a mausoleum for Hadrian and his family, it has since been converted from a tomb to a palace, castle, prison, and—finally—museum. A walk through the massive structure starts with the ascent up a 125m ramp whose dimly lit corridor is flanked by burial chambers. When you step into the light, note the central courtyard's crowning piece, the **Angel Statue** with rusted metal wings and a stone body designed by Raffaello da Montelupo. Floorplans of the castle's layout attempt to guide you through, but it's best to let yourself get lost in the staircases and rooms. If you can, make your way to the 👍**Sala di Apollo,** a mostly white room with whimsical frescoes of part-human, part-animal beasts. Once you've toured the interior, take some time on the rooftop where the panorama of Rome and view of the gleaming Sistine Chapel is one of the best in the city. The marble **Ponte Sant'Angelo** lined with statues by Bernini is best seen from this angle.

➔ Bus #23, 34, 40, 271 or 982 to P. Pia. At the end of V. della Conciliazione and at the intersection with Ponte S. Angelo. $ €8.50, EU citizens ages 18-25 €6, EU citizens under 18 and over 65 free. Audio tour €4. ⏰ Open Tu-Su 9am-7:30pm. Ticket office closes 6:30pm.

PIAZZA CAVOUR — ♿ PIAZZA

On the Lungotevere Castello

P. Cavour, cushioned between V. Triboniano and V. Ulpiano, is probably admired more from the heights of nearby monuments than from its center: most of the square's buildings are inaccessible to the public. The most imposing structure is Rome's **Supreme Court of Cassation,** where lawyers instead of lions determine the fate of those charged: there's no modern-day Colosseum here. The odd white structure on the left side is the **Chiese Valdese,** an evangelical church where the oldest existing group of non-Catholic Christians prior to the Reformation (the Waldensians) pray. If these two structures don't catch your eye from afar, then maybe the tall palms at the *piazza*'s center will, bringing you away from the gravity of St. Peter's and suggesting something a bit more playful.

🧭 From Castel Sant'Angelo, head down Lungotevere Castello away from St. Peter's Basilica. [$] Free.

TRASTEVERE

Ahhh, Trastevere. With old cobblestone streets, hidden-away trattorias, and bustling nightlife, this oft-forgotten gem of a neighborhood is not one to miss. Even if you're only in Rome a few days, ditch some of those churches you had planned to visit and head across the Tiber to enjoy more intimate *piazze*, basilicas that rival their more-famous brethren on the other side of the river, and a tight-knit community proud of their unpretentious neighborhood. Cross the **Ponte Garibaldi** to make your way directly onto **Piazza G. Belli**, which holds the triumphant statue of poet Giuseppe Gioachino Belli. Via Trastevere runs through the neighborhood, and if not the most scenic of streets, it is still a reliable place to find cheap eats or clothes. To the left, most of the streets are fairly quiet but full of restaurants and small shops. By contrast, the right side of Trastevere contains most of the neighborhood's activity—turn right onto V. della Lungaretta to arrive at **Piazza di Sant'Apollonia** and the nearby **Piazza di Santa Maria in Trastevere.** Both are full of commotion and are more touristed than the rest of the neighborhood. Just at the end of the Ponte Sisto, **Piazza Trilussa** offers proximity to nightlife spots as well as scenic views of the river, making it particularly popular with students. **Piazza San Cosimato**, off of V. Luciano Manara, boasts an outdoor market selling fresh fruits, vegetables, and fish.

👍 ISOLA TIBERINA ♿ OPEN SPACE

With most of Rome's major sights located further "inland," tourists tend to forget about Rome's river, the Fiume Tevere, and the land out yonder. On your way to Trastevere, take the tiny **Ponte Fabriccio (a.k.a. the Ponte dei Quattro Capi)**, which, in case you couldn't tell by its name, bears four stone heads, allegedly those of the architects who originally restored the bridge. You'll find yourself standing on Isola Tiberina, a small plot of land that, according to legend, is actually composed of the silt-covered bodily remains of Tarquin, an Etruscan ruler who was thrown in the river for raping the beautiful Lucretia. The island is only home to a few establishments, so most people only stay to check out the hard-to-pronounce **Fatebenefratelli Hospital**, which looks more like a church than a healing facility. If you want to stick around, head down the slope to the open expanse directly on the river. A few people might be fishing, but more will be 👍**lying in the sun** on what is the closest thing Rome has to a beach.

🧭 From V. del Teatro Marcello, walk towards the water and onto Lungomare dei Pierleoni. Turn left and cross Ponte Fabricio. [$] Free.

GIANICOLO HILL ♿ OPEN SPACE

While people-produced monuments (or at least their remains) take center stage in Central Rome, those in Trastevere are rivaled by the neighborhood's natural wonders. The highest peak in this part of Rome, Gianicolo Hill, is a large expanse of land highlighted by the **Fonte Acqua Paola,** a fountain which marks the end of an aqueduct honoring Pope Paul V. While the crystal-blue pool of water and elaborate white facade above it are marvels of human design, the 👍**surrounding landscape** really steals the show. If you continue up the winding (and steep)

V. Garibaldi, you'll come to the site of what was once the **Porta San Pancrazio** (the main gate built around Gianicolo to protect Rome from raids), which, since the French raids in the late 1800s, has been replaced. It seems the French were not always known for raising the white flag...

➔ From Fonte Aqua Paola, continue uphill, onto V. Aldo Fabrizi and enter the park. You will pass Monumento a Garibaldi on the pleasant walk. $ Free.

CHIESA DI SANTA MARIA IN TRASTEVERE ♿ CHURCH

P. Santa Maria in Trastevere ☎06 58 14 802

Located in the heart of Trastevere, this church is a tourist favorite, and for good reason: beautiful mosaics decorating the facade are matched by an equally stunning gold interior where more mosaics depicting Jesus, Mary, and a slew of other Biblical figures grace the apse. This *chiesa* was the first in Rome built exclusively for the Virgin Mary. The *piazza* out front is a lovely place to admire this Byzantine structure.

➔ From Vle. Trastevere, turn right onto V. San Francesco a Ripa and walk 5min. until you get to the piazza. $ Free. 🕐 Open M-F 9am-5:30pm.

BOTANICAL GARDENS ♿ GARDENS

Largo Cristina di Svezia 23A. ☎06 49 91 71 07

The Botanical Gardens are located on the flat area of land adjacent to Giancolo Hill. With over 3500 types of flora, ranging from bamboo in the Japanese garden to roses first grown in Rome during the Baroque Period, this oasis of green is a sharp contrast to most of Rome's drier and duller patches of natural land. Check out the **Garden for the Blind**, a star-shaped region with labels written in Braille.

➔ Walk to the end of V. Corsini until you reach Largo Cristina di Svezia. $ €4, ages 6-11 and over 59 €2. 🕐 Open Tu-Su 9:30am-6:30pm. Closed in Aug.

VILLA BORGHESE, PARIOLI, AND FLAMINIO

👍 VILLA BORGHESE ♿📶 GARDENS

Park bordered by Vle. Trinita dei Monti and V. Porta Pinciana. ☎06 32 16 564

The Villa Borghese sits north of Termini and provides a needed respite from the city's bustle. Mostly flat pathways cut through gardens, lawns, and various museums, including the **Galleria Borghese,** the **Museo Nazionale Etrusco di Villa Giulia,** and the **Galleria Nazionale d'Arte Moderna,** which actually sits right outside the park. Though most visitors choose to stroll or picnic in the park, there is also a bike rental stand just beyond the entrance of the Galleria Borghese.

➔ [M]A: Spagna or Flaminio. There are multiple entrances to the park: Porta Pinciana, Piazzale Flaminio, Vle. Belle Arti, V. Mercadante, and V. Pinciana. $ Gardens free. Bike rental €10 per day or €4 per hr. Visit 💻www.ascolbike.com for more information. 🕐 Gardens open daily Apr-Aug 7am-9pm; Sept 7am-8pm; Oct-Dec 7am-6pm; Jan-Feb 7am-6pm; Mar 7am-8pm.

GALLERIA BORGHESE 🎟♿ MUSEUM

Piazzale del Museo Borghese 5 ☎06 84 16 542 💻www.galleriaborghese.it

While the beautiful gardens in which it sits are reason enough to make the trek up to this fabulous museum, the Galleria Borghese is a must-see while in Rome. Inside the villa, Cardinal Scipione's collection includes such standouts as Bernini's *David* and the dynamic *Apollo and Daphne*, Caravaggio's gruesome *David with the Head of Goliath*, and other masterpieces by Correggio, Titian, Raphael, Veronese, and Rubens. Note that reservations are required in advance of your visit to the galleria. They are easy to make over the phone or online, but you won't be able to wander in on a whim. On par with the Vatican museums and less crowded because of the required reservation, the Galleria Borghese is a true Roman gem.

➔ Enter on V. Pinciana, near V. Isonzo. Proceed up Vle. dell'Uccelleria for about 5min. ℹ Reservations required; call ☎06 855 5952 or visit 💻www.ticketeria.it. $ €10.50, EU citizens ages 18-25

€7.25, EU citizens under 18 and over 65 €4. Tours €6, ages 9 and under free. 90min. audio tour (available in English) €5. ⏰ Open Tu-Su 9am-7pm. Reservation phone line open M-F 9am-6pm, Sa 9am-1pm. Ticket office closes 30min. before museum. Guided tours available in English at 9:10am and 11:10am

GALLERIA D'ARTE MODERNA 🎫[X] MUSEUM

Vle. delle Belle Arti 131 ☎06 32 29 81 💻www.gnam.arti.beniculturali.it

The Galleria d'Arte Moderna is not only a beautiful building but one that contains a superb collection of art dating from the past 200 years—certainly a relief to visitors who've spent days touring the sights of Ancient Rome. The museum's light-filled central room for greeting visitors offers an impressive display of works by Klimt, Mondrian, Giacometti, Balla, and Klee. Proceeding immediately ahead, you will reach the most contemporary of the rooms, which is crowned with a hanging sculpture by Calder and adorned with a number of white and black sculptural paintings by Castellani. The rest of the museum is well-organized by century and period, starting with works by Courbet, Van Gogh, Cezanne, Manet, and Degas and heading into the 20th century with a huge collection of De Chirico, Boccioni, Balla, Morandi, Miro, and Modigliani. Make sure to pass through famed modernist Marcel Duchamp's collection of ready-mades, including the famous Urinal.

🚶 From Vle. del Giardino in the Villa Borghese, veer right and exit the park onto Vle. delle Belle Arti. Museum is on the right. [$] €8, EU students 18-25 €4, ages under 18 and over 65 free. Audio tour (available in English) €4. ⏰ Open Tu-Su 8:30am-7:30pm. Ticket office closes at 7:15pm.

PINCIO [X] PANORAMIC VIEW

Near the park entrance off P. del Popolo.

Though the summit has a few sights of its own, the real motivation for climbing up this hill is the stunning vista of the P. del Popolo you will be able to view from its top. The most prominent monuments visible from the peak are the obelisk in the center of the piazza, the churches S. Maria dei Miracoli and S. Maria di Montesanto, and, looming in the distance, St. Peter's Basilica. Once you've absorbed the panorama, take some time to walk through the gardens and check out the **Idroconometro,** a clock powered by the water flowing through a group of fountains.

🚶 The fastest way to reach the top is from the steep ascent near P. del Popolo. A more scenic but slower route is through the Villa Borghese itself around V. Veneto. [$] Free.

PIAZZA BARBERINI ♿ PIAZZA

At the intersection of V. Tritone, V. Sistina, V. Barberini, and V. della Quattro Fontane

At the center of this especially busy *piazza* sit the lovely Fontana Tritone and Fontana delle Api, two Bernini fountains popular with pigeons and people. The *piazza* may not be the most restful spot, as loud cars constantly stream by, so consider heading inside to the **Palazzo Barberini** just down the street at V. delle Quattro Fontane 13, which holds the National Gallery of Arte Antica. Even if you don't venture inside, the courtyard's tall palm trees and the building's beautiful facade are worth a visit. At the Chiesa della Immacolata Concezione, the **Capuchin Crypt** *(V. Veneto 27 ☎06 48 71 185 💻www.cappucciniviaveneto.it.)* contains an awesome variety of human skulls and bones.

🚶 [M]A: Barberini. ℹ Call ☎06 32 810 for information on booking palazzo. [$] Piazza free. Palazzo €5, EU students 18-25 €2.50, EU citizens under 18 and over 65 free. ⏰ Crypt open M-W 9am-noon and 3-6pm, F-Su 9am-noon and 3-6pm. Palazzo open Tu-Su 8:30am-7:30pm.

GIARDINO BIOLOGICO 🎫♿ GARDENS

Piazzale del Giardino Zoologico 1. Entrance at Lungarno Zoologico V. Gassman, along the Vle. del Giardino ☎06 36 08 211 💻www.bioparco.it or www.listicket.it

Though a bit expensive, this biopark, located 5min. from the Galleria Borghese, is a great spot for children and families. Its collection of animals includes giraffes, lions, and an impressive collection of scaled critters within its huge Reptile House.

🚏 Walking from the Galleria Borghese, continue on Vle. dell' Uccellieria and veer left onto Vle. del Giardino. Park is on the right. $ €12.50, disabled, under 12, and over 60 €10.50, children under 1m tall free. €4 admission on W. 🕐 Open M-F 9:30am-5pm, Sa-Su 9:30am-6pm.

TERMINI AND SAN LORENZO

👍 BASILICA DI SANTA MARIA MAGGIORE

♿ CHURCH

In P. Esquilino ☎06 69 88 68 02

It's a good thing the Basilica is so close to Termini, or the slew of cheap eats and hostels might be the only first impression visitors received of the area. Just a 5min. walk from the station, this fifth-century church is a stunning combination of Baroque and classic Roman design. With its white marble artifice and huge flight of stairs, the back of the church (close to V. Cavour) might be even more stunning than the front. Although the frescoes that line the side chapels are impressive, it's the gold-coffered ceiling and wide apse that really impress. Seriously, there's a lot of gold in here. If you aren't blinded by the shininess, the 14th-century mosaics covering the *loggia* and the large *baldacchino* at the altar are also beautiful. Adjoining the basilica is a small museum containing artifacts and artwork relating to the church's history, even though the basilica itself offers enough to see. Upon leaving, check out the beautiful indigo (violet, if you prefer) stained-glass window crowning the entrance.

*🚏 ⓂTermini. Turn right onto V. Giolitti and walk down V. Cavour. **i** Modest dress required. $ Basilica free. Museum €4, EU students and over 65 €2. Loggia €5/€3. Audio tour (available in English) €4. 🕐 Basilica open daily 7am-7pm. Museum open daily 9am-6pm.*

CHIESA DI SANTA MARIA DEGLI ANGELI

♿ CHURCH

P. della Repubblica ☎06 48 80 812 💻www.santamariadegliangeliroma.it

At the crest of the expansive P. della Repubblica, this 16th-century church (Michelangelo's last, at age 86) is monumental, starting with its front doors; the façade is actually taken from the remains of Diocletian's hot baths, on which Pope Pius IV commissioned the church to be built. Half-sculpted and half-in-the-rough figures jut out of the huge doors; the bronze one on the left symbolizes the risen Christ. Throughout the interior, there are many similar statues left only partially completed. Inside, a small rotunda leads into an especially open interior whose design underwent many revisions before it was finally completed. The scarcity of seats makes it less crowded than most churches. A sundial, which leads from the east transept to the altar, was used by the Romans for centuries. Check out the schedule of sundial viewings or reserve a demonstration at the information desk.

🚏 ⓂTermini. Walk into the P. del Cinquecento and veer left toward V. Viminale. $ Sundial demonstrations should be reserved 2 days in advance, June 15-Sept 15. Call ☎06 48 70 749 for more information. 🕐 Open M-F 7am-6:30pm, Sa-Su 7am-7:30pm.

BATHS OF DIOCLETIAN

🚫♿ MUSEUM

V. Enrico de Nicola 79 ☎06 39 96 77 00

In the heart of busy Termini, the Baths of Diocletian have weathered the city grime. Begun in 298 CE by Maximianus, brother of Diocletian, the baths took nearly 10 years—and more than 40,000 Christian slaves—to build. Upon completion, they were able to accommodate 3000 people in what ended up being much more than a mere "bath"—the Diocletian complex contained libraries, gardens, gallery spaces, gyms, and even brothels. Though the baths may no longer exist in the same state of glory, a visit to them is surely worth it.

*🚏 ⓂTermini. Walk into P. dei Cinquecento; enter on V. Volturno. **i** Part of the Museo Nazionale*

Romano group; buy 1 ticket for entrance to all 4 sights over 3 days. $ €7, EU students €3.50, EU citizens under 18 and over 65 free. ⏰ Open Tu-Su 9am-7:45pm.

VIA XX SETTEMBRE ♿ STREET

Even though V. XX Settembre is mostly a functioning thoroughfare, a number of beautiful sights can be seen while walking along its length. The street merges into V. dei Quirinale on one end and V. Nomentana on the other. Between grabbing a bite and making your way to the next destination, check out the four obelisks built by the city in the 1700s to help define Rome's neighborhoods and improve traffic conditions. (Hard to believe that they needed improvement in a time that predated Vespas and the popularization of the car.) The best spot on XX Settembre from which to survey the scene is at V. delle Quattro Fontane, where you can see the monuments of **Via dei Quirinal,** the **Spanish Steps,** and **Santa Maria Maggiore.** Atop the P. San Bernardo sits the beautiful and seriously colossal **Fontana dell'Acqua Felice.**

 # ⓂTermini. Walk through P. della Rebupplica and proceed forward until you reach V. XX Settembre. $ Free.

TESTACCIO AND OSTIENSE

👍 BASILICA DI SAN PAOLO FUORI LE MURA ♿ CHURCH

Piazzale San Paolo 1 ☎06 69 88 08 00 💻www.basilicasanpaolo.org

This is the light at the end of the tunnel, but unlike the kind you might see during a near-death experience, you should definitely make your way toward this light. After a 30min. walk down the empty-ish V. Ostiense, this magnificent basilica and its gold mosaics are the shining reward you've been waiting for. The second-largest church in Rome, the often overlooked Basilica di San Paolo Fuori le Mura shares extraterritorial status with the **Vatican, Santa Maria Maggiore,** and **San Giovanni in Laterano.** Though this sounds cool, it pretty much means that if you buy a stamp from the church's gift shop, you can only mail the letter in a post box on the premises. Historically, the basilica might be most famous for housing the body of St. Paul after his beheading, but for the aesthetically inclined, the gold mosaics both inside and out steal the show. Walking in from **Portico Gregoriano** on the side, the massive arch crowning the altar is like a gold crown consisting of mosaics that depict Christ giving the benediction to surrounding apostles. Around the perimeter, 200 portraits (and counting) of past popes will leave you wondering what is to be done when space runs out. The most stunning area of all, however, is the outside courtyard, where tall palm trees sway before the gold mosaic facade upon which an image of Christ, Peter, and Paul is depicted. Despite having been constructed after a 19th-century fire that damaged the building, this more contemporary work is just as compelling as the altarpiece inside.

The quiet cloister is worth seeing if the church's main mosaics aren't enough for you: its decorated columns are similar to those in San Giovanni. Before the trek back up V. Ostiense, head to the gift shop where you can buy holy sweets and papal alcohol to fortify yourself *(€6.50-18).*

 # ⓂB: Basilica San Paolo, or bus #23 to Ostiense/LGT S. Paolo stop. i Modest dress required. $ Basilica free. Cloister €4, reduced for students and groups. 1hr. guided visits available; reserve online. ⏰ Basilica open daily 7am-6:30pm

👍 CENTRALE MONTEMARTINI MUSEUM

V. Ostiense 106 ☎06 42 88 88 88 💻www.centralmontemartini.org

You might have believed that central Rome is *the* place for seeing old ruins juxtaposed against modern constructions, but the Eternal City is nothing compared to this museum. A relatively new addition to the **Musei Capitolini** family, this building—the first public electricity plant in the city—now houses an

rome

impressive collection of Roman statues, busts, and mosaics excavated during the early 1800s. Classical marble figures stand before gigantic engines and a 15m boiler, creating a peculiar tableau that combines the ancient and the modern. After wandering through the Sala Macchina on the first floor, check out the foot from the statue of **Fortuna Huiusce Diei,** a devotional piece from 101 BCE which originally stood an impressive 8m high. The foot itself is really more like 3—in length, that is. The sea-green **Sala Caldaie** has less modern machinery, but its floor is inlaid with a reconstructed mosaic that depicts a vicious hunting scene from the fourth century.

⇞ Ⓜ B: Ostiense. A 10min. walk down the V. Ostiense. $ €4.50, EU students 18-25 €2.50, EU citizens under 18 and over 65 free. Combined ticket with Musei Capitolini €8.50/6.50. 🕐 Open Tu-Su 9am-7pm. Last entry 30min. before close.

CIMITERO ACATTOLICO PER GLI STRANIERI AND WAR CEMETERY ❂ ♿ CEMETERY

War Cemetery on V. Nicola Zabaglia beside P. Vittorio Bottego ☎06 50 99 91

Cimitero Acattolico at V. Caio Cestio 6 ☎06 57 41 900 💻www.protestantcemetery.it

We don't recommend making the trek to Ostiense for the sole purpose of seeing a cemetery, but after walking along mostly building-lined streets, these tree-filled and quiet spots are a peaceful retreat. From the outside, tall tamarind trees peek over the light pink wall of the Cimitero Acattolico, making the stroll down V. Caio Cestio all the more scenic. Inside, stray cats, more trees, and clusters of gravestones marking the death of non-Catholic foreigners compete for your attention. Notable names to look out for include John Keats (though instead of his name, the words "all that was mortal of a Young English Poet" are what you'll need to spot), Julis (son of Goethe), and socialist Antonio Gramsci. Across the street, the smaller and more refined War Cemetery is dedicated to the soldiers who died in WWII. A stone from Hadrian's Wall, the northernmost boundary of the Ancient Roman Empire, is marked to honor the soldiers.

⇞ Ⓜ A: Piramide. Walk through the Porta San Paolo and veer left. $ War cemetery free. Cimitero Acattolico €2 suggested donation. 🕐 War Cemetery open M-F 8am-3pm. Cimitero Acattolico open M-Sa 9am-5pm, Su 9am-1pm. Last entry 30min. before close.

PIAZZALE OSTIENSE ♿ PIAZZA

Piazzale Ostiense and environs

Piazzale Ostiense is the geographical epicenter of the neighborhood, most accessible by public transportation and busier than the residential streets that surround it. At the *piazzale*'s center, a curious pyramid is surrounded by speedy Vespas and pedestrians who look up at its 27m peak. Built in the first century BCE after Gaius defeated Cleopatra and her army, the **Piramide di Caio Cestio** stands like the obelisks scattered throughout the city center—a gray duckling in a pool of white Roman classicism. Right beside it, the **Porta San Paolo** stands as a reminder of Rome's ancient days when the gateway linked the city to its most important port in Ostia. The hill of dirty green beyond it is **Monte Testaccio,** a landfill which has been accumulating old terra-cotta pots (known as *testae:* note the similarity to Testaccio in name) for centuries. Of the goods which were originally traded and deposited there, the only thing which you still might find here is wine—the base of the hill is surrounded by Testaccio's best nightclubs and bars.

⇞ Ⓜ B: Piramide or bus #173 from Termini. $ Free.

SOUTHERN ROME AND THE APPIAN WAY

The Appian Way and Environs

👍 THE APPIAN WAY ♿ ANCIENT ROME

V. Appia Antica ☎06 51 35 316 💻www.parcoappiaantica.it

When you've had your way with Rome's busy *corsi*, it might be time to try the

Appian on for size. Stretching 16km from Porta San Sebastiano to Frattocchie, it tends to be a little big for most people: walking itineraries generally end around the **Tomb of Cecilia Metella,** though the road extends another 5-6 mi. Don't expect that first stretch to be all dirt roads surrounded by fields and crumbling aqueducts. Since being paved over, the Appian Way has become, somewhat unfortunately, a modern-day reincarnation of its ancient self: a very busy road. That means you'll see your fair share of whizzing cars and walking tourists as you follow the street.

In the third century, V. Appia Antica—the main branch of the trail—extended about a mile from Porta Capena to Porta S. Sebastiano. Today that stretch has become V. delle Terme di Caracalla and V. di Porta San Sebastiano, and the true "Way" officially begins after you exit the **Aurelian walls.** At the time of its use, the ancient road served as the burial ground of the highest Romans and early Christians, since they were forbidden to keep their tombs within the city walls. Legends who actually walked the road included **Virgil, Saint Peter,** and **Spartacus,** each of whom left a trail of history behind him—in the case of Spartacus, a trail of bodies. If you plan on walking this stretch, keep in mind that its cobblestone ground practically shakes with buses and scooters zooming by, and there's little shoulder reserved for pedestrians. As the road merges into V. Appia Antica, the din doesn't stop until you reach the tourist office, where you'll need to make a decision about what roads to take. For the most scenic path, head up the slightly inclined road leading to San Callisto *(closed W)*, where you can see countryside and bushes of pink flowers from the elevated path. V. Appia Antica and V. Ardeatina on either side are traversed by buses.

The main attractions on this initial strip are the third-century catacombs, underground passageways full of bodies, sarcophagi, and paintings. For the more nature-inclined traveler, the true attractions will not start until after **Cecilia Metella,** where you can walk on the road's original paving stones and gaze at miles of unsullied land. If that sounds more appealing to you but you don't want to wander that far south, consider walking down V. della Caffarella (to the left of V. Appia Antica) and the pedestrian trails surrounding it instead of hitting the catacombs. (And at a hefty fee of €8 each, by bypassing them completely, you'll be seeing fewer bones of the dead-person variety and more of the cash-monies kind.) Either way, bring yourself a picnic lunch to avoid a stop at the overpriced restaurants along the way.

✠ ⓂA: San Giovanni. Head through Porta San Giovanni and into the piazza. Take bus #218; to reach the info office, push the button after you turn left onto V. Appia Antica, right before Domine Quo Vadis. The bus continues up V. Ardeatina and drops you off near the S. Domitilla and S. Calisto Catacombs. Alternatively, take ⓂB: Circo Massimo or Piramide, then bus #118, which runs along V. Appia Antica to the S. Sebastiano Catacombs. If you want to walk, head down V. delle Terme di Caracalla from the Circo Massimo. At Piazzale Numa Pompilio, veer right onto V. di Porta S. Sebastiano, through the city wall and onto V. Appia Antica. *i* Info office is located at V. Appia Antica 42, right before Domine Quo Vadis. It offers bike rental, free maps, historical pamphlets, a self-service bus ticket machine, and opportunities for activities along the way. For information on Archeobus tours leaving from Termini, call ☎800 281 281 or visit ▣www.trambusopen. com. Ⓢ Road and park free. Bike rental €3 per hr., €10 per day. Archeobus taking you from Termini through the park with audio tour €10. ⧗ Info office open in summer M-Sa 9:30am-1:30pm and 2-5:30pm, Su 9:30am-5:30pm; in fall, winter, and spring M-Sa 9:30am-1:30pm and 2-4:30pm, Su 9:30am-4:30pm. Road is closed to cars on Su, making it the best day to walk the trail. Archeobus tours every 30min. 9:30am-4pm.

CATACOMBO DI SAN SEBASTIANO   ⊕⊗ ANCIENT ROME

V. Appia Antica 136   ☎06 78 50 350 ▣www.catacombe.org

Though not quite as long as San Callisto, the 160,000 tombs making up San Sebastiano's catacombs give them a weighty status. Among the thousands of bodies, those of Saints Peter and Paul are perhaps most renowned, placed here during a harsh period of Christian persecution in the third century. Though the catacombs comprise four levels, only the second is accessible to tourist crowds—check out the symbols lining the wall. If you need something to take away as a souvenir, head to the gift shop for some jewelry reproductions.

➡ Bus #218 to stop near San Callisto and Santa Domitilla. Walk down V. Sette Chiese to V. Appia Antica and turn right. i Catacombs accessible only on guided tours (available in English). Tours leave every 30min. from the ticket office. $ €8, ages 6-15 €5. 🕒 Open M-W 9am-noon and 2-5pm, F-Su 9am-noon and 2-5pm. Closed Nov 22-Dec 20.

BASILICA DI SAN SEBASTIANO 👍⊗ CHURCH

V. Appia Antica 136 🖥www.catacombe.org

One of the road's few respites that doesn't require a subterranean retreat, an entrance fee, and a tour guide to appreciate, the basilica, reflecting its somewhat modern restructuring (17th-century "modern," that is), is not as dark and ornate as some of Rome's more central churches but attracts a large crowd to admire its Bernini masterpiece, **Jesus Christ the Redeemer,** finished when the Baroque master had reached the ripe old age of 81. Look up to the ceiling for a magnificent wood relief of St. Sebastian pincushioned with arrows sticking out from his sides. It would seem that the Roman army had a pretty harsh "don't ask, don't tell" policy when it came to religious matters. Poor Captain Sebastian was shot with arrows and left to die after the military brass discovered that he was actually a Christian. When he managed to survive the barrage of projectiles, his persecutors resorted to the next best thing: death by clubbing.

➡ Bus #218 to stop near San Callisto and Santa Domitilla. Walk down V. Sette Chiese to V. Appia Antica and right. $ Free. 🕒 Open daily 8am-6pm.

CATACOMBO SAN CALLISTO 👍⊗ ANCIENT ROME

V. Appia Antica 110 ☎06 51 30 15 80 🖥www.sdb.org

Twenty kilometers long and 20m deep, the Catacombs of San Callisto could be their *own* Appian Way. As Rome's oldest burial ground for Christians, the catacombs contain a mighty collection of corpses: 56 martyrs and 18 saints, many of whom were popes. If the thought of dead bodies isn't so aesthetically pleasing to you, check out the wall paintings which line the narrow passageways. There's a copy of *The Good Shepherd* at the entrance.

➡ From P. di San Giovanni in Laterano, take bus #218 to Fosse Ardeatine. From Circo Massimo or Ostiense, take bus #118 to Catacombe di San Callisto. i Catacombs accessible only on guided tours (available in English). Tours leave every 30min. from the ticket office. $ €8, ages 6-15 €5. 🕒 Open Mar-Jan M-Tu 9am-noon and 2-5pm, Th-Su 9am-noon and 2-5pm.

PORTA SAN SEBASTIANO AND MUSEO DELLA MURA 👍⊗ MUSEUM, ANCIENT ROME

V. di Porta San Sebastiano 18 ☎06 70 47 52 84 🖥www.museodellemuraroma.it

At the end of the car-crammed path leading to the Appian Way's start, this massive archway, the largest and best-preserved from the original Aurelian walls, remains. You've survived the cars and can now enjoy the small museum inside, but back in the third century, invaders would meet their death here. After being trapped inside, they would be massacred by archers. While the museum is intriguing, the scenic view offered from its terrace is a particular highlight if you expect to spend the rest of the afternoon in underground catacombs.

➡ Bus #218. Get off at intersection of V. Mura Latine and V. Appia Antica. $ €3, EU citizens ages 18-25 €1.50, under 18 and over 65 free. 🕒 Open Tu-Su 9am-2pm. Last entry 30min. before close.

DOMINE QUO VADIS? ⊗ CHURCH

At the intersection of V. Appia Antica and V. Ardeatina ☎06 51 20 441 🖥www.catacombe.org

Even its questioning name reflects the speculation that surrounds this tiny church. Supposedly, Christ's **footprints** are set in stone up the middle aisle, though San Sebastiano down the way claims the same novelty. (Sounds like something we've heard before at the Vatican.) The church's name derives from the question St. Peter asked Christ when he feared the Lord was fleeing Rome. Christ replied he was returning to the city to be crucified. St. Peter was eventually dealt that very same fate, though he requested to be hung upside down, not believing himself enough of his master's equal to meet death in the same way. Though speculation surrounds the footprints, the tourist office's brochures indicate that this church is winning the debate.

Bus #218. $ Free. Open in summer M-Sa 8am-7:30pm, Su 8:15am-7:40pm; in winter M-Sa 8am-6:30pm, Su 8:15am-6:45pm.

Other Sights

BASILICA DI SAN GIOVANNI IN LATERANO — CHURCH

P. San Giovanni in Laterano 4 ☎06 69 88 64 33

Practically off the radar in central Rome, San Giovanni in Laterano is hardly something to be overlooked. Before St. Peter's became such a hot spot, this massive basilica was the home of the papacy and today shares its extraterritoriality (along with the **Basilica di San Paolo Fuori le Mure**). If you're approaching from the side door near V. Merulana, note the beautiful frescoed ceiling on the outside portico. From the main entrance, the doors, moved from the Roman Senate House in the Roman Forum, attract a bigger crowd. Big windows and a white mosaic floor make the nave feel lighter than that of St. Peter's (though the lack of huge crowds also helps). The dynamic statues of apostles glaring down from their elevated position make you feel just as small and inconsequential, however. At the nave's end, you might hear the chink of coins being thrown into the crypt of **Pope Martin V.** The most striking (and fortunate) difference between San Giovanni and St. Peter's is the accessibility of the gold *baldacchino*, which can be viewed up close and completely circled. Decorated by **Giotto,** this canopy of state and its "roof" painted in blue sky and gold stars provide reason enough to make the trip to Laterano.

[M]A: San Giovanni or bus #16 from Termini. i For information about the Museo della Basilica, call ☎06 69 88 64 09. $ Basilica free. Cloister €2, students €1. Museo della Basilica €1. Audio tour €5. Basilica open daily 7am-6:30pm. Cloister open daily 9am-6pm. Museo della Basilica open M-F 9:30am-6:15pm, Sa 9:30am-6pm.

CHIESA DI SAN CLEMENTE — CHURCH

P. San Clemente ☎06 77 40 021 www.basilicasanclemente.com

Without knowing anything factual about this small church, you can still appreciate its unique layout, frescoes, and mosaics, all of which trump some basilicas twice its size. Masses, conducted in Italian, are held in the church's nave, curiously enclosed by an intricately engraved stone wall. The church's wooden pews face each other, adding to the intimacy of the service, and golden mosaics bordered by an aquamarine strip and 12 sheep are as beautiful as they are didactic. Near the back, the **Chapel of Santa Caterina** is decorated with Masolino's delicate 15th-century frescoes—their interplay of rendered and flat forms keeps you staring. Though the art on the wall is enough to satiate the eye, head down to the fourth-century lower basilica for some history to satisfy your intellectual tummy. The underground area now consists of a labyrinth of passageways, built to support the basilica above. The remains of original frescoes might take more effort to discern than the brighter ones upstairs, but they evoke more curiosity.

[M]B: Colosseo or bus #85 or 87. $ Basilica free. Excavations €5, students €3.50. Basilica open M-Sa 9am-12:30pm and 3-6pm, Su 10am-12:30pm and 3-6pm. Lower basilica and excavations open M-Sa 9am-12:30pm and 3-6pm, Su noon-6pm. Last entry 20min. before close.

CHIESA DEI SANTI GIOVANNI E PAOLO — 🚫📷🚫♿ CHURCH

P. San Giovanni e Paolo — ☎06 70 45 45 44 💻www.caseromane.it

Dusty meets very bright and sparkly at Chiesa dei Santi Giovanni e Paolo. The facade is nothing to gawk at, but the crystal chandeliers adorning this 12th-century basilica make one wonder whether this is a palace or a site of religious worship. Head back to the **Case Romane,** where even richer decoration—this time slightly more traditional—graces the foundation for the original fifth-century church. Beautiful wall paintings can also be found depicting Roman life as it was carried out between the third and 12th centuries. Surprisingly, things look nicer than they do bloody.

🚏 ⓂB: Colosseo. From the Colosseum, take V. Claudia and turn right onto V. di San Paolo della Croce. The basilica is in the courtyard, while the Case Romane entrance is to its left, through the archway. $ €6, reduced €4, under 12 free. ⏰ Open daily 8:30am-noon and 3:30-6:30pm. Office of the church open M-Th 9-11:30am and 4-6pm, Sa 9-11:30am and 4-6pm. Case Romano open M 10am-1pm and 3-6pm, Th-Su 10am-1pm and 3-6pm.

CHIESA DEI SANTI QUATTRO CORONATI — 🚫♿ CHURCH

V. dei Santissimi Quattro Coronati 20

Up a steep hill, this small church's peaceful interior makes the trek well worth it. From the austere courtyard, turn right to reach the 13th-century **cloister:** after ringing the bell, you'll be met by a nun requesting a €1 donation before letting you into the grounds. If the simplicity of the cloister has you seeking something a bit flashier, head to the **chapel,** where a bright 13th-century fresco depicts the life of Constantine. Inside the basilica itself, more paintings line the altar and give some life to the otherwise quite dark interior. The church feels like a retreat from the busy city because that's what it was meant to be: over 800 years ago, it served as a refuge for popes under siege thanks to its strategic location near the Lateran Palace.

🚏 ⓂB: Colosseo. Head up V. Labicana, turn right onto V. dei Normanni, and walk up the steep hill of V. dei Santissimi Quattro Coronati. ℹ Ring bell to enter cloister and a nun will let you in. $ Basilica free. Cloister requested donation €1. ⏰ Basilica and cloister open M-Sa 6:15am-8pm, Su 6:45am-12:30pm and 3-7:30pm. Chapel open M-Sa 9am-noon and 4:30-6pm, Su 9-10:40am and 4-5:45pm. Crypt open M-F; ask at cloister for admittance.

VIA NOMENTANA

V. Nomentana is a sight in itself, even if you don't hit any real "sights" along the walk. Lined with beautiful houses (that were ironically once used as farms), it is worth an afternoon stroll if you want to get out of the busy city center.

👍 PORTA PIA — ♿ MONUMENT

Piazzale Porta Pia

The magnificent Porta Pia marks the end of **Via XX Settembre** and the start of **Via Nomentana,** a tree-lined street that leads out of the city center. Michelangelo was commissioned by Pope Pius IV to construct this gate to replace the Porta Nomentana, which was not accessible at the time. There is much debate about the degree to which Michelangelo's plan was altered, especially because he died shortly before the gate's completion. Today, Porta Pia marks the end of Termini and the beginning of the more residential zones beyond. At the center, a statue of La Patria di Bersaglieri presides over an ideal spot in which one can admire the *piazza* or grab a lunch break.

🚏 ⓂA: Repubblica. Turn right onto V. XX Settembre and proceed straight until you reach the Porta Pia; after that, the street becomes V. Nomentana. $ Free.

VILLA TORLONIA — ♿ MUSEUM

V. Nomentana 70 — ☎06 06 08 💻www.museivillatorlonia.it

The Villa Torlonia is a beautiful complex of buildings and park grounds, originally owned by the wealthy Pamphilj family and used as a farm. It wasn't until Giovanni Torlonia acquired the farm that the villa came to resemble a palace rather than an agricultural ground. In 1925, Mussolini co-opted the property, paying a grand total of one lira (the equivalent of about a penny) to the Torlonia family. Since its abandonment in 1943, the house and park grounds have undergone drastic changes and are now open to the public as a group of museums. The Casino Nobile is perhaps the most prominent of the buildings and was the primary home of the family, making it the most ornate and expansive building of the complex's trio. The Casina delle Civette is renowned for its Art Deco work and stunning stained-glass windows, while the Casino dei Principi contains gorgeous mosaic floors and amazing marble reliefs on the doors. Even if you don't venture into the museums, a walk in the park is more than pleasant.

➡ From Piazzale Porta Pia, walk about 10min. down V. Nomentana. ℹ For tickets or reservations call ☎06 06 08 from 9am-9pm. $ Casina delle Civette €3, EU students 18-25 €1.50. Casino Nobile and show €7/5; Casino Nobile, Casina della Civette, Casino dei Principi, and show €9/5.50. EU citizens under 18 and over 65 free. ⏰ Open from 1st-last Sa in Mar and 1st-last Sa in Oct 9am-5:30pm; from last Su in Oct-Sept 30 9am-7pm; from last Su in Oct-Feb 28 9am-4:30pm. Ticket booth closes 45min. before museum closing.

MAUSOLEUM OF COSTANZA

⛪ CHURCH

V. Nomentana 349 ☎06 86 20 54 56

This mosaic-covered fourth-century church was named after Constantine's daughter and built as a mausoleum after her conversion to Christianity. It was later transformed into a baptistery and then church, which is what it functions as today for viewers who make the effort to see it. Inside, beautiful mosaics, especially over the upper domes, tell early Christian stories in elaborate layouts of animals and other earthy designs.

➡ [M]Termini. Either walk 2km down V. Nomentana or take the #36 bus. $ Free. ⏰ Open M 9am-noon, Tu-Sa 9am-noon and 4-6pm, Su 4-6pm.

food

If Italy is the king of fine food, then Rome is its crown jewel. The sheer number of trattorias, cafes, *alimentari* (local grocery stores), *osterie*, *tavole calde* (cafeterias), pizzerias, and *gelaterie* is enough reason to be overwhelmed without even picking up your fork. With so many options, it's tempting to simply settle for the most convenient—but don't. Always head away from the blocks immediately surrounding major sights: food here is overpriced and usually not well made. Avoid "tourist menus" with bright photos illustrating the plates and English translations. Restaurants with nonstop hours (no midday closing) are often those that cater to tourists rather than locals. When there seems to be no high-quality, cheap meal around, look for *panificii* (bakeries) or supermarkets where you can always pick up fresh breads or pastries to tide you over. Be aware that sitting at a table (instead of at the *banca*—bar) will knock up the bill as much as €2. Bread and water doesn't come with your meal either, but to make up for the extra €5 euro you'll be shelling out, a tip is not usually expected of customers.

Roman menus usually contain *primi* ranging from classics—*spaghetti alla carbonara* anyone?—to more Roman specialties. Local favorites, particularly during the summer when the ingredients are in season, include *carciofi alla giudia* (deep-fried artichokes) and *fiori di zucca* (stuffed, fried zucchini flowers). Though a Roman might find it hard to believe you could ever tire of the city's cuisine, cravings for ethnic food can be satisfied by one of Rome's African or Middle Eastern eateries. You might also try sampling the fare at establishments that focus on vegetarian food. Despite Rome's size and variety, however, certain cuisines remain woefully underrepresented—the few Chinese, Japanese, and Indian restaurants in the city tend to be overpriced and may differ markedly from what you'd find in the rest of the Western (or for that matter, the Eastern) world.

ANCIENT CITY

It's a shame that eating's necessary. Well, not really, but since everyone has to do it—and nearly everyone in Rome comes to the Ancient City—restaurants in this region are often overcrowded and overpriced. For the best deals, avoid places closest to the sights and meander down some of the quieter streets.

PIZZERIA DA MILVIO — PIZZERIA ①

V. dei Serpenti 7 ☎06 48 93 01 45

A sign that reads, "40 Types of Pizze e Pane," hangs above this pizzeria's bright red walls, a little reminder to passersby that this is the spot for variety, convenience, and flavor. Architecture students crowd the casual stools in back for simple *primi* like *pomodoro con riso (€5)* and *secondi (€6)* served from hot trays. Up front, the friendly servers cut dozens of thin-crust pizzas into slices sold by the ounce. Be ready to eat on the go; lunch is the busiest hour.

From V. Cavour, turn onto V. dei Serpenti and walk 2min. $ Primi €5; secondi €6. Pizza €0.80-1.40 per etto. Open daily 7am-midnight.

LA CUCCUMA — RISTORANTE ①

V. Merulana 221 ☎06 77 20 13 61

Even if you're not sitting at their outdoor tables, La Cuccuma's warmly colored walls, arched ceilings, and airy interior will make you feel like you're in the warm Roman sun. The €9 fixed meal *(primi, secondi, contorni, and bread)* is hard-to-beat with huge portions. Still, this restaurant threatens to outdo itself, selling thin-crust pizza by the kilo to hungry students looking for a meal on the go. Generous slices loaded with toppings will set you back less than €4.

[M]A: Vittorio Emanuele. Walk down V. d Statuto, and turn right onto V. Merulana. $ Pizza €8-12.90 per kg. Open daily 11am-midnight.

ANTICA BIRRERIA PERONI — RISTORANTE, DELI ②

V. San Marcello 19 ☎06 67 95 310 www.anticabirreriaperoni.net

Pizza and panini may abound in Rome, but far harder to come by are the German-Italian plates Antica Birreria Peroni has been making for over 100 years. This popular establishment's tiny interior feels a bit like an old-fashioned candy shop—albeit, a candy shop filled with adults instead of children and beer instead of sweets. It is constantly teeming with customers ordering takeout plates like grilled pork sausage *(€4)* or the smoked pork with sauerkraut *(€10)*. Four types of beer on tap go for as little as €3 to wash down the wurstel *(€6.50-13)*. Be ready to stand or scramble for one of the few stools at the bar.

From the Vittorio Emanuele monument, turn right on V. Cesare Battisti, left into P. dei Santissimi Apostoli, and walk 2 blocks down. $ Primi €5-7; secondi €4-19. Buffet €3.50-6.50. Open M-Sa noon-midnight.

LA TAVERNA DA TONINO E LUCIA — RISTORANTE ③

V. Madonna dei Monti 79 ☎06 47 45 325

You'll feel like you're in some Italian *madre*'s home as soon as you walk into this local favorite: mouthwatering aromas, a view into the kitchen, and a cork-lined wall full of pictures and lights give La Taverna da Tonino e Lucia its cozy feel. Tight quarters may just have you becoming *amici* with your neighbors at the next table by meal's end, but that's par for the course here where the regulars already know each other. The small menu's limited selection is actually a blessing in disguise—the plates are so good that a bigger selection might make choosing impossible. Try the veal rolls with tomato sauce or the specially recommended *paglia ai funghi*.

food . ancient city

➤ ⓂB: Cavour. Walk down V. Cavour towards the Fori Imperiali, turn right onto V. dei Serpenti and left onto V. Madonna dei Monti. $ Pasta €8, meat €9-13. ⏰ Open M-Sa noon-2:30pm, 7-10:30pm.

LA CARBONARA 💳🚭🍷 RISTORANTE ❸

V. Panisperna 214 ☎06 48 25 176 💻www.lacarbonara.it

The wall of handwritten comments and the massive collection of wine corks beside it should give you an idea of how long this standby has been around (try over 100 years). Despite its history and fame, La Carbonara has remained well priced and down to earth—just read some of the comments made by customers and family members as you gobble down classics like *carciofi alla giudia* (fried artichoke) and *cacio e pepe* (cheese and peppers). If you like what you get (and you surely will), don't hesitate to scribble your own sweet nothings on the wall. Just try to compose something a bit more poetic than the graffiti on your hostel bunk bed.

➤ From S. Maria Maggiore, walk 5min. down V. Panisperna. $ Primi €6-9; secondi €9-15. ⏰ Open M-Sa 12:30pm-2:30pm and 7pm-11pm.

IL GELATONE 💳🚭 GELATERIA ❶

V. dei Serpenti 28 ☎06 48 20 187

Il Gelatone deserves every bit of its name: the suffix "*one*," which means big, translates to plentiful scoops and an expansive selection of flavors. Twenty-eight types of sorbet, more than 30 creamier *gelati*, and four flavors of yogurt make ordering hard—it's a good thing even small cones *(€2)* come with a choice of three flavors. To make matters better (or worse, if you have a hard time making up your mind), you can top off your frosty delight with anything from meringue to pistachio to fresh fruit, whipped cream, and chocolate.

➤ From the Fori Imperiali, walk up V. Cavour and make a left onto V. dei Serpenti. $ Cones or cups €2-4. ⏰ Open daily 10am-10pm.

GELATERIA ORNELLI 💳♿ GELATERIA ❶

V. Menetura 232/233 ☎06 48 91 30 66 💻www.ornelli.it

Gelaterie in Rome may be common, but ones serving varieties as unique as *soia* (soy) and homemade yogurt are not. Try a refreshing cup of yogurt and fresh fruit *(€2.50)* or a frozen variety topped with your choice of crunchy additions, such as cereal. For the less adventurous, more than 30 "regular" flavors are served in generous form and topped with *panna*.

➤ From S. Maria Maggiore, walk down V. Merulana. $ 2 flavors with whipped cream €1.50, 3 flavors €2. Fruit cups €2.50-4.50. ⏰ Open daily 11am-11:30pm.

HOSTARIA I BUONI AMICI 💳🚭🍷❄ RISTORANTE ❷

V. Aleardo Aleardi ☎06 70 49 19 93

Hand-decorated plates, countless bottles of wine, and quirky paintings line the walls of this tightly-packed, locally loved spot where *buoni amici* do indeed come to dine and drink. The plaid-covered tables are small, but the servings are large; pasta plates like *bucatini* with bacon, cheese, and chili are hot in more ways than one *(€7)*.

➤ ⓂB: Colosseo. From the Colosseum, take V. Labicana; then take a right on V. Merulana and a left on V. Aleardo Aleardi. $ Primi €7-8; secondi €7-12. ⏰ Open M-Sa 12:30-4pm and 7:15pm-midnight.

HOSTARIA DA NERONE 💳♿🍷❄ RISTORANTE ❸

V. delle Terme di Tito 496 ☎06 48 179 52

There's something golden about this place—whether its the yellow decor, the sunny outdoor seating, or the stellar food, this place radiates quality. Etchings of the Colosseum and a menu fit for a gladiator will remind you that this ancient landmark is nearby. Full of intriguing (some might say squirm-inducing) meat dishes such as buttered brains with mushrooms *(€12)*, Ostaria da Nerone's list of dishes will even pique the curiosity of Rome's most carnivorous visitors. Walk off the heavy meal with a stroll through Domus Aurea, which awaits you right across the street.

[M]B: Colosseo. From the Colosseum, take V. Nicola Salví and turn left onto V. Terme di Tito. $ Primi €9.50-10; secondi €7-12. ⏰ Open M-Sa noon-3pm and 7-11pm.

WANTED "IL POSTO RICERCATO" RISTORANTE ❸

V. dei Serpenti 166-168 ☎06 48 93 01 18

In accordance with this restaurant's name, their homemade desserts, Moretti beer served on tap, and, oh yeah, food are indeed "wanted" by those who frequent the place. Colorful beer flasks and decorative lights—some of which are nearly 2 ft. tall—line the spacious interior that includes a wooden pizza oven and a covered patio in back. While eating hearty plates like pasta bags stuffed with cheese, pears, and walnut sauce *(€9)*. You'll probably be eyeing the freshly baked desserts sitting in the central glass display case or maybe, on a hot summer's day, the beer beckoning from the bar.

From V. Cavour, turn right onto V. dei Serpenti; restaurant is on the right. $ Primi €8-9; secondi €8-18. Pizza €5.50-9.50. ⏰ Open daily noon-midnight.

LUZZI RISTORANTE ❸

V. San Giovanni in Laterano 88 ☎06 70 96 332

With the Colosseum in plain sight and plenty of overpriced restaurants in the vicinity, Luzzi is a welcome relief. Plastic menus and chairs, a lively staff, and no-frills outdoor seating give this restaurant an unassuming vibe that matches its modest prices and playful photos of Rome that adorn the walls. Inside, small tables crowd around an open brick oven where your pizza is likely being cooked to hot perfection, but if you're feeling a need for pasta, try out Luzzi's take on the classic pasta *all'amatriciana*.

[M]B: Colosseo. From the Colosseum, walk down V. San Giovanni in Laterano about 5min. $ Cover €1. Primi €5-7; secondi €5-11. ⏰ Open M-Tu noon-midnight, Th-Su noon-midnight.

CENTRO STORICO

Catering to hungry tourists, food in the Centro Storico tend to be overpriced. Your best bet for a quick meal is to head to a *panificio*, *pasticerria*, or pizzeria and eat your grub in a nearby *piazza*. For a sit-down meal, try to wander down narrow and out-of-the way streets rather than stay in more central regions.

DAR FILETTARO A SANTA BARBARA FISH ❶

Largo dei Librari 88 ☎06 68 64 018

We're glad that some places never change. Despite its fame and hordes of customers—families and fancily clad couples alike—Dar Filettaro a Santa Barbara has remained reliably excellent. The *piazza* fills with the sound of chatter from those who dine and those in line. The unadorned interior gets even louder with the sound of happy customers. It won't be hard to make an order: the one-sheet menu features only salad, *antipasti*, and the classic fried cod fillet. Plus, nearly everything is €5, so feel free to leave your calculator at home. Draft beer *(€2.50 per pint)* and wine might make the wait seem shorter. Once you've eaten at this simple eatery, you'll be convinced that patience is a virtue...or at least the path to a good meal.

From Campo dei Fiori, walk down V. dei Giubbonari and turn left onto the tiny Largo dei Librari. $ Salads, antipasti, and fried fish €5. Desserts €0.50-3.50. Beer €2.50-4.50. ⏰ Open M-Sa 5:30-11:30pm.

FORNO MARCO ROSCIOLI BAKERY ❷

V. dei Chiavari ☎06 68 64 045 www.anticofornoroscioli.com

If you can find a stool at this bakery, grocery, and fresh food "deli," grab it or else you'll be forced to eat standing at one of the beer barrel tables outside (which frankly, isn't too bad of an option). Most people grab a slice of something to go—a strip of thin-crust pizza or *kranz*, a flaky, twisted roll with almonds and

food . centro storico

eternal etiquette

Fancy eating out in Rome but don't really know the etiquette or are scared of making a mistake while ordering? *Let's Go* is here to rescue you with some tips on how to avoid an *errore* when eating in Italy:

1) No cheese on seafood pastas. Even though you may love sprinkling parmesan on all of your spaghetti back home, no matter the topping, if you ask your server to do so in Rome, expect to see a baffled expression on his or her face. Romans feel that the strong taste of cheese will dampen the fish's flavor and ruin the pasta.

2) No coffee or cappuccino after noon. While this rule isn't set in stone, you will get some odd looks from the locals if you have a cup of coffee in your hand at 2pm.

3) Thirsty? Buy wine, not water or soda. You'll save money, since some wine is cheaper than bottled water or your favorite cola. If you don't know where to look, buying a Gatorade from a street vendor can set you back as much as €8, while wine will cost less than that. Too much of the good stuff may dehydrate you, though, so even when booze is the right choice for your wallet, it still might not be the best thing for your body.

4) Craving an omelette this morning? Well too bad, because Romans eat their eggs for lunch and dinner. Early-rising Americans will have to wait to get their normal breakfast. Swap your afternoon coffee with your morning scramble instead.

5) Need to get the edge off with a beer or two, but it's only noon? Never fear, as having a couple of beers or wine with lunch is perfectly acceptable in Italy. Just don't toss back too much, as public drunkenness is looked down upon.

raisins. But the best deals are Forno's fresh plates of *primi*, like its cold rice salad and hot tomato gnocchi, which customers order at the counter according to portion size as they stealthily nab one of the coveted stools. At only €5-7 a plate, Forno's prices beat those of any restaurant around.

➤ From Campo di Fiori, walk down V. dei Giubbonari and turn left onto V. dei Chiavari. $ Primi €5-7. Pizza €9.50-18 per kg. Strudel €1.80 per etto. 🕑 Open M-Sa 7am-8pm.

GELATERIA DEL TEATRO 💳🚭❄ GELATERIA ❶

V. di San Simone 70 ☎06 45 47 880

Ever wondered what makes Italian gelato so darn good? Well, much like Willy Wonka, the friendly owners here offer customers a peek into the magic makings of their product—and it really is a *teatro*-tastic experience watching fruit and milk get churned into creamy perfection. The result of Gelateria Del Teatro's alchemy? Over 40 flavors of truly unique gelato, and the owners pride themselves on individually developing each one. After the show, indulge in varieties like garden sage with raspberry, lemon cheese cake, or ricotta, fig, and almond, which if you hadn't seen it made, would seem like the result of some superhuman culinary feats.

➤ From P. Navona, turn left onto V. dei Coronari and look for the tiny V. di San Simone on the left. i Free tours offered for groups; call (or unwrap a golden ticket) to reserve a spot. Credit cards accepted for purchases over €20. $ Cones and cups €2-8. 🕑 Open daily noon-midnight.

PIZZERIA DA BAFFETTO ♿🍸 PIZZERIA ❷

V. del Governo Vecchio 114 ☎06 68 61 617

At Pizzeria da Baffetto, the doors stay sealed and the menu stays hidden until the server lets you in. When the doors do open, a cloud of warm, pizza-infused air slips out to tempt the many eager patrons waiting in line. The service here may be brusque, but that's because they need a Soup-Nazi demeanor to control the crowds waiting for a table. This pizzeria cooks up some of the best pizza in the city, served in a no-frills, packed dining room. While you're in line, check out the drawings and letters plastered on the restaurant's window by loving customers—a decorating motif which, funnily, seems to double as a tactic to keep you from seeing inside.

✈ *From P. Navona, exit onto P. Pasquina and continue as it becomes V. del Governo Vecchio.* ⓘ *Long waits and no reservations; arrive early if you want a table.* ⓢ *Pizza €5-9.* ⓩ *Open M-W 6:30pm-12:30am, Th-Su 6:30pm-12:30am.*

CUL DE SAC ♨♿♍♨ RISTORANTE ❷

P. Pasquino 73 ☎06 68 80 10 94

When it's so close to Rome's most famous *piazza* (P. Navona, if you weren't sure), it's surprising that Cul de Sac's fresh mix of international flavors is the only touristy thing about the place. Though Roman classics abound, the "international thing" seems to be catching: try the *escargots alla bourguignonne (€6.60)*, an order of *baba ghanoush (€6.20)*, or a cup of hot chocolate made with cocoa from Ghana, Ecuador, Venezuela, and Trinidad. The cool marble bar up front is surrounded by hundreds of wine bottles to pair with the dishes on the diverse menu (written in four languages). Wooden benches and the vine-decorated walls and floors create a laid-back, picnic feel.

✈ *From P. Navona, walk onto P. Pasquino.* ⓢ *Primi €7.10-8.90; secondi €6.70-9.80. Desserts €4.30.* ⓩ *Open daily noon-4pm and 6pm-12:30am.*

PIZZERIA TAVOLA CALDA ♨♿ PIZZERIA ❷

C. Vittorio Emanuele II 186/188 ☎06 68 80 62 29

Haphazard and playful decor creates a relaxed vibe in which to gobble down some really fine food. Though pizza is sold by the slice, the best deal is to order a "sort of" round pie and cheap beer *(€2)* to eat at one of the colorful tables. Classic *primi*, changed daily and priced by portion size, are dished up from behind the counter. As casual and fun as the guys who work here, this place is "lunch on the go"—just at a table.

✈ *From Campo dei Fiori, head towards C. Vittorio Emanuele II.* ⓢ *Round pizza €3.50-6, by the slice €9-14 per kg. Primi €4; secondi €5.50. Beer €2-3.* ⓩ *Open daily 10am-10pm.*

IL CORALLO ♨♿♍♨ RISTORANTE ❹

V. del Corallo 10/11 ☎06 68 30 77 03

Even on a warm night, every table inside Il Corallo will be full, and the outside patio will have filled up long ago. The warm aroma is enough to draw you in the first time, and the generous portions will hook you for good. Their seafood specialties, like the creamy stock-fish mousse or pasta with orange and crab *(€13)*, offer creative twists on classics. Sandy-colored brick and dark wooden rafters give the place a cozy, tavern-y feel.

✈ *From P. Navona, exit onto V. di Sant'Agnese di Agone; continue as it becomes V. di Tor Millina, and veer left looking for V. del Corallo.* ⓢ *Primi €10-13; secondi €15-22. Pizza €5-10.* ⓩ *Open daily noon-3:30pm and 7pm-1am.*

ANTICA TRATTORIA DE PIETRO AL PANTHEON ♨♿♍♨ RISTORANTE ❸

V. dei Pastini ☎06 67 89 940

In a stream of "classic Italian restaurants" on the way to the Pantheon, this place stands out in both age and value. The friendly owner—who's taken on the family business that began in 1842—doesn't let the crowds perturb him. And now, yes, it's time for all the classics: grilled meats and pastas (most of which are homemade), *antipasti*, and wine. The menu may consist of old standbys, but

food . centro storico

they're doing something different here: serving quality food at a good value in a neighborhood that all too often caters to (and takes advantage of) a tourist crowd.

➤ From P. della Rotonda outside the Pantheon, turn onto V. dei Pastini. $ Primi €8-10; secondi €8-18. ⏰ Open daily noon-3:15pm and 6:15-11:15pm.

LA LOCANDA DEL PELLEGRINO
💳🚭🍸 MEDITERRANEAN [4]

V. del Pellegrino 107 ☎06 68 72 776 💻www.lalocandadelpellegrino.it

Slow down at this relaxing Mediterranean restaurant for some grains that are (finally!) not in the form of spaghetti: the chef's specialty is a two-person plate of couscous with vegetables or fish. Even if you opt for a smaller dish, fish and veggies will remain the theme in unique combinations like *cavatelli* with artichoke sauce, saffron and *pinoli*, or a plate of octopus and potatoes. The dim hanging lights and calming music might just have you convinced that the Mediterranean Sea is lapping at the door.

➤ Exit Campo dei Fiori into P. Teatro di Pompeo and look for V. del Pellegrino on the left. $ Primi €8-20; secondi €13-19. Couscous special €45 for 2 people. ⏰ Open daily noon-3:30pm and 6:30pm-midnight.

IL FORNAIO
🚭 BAKERY [1]

V. del Baullari 5/7 ☎06 68 80 39 47

Take a break from that gelato diet and try one of the decadent pastries stacked high at this bakery. Their *foresta al cioccolato* is exactly what it sounds like—a forest of shaved and flaked chocolate dusted with confectioner's sugar. If you're tired of the savory ravioli found on every restaurant menu, try their famous variation, the *ravioli ricotta cioccolata*, a large "pouch" stuffed with ooey gooey goodness.

➤ From P. Navona, head to C. Vittorio Emanuele II; V.dei Baullari is just off of it. $ Cookies €18 per kg. Cannoli and sweet ravioli €2. Pizza €7-18 per kg. Calzones €2.50. ⏰ Open daily 8am-10pm.

rome

SANT'EUSTACHIO IL CAFFE
🚭 CAFE [1]

P. Sant'Eustachio 82 ☎06 68 80 20 48 💻www.santeustachioilcaffe.it

Before even stepping inside this tiny cafe (and you'll probably be outside for a while, as it's often packed), you'll smell its signature product. Now, they do coffee well in Italy generally, but at the age of 72, this place has reached a level of superbness that shines even by Italian standards. Served sweet (request before ordering if you don't want sugar), the drinks here come in decadent varieties such as *mousse al caffe (€2.70-6.50)* or *granita al caffe (€4-6.50)*. While you probably won't make it like they do, they sell their beans by the kg if you want to give it a shot *(€24-26 per kg)*. Drink your joe while standing, or pay as much as €2 more to enjoy it at a table outside.

➤ From the Pantheon, head onto Salita de Crescenzi and make an immediate left into P. Sant'Eustachio. Look for a crowd and sniff around for coffee. $ Capuccino or coffee €2.40 at bar, 4.90 at table. Pastries €1-3. ⏰ Open M-Th 8:30am-1am, F 8:30am-1:30am, Sa 8:30am-2am, Su 8:30am-1am.

PIAZZA DI SPAGNA

Between Prada, the Spanish Steps, and the teems of tourists frequenting both, it might be hard to find a tasty and economical bite midday. For lunch, try heading to *panifici* (bakeries) or pizzerias and eating on the *piazze*. For dinner, veer onto smaller streets for better quality and service, even if it will cost you a bit more.

GUSTO
💳♿🍸 RISTORANTE, BAR [3]

V. della Frezza 23 and P. Augusto Imperatore 9 ☎06 32 26 273 💻www.gusto.it

The difference between good taste and bad is as clear as black and white—and by taste we mean flavor *and* style. Black-clad waiters whisk around Gusto's white, brick interior that's divided between a wine lounge and a sit-down restaurant opening onto P. Augusto Imperatore. Tall mirrors make the place feel even bigger than it is, but petite tables near the bar bring it back to life-size for you and your date. On the *piazza* side of things, your best bet is one of the stellar pizzas cranked out of their open brick oven. The real action (and the best deal), however, is to be found at the bar during nightly happy hours: Gusto's buffet of gourmet treats like vegetable couscous and curious black-bread *tramezzini* is better than a sit-down meal. If it weren't for the accompanying cocktails, you'd swear your mom was feeding you right out of her kitchen.

*Directly across from Mausoleo Augusto on the piazza or, from P. del Popolo, exit onto V. di Ripetta and turn left onto V. della Frezza. **i** Happy hour buffet with drink €10. Pizzeria and restaurant are on piazza side; enoteca is on V. della Frezza side. $ Primi €10; secondi €10-18.50. Pizza €6-9.50. Beer €3-5.50. Wine €4.50-12. Cocktails €9. ⏰ Open daily 10am-2am. Happy hour daily 6-9pm.*

FRASCHETTERIA BRUNETTI — RISTORANTE ❷

V. Angelo Brunetti 25b ☎06 32 14 103 www.fraschetteriabrunetti.it

Save your messiness for a melting gelato after dinner—there'll be no greasy pizza fingers or spaghetti mishaps here. Instead, Fraschetteria Brunetti focuses primarily on baked pasta dishes, including 11 types of lasagna in varieties that you won't find anywhere else; try the rich gorgonzola and walnut. Covered in handwritten notes from loyal patrons, this place is legit, managing to avoid jacked-up prices and watered-down cuisine despite its proximity to the sights.

*[M]A: Flaminio. From P. del Popolo, exit onto V. di Ripetta and turn right onto V. Angelo Brunetti. **i** Fixed lunch of entree, coffee, and drink €7.50. $ Primi €8. Panini €3.50. Cocktails €4. ⏰ Open M-Sa 11am-midnight, but may close earlier or later depending on the crowd.*

CAMBI — PIZZERIA, BAKERY ❶

V. del Leoncino 30 ☎06 68 78 081

Better than a cheapo pizzeria and cheaper than a sit-down restaurant. The mix of salty and sweet scents perfuming the area has most folks starting with a loaded slice of pizza and following it up with a €1 fruit torte. But don't overlook their real specialties: unleavened bread (hard bread lightly doused in oil) and *crostata* (cookies filled with chocolate or fruit). When you see tourists paying three times the price down the street, your meal will taste even better.

*From Ara Pacis/Mausoleo Augusto, walk down V. Tomacelli and turn right onto V. Leoncino. **i** No seating. Only vegetable oil used. Also sells basic groceries. $ Cookies €0.80, €33 per kg. Panini €3.50. Pizza €7.50-15 per kg. Crostatine €11. ⏰ Open M-Sa 8am-8pm.*

BAR SAN MARCELLO — CAFE ❶

V. D. San Marcello 37-8 ☎06 69 92 33 15

Don't let the curt service turn you off from this small *tavola calda*, a lunchtime favorite among local workers. The ratio of Italians to tourists means you won't hear much English as you munch on fresh pasta salads, grilled fish, or panini. Take advantage of the linguistic discrepancy: with the **Trevi Fountain** right around the corner, you can easily get your full share of English chatter for the day just a short walk away.

*From Palazzo Venezia, take V. del Corso; turn right onto V. S.S. Apostoli and left onto V. D. San Marcello. **i** Takeout available. Limited seating in back. $ Panini €3.50-4. Primi €4-5. ⏰ Open daily 6am-5:30pm.*

FIASCHETTERIA BELTRAMME — RISTORANTE ❸

V. della Croce 39

When a restaurant has managed to limit its menu to one page and survive for over 100 years without a phone, you know it's doing something right. Don't expect creative culinary concoctions but classic dishes made with family love. Their *cacio e pepe* might be some of the best in the neighborhood, and locals will let you know it when you end up sitting next to them in the restaurant's close quarters. We're glad that despite the modern fashion flash surrounding it, this traditional standby hasn't changed.

✠ Ⓜ A: Spagna. From the Spanish Steps, take V. Condotti; turn right onto V. Belsiana and right onto V. delle Croce. Ⓢ Primi €10; secondi €15-18; verdure and contorni €6-10. Ⓣ Open M-Sa noon-2:30pm and 7-10:30pm.

NATURIST CLUB
✦✧⊗Ⓨ RISTORANTE, VEGETARIAN ❸

V. della Vita 14, 4th fl.
☎06 67 92 509

Like its street name, this restaurant is all about "la vita"—that is, saving a few vite by serving up an entirely macrobiotic menu. Climb up four well-worn flights of stairs (which might be part of the health kick) to enjoy totally atypical Roman fare like ravioli stuffed with creamy tofu and pesto (€8) or seitan escalope with grilled vegetables (€9). Despite their exotic twists, dishes here taste like they might have been made at any one of the trattorias down the street. Those skeptical of macrobiotic food might find that this place changes their mind.

✠ Directly off V. del Corso around P. San Lorenzo in Lucina; turn right onto V. della Vita from V. del Corso and look for #14. Buzz and walk to 4th fl. ℹ 90% organic and totally macrobiotic; fish is the only non-vegetarian option. Ⓢ Primi €8-9; secondi €9-11. Fixed vegetarian meal €14; lunch/dinner combo €8-10/€20-25. Organic wine €12-16 per bottle. Ⓣ Open M-F 12:30-3pm and 7-10:30pm.

F.LLI FABRI
✦♿Ⓨ DELI ❷

V. della Croce 27-28
☎06 67 90 612 📧www.fabbi.it

Save your euro for Dolce and Gabbana down the street, and get your real dolce on the cheap at this corner deli. A few slices of their prosciutto di parma and mozzarella di bufala along with some homemade pesto (all sold by weight) make the perfect snack to be enjoyed in the piazza down the way. If all that food has inspired your inner chef, pick up some homemade ravioli or gnocchi and a bottle of imported olive oil for the stove. Also sells grocery staples like milk and beer.

✠ Ⓜ A: Spagna. Walk down V. della Croce. Ⓢ Homemade pasta €8.80-22 per kg. Cheese €8.95-23 per kg. Smoked meats €14.30-27.30 per kg. Ⓣ Open M-Sa 8am-7:40pm.

JEWISH GHETTO

Though the Jewish Ghetto is one of the smaller neighborhoods in Rome, it is rich in fine cuisine and character. Most restaurants are on V. del Portico d'Ottavia, and while not exactly cheap, they are a great alternative to classic Italian fare if that's all you've been eating. Most are kosher and closed early Friday through Saturday.

🔲 ANTICO FORNO DEL GHETTO
⊗⊗ BAKERY, GROCERY ❶

P. Costaguti 31
☎06 68 80 30 12

You don't have to resort to a slice of pizza in order to avoid the overpriced plates of a sit-down restaurant: grab a loaf of to-die-for bread, a few slices of smoked meat, and a hunk of cheese at this family-run neighborhood staple instead. Locals flock to the small store to buy anything from fresh pasta to cookies and milk to a hot slice of flatbread or focaccia topped with veggies.

✠ From Ponte Garibaldi, walk down V. Arenula, turn right onto V. S. Maria d. Pianto and into P. Costaguti. ℹ Only pizza and bread guaranteed kosher. Cheese, bread, cookies, and meat sold by lb. Ⓢ Pizza and focaccia €1.20-2 per piece, €7.70-9.70 per kg. Ⓣ Open M-F 7:45am-2:30pm and 5-8pm, Sa-Su 7:45am-1pm.

LA TAVERNA DEL GHETTO
✦♿⛩ KOSHER ❹

V. del Portico d'Ottavia 7/b-8
☎06 68 80 97 71 📧www.latavernadelghetto.com

The small dining area out front might have you thinking that this is an intimate cafe with Middle Eastern music and delicious food to match. But head around the block, and you'll see that this popular spot opens up into an expansive dining space that can play host to bigger parties and more festive dining. The first kosher restaurant in Rome, La Taverna del Ghetto is an expert in the classics: *bacala* (fried catfish), *fiori di zucca*, and any variation of artichoke. Soy-based desserts are dairy-free and pleasantly mild after an otherwise heavy meal.

☙ From Teatro Marcello, walk down V. del Piscaro and veer right as it becomes V. del Portico d'Ottavia. *i* Strictly kosher. Ⓢ Primi €11.50; secondi €15.90-19.50. Ⓩ Open M-Th noon-11pm, F noon-4pm, Sa 9-11pm, Su noon-11pm.

PASTICCERIA BOCCIONE LIMENTANI ⊛⛦ BAKERY ❷
V. Portico D'Ottavio 1 ☎06 68 78 637

This tiny, unadorned *pasticceria* doesn't need the cuteness factor to promote itself: its small assortment of baked goods is strong enough to bring customers running, no advertisements needed. Only about four products are made here—freshly baked tortes and a range of biscottini with nuts and fruits—so all you have to do is know what you want, order, and enjoy.

☙ Right on the corner of V. Portico D'Ottavio; look for numbers, as it's practically unmarked. Ⓢ Cookies around €18 per kg. Tortes €18-22 each. Ⓩ Open M-Th 7:30am-7:30pm, F 7:30am-3:30pm, Su 7:30am-7:30pm.

KOSHER BISTROT CAFE ⊛⛦♈⌂ CAFE, KOSHER ❸
V. Santa Maria del Pianto 68/69 ☎06 68 64 398

This cheerful and brightly lit cafe doubles as an early evening spot for mixed drinks and an anytime spot for delicious kosher food. Picnic-like wooden tables on the street are often full of locals munching on finger food with their wine or enjoying fuller plates like curry chicken with artichokes. The modern interior has a full bar and a few shelves with packaged food items for sale.

☙ From Ponte Garibaldi, walk up V. Arenula and turn right onto V. Santa Maria del Pianto. Ⓢ Primi €9-11; secondi €8-9. Beer and wine €6-7. Mixed drinks €7-8. Ⓩ Open M-Th 9am-9pm, F 9am-sundown, Su 9am-9pm. Aperitivo happy hour 5-9pm.

NONNA BETTA CUCINA KOSHER ⊛⛦♈⌂ KOSHER ❹
V. Portico d'Ottavia 16 ☎06 68 80 62 63 ▥www.nonnabetta.it

Famous for its fine selection of Roman kosher food, this bustling restaurant is great for a sit-down meal. The handwritten menu has an ample selection of vegetarian plates like baked artichokes with mozzarella—in fact, artichokes are in nearly every dish (look for *carciofi alla giudia*). If you're seeking a lighter plate, consider an order of *baba ghanoush* or hummus *(€3)* or a focaccia stuffed with falafel *(€6)*. Pictures of the old ghetto lining the walls and an amiable staff eager to discuss the history and significance of the fried artichoke will remind you of this neighborhood's rich history.

☙ From Teatro Marcello, walk down V. del Piscaro and veer right as it becomes V. del Portico d'Ottavia. Ⓢ Primi €8-11; secondi €9-18. Ⓩ Open M-Th 10am-3:30pm and 6:30-11:30pm, F 10:30am-3:30pm, Su 10am-3:30pm and 6:30-11:30pm.

PANE VINO E SAN DANIELE ⊛⊗♈❄ RISTORANTE, ENOTECA ❸
P. Mattei 16 ☎06 68 77 147 ▥www.panevinospa.it

You won't see the classic *primi* and *secondi* format at this dark and diverse *enoteca* and restaurant. Instead, the menu features plates with regal names like the *piatto del re* (a large plate of raw prosciutto) or *la duca*. All the food and wine on the menu hails from the San Daniele region, and there is an ample selection of polenta plates as well as *sformato*, an egg-based casserole stuffed with vegetables, cheese, and meat. Sea-green walls and dark wooden tables scattered throughout the low-ceilinged, dimly lit space create a grandiose but quirky feel.

☙ In P. Mattei. Ⓢ Salads €7-8.50. Sformati €9.50. Wine €4-7.50 per glass. Ⓩ Open M-Sa 9:30am-2am. Kitchen closes at 10:30pm.

food • jewish ghetto

VATICAN CITY

The longest line in Rome eventually becomes a hungry crowd. The selection of neighborhood trattorias and small stores that lines the quieter streets outside the Vatican walls won't disappoint, but the bright English menus and beckoning waiters closer to the museums will.

👍 CACIO E PEPE — 🌱♿☀ RISTORANTE [3]

V. Avezzana 11 ☎06 32 17 268 💻www.cacioepeperistorante.com

If you're in the area (and by that, we mean as far as 1 mi. away), it will be well worth your time to trek to this true trattoria. Welcoming owner Gianni will personally seat you and make sure your *cacio e pepe* (fresh egg pasta topped with oil, grated cheese, and black pepper) is everything it should be: big, flavorful, and perfectly *al dente.* Its popularity with locals instead of tourists has kept the vibe casual and the service as good as the food...and that's saying a lot.

🧭 [M]A: Lepanto. From Metro, walk up V. Lepanto (away from the Vatican), turn right on Vle. delle Millizie and left onto V. Avezzana, a 5min. walk. $ Primi €8; secondi €9-10. 🕐 Open M-F 12:30-3pm and 7:30-11:30pm, Sa 12:30-3pm.

👍 OLD BRIDGE GELATERIA — 🌱♿ GELATERIA [1]

V. Bastioni di Michelangelo 3/5 ☎06 38 72 30 26 💻www.gelateriaoldbridge.com

Gelato so sinfully good you might need to visit the Vatican just to confess it. Despite being practically on the doorstep of the most touristed sight in the city, this hole-in-the-wall *gelateria* has thankfully remained just that. It's tiny and unadorned yet amazingly good. Beware: lines may rival those of the Vatican, but the size of your order (huge) will make the wait worthwhile.

🧭 Off P. Risorgimento and across the street from the line to the Vatican Museums. $ Cones €1.50-3; cups €3-4. 🕐 Open M 3pm-2am, Tu-Su 9am-2am.

FA BIO — 🌱♿❄ CAFE, ORGANIC [1]

V. Germanico 43 ☎06 64 52 58 10 💻www.fa-bio.com

If you're going to pay €4 for a panini, it might as well be organic, right? And if all that pizza and gelato have you craving something green, then Fa Bio will be your Eden. Just walking in, you'll be refreshed by the smell of blended smoothies and fresh salads alone. Organic pie *(€1.50),* hearty tofu salads *(€4.50),* and bread that is, for once, not white are enough to sustain you for a heavy afternoon of sightseeing. If you still need a pick-me-up after the 4hr. waits, reenergize with "*L'energizzante*," a potent shake of milk, pear, ginger, and cacao.

🧭 [M]A: Ottaviano. Walk down V. Ottaviano and turn left onto V. Germanico. ℹ All food organic. $ Panini €4. Salads €4.50. Cookies €0.50-1. Fruit juices and smoothies €3.50. 🕐 Open in summer M-Sa 9am-8pm; in winter M-Sa 9am-5pm.

FABBRICA MARRONS GLACES GIULIANI — 🛍♿❄ CIOCCOLATERIA [2]

V. Paolo Emilio 67 ☎06 32 43 548 💻www.marronglaces.it

This is the kind of place you visit first for yourself, second to do some gift-shopping for friends back home, and third...for yourself again. The shop's old school '40s feel adds to the delight of ordering your sweet confections from the family owners. Their specialties—*marron glacés* (candied chestnuts) and chocolate—are the perfect match of sweet and rich. Though they might not make a boxed trip home to your folks, the candied fruits are stellar—shiny and big as crown jewels.

🧭 [M]A: Lepanto. Take Vle. Giulio Cesare toward the Vatican and turn left onto V. Paolo Emilio. $ Marron Glacés €3.50 per etto. Candied fruit €4.50 per etto. Chocolates €4.50 per etto. 🕐 Open in summer M-Sa 8:30am-1pm and 3:30pm-7:30pm; in winter M-Sa 8:30am-8pm, Su 9am-1pm.

FORNO TACIO — 🌱🚭 BAKERY [1]

V. Tacito 20 ☎06 32 35 133

If melting gelato is making you sticky, try a warm pastry from this local bakery and grocer. Their waffle-shaped *ferratelle* cookies (€15 per kg) are mild and crispy, while their flaky *fiocchetti* twists are a lighter alternative to the standard croissant (€0.85). To slow the sugar rush, excellent pizza (less greasy and better priced than the standard slice) and bread are great taken hot or cold.

⚡ Ⓜ A: Lepanto. Walk down V. Ezio and continue straight as it becomes V. Tacito. *i* Also sells basic groceries. No seating. Ⓢ Pizza €7-13 per kg. Cookies €9.50 per kg. Fruit and cream tarts €1.50 each. 🕐 Open M-F 8am-2pm and 5-8pm, Su 8am-2pm and 5-8pm.

LE ARANCINE
🌐⊗ CAFE ❶

V. Marcantonio Colonna 38 ☎06 32 02 395 ◾www.mondoarancina.it

Diverge from the standard pizza lunch and try this bright orange restaurant's namesake product, the *arancino*, a fried rice ball stuffed with mozzarella, meat, or vegetables. Named for their resemblance to an orange (*arancia*), these rich balls are anything but sweet. The "*vulcano*" is a savory blend of black cuttlefish pasta and fresh tomatoes. If even the more mainstream *arancine* are too much for you, their substantial selection of other fried goodies like *crocche* (potato with cheese) and pizza are safe bets.

⚡ Ⓜ A: Lepanto. Walk down V. Marcantonio Colonna. Ⓢ Arancine €2.20. Pizza €9-15.50 per kg. Calzones €2.30. 🕐 Open daily 9am-1am.

WINE BAR DE' PENITENZIERI
⊘⊗Ⓨ CAFE, BAR ❸

V. dei Penitenzieri 16/A ☎06 68 75 350

Before hitting the inescapable nest of pizzerias surrounding the Vatican, grab a bite at this small but hugely popular lunch spot. The stand-up bar makes it easy to munch on a panino (€4-5) and sip your cappuccino (€0.90-2.50) without having to pay for table service. A rotating list of classics—mostly pastas and salads—is reserved for those who nab a seat in the adjoining room. If you don't want real sustenance, have a cocktail instead. Hey, you're not in St. Peter's yet.

⚡ From St. Peter's, take V. della Conciliazione toward the river, turn right onto V. dei Cavalieri del San Sepolcro, and keep straight as it becomes V. Penitenzieri. Ⓢ Primi and meat-and-cheese plates €10. Panini €4-5. Beer €3-4.50. Wine €3.50-4. Cocktails €6. 🕐 Open M-Sa 6am-8:30pm.

L'ARCHETTO
⊘⊗⊿ PIZZERIA ❷

V. Germanico 105 ☎06 32 31 163

Tired of the same old pizza toppings and overpriced slices? Order one in the round from a menu that trumps the regular list. Try L'Archetto's namesake specialty with cooked mozzarella, arugula, sausage, and peppers or, for a smaller bite, an order of bruschetta (€1.50-2.80). Though the setting might not be anything special, their lunch special—€8 *primo* with a choice of soup—makes the pizzeria popular with the economically minded and hungry midday crowd.

⚡ Ⓜ A: Ottaviano. Walk V. Ottaviano toward the Vatican and turn left onto V. Germanico. *i* Primi served only at lunch. Ⓢ Bruschette €1.50-2.80. Pizza €3.50-8. Primi with soup €8. 🕐 Open daily 12:30-3pm and 7pm-midnight.

TRASTEVERE

There are plenty of dining options in Trastevere, whether you want a luxurious sit-down meal, a bite on the go, or something in between. While the *piazze* are full of great choices, explore smaller side streets for some of the harder-to-find gems.

🍴 LA RENELLA
🌐♿ PIZZERIA, BAKERY ❶

V. del Politeama 27 ☎06 58 17 265

La Renella is as close to a true neighborhood eatery as you're likely to find, with locals coming here at all hours of the day for everything from their morning bread to lunchtime pizza to after-dinner cookies. The handwritten menu looks like it hasn't changed for years, but with Roman classics like the *fiori di zucchini* (huge orange petals topped with anchovies and cheese), why should it? The wall is covered in flyers for local events, apartments for rent, and job offerings, so if you're not in the mood to eat, at least come in to browse through the neighborhood happenings. You may not walk away having found a new apartment, but in all likelihood, you'll have succumbed to the tempting call of La Renella's marmalade-and-chocolate fagotini cookies *(€14 per kg)*.

From P. Trilussa, walk down V. della Renella; the front entrance is here, but there's also a back entrance on V. del Politeama. $ Pizza €5-12 per kg, sweet tortes and crostate €10-18 per kg, biscotti €10-16 per kg. ⏰ Open daily 7am-10pm (closing time can be variable).

SIVEN ♿ PIZZERIA, DELI ❶

V. San Francesco a Ripa 137 ☎06 58 97 110

There's hardly a moment of the day when someone isn't entering or exiting this tiny spot, where cheap pizza and hot pasta *primi* are sold by weight. Lasagna, gnocchi, eggplant parmigiano, and calzones would make meals on their own, but most people come away with a few slices of thin-crust pizza, loaded with all the standards—think zucchini, potatoes, mushrooms, or steak. There's nowhere to sit and the service is fast, so be ready to eat on the go. And make sure you know what you want, or you'll just get in the way of the regulars behind you.

From Vle. Trastevere, turn right onto V. San Francesco a Ripa. $ Pasta €0.75-0.80 per etto, calzones €2.50, pizza €1-1.30 per etto. ⏰ Open M-Sa 9am-10pm.

LE FATE ♿ 📶 🍸 ❄ RISTORANTE ❸

Vle. Trastevere 130 ☎06 58 00 971 💻www.lefaterestaurant.it

Inspired by the fable of Aurora, this festive restaurant has taken on the themes of love and solidarity in both its ambience and the quality of its food. The warmly lit dining area has the feel of a woodland cottage, with a bookshelf of cookbooks in the corner, twinkling star lights, and a string of vines covering the wall. All ingredients come from Lazio, so you can expect especially fresh plates; the homemade gnocchi with steak, cream, spinach, and ricotta is as rich in flavor as Princess Aurora was in gold. Students who aren't blessed with riches like the fairytale heroine should take advantage of the €10 meal, complete with bruschetta, pasta, dessert, and a glass of wine. Just say the magic word (or show your student ID).

About 15min. down Vle. Trastevere from P. G. Belli. ℹ Free Wi-Fi. Inquire about cooking classes and apartment rentals for students. $ Primi €10-13; secondi €12-25. ⏰ Open daily 6-11pm.

PIZZERIA DA SIMONE ♿ PIZZERIA, DELI ❶

V. Giacinto Carini 50 ☎06 58 14 980

After a long trek up to Ponte Acqua Paola and the surrounding gardens, there's no better way to replenish yourself than with a hot slice of Da Simone's pizza. Pies topped with anything from shrimp to the more classic sun-dried tomatoes and *mozzarella di bufala* go for about €1.50-4 per slice. Down the counter, you'll find freshly-made pasta dishes, steamed vegetables *(€12-16.90 per kg)*, and huge legs of chicken *(€3)* that are filling enough to be a complete dinner. If you're hoping to grab dinner here, be ready to take your food and make a picnic of it in the park, as there's no seating.

From the Porta San Pancrazio on Giancolo Hill, walk downhill on V. Giancinto Carini for about 7min. $ Pizza €6.96-16.90 per kg. ⏰ Open M-Sa 7am-8pm.

CASETTA DI TRASTEVERE ♿ 🍸 ☀ RISTORANTE ❷

P. de Renzi, 31/32 ☎06 58 00 158

Inside is like outside at this budget-friendly restaurant. A hanging clothesline, painted Italian facade and terra-cotta rooftop transform the spacious interior of Casetta di Trastevere into just what its name implies—a *casetta*, or little house. Upstairs, a banquet-sized table serves especially large groups, but downstairs, smaller clusters of students consistently fill the tables. With the cheapest pizza in town *(marinara pie €3)*, this little house is a very, very, very fine house, allowing you to save your euro for Trastevere's teeming nightlife just down the street.

From S. Maria in Trastevere, walk down V. di Piede until you hit V. della Pelliccia. P. de Renzi is just beyond. $ Pizza €3-6. Primi €5-8; secondi €5-16; dessert €3-5. Open daily noon-11:30pm.

BISCOTTIFICIO ARTIGIANO BAKERY ❶

V. della Luce 21 ☎06 58 03 926

With piles on piles of freshly baked cookies, this place seems more like a factory than a humble bakery. With no seats or decorations to speak of, Biscottificio Artigiano's success rests solely on its scrumptious cookies and ever-growing reputation. (Note the wall of newspaper clippings.) Try the paper-thin *stracetti*—a slightly sweet cookie made from nuts and eggs. Family-run for over a century, this bakery cooks with recipes that are like no one else's in Rome.

From P. Sonnino, take V. Giulio Cesare Santini and turn left on V. della Luce. $ Most cookies €7.5-16 per kg. Rustic and fruit tortes €15. Open M-Sa 8am-8pm and Su 9:30am-2pm.

HOSTARIA DAR BUTTERO RISTORANTE ❸

V. della Lungaretta 156 ☎06 58 00 517

Amidst hanging tools, framed sketches and paintings, dangling lamps, and polaroid snapshots, you'll find classic Roman cuisine at this popular local lunchtime spot. The eclectic decor speaks to the owner's time spent collecting artwork and furniture throughout Italy, the fruits of which have been assembled into a cozy nest of a restaurant. Specialties of the house include *Rigatoni alla Buttero*, a rich dish of pancetta, mushrooms, and tomatoes covered in parmesan and butter *(€8)*. If your eyes need a break from the impressive array of objects inside, head to the peaceful indoor garden that is covered in vines.

From P. San Sonnino, turn left onto V. della Lungaretta. $ Pizza (only in evenings) €5-7. Primi €6-10; secondi €7-15. Open M-Sa noon-3pm and 7-11pm.

AI SPAGHETTARI RISTORANTE ❹

P. San Cosimato 57/60 ☎06 58 00 450 www.aispaghettari.it

With photos of Alberto Sordi and Al Pacino lining the walls, this place is obviously loved by at least a few Italians. Since 1896, Ai Spaghettari has served a hearty mix of meat and seafood on its casual patio overlooking the small *piazza*. Don't fill up on the huge selection of *bruschette (€2.50-4)* before you try the restaurant's classic "Ai Spaghettari" pizza, which is topped with tuna, rocket, balls of fresh cheese, and tomato *(€9)*. Rivaling the menu, huge barrels of wine just inside the building make this a viable alternative for late-night drinks.

From Vle. Trastevere, turn right onto V. San Francesco a Ripa and then left onto V. Natale d. Grande until you reach P. San Cosimato; veer right on the piazza. $ Primi €8.70-10.50; secondi €13.50-18.50. Pizza €6.50-9.50. Open M-Tu 5pm-12:30am and W-Su noon-12:30am.

IL GALEONE CORSETTI SEAFOOD ❺

P. San Cosimato 27 ☎06 58 09 009 www.corsettigaleone.it

A galleon-turned-cruise ship, this elegant restaurant serves seafood in style. Jazz, stripped white wood, and waiters in matching uniforms give the place an upscale, though relaxed, feel. The *spaghetti alla corsetti (seafood in white sauce; €16)* comes highly recommended when paired with one of over 100 wines hailing from Trentino Alto-Adige, Campania, and everywhere in between.

From Vle. Trastevere, turn right onto V. San Francesco a Ripa, and left onto V. Natale d. Grande until you reach P. San Cosimato; restaurant is on the center-left side of thepiazza. $ Primi and secondi €11-50. Open daily noon-3:30pm and 7:30pm-midnight.

VILLA BORGHESE, PARIOLI, AND FLAMINIO

Food in this area is best eaten away from the dinner table. In other words, because it is primarily a residential area surrounded by park, eating out tends to be pricey. Your best bet is to pack a picnic beforehand and eat it in one of the lovely gardens.

STAROCIA LUNCH BAR
🚫💳♿🍸⛅ CAFE [1]

V. Sicilia 121 ☎06 48 84 986

Pop into this bustling, modern cafe after a stroll in the Villa Borghese. Chic white decor and a small patio out front distinguish it from other food bars offering the same, standard fare. Fresh (and huge) panini, pasta, mixed drinks, and coffee are surprisingly well-priced given Starocia's hip vibe. Especially popular with the lunch crowd, though its evening happy hour buffet for only €4 (€6 with wine) means you'll probably make it your dinner spot.

🧭 Walking south on V. Po (away from the Villa Borghese), make a right onto V. Sicilia. ℹ Happy hour buffet €4, with wine €6. $ Pasta and secondi €4-7. Tramezzini and panini €1.80-3. Coffee €0.80-1.80. Mixed drinks €4.50-5.50. ⏰ Open M-Sa 5:15am-9:30pm. Happy hour M-Sa 6pm.

BUBI'S
💳♿🍸⛅ RISTORANTE [4]

V. G.V. Gravina 7-9 ☎06 32 60 05 10 💻www.bubis.it

The small menu and serene pistachio walls of this elegant restaurant cater to diners with refined taste. Terrace seating behind a wall of leaves is great for a more intimate meal and makes you feel far removed from the busy V. Flaminia. Though specializing in classic Roman cuisine, the restaurant serves entrees like *straccetti di pollo* with curry and Canadian rice as well as a range of gourmet hamburgers that add a little bit of international flare.

🧭 ⓂA: Flaminio or tram #19 to Belle Arti. Walk up V. Flaminio from the Metro for about 5min. and turn left onto V. G.V. Gravina. $ Primi €9-12; secondi €12-18. Panini €12-14. ⏰ Open M-Sa 12:30-3pm and 8-11pm.

TREE BAR
💳♿🍸⛅ CAFE [2]

V. Flaminia 226 ☎06 32 65 27 54

If you're in the park and want to feast somewhere besides a picnic bench, this classy lunch bar does the trick. The white pebbles, glass "walls," and wooden decor (even the lanterns are made of wood, but try to banish those thoughts of potential fire hazard from your mind) make you feel like you're at a vacation house and should be sunbathing by the pool. But save that for outside—the art magazines, chic bar, and plush green couches inside create an upscale vibe. Healthy entrees and finger foods are listed on the chalkboard menu, which is posted on a column in the center of the room.

🧭 ⓂB: Flaminio. Walk about 25min. up V. Flaminia. Or tram #2 to Belle Arti. $ Primi and secondi €6-16. ⏰ Open M 6pm-2am, Tu-Su 10:30am-2am.

RISTORANTE AL BORGHETTO
💳♿🍸❄⛅ RISTORANTE [4]

V. Flaminia 77 ☎06 32 02 397

A quality alternative to some fancier spots nearby, this modest restaurant serves delicious and more original takes on Roman classics. A great variety of vegetarian plates includes the orecchiette with eggplant, mint, ricotta, and walnuts. Fish lovers will appreciate the pesto *taglioni* with octopus for a little variation on standard *primi*. The small, yellow- and scarlet-accented interior creates a welcoming atmosphere.

🧭 ⓂA: Flaminio. Walk 5min. up V. Flaminia. $ Primi €8.50-13; secondi €14-18.50. ⏰ Open M-Sa 12:30-3pm and 7:30pm-midnight.

IL MARGUTTA RISTORANTE
💳🚫♿🍸❄ VEGETARIAN [3]

V. Margutta ☎06 32 65 05 77 💻www.ilmargutta.it

Vegetarians, rejoice! (Even vegans can let out a shout of joy.) The expansive interior of this meatless restaurant, accented by tall potted plants to match the green cuisine, creates a surprisingly sophisticated feel. Black circular booths mixed with small, orange tables welcome both bigger parties and couples. Those tired of white pasta can feast on refreshing plates like buckwheat noodles topped with strawberries, asparagus, and gorgonzola. For a protein kick, try the seitan escalope with lemon and Cartizze sauce. Though a single entree will probably fill you up, full tasting menus are offered for those who can't get enough. The Sunday festivity brunch features a huge buffet with live music *(€25)*.

🧭 [M]A: Flaminio. From Piazzale Flaminia, walk into P. del Popolo and veer left onto V. del Babuino. Proceed 5min. and turn left onto the small alley street, V. Margutta. $ Primi €10-12; secondi €11-14. Lunch buffet €12-18. ⏰ Open daily 12:30-3:30pm and 7:30-11:30pm.

TERMINI AND SAN LORENZO

Termini and its surrounding region are dominated by restaurants representing both extremes of the price range: cheap eats and over-priced tourist menus catering to hungry travelers. Avoid restaurants immediately surrounding the station and head into some side streets for higher quality options. Hostel dwellers with kitchen access should make the huge **SMA grocery store** *(⏰ Open M-Sa 8am-9pm, Su 8:30am-8:30pm)* located downstairs next to the Coin store on V. Esquilino, right on the corner of P. Santa Maria Maggiore, their friend. There's also an **indoor market** filled with merchants selling fish, meat, fruit, vegetables, and various canned goods at V. Giolitti 271/A *(alternative entrance on V. Principe Amadeo 188 ⏰ Open M 5am-3pm, Tu 5am-5pm, W-Th 5am-3pm, F-Sa 5am-5pm)*.

👍 ANTICA PIZZERIA DE ROMA — 💳♿❄ PIZZERIA ❶

V. XX Settembre 41 — ☎06 48 74 624 💻www.mcmab.net

Businessmen may take home a big paycheck, but that doesn't mean they don't like bargains when they see them: midday, this tiny pizzeria is full of men in suits, munching some of the best-priced and freshest pizza in the neighborhood. Though this pizzeria offers the same standard fare that infiltrates all of Rome (thin crust pizza sold by weight), watching the workers cut, weigh, and serve up fresh pies like a science (or whip out an individual one in less than 10min.) is a real pleasure—and you haven't even taken your first bite. Once you do, you'll be ready to join the businessmen every day.

🧭 From P. della Repubblica, walk down V. V. E. Orlando and turn right onto V. XX Settembre. Proceed 7min. $ Individual pizzas €2.20-5.50, €0.70-2 per etto. ⏰ Open daily 8am-9:30pm.

PASTICCERIA STRABBIONI ROMA — 💳♿🍸☀ CAFE, PASTICCERIA ❷

V. Servio Tullio 2a-2b — ☎06 48 73 965

Not much has changed at Strabbioni since it opened in 1888: not the hand-painted flowers gracing the ceiling or the old-fashioned lamps, and definitely not the good service and food. (While *Let's Go* might not have been around in 1888, we're pretty sure this place would have merited a listing in *Let's Go Grand Tour 1889*.) The second-oldest bar of its type still in Rome, this is the place where locals come for a cheap lunch (*primi* classics are written daily on a chalkboard outside), a freshly baked pastry, or even an afternoon mixed drink. At only €3.50-4 a drink, how can you resist? Enjoy a specialty like the *budino di riso*, a small rice pudding cake, in the casual seating outside or while standing at the wooden bar as you chat with the staff.

🧭 From Porta Pia, walk down V. XX Settembre and make a right onto V. Servio Tullio. $ Primi €6-7; secondi €8. Pastries €0.80-3. ⏰ Open M-Sa 7am-8pm.

FASSINO — 💳♿🍸 CAFE, GELATERIA ❷

V. Bergamo 24 — ☎06 85 49 117

The folks at Fassino will have you know gelato isn't just a summer thing. Their famous *Brivido Caldo* reinvents the favorite frozen treat, sticking a cookie in its middle and turning it into a hot delight topped off with whipped cream. If it's a winter month, try their richest flavor, the *cioccolato* with brandy and cream. If it's summer, their original *cioccarancio* (dark chocolate and orange) is to die for. After the sugar rush (or before, if you're one of those people who's been brainwashed into the dessert-after-dinner rule), settle down for a savory crepe, which the Sicilian owner makes with no butter fat—only extra virgin olive oil—for a lighter taste. Though their fixed lunch meal *(a crepe, drink, dessert, and coffee; €8.50)* is a steal, consider coming in the evening when a classical pianist plays until the customers leave.

☩ *From the end of V. XX Settembre, turn left onto V. Piave and walk until you hit P. Fiume. Turn right onto V. Bergamo.* **i** *Live music M-W, F, Su 10pm-closing.* Ⓢ *Gelato €1.50-3. Brivido Caldo €3 (winter only). Mixed drinks €4.50-5.* Ⓣ *Open M-F 9:30am-1am, Sa 3:30pm-1am, Su 9:30am-1:30pm and 3:30pm-1am.*

RISTORANTE DA GIOVANNI   ✦⊗♈ RISTORANTE ❸
V. A Salandra 1   ☎06 48 59 50

A hand-written menu, shelf of old typewriters, and even a hanging carcass greet customers at this subterranean trattoria. Don't worry: the meat is dangling in the kitchen, ensuring that your entree will be that much fresher. With only a few windows near the ceiling and a wood-lined interior, this family-run Roman restaurant oozes with dark warmth that matches its classic dishes. You've seen it written dozens of times at numerous establishments, but you'll never get tired of Da Giovanni's *cacio e pepe*, which they've been making for over 50 years.

☩ *From P. della Repubblica, walk up V. V. E. Orlando and turn right onto V. XX Settembre. Walk 5min. and turn left onto V. M Pagano; veer left onto V. A. Salandra.* Ⓢ *Primi €5.50-6.50; secondi €4.50-12.* Ⓣ *Open M-Sa noon-3pm and 7-10:30pm.*

RISTORANTE AFRICA   ✦♿♈ AFRICAN ❸
V. Gaeta 26-28   ☎06 49 41 077

The area around Termini abounds with cheap, international dives, but this African restaurant distinguishes itself with better quality food and a more welcoming decor. The friendly staff will be happy to recommend a dish to the customer ignorant of African cuisine or Italian, but English translations provide ample assistance. Vegetarians can finally feast on something other than pasta: the *aliccia* is a healthy dish of puréed vegetables simmered in onion and herb sauce and served with traditional African bread *(€9)*. Bright orange walls, carved wooden seats, and African sculptures bring you out of Italy, at least for the hour you're here to eat.

☩ Ⓜ*Termini. Walk in the direction of P. del Cinquecento and turn right onto V. Gaeta.* Ⓢ *Appetizers €3-4; entrees €9-12.* Ⓣ *Open M-Sa 8am-midnight.*

LA FAMIGLIA   ✦♿♈⌂ RISTORANTE ❸
V. Calatafimi 11   ☎06 48 54 39

Trattorias are about as common as hotels in Termini...which means they're essentially everywhere. Though La Famiglia offers the same classic fare you'll find elsewhere, its location on a quieter street, its surprisingly good prices, and its bright, white decor make it a superior choice. Patio seating behind tall plants offers even more privacy to diners seeking something a bit more romantic. A huge menu of pizza, homemade pasta, fish, and meat is made even more affordable by the freshly prepared buffet option.

☩ Ⓜ*Termini. Walk up V. Volturno and turn right onto V. Calatafimi.* Ⓢ *Primi €5-8; secondi €6-18. Small self-service plates €6.50, large €8.50.* Ⓣ *Open daily noon-4pm and 6-11pm.*

PIZZERIA DEL SECOLO   ⊗⊗♈ PIZZERIA ❶
V. Palestro 62   ☎06 44 57 606

A favorite among nearby hostel dwellers, this corner spot serves up 27 varieties of thin-crust and filled pizza, including one loaded with nutella. Grab a slice or a cheap *primi* before ordering a few cups of even better-priced Peroni beer *(€2.50)*.

☩ Ⓜ*Termini. Take V. Milazzo 4 blocks and turn left onto V. Palestro.* Ⓢ *Pizza by the slice €0.70-1.10 per etto; whole pizzas €4.50-6. Primi €5-7.* Ⓣ *Open daily 8am-midnight.*

rome

TESTACCIO AND OSTIENSE

Testaccio is known among Roman residents as one of the best spots for high-quality, well-priced food. Its location farther from the sights means it evades the tourist crowds of the city center. Whether you want an upscale restaurant or a cheaper trattoria, you won't have any trouble finding it here.

👍 IL NOVECENTO — RISTORANTE ❸

V. dei Conciatori 10 ☎06 57 25 04 45 🖥www.9cento.com

Fresh. Homemade. Family-run. You've heard these adjectives used all too often to describe Italian cuisine, but here, they actually come to life. Watch the owner's son roll out pasta dough, cut it into *tagliatelle*, and dump it into boiling water before it ends up on your plate topped with their own pesto *(€9)*. If pasta isn't your thing, then how about pizza or roasted meat—again, you can see both sliced and diced minutes before you eat them. Though the wood-lined rooms up front are especially cozy, try to grab a table in the huge dining room in back so you can take in all the kitchen action.

 # Ⓜ B: Piramide. Walk down V. Ostiense and make a right onto V. dei Conciatori. $ Primi €8-10; secondi €12-18. Pizzas €5-9 (only at dinner). ⏰ Open M-F 12:30-2:30pm and 7:30-11pm, Sa-Su 7:30-11pm.

👍 FARINANDO — PIZZERIA, PANIFICIO ❷

V. Lucca della Robbia 30 ☎06 57 50 674

At Farinando, you can get top-notch pizza by the kilo or pie, huge calzones, and anything from cookies to fruit tarts without having to pay for expensive table service or retreat to a park bench. Stock up before hitting the long V. Ostiense for some sightseeing.

 # Ⓜ B: Piramide. Walk up V. Marmorata; turn left onto V. Galvani and right onto V. Lucca della Robbia. $ Calzones €3. Whole pizza €4-7, €7-18 per kg. ⏰ Open M-Th 7:30am-2pm and 4:30-8:30pm, F 7:30am-9pm, Sa 5-9pm.

LA MAISON DE L'ENTRECÔTE — RISTORANTE, ENOTECA ❸

P. Gazometro 1 ☎06 57 43 091 🖥www.lamaisondelentrecote.it

You don't need a plane ride or a time machine if you want to return to bohemian Paris: just retreat to Le Maison's dim downstairs, where stained-glass lamps and slow music put you at ease. The small menu lets you pair classic French dishes like cheesy onion soup *(€7)* with Italian staples. Try their *crema* gelato topped with Grand Marnier. Check out the antique mirror and the 10% discounted menu scribbled atop it, then check yourself to see if your cheeks are pink like Moulin Rouge from the wine you've hopefully been sipping.

 # Ⓜ B: Ostiense. Walk down V. Marmorata away from Piramide for 5min. and turn right onto P. Gazometro. $ Primi €7-10. Salads €5-7. Meats €9-14. Beer €4. Cocktails €6. Wine by the bottle €12-16. ⏰ Open Tu-Th 1-3pm and 8pm-midnight, F-Sa 8pm-midnight.

OSTERIA DEGLI AMICI — RISTORANTE ❸

V. Nicola Zabaglia 25 ☎06 57 81 466 🖥www.osteriadegliamici.info

Besides the excellent cheese-topped pasta dishes, there's nothing cheesy about this place. Enjoy hot saffron risotto sprinkled with smoked Scamorza cheese and drizzled in balsamic vinegar while downing a glass of their stellar wine (whose cork might get added to the gigantic collection up front). If the relaxed setting makes you want to linger, split a spicy chocolate souffle—almost as hot as the entrees—with your *amici*, who's hopefully bringing the heat as well.

 # Ⓜ B: Piramide. Walk up V. Marmorata; turn right onto V. Luigi Vanvitelli and left onto V. Nicola Zabaglia. $ Primi €7-9; secondi €12-16. ⏰ Open W-Su 12:30-3pm and 7:30pm-midnight.

L'OASI DI BIRRA — RISTORANTE ❷

P. Testaccio 40 ☎06 57 46 122

Most liquor menus round off their selection at a few pages, but this two-floor mecca of food and alcohol has six pages devoted to Belgian beer *alone*. It requires a book to catalogue the rest of their international collection, which also includes wine, grappa, rum, and whiskey. The floor-to-ceiling bottles (both upstairs and down) probably make up less than 10% of their actual collection. The best way to tackle the menu is to order a bottle for the table (some upwards of €200) and match it up with a few six- or eight-variety plates of *salumi*, cheese, or bruschetta which come in nearly as many combinations as the alcohol. If you're bad at making decisions, drop in during happy hour when you can endlessly sample the goods for only €10 at the *aperitivo* buffet.

♯ Ⓜ️B: Piramide. Walk up V. Marmorata and turn left onto P. Testaccio. *i* Also carries a small selection of bottled food products. Ⓢ Bruschette €8. Salumi and formaggi plates of 6-8 types €16-19. Draft beer €4-10. Wine €12-200+ per bottle. ☒ Open M-Sa 4:30pm-12:30am, Su 7:30pm-12:30am. Happy hour nightly 5-8:30pm.

FELICE A TESTACCIO   🛵⊗♿️💲 RISTORANTE ❸

V. Mastro Giorgio 29   ☎06 57 46 800 🖳www.feliceatestaccio.com

Sunday, Monday happy days...except replace happy with *felice* and make that *every day* at this place. Part of a rotating selection of seven entrees each day, the plates here are among the freshest and best in Testaccio. If you're picky, choose your day wisely: F is particularly fish heavy (and consequently more expensive), while W might be a good day for vegetarians given that it's the day they serve up their special rigatoni pasta and Roman broccoli *(only in season; €10)*. If you haven't gotten your hands on the menu beforehand, you can count on finding an assortment of Roman standards—prepared far above standard—which are made daily and are the only things served Su.

♯ Ⓜ️B: Piramide. Walk up V. Marmorata; turn left onto V. Galvani and right onto V. Mastro Giorgio. Ⓢ Primi €8-10; secondi €13-22. ☒ Open M-Sa 12:30-2:45pm and 8-11:30pm, Su 12:30-2:45pm.

CACIO E COCCI   🛵♿️💲 RISTORANTE ❸

V. del Gazometro 36   ☎06 57 46 419

In case you didn't know you were in an *hostaria*, there's a 5 ft. sign hanging on the yellow walls reminding you where you are. Cacio e Cocci has been making traditional Roman dishes since 1944; pick up a menu and you'll see a 1960 (the year the sign was inaugurated) shot of the restaurant and its proud mother. Since then, specialties like the ricotta ravioli with oranges *(€10)* and fresh fish plates like spaghetti with clams, zucchini, and saffron keep locals streaming in. Though it could be a casual dinner spot, the best deal is the €9 lunch menu, which includes a *contorno*, *primo*, water, and coffee.

♯ Ⓜ️B: Ostiense. Walk down V. Ostiense; turn right onto V. dei Magazzini Generali and immediately left onto V. del Gazometro. Ⓢ Primi €7.50-11; secondi €9-16. ☒ Open M-Sa noon-3pm and 7-11:30pm.

LINARI   🛵♿️💲 CAFE ❶

V. Nicola Zabaglia 9   ☎06 57 82 358 🖳www.pasticcerialinari.it

If you closed your eyes, the sound of clinking plates and busy counter orders might have you thinking you were in an American diner. In fact, with its small tables, counter stools, and sunny feel, Linari isn't far off. Instead of ordering a banana split or sundae, you'd be best off indulging in homemade gelato atop apple strudel or perhaps one of the fresh-made, heavenly pralines *(€5 per etto)*. Nab a table at breakfast or lunch or stand at the bar Frank Sinatra style while sipping on a happy hour cocktail *(€4)*.

♯ Ⓜ️B: Piramide. Walk up V. Marmorata; turn right onto V. Luigi Vanvitelli and left onto V. Nicola Zabaglia. *i* Seating only at breakfast and lunch. Happy hour buffet with drink €6. Ⓢ Gelato €2-2.50. Primi €4.50-5. Pizza €12 per kg. Pastries €18-20 per kg. ☒ Open M 6:30am-9:30pm, W-Su 6:30am-9:30pm. Happy hour 6-9pm.

nightlife

d-squared

Drinking and dining are two of Italy's most famous attractions. For all the great cuisine on offer, however, sit-down meals in Italy can equal time and money. If you're looking to save on both those fronts while indulging your stomach and liver (livers *want* alcohol, right?), the Italians are have something to help you out: the *aperitivo* happy hour. This works as follows. Anytime after 5:30pm, most places put out a buffet spread containing anything from finger food to *primi,* into which customers are free to dive after purchasing a drink. Though you don't get the service of a sit-down meal, the food is often extremely fresh and well-made, the vibe is casual, and the value unbeatable: as much food as you want and well-priced cocktails for under €10. The only thing to prevent you from loading up your plate with refill after refill is pride. After your fifth trip back to the food table in the course of two hours, you'll probably realize you don't have too much of that.

Don't spend all your euro and energy at the museums—Rome's nightlife is varied and vast, giving you a whole other itinerary to attack after the guards go home and the cats come out to prowl the ruins. Generally, you'll be able to find whatever nightlife you're into, though each neighborhood has its own flavor and characteristic selection. The only areas where your nights might end a bit early are, unsurprisingly, Vatican City and the region near Villa Borghese.

Enoteche (wine bars, often with *aperitivi*) are scattered throughout the city but are especially prevalent in the **Ancient City** and **Centro Storico.** They generally cater to an older crowd seeking high-quality drinks and low-key conversation.

Irish pubs and American-style bars populate **Trastevere,** busy *corsi* (Vittorio Emanuele, V. del Corso, V. Nazionale, etc.), and the area around **Termini.** They often have weekly specials (karaoke and quiz nights) and air sporting events. Note that "bar" in Italy generally refers to a cafe where you can buy alcoholic beverages but which is mostly a daytime spot for food. Cocktail bars and lounges are called "American bars." More upscale lounges are common in the area around **Piazza di Spagna,** where they're about all you'll find.

The ragers in your party should head to **Testaccio,** known for some of the best discos in the city, most of which are conveniently clustered around the base of Monte Testaccio. If you're up for the trek, take a night bus to **Ostia,** Rome's closest beach, and enjoy plenty of opportunities for dancing and lounging on the sand as the morning sun rises. Go with a group, though, as the long stretches between discos tend to be isolated at odd hours.

Speaking of beaches, many clubs migrate to the sandy shore starting in late May and continuing through August. Check out **Gilda on the Beach** (*Lungomare di Ponente 11 in Fregene* ☎*06 66 56 06 49).*

While indoor venues such as bars, clubs, and discos can provide a fun setting for your evening pursuits, they expectedly rake up a large bill: cover fees and pricey cocktails may have you broke after a few nights. As an alternative, head to **Campo dei Fiori, Piazza Santa Maria in Trastevere, Piazza Colonna** (outside the Pantheon), or the **Spanish Steps** for an inevitably large crowd (even on a "tame" Tuesday), impromptu live performances, and an evening before some of Rome's greatest monuments without the constant flash of photos. (It's okay to snap your camera during the day, but you'd just be the lame tourist at night.) Alcohol by the bottle is surprisingly cheap at the supermarket and drinking outside is as common as smoking, for better or worse. Crack open a Peroni or a bottle of wine and make your own nightlife on the *piazza*. A note to the overzealous, underage American tourist, however: getting wasted is not looked upon favorably by the Italian populace. Drinking is as much a part of the culture as eating, so there's little sense in overdoing it on a single night. Hopefully, you'll grow out of the beer pong, pub crawl, and open-bar phase after one night of trying each.

ANCIENT CITY

Nightlife in the Ancient City is confined mostly to Irish pubs, upscale wine bars, and small cafes open until the late hours. While there's nothing like walking down a cobblestone street after a few glasses of wine, if you're looking for young, pumping clubs, head elsewhere.

ICE CLUB — CLUB, BAR

V. Madonna dei Monti 18/19 ☎06 97 84 55 81 www.iceclubroma.it

Gelato isn't the only way to cool off from the hot Roman sun: enter Ice Club, the only bar in Italy made entirely of ice. For €15, you get a silver cloak, a pair of gloves, and one free drink at what may be Rome's (literally) coolest spot, an ice tube of colored lights, pulsing music, and stellar drinks. Vodka goes down smooth as, you guessed it, ice and not only because it's served in an ice cup: with over 40 flavors ranging from strawberries and cream to chocolate, you'll never know you're drinking your liquor straight. Clearly, this is how the place keeps its clientele, since after a few shots, it's hard to tell that the temperature is below freezing.

From the Fori Imperiali, turn right onto V. Madonna dei Monti. *i M, W-F, and Su drop by between 6-9pm and get in free after 11pm. Open bar Tu €15. Buy 1 shot, get 4 free Th. Credit cards accepted for cover. Cash only at the bar (because credit cards would just be impractical in that weather).* *$ Cover €15; includes 1 drink. Shots €2.50. Straight vodka €7. Mixed drinks €8. Ice luge €10.* *Open daily 6pm-2am.*

rome

SCHOLAR'S LOUNGE — BAR

V. del Plebiscito 101/b ☎06 69 20 22 08 www.scholarsloungerome.com

There'll be no scholars reading here: with nine TVs (including two that are over 5 ft. wide) and over 250 kinds of whiskey (the biggest collection in Italy), they're probably dancing on the table. Don't bother bringing your Italian phrasebook, because the Irish bartenders, huge Irish flag hanging over the bar, and steady stream of Irish dishes *(beef in Guinness stew, €9.50)* make this a bit of Dublin on the Tiber. Although you can keep it cheap at only €3.50 for a pint of beer, those looking for a splurge should check out the whiskey list: a shot of Jameson Rarest Vintage Reserve goes for a whopping €133.50. Ask to see their private collection, which might as well be at a museum.

From P. Venezia, follow V. del Plebiscito to just where it intersects V. del Corso. *i Live music Th-F. Karaoke on Tu and Su.* *$ Pints €3.50-5.50. Mixed drinks €7.50-9.50, €5 during the day. Student specials: long drinks €4.50, shots €1.* *Open daily 11am-3:30am. Happy hour until 8pm.*

LIBRERIA CAFÉ — CAFE

V. degli Zingari 36 ☎33 97 22 46 22

Libreria's "business card" is a bookmark, just in case you want to remember the address—or perhaps the page number—where you left off. You'll find yourself in relaxed company at this bohemian cafe, accoutered with draped cloths, antique couches, votive candles, lamps that might as well have come from a Lewis Carroll novel, and, of course, walls of books by Karl Marx, Victor Hugo, Freud, and any number of Italian authors. Check out the coffered ceiling of the stone "den" downstairs, which, surprisingly, is brighter, if a bit musty. Smooth jazz playing in the background will feel even smoother after a glass of one of the 47 varieties of wine (€5) offered. If you do, in fact, want to read, try a cup of tea instead, hailing from Russia, Japan, or even South Africa (€5).

♯ ⓜB: Cavour. From V. Cavour, turn right onto P. degli Zingari and left onto V. degli Zingari. ⓢ Beer €3-5. Wine €5. Mixed drinks €5-6. Appetizers €6-10. ⏰ Open M 6pm-2am and W-Su 6pm-2am. Aperitivo buffet 7-9pm, €8.

STUDIO 33 LE BAIN
♥க♥❀ CLUB

V. delle Botteghe Oscure 33 ☎06 68 65 673 🖳www.studiolebain.it

If the Roman gods ever came down to earth, they might choose this grandiose spot to make their landing. Elegant white tables and fresh flowers juxtaposed beside playful neon paintings and suave gold cushions should clue you in to the mixed crowd which comes here—both sophisticated adults looking for fine food and younger *ragazze* seeking pumping tunes. During the day, full breakfast and brunch are served in the creamy-colored central hall. Starting at 7pm, crowds cluster around one of two bars for aperitifs (€7), mixed drinks (€7), and conversation. *Dopo cena*, expect a louder and more experimental mix during the week.

♯ From C. Vittorio Emanuele, turn right onto P. del Gesu; head down V. Celsa, then turn left onto V. d. Botteghe Oscure. ⓢ Mixed drinks €10. Primi €10-16; secondi €15-18. Buffet lunch €10. ⏰ Open daily 7am-2am.

FINNEGAN PUB
🎯❀♥ BAR

V. Leonina 66 ☎06 47 47 026 🖳www.finneganpub.com

There's a pool table and dart board, flat-screen TVs showing soccer, and live Irish music at this dark and rowdy bar—what more could you want? Perhaps drafts starting at €3 and spirits at €3.50? (No mixed drinks—the Irish drink it straight.) International currency left by customers trails across the ceiling, while enough jerseys to clothe the entire Italian soccer team adorn the walls. All this memorabilia is here to remind folks where they are: a spot that teems with Italians and expats getting their fill of beer, sport, and fun.

♯ Coming from the Fori Imperiali, walk down V. Madonna dei Monti until it becomes V. Leonina *i* Live music on F ranging from jazz to Irish fiddle to folk. ⓢ Wine €2.50-5.50. Drafts €3-6. Spirits €3.50-4.50. ⏰ Open M-Th 1pm-12:30am, Sa noon-1am, Su noon-12:30pm.

CAVOUR 313
♥க♥ ENOTECA

V. Cavour 313 ☎06 67 54 96

The 100 varieties of wine, savory plates, and numerous awards honoring Cavour 313's classy offerings make it the spot of choice for those whose idea of a night out consists of fine food and even finer wine. The wine collection, conveniently on file up front in good library fashion, hails from all over Italy, as do *golosità* plates like the Calabrian—a mix of hot salami, sun-dried tomatoes with herbs, and olives. For something to offset the salty offerings, try a bit of gorgonzola cheese with honey and sweet marsala wine (€8). Cozy wooden booths can make your dining experience not only more private, but also less noisy.

♯ Midway up V. Cavour coming from V. dei Fori Imperiali ⓢ Wine €3.50-8. Mixed cheese plates €8-12, meat plates €8-10. ⏰ Open M-Sa 12:30-2:45pm and 7:30pm-12:30am.

CENTRO STORICO

The Centro Storico might be old, but it packs in a young crowd at night. One of the best places to find bars and clubs, both in terms of location and quality, this area remains fairly safe after sunset due to its bustle at most hours. If you don't feel like heading inside, check out the Campo dei Fiori, where many spend the evening enjoying the outdoor scenery.

🅢 DRUNKEN SHIP
♥க♥❀♬ BAR, CLUB

Campo dei Fiori 20/21 ☎06 68 30 05 35 🖳www.drunkenship.com

Wait, is this the campo or the campus? Walking into Drunken Ship, you might very well think you're back at college, as it comes complete with nightly beer pong, TVs airing sports games, a DJ spinning Top 40 tunes, and a raucous crowd of students ready to enjoy it all. Great weekly specials, including Wednesday night power hours and Pitcher Night Thursdays *(€10)*, make this one of the most popular spots for young internationals aching for some university-style fun.

☩ *In Campo dei Fiori.* ℹ *M-Th half-price drinks for women until 11pm, Tu buy-1-get-1-free until 11pm; check online for more specials. Student discounts nightly. Happy hour pint of wine with free buffet €4.* Ⓢ *Shots €3-6. Long drinks €6. Mixed drinks €7.* 🕐 *Open M-Th 3pm-2am, F-Sa 10am-2am, Su 3pm-2am. Happy hour M F 4-8pm.*

▧ SOCIETE LUTECE ⬤♿☂⛱ BAR

P. di Montevecchio 17 ☎06 68 30 14 72

The total opposite of an American-college-student-ridden bar, Societe Lutece attracts an artsy late 20s to early 40s crowd. Homemade bags made from recycled material hang from the ceiling, and the menu is a fabric-covered panel of wood into which prices are etched. To complete the natural feel, all food and drinks are organic or locally produced. If you're hunting for high-quality and low-stress nightlife, how could you look any further than this place's nut colada *(€8)*?

☩ *From P. Navona, exit and turn left onto V. Coronari; continue and make a sharp left onto V. Montevecchio.* ℹ *Happy hour drinks with free buffet €8.* Ⓢ *Beer €5. Wine €6. Mixed drinks €8.* 🕐 *Open Tu-Su 6pm-2am. Aperitivo 6:30-10pm.*

MOOD ⬤⊗☂✷ CLUB

C. Vittorio Emanuele 205 ☎329 06 42 240

It may be painted entirely silver, but it meets the golden standard as far as Roman discos go. Room after room in Mood's cavernous downstairs lets guests choose between lounging or dancing. But with the stereo blaring Top 40 early on and drinks flowing generously (student specials abound), most people will be up on the floor by the time 1am rolls around. Because it's downstairs, the Centro Storico's 2am norm for closing may as well not exist.

☩ *Near Campo dei Fiori.* ℹ *Americans get in free. 2 drinks for €10 or open bar €15 until 1am. €2 shots for ladies. Student specials; show ID.* Ⓢ *Mixed drinks €10.* 🕐 *Open daily 11pm-4am.*

FLUID ⬤⊗☂✷ BAR, CLUB

V. del Governo Vecchio 46 ☎06 68 32 361 🖳www.fluideventi.com

Fluid seems to be working a "natural" theme—though the fake tree branches, caged rocks, and faux ice cube stools don't exactly scream "crunchy granola." With a lounge early in the evening and an upbeat DJ set later in the night, this is the place to come for post-dinner drinks and company. The drink menu, which is essentially a book of cocktails, features unorthodox mixes, like the cinnamon red: a smoothie of *cannella rossa* liqueur, yogurt, *crema di limone*, and whipped cream *(€7.50)*.

☩ *From P. Navona, exit onto P. Pasquina and continue as it becomes V. del Governo Vecchio.* ℹ *DJ nightly. Aperitivo drink and buffet €7.50.* Ⓢ *Beer €5-6. Mixed drinks €7.50.* 🕐 *Open daily 6pm-2am. Aperitivo hour 6-10pm.*

ARISTOCAMPO ⬤♿☂⛱ BAR

P. Campo dei Fiori

On the doorstep of Campo dei Fiori, this fast-paced bar gets crowded early thanks to its better-than-average *aperitivo* buffet. Pumping music pulses from the small bar inside, but most of the action is on the patio where nearly every stool is occupied. Great panini—good for carni-, herbi-, and omnivores—satisfies those late night cravings wrought by yet another cocktail.

☩ *In Campo dei Fiori.* ℹ *Aperitivo drink and buffet €5.* Ⓢ *Beer €5-6. Mixed drinks €7. Panini €4-5. Salads €8.* 🕐 *Open daily noon-2am. Aperitivo hour 6-8pm.*

ANIMA

⬥⊗✧❀ CLUB, BAR

V. di Santa Maria dell'Anima 57

Anima's copper entrance leads into a dim lounge, complete with black lights, low couches, and two bars. Lounge music plays in the early evening as a mixed crowd of students and 20-somethings wander in. Starting around midnight, the dance floor heats up with house and commercial tunes spinning until the wee hours. Head up the tiny spiral staircase if you want to step off the floor and people-watch from above.

⚑ *From P. Navona, turn left onto V. di Santa Maria della'Anima.* *i* *Ladies' night 2-for-1 drinks on M. Open bar Th and Su. Happy hour beer €2.50, mixed drinks €4.50.* Ⓢ *Beer €4-5. Mixed drinks €6, €10 after midnight.* ⚇ *Open daily 7pm-4am. Happy hour 7-10pm.*

ABBEY THEATRE

⬥♿((ᵖ))✧ IRISH PUB

V. del Governo Vecchio 51/53 ☎06 68 61 341 ▣www.abbey-rome.com

A traditional Irish pub where you can get your fair share of bar food, soccer, (American football?!), and great drinks—try a "mixed beer" special like the hard cider and grenadine *(€5.50).* The wooden interior is huge but fills up quickly during big games. Comedy nights (in English) cater particularly to an international crowd, but monthly specials like an open mike and a night of live Irish music bring everyone from expats to locals.

⚑ *From P. Navona, exit onto P. Pasquina and continue as it becomes V. del Governo Vecchio.* Ⓢ *Shots €4-6.50. Beer €5.50-6. Mixed drinks €7.* ⚇ *Open daily noon-2am. Happy hour noon-8pm.*

SALOTTO 42

⬥⊗✧❀ BAR

P. di Pietra 42 ☎06 67 85 804 ▣www.saloto42.it

The folks at the swanky Salotto 42 had it right: combine ancient pillars with refined, modern decor, a splash of wine, and a bit of Asian flare (check out the sushi appetizers), and you can't go wrong. The classy crowd that convenes at this dim lounge might bump shoulders inside, but the real place to see—and be seen—is the *piazza* outside. The sleek black furnishings inside might be snazzy, but they don't quite compare to classic Roman architecture. Luckily, Hadrian's Temple is just around the corner.

⚑ *From the Pantheon, turn right onto V. di Pastini and veer left towards the Tempio Adriano.* Ⓢ *Beer €6. Mixed drinks €10. Free buffet with drink purchase during aperitivo.* ⚇ *Open Tu-Sa 10am-2am, Su 10am-midnight. Aperitivo 7-9pm.*

PIAZZA DI SPAGNA

There's a reason the Spanish Steps are so popular at night, and it's not their beauty (though that's a definite perk). Young travelers seeking nightlife in this neighborhood would rather lounge on the steps than pay €15 for drinks and light music at a lounge nearby. There's no reason to stay in this neighborhood for a night out, unless you like walking down empty streets of closed boutiques or rubbing shoulders with businessmen and the residents of five-star hotels.

ANTICA ENOTECA DI V. DELLA CROCE

⬥♿✧⊿ ENOTECA

V. della Croce 76b ☎06 67 90 896

Escape the pretentiousness of the surrounding snazzy bars and head to this old-fashioned *enoteca* for a drink and a meal. The airy feel set by tall ceilings and rustic arches is refreshing compared to nearby places. A plate of homemade pasta with duck sauce and a glass of wine will cost you less than €15 and can be enjoyed in comfort at the long bar or a small side table. Unfortunately, there's no happy hour, but that just means you can enjoy €5 draft pints at 3pm.

⚑ Ⓜ*A: Spagna. From the Spanish Steps, walk down V. della Croce.* Ⓢ *Wine €4-10 per glass (also available by the bottle). Beer €5. Cocktails €8. Primi €8-9; secondi €12-16.* ⚇ *Open daily 11am-1am.*

GILDA
♣⊗♈♨ CLUB

V. Mario dè Fiori 97   ☎06 67 84 838 ■www.gildabar.it

We don't think the gold walls and chichi leather couches are a coincidence—dress sharply and prepare to schmooze with Rome's elite (or those with aspirations). One of the city's most famous discos, this upscale spot caters to an exclusive crowd wanting only the best cocktails and music. Pay for a table or rent a private room while you sip that martini and wait for the dance floor to fill up with stylishly-clad clubbers. Colored lights, multiple stereos, and ceilings rivaling St. Peter's in height don't disappoint. Our advice: if you make it here, just forget that "budget" thing and resign yourself to weeping in the morning.

♯ Ⓜ️A: Spagna. From the Spanish Steps, walk down V. Condotti and turn left onto V. Mario de Fiori. i Disco open from Sept to mid-June; moves to the beach at Ostia during the summer. Happy hour buffet with drink €8. Ⓢ €20-30 for a table, includes 1 drink. Cocktails €15. ☼ Disco open Sept-June Th-Su midnight-4am. Restaurant open daily from noon. Happy hour 5-9pm.

ELEGANCE CAFE
♣&♈♨♨ BAR

V. Vittorio Veneto 83/85/87   ☎06 42 01 67 45

If elegance means expensive cocktails served by waiters in bowties, then this cafe earns its name. As you might expect of a place surrounded by four-star hotels and catering to rich vacationers, Elegance can't really escape pretentiousness. Colored lights slowly change in sync with the refrains of live piano each night; unfortunately, the music feels like the soundtrack to a 1980s soap opera in which you are the star. From the outside patio, the music isn't quite as overbearing and the high-end modern sculptures will be in your peripheral vision. After a cocktail and a song, you and your wallet will be through.

♯ Ⓜ️A: Barberini. From P. Barberini, walk up V. Vittorio Veneto. i Live piano nightly 9pm-midnight. Ⓢ Cocktails €10-12.50. ☼ Open daily 7:30am-1am. Happy hour 6-9pm.

TRASTEVERE

Trastevere is home to some of the best nightlife in the city—student and otherwise. Whether you want a small bar, a classy lounge, or somewhere where you can move around a bit, make the trek over the river and get ready for a late night.

▩ FRENI E FRIZIONI
♣&♈♨ BAR

V. del Politeama 4-6   ☎06 45 49 74 99 ■www.freniefrizioni.com

To find this place, don't look for a street number: turn your head skyward until you spy a jam-packed bar. Located just up the stairs off Via del Politeama, Freni e Frizioni has essentially created its own *piazza*. (And you thought only high Roman authorities could do that.) The white interior, decorated with art work and bookshelves, feels more like a living room than a lounge. The extensive bar is only a precursor to the *aperitivo* room in back—a dining table to rival that of the Last Supper's, constantly replenished with fresh entrees served directly from the pots they were cooked in, awaits you. Check out the "shelf" of wooden drawers bearing foreign words, upon which international dips like Tzatiki and *salsa tonnata* are served. The outside *piazza* is possibly even more popular than the interior and is perfect for literally "looking down" on the world.

♯ From P. Trilussa, head down the tiny V. del Politeama and look for the steps (and the crowd) on the left. i Happy hour €6-10. Ⓢ Wine €6. Mixed drinks €7-8. ☼ Open daily 6:30pm-2am. Aperitivo happy hour 6:30-10:30pm.

▩ CAFE FRIENDS
♣&((♈))♨♨ CAFE, BAR, CLUB

P. Trilussa 34   ☎06 58 16 111 ■www.cafefriends.it

Like good friends (well, even mere acquaintances) should, the servers here know your name. Locals and international students alike crowd this hip cafe-lounge at all hours of the day. Fully decked out with a swanky silver bar, stylish cartooned walls, and spacious indoor and patio seating, Cafe Friends caters to more

American tastes: a full breakfast is served daily 8:30am-12:30pm. But abandon those early-morning ways for the more typically Italian *aperitivo* mixed-drink buffet, served nightly 7-10pm *(€6-8)*, which draws the biggest crowd. The special Friends drinks, like the "Zombie" *(rum, Jamaicano, cherry brandy, orange juice, and lime; €6.50)* will keep you going to music that blasts all the way into the early evening and gets cranked even louder on the weekends.

 # From Ponte Sisto, head into P. Trilussa. ℹ Free Wi-Fi. $ Beer €3.50-5. Martinis €7. Mixed drinks €8. 15% discount for international students with ID. ⏰ Open M-Sa 7am-2am, Su 6:30pm-2am.

PEPATO 💳♿🍸☁ BAR

V. del Politeama 8 ☎06 58 33 52 54

Follow the illuminated red Pepato sign into this dim haven of drinks and music, where predominantly black decor sets a sophisticated vibe. Sleek black stools line the silver bar where young staff serve Pepato specials like the "Royal," a powerful mix of Absolut Peppar, peach vodka, and champagne *(€7)*. Although there are plenty of couches and tucked-away corners for sitting, rock and house tunes blaring on the stereo will probably have you moving before the night is out. The wooden patio outside offers some reprieve from the pulsing interior, reminding you that you are on a historic, cobblestone street in a good ol' Catholic city.

 # From Ponte Sisto, turn left onto Lungotevere Raffaello Sanzio; head down the stairs in the piazza on the right, and make a left. $ Shots €3. Beer €4-7. Wine €5-7. Mixed drinks €6. ⏰ Open Tu-Su 6:30pm-1am. Aperitivo buffet with drinks 6:30-10pm, €10.

GOOD CAFFE 💳♿📶🍸☁ CAFE, BAR

V. di San Dorotea 8/9 ☎06 97 27 79 79 🖥www.goodcaffe.it

Alcohol really finds a home here—a refrigerator full of white wine, a bookshelf full of red, and an armoire of liquor make the place especially homey. Of course, the twinkling lights, colorful chandeliers, and festive red walls don't take away from the comfy feel. Most customers come for casual conversation over drinks, but live jazz and blues Monday and Thursday and a DJ on weekend nights make Good Caffe a better-than-good place to check out any night.

 # From P. San G. de Matha, take V. di San Dorotea as it veers left. ℹ Free Wi-Fi. $ Beer on tap €4.50-7. Mixed drinks €8. ⏰ Open daily 8am-2am. Happy hour aperitivo 7-9pm, €5 with wine, €8 with mixed drinks.

BEIGE 🚭♿🍸❄ BAR

V. Politeama 13-14 ☎06 58 33 06 86 🖥www.beigeroma.com

Somehow swanky black and white decor equals...Beige? Distinguishing itself from some of the more low-key establishments nearby with its plush stools, modern black arches, and dark green lounge, Beige caters to a sophisticated crowd all evening long. Its 12+ page menu, organized solely into pre- and post-dinner beverages, gives a drink to match nearly every hour until 2am. Mellow music and plenty of seats.

 # From Ponte Sisto, turn left onto Lungotevere Raffaello Sanzio, head down the stairs in the piazza on the right, and make a left. $ Mixed drinks €8. ⏰ Open Tu-Su 7:30pm-2am. Aperitivo happy hour 7:30pm-10:30pm.

BACCANALE 💳♿🍸☁ BAR

V. della Lungaretta 81 ☎06 45 44 82 68

While many places down the way may tout classier decor, none can approach Baccanale's prices or spirit. Bacchus would indeed be proud. The dark interior is made more colorful by dozens of alcohol flags and posters, an entire row of Aperol and Bacardi lining the wall, and a display of currency donated by the teems of international students that have visited over the years. Though their famous mojitos go for only €5, if you're with a crowd, you might consider ordering a pitcher for a mere €15 or 2L of Peroni for €18. Pop and R and B during the evening keep the crowds young.

✂ *From Vle. Trastevere, turn right onto V. della Lungaretta.* Ⓢ *Drafts €3.50-5. Mixed drinks €5-7.* ⌚ *Open Tu-Su 9:30am-2am.*

MA CHE SIETE VENUTI A FÀ
⊗ ⚹ ♈ BAR

V. Benedetta 25

Cocktails? Wine? Forget it all. Ma Che Siete Venuti A Fà's 16 taps and keg-lined interior will make you fall in love with beer—and only beer—all over again; even the lamps are made from recycled beer bottles. There is no "special" because, according to the friendly owner, they're all special; check out the chalkboard menu up front to order one of their constantly changing international brews. Customers can either retreat to what is essentially a wooden box in back or spill out onto the street as crowds accumulate in the early evening. Quiet music and tight quarters make casual conversation with *amici* about the only thing possible.

✂ *From P. Trilussa, turn right onto V. Benedetta.* Ⓢ *Bottled beer €3.50-5, draft €4-6.* ⌚ *Open daily 3pm-2am.*

NY.LON
✎ ⚹ ♈ ⌂ BAR

Lungotevere Raffaello Sanzio 8b ☎06 58 34 06 92 🖳www.nylonroma.it

If its name indicates anything, NY.LON will seem somewhat like a hip downtown loft in NY—exposed white brick, sky-high ceilings, and a slightly raw but modern feel. The red-lit bar and matching couches fill up around 7pm for a happy hour of fresh *aperitivo* and drinks (€10 nightly until 10:30pm). Thursdays, a live band sets up camp downstairs. The slightly quieter upstairs gives customers even more options.

✂ *From Ponte Garibaldi, turn right onto L. Raffaello Sanzio and walk 5min.* Ⓢ *Beer and wine €6. Mixed drinks €8.* ⌚ *Open M 7pm-2am, W-Su 7pm-2am.*

CANTINA PARADISO
✎ ⚹ (ⁱ⁾) ❄ ⚙ CAFE, BAR

V. San Francesco a Ripa 73 ☎06 58 99 799

It really is a little paradise here—stripped wooden tables topped with tiny lamps, red chandeliers and roses, cowprint stools, and purple beach chairs make for an unusual mix of rustic and couture. A lounge, wine bar, and cafe all in one, customers come to work (free Wi-Fi), dine (vegetarian buffet €5, with drink €7), or kick back for a mixed drink on the outside patio where you'll find a bit of beach and a bit of "cozy."

✂ *From P. San Sonnino, walk down Vle. Trastevere and turn left onto V. San Francesco a Ripa.* Ⓢ *Beer €4. Wine €5. Mixed drinks €8-10.* ⌚ *Open daily noon-2am. Aperitivo buffet 6-9pm.*

D. J. BAR
⊗ ⚹ ♈ CLUB, BAR

Vicolo del Cinque 60 ☎338 85 98 578

Who ever said size matters? Although the tiny upstairs occupies just barely a street corner, this place pulls a big punch with its loud music, colored lights, and over 100 types of mixed drinks. Cool black-and-white wallpaper decorates the upstairs, and a DJ blaring commercial tunes pumps up the crowd. The swanky green bar with lit-up Red Bulls fills up around 10pm, while the bigger arena downstairs gets crowded when people start wanting to dance.

✂ *From Santa Maria in Trastevere, veer into P. San Egidio and turn right onto Vicolo del Cinque.* Ⓢ *Shots €3. Beer €5. Mixed drinks €7.* ⌚ *Open daily 5pm-2am. Happy hour F-Sa 7-10pm.*

M8 BAR
⚹ ⊗ ♈ BAR

V. Benedetta 17 ☎06 58 33 16 45 🖳www.m8bar.com

A human-sized beer bottle towers over the entrance of M8, a brick-lined, warmly lit bar and lounge that feels a little bit like a cave. Upstairs, DJs spin house and commercial tunes (F-Sa), while a diverse crowd sips sweet specials like the "Mate" (vodka, sambuca, aperol, grenadine, and an orange). For a quieter and more intimate setting, descend the steep staircase to two curtain-enclosed lounges.

✢ *From P. San Malva, turn left onto V. Benedetta.* ⓘ *Foreign-language exchange conversations on Th night. Free Wi-Fi.*Ⓢ *Shots €3. Draft beer €3.5-5. Mixed drinks €7.* ⓩ *Open daily 7:30pm-2am. Aperitivo buffet daily 6:30-9:30pm, €5 euro buffet only, €7 with 1 drink.*

ENOTECA TRASTEVERE
🍴♿️♀⌂ ENOTECA

V. della Lungaretta 86   ☎06 58 85 659 🌐www.enotecatrastevere.it

A quote by Oscar Wilde hangs on one of Enoteca Trastevere's stripped brick walls: "Life is too short to drink mediocre wine." Enoteca Trastevere ensures that you won't: bookshelves filled with bottle after bottle treat customers to only the best. Though you can choose from one of their standby varieties, check out the weekly special menu (with dessert suggestions to match) on your little table. Indeed, it's hard to resist ordering a limoncello custard cake to go with your glass (€5) when the dessert case is right in sight. If the old-fashioned interior feels a bit dim for you, head outside to the comfy couches shaded by umbrellas and plants.

✢ *From Largo San G. de Matha, turn right onto V. della Lungaretta.* Ⓢ *Hard liquor €3.50-6.50. Wine €3.5-10. Mixed drinks €6.50-8. Desserts €5-7.* ⓩ *Open M-Th noon-1am, F-Sa noon-2am, Su noon-1am. Happy hour M-F 6-8:30pm.*

TERMINI AND SAN LORENZO

There are plenty of bars surrounding Termini, most of them close to hostels and thus especially popular with students. If staying out late, travel with a group and watch your purse. Stay away from the station as much as possible.

AI TRE SCALINI
🍴⊘♿(((•))) ♀ CAFE, ENOTECA

V. Panisperna 251   ☎06 48 90 74 95

Look down V. Panisperna and you'll see two things: a hanging curtain of vines and a crowd of people. The *sorridenti* customers at this socially-conscious *enoteca* and cafe often spill out onto the street, wine glass in hand. Inside, the giant blackboard menu features only locally grown and seasonally harvested products hailing from Lazio. Their *bufala con miele di tartufo (€6)* is especially good. The beverage selection is just as sustainable, including organic and hand-cultivated wines (the Sangiovese was made by prison inmates); the restaurant also refuses to sell bottled mineral water. Blues in the background, frescoed walls, tiny tables, and dim lights make this the perfect spot for casual conversation, a game of chess (check out their antique set), or some Roman history catch-up (their mini bookshelf should help). Before leaving, make sure to sign the guestbook, which has more than four years of scribbles in it, and check out the *piscina* (male toilet), where vintage photos of nude women tastefully decorate the wall. (Don't ask how *Let's Go*'s female researcher learned about these.)

✢ *From the intersection of V. XIV Maggio and V. Nazionale (near Trajan's column), walk up V. Pa- nisperna.* ⓘ *Free Wi-Fi. 10% discount at lunch hours.* Ⓢ *Beer on tap €3-5. Wine €3.50-6 per glass, €11-70/bottle. Sfizi (bite-sized appetizers) €2.50-3; primi €3-8.* ⓩ *Open M-F noon-1am, Sa-Su 6pm-1am. Aperitivo hour 6-9pm.*

YELLOW BAR
🍴♿️♀⌂ CAFE, BAR

V. Palestro 40   ☎06 49 38 26 82 💻www.the-yellow.com

Feeling a bit homesick for college, or perhaps just your home country? What- ever locale you have a hankering for, the international folks at Yellow Bar are sure to cure your case of the blues. Next door to its hopping hostel, this bar caters to a mixed crowd of travelers and students who come for cheap drinks, relaxed music, and good company. Order one of their special mixed drinks like the 🟡Chuck Norris Roundhouse Kick to the Face Crazy Shot (don't ask what's in it... just drink up) before heading downstairs to the beer pong room, fully equipped with two regulation-size tables and an official list of house rules. If you have to sit out a couple of rounds, be sure to scribble something on the white brick already covered in both lewd and lovely comments from past travelers. After the long night (or, shall we say, early morning), there's nothing like a "full American Breakfast" to get your day going...or perhaps prepare you for a nap.

♯ Ⓜ*Termini. From V. Marsala, near track 1, walk down V. Marghera and then turn left onto V. Palestro. i Pub quiz on W €5. Open bar on F €15. Ⓢ Mixed drinks €8. Beer pong pitchers €14.50. Happy hour spirits €2.50; wine €1.50. ⏰ Open daily 7:30am-2am. Kitchen open 7:30am-noon. Happy hour 3-9pm.*

TWINS
⟶⊗♀❄ BAR, CLUB

V. Giolitti 67   ☎366 13 58 140 or 06 48 24 932 🖥www.twinbar.com

Flashing lights, loud music, and red walls set a lively stage for the international crowd that packs Twins every night. Located just outside of Termini's station, this club is as busy as the street outside. The front bars cater to those seeking more of a lounge, while the back room and its private outdoor courtyard pack it in with loud beats and dancing. Nightly themes ranging from Brazilian to house music keep the crowd mixed. One of the stops on a €20 pub crawl featuring two long drinks at each club (check website for details). Though it's easy to get carried away here, keep your wits about you and your wallet close to your body—Termini's station is known for pickpockets.

♯ Ⓜ*B: Right outside of station. i Latin night on Tu. Brazilian night on Th. House/Commercial most other nights. Ⓢ Beer €3.50-5. Mixed drinks €8. Primi €7-13; secondi €12-23. ⏰ Open daily 6am-2am. Happy hour 5-7pm.*

DRUID'S DEN
⟶♿♀☂ IRISH PUB

V. San Martino ai Monti 28   ☎06 48 90 47 81 🖥www.druidspubrome.com

Wait, we're in Italy? You'd never know it in this green-lit Irish pub, the second oldest in the country. The brick walls are lined with memorabilia from the owner's frequent trips back home, an assortment ranging from flags to wooden place-name placards. Popular mostly with Italians and expats in the neighborhood, this is the place to come for quality drinks against a backdrop of national soccer games (though they've been known to take homesick American requests for baseball) or traditional live Irish music, depending on the night.

♯ Ⓜ*B: Cavour. Walk down V. Giovanni and veer left onto V. San Martino ai Monti. i Live music F-Sa around 10pm. Ⓢ Special whiskeys €4-5. Mixed drinks €4.50. Drafts €5.50. Happy hour prices about €1 less. ⏰ Open daily 5pm-2am. Happy hour 5-8:30pm.*

L'ISOLA CHE NON C'È
⟶♿(ⁿ)♀☂ LIBRERIA

V. San Martino ai Monti 7/A   ☎06 48 82 134

Lavender walls and a sleek wooden catwalk lined with books and bottles make up the little *isola* that, according to its name, "is not here." (Maybe that's because it's a paradise?) Books are only a starting point for discussion, an excuse for intellectual folk to gather over good wine and food. Occasional lectures on environmental concerns and live music on select nights provide other reasons to pop by this place and see what's going on. While classically Italian in its low-key style, Isola's tiny menu is a bit spunkier, with specials like smoked swordfish and pineapple or vegetarian delights like tabbouleh with zucchini.

♯ Ⓜ*B: Cavour. Walk down V. Giovanni and veer left onto V. San Martino ai Monti. i Free Wi-Fi. Live music most Th and Sa. Free buffet with purchase of a drink. Ⓢ Wine and beer €3-5. Mixed drinks €4-8. Primi €7-11. ⏰ Open M-Th 11am-midnight, F-Sa 11am-2am.*

THE FIDDLER'S ELBOW
⟶♿♀☂ IRISH PUB

V. dell'Olmata 43   ☎06 48 72 110 🖥www.thefiddlerselbow.com

So, what exactly is a "fiddler's elbow"? A musician might say it's a sore elbow caused from the up-and-down motion of playing the fiddle, but a good Irishman will tell you it's actually the result of raising beer flask to mouth so often that the elbow stiffens. They're more prone to the latter injury here, the oldest Irish pub in Rome, which has been liquoring up The Eternal City since 1976. Renowned in the neighborhood for its family history, congenial company, and great drinks, this pub brings in everyone from the backpacker to the neighborhood expat to the sophisticated businessman stopping in after a day's work. The wooden interior is speckled with objects from the Emerald isle and full of loud conversation. Locals love playing piano on open-mike night.

*[M]Termini. Walk toward P. Santa Maggiore and then down V. Paolina. Turn left onto W. Quattro Cantoni and left onto V. Olmata. **i** Open mike Th at 10pm. Pool and dart room in back. $ Beer €5-5.50, €4-4.50 during happy hour. ⏰ Open daily 5pm-2am. Happy hour 5-8:30pm.*

OLD STATION PUB AND CLUB — CAFE, CLUB

P. Santa Maria Maggiore ☎06 47 46 612 🖥www.oldstationmusicpub.it

You'd never know that beneath the old-fashioned cafe upstairs a raucous party of 20-somethings is raging. Come here for gelato, panini, and coffee with your parents; come for body shots, mixed drinks, and dancing until 4am with your friends. Beats ranging from reggae to house to R and B spin every night in the wooden "den" downstairs, where people either dance or lounge in one of the three rooms. Check out their website for themed parties and special events.

*On the corner of P. Santa Maria Maggiore. **i** Karaoke on W. $ Cover €10; includes 2 drinks. Shots €3-4. Beer €5-6. Mixed drinks €8. ⏰ Cafe open daily 7am-11pm. Bar and club open daily 9pm-4am.*

CHARITY CAFE JAZZ CLUB — BAR, JAZZ CLUB

V. Panisperna 68 ☎06 47 82 58 81 🖥www.charitycafe.it

Though the long black benches are lined up like pews, you won't hear any classical choir here—only exceptional live jazz, all night, every night. The terra-cotta walls are covered with pictures of famed musicians as well as scribbles from past customers singing their praise. Great, well-priced drinks during happy hour make the jazz sound even smoother.

*From the intersection of V. XIV Maggio and V. Nazionale (near Trajan's column), walk up V. Panisperna. **i** Check their monthly calendar for a schedule of nightly shows. $ Beer €6-7, during happy hour €3.50-4.50. Mixed drinks €8/4.50. ⏰ Open in summer M-Sa 6pm-2am; in winter daily 6pm-2am. Happy hour daily 6-9pm.*

DRUID'S ROCK — IRISH PUB

P. dell'Esquilino 1 ☎06 47 41 326 🖥www.druidspubrome.com

Conveniently located and laid-back, this Irish pub is the place to shoot the breeze, midday or midnight. The tall ceilings and outdoor seats overlooking the *piazza* create an especially open feeling, while live rock Friday and Saturday nights gives the place a bit more bite. If you don't choose one of the bar stools or small wooden tables, head upstairs where blue lights, eclectic decor, and a pool table give some kick to the place.

*On P. Esquilino, behind Basilica Santa Maria Maggiore. **i** Live music F-Sa. $ Beer pints €5.50. Mixed drinks €5. ⏰ Open daily noon-2am. Happy hour noon-8pm.*

TRIMANI WINE BAR — ENOTECA

V. Cernaia 37-B ☎06 44 69 630 🖥www.trimani.com

In the nest of mediocre trattorias and pubs that crowd Termini, this slightly upscale wine bar comes as a welcome surprise. The list of wine (which is practically a book) consists primarily of bottles to be split with your table (some, upwards of €200), though the first page features 20 varieties sold by the glass and organized according to the "four Cs": cult, chic, classic, and casual... one to match every mood? Delicious platters of cheese, *salumi*, and meats are great for satisfying a post-drink appetite.

*From P. Indipendenza, walk up V. Goito and turn right onto V. Cernaia. **i** Buy 1 glass get 1 free during happy hour. $ Wine €3.50-23 per glass; also sold by the bottle. Mixed drinks €9. Primi,* *secondi, and antipasti €7-14.* ☼ *Open M-Sa 11:30am-3pm and 5:30pm-12:30am. Happy hour 11:30am-12:30pm and 5:30-7pm.*

TESTACCIO AND OSTIENSE

Off Rome's central map, Testaccio and Ostiense cater to in-the-know partygoers: locals who've sought out the best clubs and the savvy tourists or students who've sought out the locals. The strip of clubs, restaurants, and lounges surrounding **Via di Monte Testaccio** begs to be explored, though as the evening rolls on longer lines make it harder to gain admission. The streets closer to the train station tend to have smaller, low-key establishments that stay open late, an option if you don't feel like heavy-duty clubbing.

▨ CONTE STACCIO
●⊗♥❄☃ BAR, CONCERT VENUE

V. di Monte Testaccio 65/b   ☎06 57 28 97 12 ▣www.myspace.com/contestaccio

If bumping and grinding to DJ'd music isn't your thing, then you'll probably love Conte Staccio. Live music ranging from indie rock to electro-funk draws a mixed crowd of internationals and not-so-mainstream students and locals. Two rooms—one with a stage, the other with tables for late-night nibbles—give you the option to enjoy the music from afar or rock out up close, though the smallish quarters mean that the huge stereos might blow your ears out before long, regardless of room. Head to the outdoor steps if you need a break from the music, but chances are the crowd outside will be just as packed.

✄ ⓂB: Piramide. Walk up V. Marmorata towards the river, turn left onto V. Galvani ,and veer left onto V. di Monte Testaccio. ⑤ Beer €2.50-5. Wine €3-5. Cocktails €6-7. Pasta €8. Secondi €10. ☼ Open daily 8pm-5am. Restaurant 8pm-3am. Music 11pm-5am.

▨ AKAB
●⚥♥❄☃ CLUB

V. di Monte Testaccio 69   ☎06 57 25 05 85 ▣www.akabcave.com

It's hard to tell what's inside and what's out at Akab, where the switch is so subtle that you don't know if your feeling is a cool summer breeze or some powerful A/C. During the summer most of the action starts in the central room, as live bands warm up the crowd and customers load up at the blue-lit bar staffed by buff bartenders. When the DJ starts, head back to room after room of dimly lit lounges and dance halls that, with ramps and flashing lights galore, feel somewhat like a psychedelic amusement park for adults. During the winter, the neon-colored upstairs lounge opens to accommodate the crowds. Though the cover and drinks cost a pretty penny, you'll be paying for one of Testaccio's hottest clubs and crowds.

✄ ⓂB: Piramide. Walk up V. Marmorata towards the river, turn left onto V. Galvani, and veer left onto V. di Monte Testaccio. ⓘ Beer €5 on Tu. Electronic on Tu. House on Th. Rock on F. Commercial and house on Sa. ⑤ Cover €10-20 on F-Sa includes 1 drink, free some other nights. Cocktails and beer €10. ☼ Open Tu 11:30pm-4:30am, Th-Sa 11:30pm-4:30am.

COYOTE
●⊗♥☃ BAR, CLUB

V. di Monte Testaccio 48/B   ☎340 24 45 874 ▣www.coyotebar.it

Cowboys might ride off into the sinking western sun; but night visitors at Coyote will wander home as the sun rises in the east. Get here early to avoid Colosseum-sized lines and an entrance fee to match. Once inside, ascend the curving ramp to a huge outdoor patio where beer flows generously under green and red lights. Once the clock strikes midnight, what started out as a casual cocktail bar becomes a full-fledged disco spinning house, Latin, and Top 40 tunes. The wooden floors give the place an extra bounce as the stereo cranks up and the crowds begin to move. If you're sober enough before leaving, check out the trail of American license plates lining the wall—last time we checked, the eastern seaboard was heavily outweighed by the wild west and the sultry south. New Yorkers, donate a plate, please?

✂ Ⓜ B: Piramide. Walk up V. Marmorata toward the river, turn left onto V. Galvani, and veer left onto V. di Monte Testaccio. *i* No food—hit Top 5 downstairs if you get hungry. Ⓢ Cover €10 F-Sa after midnight. Beer and wine €5. Cocktails €8. ⏰ Open daily 9pm-5am. Bar 9pm-midnight. Disco midnight-5am.

ON THE ROX

🍷♿️ BAR

V. Galvani 54   ☎06 45 49 29 75

The lively crowd that frequents this huge lounge still "rox" out big time, even if the place isn't technically a club. Rustic arches offset by twinkling chandeliers give the place a spunky vibe that matches its nightly mix of students and locals. Pop music plays in the background, but the real buzz comes from conversation and the cheers of customers watching sports on the flatscreen TVs. With great nightly specials, even Tu becomes an ideal day for a night out.

✂ Ⓜ B: Piramide. Walk up V. Marmorata to the river and turn left onto V. Galvani. *i* Pitcher night on M, €10. Buy 1 get 1 free on W. Ladies' night 2-for-1 cocktails on Th. Live music 4 nights per week in the winter. Student special long drinks €5. Happy hour buffet €7. Ⓢ Shots €2.50. Beer €4. Cocktails €6. Food €6-8. ⏰ Open M-W 6pm-4am, Th-Su 6pm-5am. Happy hour daily 6-10pm.

LA CASA DELLA PACE

CULTURAL CENTER, CONCERT VENUE

V. di Monte Testaccio 22   ☎329 54 66 296 🖳www.myspace.com/bigbang

More than a nightlife haven for artsy and intellectual folks, this "House of Peace" holds multicultural events, art exhibitions, and live music performances throughout the year. In the evening, join a truly mixed crowd on any of the floors as live music ranging from reggae to electro-funk plays on the stripped-wood dance floor. Multiple adjoining rooms, including the upstairs gallery space, slowly fill up with beer sippers, conversationalists, performers, and artists. Drop by Friday or Saturday for La Casa's "Big Bang" nights or check online for a schedule of upcoming events. Be sure to try out the 📷mosaic-tiled bathroom, which rivals some of Rome's greatest—bathrooms, that is.

✂ Ⓜ B: Piramide. Walk up V. Marmorata towards the river, turn left onto V. Galvani, and veer left onto V. di Monte Testaccio. *i* €7 membership card required to enter; buy at the desk, and re-use for all events. Ⓢ Shots €2.50. Beer €2.50-4. Cocktails €6. ⏰ Open M-Th 3-10pm, F-Sa 10pm-5am, Su 3-10pm.

CARUSO

CLUB, LATIN

V. di Monte Testaccio 36   ☎06 57 45 019 🖳www.carusocafe.com

Move your hips to merengue rather than the same old pop mix. The distinctive orange glow in this club's cluster of dance rooms will warm you up for dancing; cool (though slightly pricey) drinks and strong A/C will cool you down when things get too hot. Plenty of tables and padded chairs sit beside rather random Buddha sculptures, so take this opportunity to lounge next to the big enlightened guy. Live bands take the small stage when the DJ steps down.

✂ Ⓜ B: Piramide. Walk up V. Marmorata toward the river, turn left onto V. Galvani, and veer left onto V. di Monte Testaccio. *i* Live and DJ'd Latin music. Ⓢ Cover Su-Th €8; F-Sa €10; includes 1st drink. Beer €6. Cocktails €6-11. ⏰ Open M-Th 11pm-2am, F-Sa 11pm-4am, Su 11pm-2am.

KETUMBAR

BAR

V. Galvani 24   ☎06 57 30 53 38 🖳www.ketumbar.it

Close in proximity but far in style from the rowdier bars and discos that surround it, this upscale lounge serves a fusion of Mediterranean and Japanese cuisine that is matched with well-made cocktails and wine. No need to rub shoulders here—a cavernous interior lit only by hanging votive-candle lamps lets you lounge with your date in relative privacy. Though pricey, sushi-inspired plates like the Tori Kara Rolls (fried chicken, cheese, and special salad) offer the rare finger food that won't leave your hands greasy and will still please your belly.

nightlife • testaccio and ostiense

♯ Ⓜ B: Piramide. Walk up V. Marmorata toward the river and turn left onto V. Galvani. *i* Happy hour buffet €8-10. Ⓢ Beer and wine €5. Cocktails €8-10. Primi €8-12; secondi €12-18. Japanese plates €7-34. ✿ Open daily 8pm-4am. Happy hour 8-10pm.

TOP FIVE
◆⊗❡✿☾ RISTORANTE, BAR

V. di Monte Testaccio 46/48   ☎06 57 45 453 🔲www.topfivebar.it

When your stomach starts to growl after a night of clubbing, Top Five will be your top priority. Right beneath the thumping **Coyote** (see above), this bright American restaurant-bar satisfies late-night pizza cravings (or perhaps early morning breakfast calls). Kick back like a cowpoke beside an old American movie poster while enjoying €2 pizza or panini. Once your stomach is sufficiently lined, it might be time for another drink. At these prices, another stiff one is hard to turn down, even if your liver is begging you to stop.

♯ Ⓜ B: Piramide. Walk up V. Marmorata towards the river, turn left onto V. Galvani, and veer left onto V. di Monte Testaccio. *i* Happy hour shots and beer pints €4; cocktails €6. Ⓢ Beer €4-6. Cocktails €8. Food €2-8. ✿ Open Tu-Su 8pm-5am. Happy hour 8:30-11pm.

VIA NOMENTANA

V. Nomentana is near the cluster of hostels surrounding Termini, making it a great option for students wanting to venture a bit further. Good bars and discotecas which open and close seasonally are always popping up. Many of the winter clubs close once summer hits and students at Erasmus go home, so bars are generally a more sure-fire option throughout the year.

BOEME
◆⊗❡✿ CLUB

V. Velletri 13   ☎06 84 12 212 🔲www.boeme.it

An expansive downstairs disco lined entirely in black and white stripes and funky flowered wallpaper brings in a happening crowd on the weekends. Multiple platforms for dancing, flashing lights, a sound system blaring house and Top 40 hits, a huge bar, and neon accents create a psychedelic experience for partiers willing to drop a few euro.

♯ From P. Fiume, walk up V. Nizza and turn left onto V. Velletri. Ⓢ Cover €15-20; includes first drink. Drinks €10. ✿ Open F-Sa 11pm-5am.

NEW AGE CAFE
⊛♿❡☾ BAR, CAFE

V. Nizza 23

Whether it's 3am or 3pm, this corner cafe will have music playing and beverages of some sort flowing. The extensive menu features everything from 7am eggs and panini to an extensive buffet of complimentary appetizers during their nightly happy hour. Lounge on the outdoor patio, climb the spiral staircase to the mini balcony up top, or grab a stool at the bar while you sip your mixed drink or cappuccino. This little island in the middle of the city is made for relaxation at midday or drinks at midnight. Even if the caffeine doesn't pick you up, the upbeat, commercial tunes playing from dawn to...dawn certainly will.

♯ From P. Fiume, walk down V. Nizza. Ⓢ Shots €2.30. Draft beer €3.50-5; L €12. Mixed drinks €6.50. Lunch panini and primi €3-5. ✿ Open daily 7am-4:30am. Aperitivo bar 6:30-9:30pm.

arts and culture

"Arts and culture?" you ask. "Isn't that Rome, *itself*?" Psshh. Well, yes, Renaissance paintings, archaeological ruins, and Catholic churches do count. But aside from these antiquated lures, Rome offers an entertainment scene that makes it much more than a city of yore. Soccer games might not quite compare to man-fights-lion spectacles, but with hundreds of screaming Italians around, it comes close. If you need more ideas, check Rome's city website (🔲www.060608.it) for a schedule of upcoming events ranging from live music to festivals. Other good resources are *Romac'è*

(🔲www.romace.it) and 🔲www.aguestinrome.com. Or just wander the streets scouting out advertisements and flyers, which are nearly as common as ruins. In Rome, it's definitely possible to experience "arts and culture" in places where an alarm won't go off when you get too close.

JAZZ

Unfortunately, most jazz places close during the summer months, either re-opening in September or heading outdoors. **Alexanderplatz Jazz Club,** one of Rome's most popular of its kind and Italy's oldest, shuts its doors mid-June and hosts a spectacular program of outdoor performances at the Villa Celimontana. *(☎06 58 33 57 81; call M-F 9:30am-5:30pm* *🚇 Ⓜ︎B: Colosseo. Concerts at V. della Navicella. i Ticket sales at V. della Navicella start at 7:30pm. Ⓓ Doors open at 9pm; shows start at 10:10pm.)* At other times of the year, Alexanderplatz can be found at V. Ostia 9. *(☎06 58 33 57 81 9:30am-2pm, ☎06 39 74 21 71 6pm on. Ⓢ Monthly card €10, yearly €30. Ⓓ Open 8pm-2am; concerts at 10pm.)* For a current schedule of other jazz events check out 🔲www.romace.it, 🔲www.romajazz.com, or 🔲www.casajazz.it.

🔲 FONCLEA   ✈👁⊗⚲Ⓨ VATICAN CITY
V. Crescenzio 82A   ☎06 68 96 302 🔲www.fonclea.it
Crowds linger on the street and trickle down the steps into this den of live jazz and food. Amid hanging skis and teapots, nightly performers pay homage to anything from swing to The Beatles. Munch on chips and guacamole during the *aperitivo* hour while trumpeters and saxophonists warm up their lips. Drinks and food are a bit overpriced, but with music this good, who's thinking of eating?
🚇 Ⓜ︎A: Ottaviano. From P. Risorgimento, head away from the Vatican on V. Cresenzio. Ⓢ Cover F-Sa €6. Beer €7. Cocktails €10. Ⓓ Open from mid-Sept to mid-June M-Th 7pm-2am, F-Sa 7pm-3am, Su 7pm-2am. Music at 9:30pm. Aperitivo buffet 7-8:30pm.

CHARITY CAFE JAZZ CLUB   ✈⊗Ⓨ❄ TERMINI
V. Panisperna 68   ☎06 47 82 58 81 🔲www.charitycafe.it
Charity's a rarity in that its open year-round (never mind that people are stingy). See listing in **Nightlife**.
🚇 Ⓜ︎B: Cavour. From the intersection of V. XIV Maggio and V. Nazionale (near Trajan's column), walk up V. Panisperna. Ⓢ Beer €6-7. Cocktails from €8. Ⓓ Open in summer M-Sa 6pm-2am; in fall, winter, and spring daily 6pm-2am.

BIG MAMA   ✈♿Ⓨ TRASTEVERE
Vicolo San Francesco a Ripa 18   ☎06 58 12 551 🔲www.bigmama.it
She's not just a "Mama"—when it comes to the blues, she's a *big* mama. Nightly concerts by aspiring and well-known performers including jazz and blues guitarist Scott Henderson and rock singer-songwriter Elliott Murphy make this self-proclaimed "House of Blues" a place for all kinds of musical fare.
🚌 Bus #75 or 170 or tram #8. From P. Garibaldi, walk down Vle. Trastevere, turn left onto V. San Francesco a Ripa, and veer right onto the tiny vicolo. Ⓢ Year-long membership card (€14) or monthly card (€8) grants free admission to most shows. A few big shows require an additional ticket fee. Ⓓ Open daily from late Sept to late May 9pm-1:30am. Music at 10:30pm.

CLASSICAL MUSIC AND OPERA

TEATRO DELL'OPERA   ✈♿ TERMINI
P. Beniamino Gigli 7   ☎06 48 16 02 55 or 06 48 17 003 🔲www.operaroma.it
Once you've caught a glimpse of the 6m chandelier and frescoes by **Annibale Brugnoli** gracing this four-tier theater, you'll be happy you shelled out the extra euro even if arias, pirouettes, and musical overtures aren't exactly your thing. If you really did just come for the opera and ballet, you might consider Teatro dell'Opera's affiliated newer and less ornate **Teatro Nazionale** across the street, which has cheaper tickets. From June 30 to early fall, additional performances are held outdoors at the **Baths of Caracalla** *(Terme di Caracalla).*

culture on the tiber

One hardly needs a map to arrive at a *piazza* or historical site while in Rome: the streets are as dotted with churches and statues as they are with *gelaterie.* A real reason to take out the map again is to navigate a 450m section of the Tiber River, which, since 2005, has been the site of a different type of *piazza.* "Piazza Tevere," a straight strip of water between Ponte Sisto and Ponte Mazzini, has become a nexus of contemporary art installations ranging from projected animations inspired by Roman history to live music and performances.

Each year, the project ("Tevereterno") brings together an international group of artists to create public pieces that deal with modern-day cultural and environmental concerns. Envisioned as a way to revitalize the Tiber, which had for many years been a forgotten resource for Romans and tourists, Teverterno provides a refreshing chance to see current work in a setting other than a museum or gallery. Everyone loves a fresco, but larger-than-life projections of the historic she-wolf on the river's embankment walls are hard to beat. For more information and a schedule of installations, visit 💻www.tevereterno.it.

*🚏 Ⓜ A: Repubblica. Walk down V. Nazionale, then turn left onto V. Firenze and left onto V. del Viminale. **i** 2nd location (Teatro Nazionale) at V. del Viminale 51. Tickets can also be bought online at 💻www.amitsrl.it. [$] At Teatro dell'Opera opera €17-130, ballet €11-65; at Teatro Nazionale opera €30, ballet €20. Students and over 65 receive 25% discount. Check website for last-minute tickets with 25% discount. ⏰ Regular box office open Tu-Sa 9am-5pm, Su 9am-1:30pm, and 1hr. before performance-15min. after its start. Box office for Baths of Caracalla open Tu-Sa 10am-4pm, Su 9am-1:30pm.*

ACCADEMIA NAZIONALE DI SANTA CECILIA — 🎫 VILLA BORGHESE

Vle. Pietro de Coubertin 30 ☎06 80 82 058; ☎06 89 29 82 for tickets 💻www.santacecilia.it

Founded in 1585 as a conservatory, the Accademia is now both a place of training for aspiring and renowned musicians and a professional symphonic orchestra. Past conductors have included **Debussy, Strauss, Stravinsky,** and **Toscanini.** Concerts are held in three massive halls located in the Parco della Musica near Flaminio, so if you're as much into the great outdoors as you are into music, this is the perfect venue.

*🚏 Ⓜ A: Flaminio and then tram #2 to P. Euclide. Or take the special line "M" from Termini (every 15min. starting at 5pm) to Auditorium. Last bus after last performance. **i** Box office at Largo Luciano Berio 3. [$] Tickets €18-47. ⏰ Box office open daily 11am-8pm.*

TEATRO FLAIANO — 🎫♿ CENTRO STORICO

V. Santo Stefano del Cacco 15 ☎06 67 96 496 💻www.piccolalirica.com

Contemporary and innovative takes on traditional opera give this small theater a definite edge on other companies. Shows are kept short—around 90min.—and highlight particularly melodramatic moments of already melodramatic works, including *Tosca* and *Carmen* in recent seasons. If you don't want to sit through three hours of arias, the productions' brevity and creative interpretations will certainly please.

🚏 Tram #8. From V. Corso Vittorio Emanuele II, turn left onto V. del Gesu and right onto V. Santo Stefano del Cacco. [$] Tickets €44-60. ⏰ Box office open Tu-Sa 3-7pm; general office open Tu-Sa 11am-7pm. Shows at 8pm.

ROCK AND POP

Live music can be heard throughout the city. 🖥www.060608.it is a great resource for information on upcoming shows.

ROMA INCONTRA IL MONDO — 🎫♿ VILLA BORGHESE, PARIOLI, FLAMINIO

Villa Ada at V. di Ponte Salario ☎06 41 73 47 12 🖥www.villaada.org

This venue hosts an eclectic mix of rock, reggae, folk, and ethnic music at the large outdoor grounds of Villa Ada, near the Villa Borghese. Most of the acts are international performers on tour, many hailing from as nearby (if you can call it that) as Africa to as far away as Australia. Recent ones include Habib Koite and Bamada (Mali), Luciano (Jamaica), and local Christina Dona.

➜ Ⓜ︎A: Flaminio, then Ferrovie Urbane bound for Civitacastellana; get off at Campi Sportivi. Enter the park at Vle. della Moschea and veer right down the winding V. di Ponte Salario. $ Tickets €5-15. ⏰ Concerts from mid-June to early Aug. Concert area opens at 8pm; concerts start at 10pm and usually last until 2am.

FIESTA — 🎫♿ SOUTHERN ROME

Ippodrome delle Capanelle, V. Appia Nuova 1245 ☎348 88 89 950 🖥www.fiesta.it

This huge concert venue complete with restaurant, bar, disco, and lounge area features popular Latin performers most nights of the week. The festival wouldn't be complete without crowds in the thousands and so much dancing that your hips will start to feel like an 80-year-old's. Big names include Don Omar, La India, Los 4, and the legendary **Ricky Martin.**

➜ Bus #664 to Colli Albani or Ⓜ︎A: Cinecittà and then bus #654 down V. delle Capanelle. i Buy tickets online at 🖥www.greenticket.it or 🖥www.ticketone.it or in person at concert venue. $ Tickets €10-35. Weekday performances usually cheaper than weekends. ⏰ Concerts June-Aug at 9:30pm. Concert venue open for ticket sale M-Th 8:30pm-1am, F-Sa 8:30pm-2am, Su 8:30pm-1am.

SPECTATOR SPORTS

STADIO OLIMPICO — ♿ OUTSKIRTS

V. del Foro Italico 1 🖥www.asroma.it, www.sslazio.it

Soccer matches—the favorite game of the Romans since their gladiator days—are held here. The stadium serves as the battleground for **A.S. Roma** and **S.S. Lazio.** The easiest way to tell them apart is by color (red and sky blue, respectively). Tickets aren't easy to come by: check the spots below or ask around.

➜ Ⓜ︎A: Ottaviano. Then take bus #32 to Piazzale della Farnesina. i Tickets can be purchased at the stadium, online at sites like 🖥www.listicket.it, or at various ticketing spots around the city such as Lazio Point (V. Farini 34/36 ☎06 48 26 688). $ Tickets €20-80. ⏰ Most matches Sept-May Su afternoons. Lazio Point box office open daily 9pm-1am and 2:30-6pm.

shopping

When it comes to shopping, it would be significantly easier to make a list of what Rome *doesn't* have than what it does. Fashionista, artista, or "intelligista," you won't leave Rome unsatisfied, though your pocketbook might be significantly lighter. European chains like **United Colors of Benetton, Tezenis, Motivi,** and even **H and M** speckle the city. Those with a taste for high fashion should head to the Piazza di Spagna region, Rome's equivalent of Fifth Ave., which is home to the regular gamut of designer stores: **D and G, Valentino,** and **Prada,** to name a few. Smaller (though no less costly) boutiques dominate the Centro Storico. Major thoroughfares like V. del Corso, C. Cavour, V. Nazionale, and V. Cola di Rienzo abound with cheap clothing stores touting a similar collection of tight, teeny-bopper glitz and fare that comes unattached to a brand name. The regions around Termini, Vle. Trastevere, and the Vatican contain a fair number of street vendors selling shoes, lingerie, dresses, and sunglasses, usually for under €15, though established open-air markets will have a bigger selection.

DEPARTMENT STORES

Everyone needs a department store to stock the basics, whether that means Gucci underwear at discounted prices or jeans and a sweater to cover up at the Vatican. Expect to find everything from makeup to household products to entire clothing wardrobes at most stores.

⬛ LA RINASCENTE ⬛⊗❄ PIAZZA DI SPAGNA
P. Colonna 195/199 ☎06 67 84 209 ▣www.rinascente.it
Glamorous, big, and well-stocked, La Rinascente allows you to save a couple of euro by offering those coveted designer brands from around the block on V. dei Condotti on their discounted clothes racks. A good selection of makeup and accessories on the first floor makes way for clothing upstairs and down. With the designer selection of lingerie, you could be spending three times the money on one third the material. Has a tax refund office.
✂ Bus #116. ⏰ Open daily 10am-9pm.

COIN ⬛♿❄ VATICAN CITY
V. Cola di Rienzo 173 ☎06 36 00 42 98 ▣www.coin.it
With a generous selection of everything you might need in both designer and basic varieties, COIN is a good place to come for hours of rack-sorting, bargain-hunting, euro-dropping, and, if that line at the Vatican has left you in need, peeing.
✂ Ⓜ️A: Ottaviano. Head down V. Ottaviano and turn onto V. Cola di Rienzo from P. Risorgimento. ⏰ Open M-Sa 10am-8pm, Su 10:30am-8pm.

spagna stores

It's not Milan. It's not Paris. It's Rome—and that's no small thing. The area around Piazza di Spagna has all the glitz you might want—ice-cold stores with ice-cold staff hovering about making sure you don't paw through their precious items. You'd think you were in another museum or something. Here's where to find the priciest and snobbiest of stores:

- **DOLCE AND GABBANA.** (P. di Spagna 94 ☎06 69 38 08 70 ▣www.dolcegabbana.it ⏰ Open M-Sa 10:30am-7:30pm, Su 10:30am-2:30pm and 3:30-7:30pm.)

- **EMPORIO ARMANI.** (V. del Babuino 140 ☎06 32 21 581 ▣www.giorgioarmani.com ⏰ Open M-Sa 10am-7pm.)

- **GUCCI.** (V. dei Condotti 8 ☎06 679 0405 ▣www.gucci.com ⏰ Open M-Sa 10am-7:30pm, Su 10am-7pm.)

- **PRADA.** (V. dei Condotti 92/95 ☎06 679 0897 ▣www.prada.com ⏰ Open M-F 10am-7:30pm, Sa 10am-8pm, Su 10am-7:30pm.)

- **VALENTINO.** (V. del Babuino 61 and V. dei Condotti 15 ☎06 36 00 19 06 and ☎06 67 39 420 ▣www.valentino.com ⏰ Open daily 10am-7pm.)

- **VERSACE.** (V. Bocca di Leone 26/27 ☎06 67 80 521 ▣www.versace.com ⏰ Open M-Sa 10am-7pm, Su 2pm-7pm.)

rome

UPIM
V. Gioberti 64

🍴🚾❄ TERMINI
☎06 44 65 579 💻www.upim.it

Come here to dress your house rather than your bod. A well-priced selection of furniture, cookware, bedding, and toys outdoes the basic clothing, most of which is seasonal. Dress up the simple lines of the store's garments with some makeup, which has taken over the first floor in full force.

✚ *Near Termini, across from Basilica Santa Maria Maggiore.* ⏰ *Open M-Sa 9am-8:30pm, Su 9:30am-8:30pm.*

OVIESSE
Vle. Trastevere 62

🍴🚾❄ TRASTEVERE
☎06 58 33 36 33 💻www.oviesse.com

Oviesse stocks a somewhat small collection of cheap, seasonal clothes for women and men: it's nothing special, but hey, you're wearing something, right? You might smell better than you look—the adjoining perfumerie's collection is comparable in size. There's also plenty of clothes for children and babies in case their fashion is more important than yours. Custom tailoring available.

✚ *Tram #8 down Vle. Trastevere.* ℹ *Huge BILLA supermarket downstairs with great prices.* ⏰ *Open M-Sa 8:30am-8pm, Su 9:30am-1:30pm and 4-8pm.*

OUTDOOR MARKETS

One of the few things that tourists and locals appreciate with equal enthusiasm are Rome's outdoor markets. You can find real bargains if you're willing to rifle through the crowds and stacks. With early hours on both their opening and closing ends, make sure you set that alarm. It's best to stick to official markets rather than take on merchants who set up shop individually. The fine for buying fake designer products rests on the buyer, not the seller, and can reach into the hundreds of thousands of euro.

🏛 PORTA PORTESE
From P. di Porta Portese to P. Ippolito Nievo

🍴♿ TRASTEVERE
💻www.portaportesemarket.it

The legs of this U-shaped market seem to extend forever and are of markedly different qualities. The longer V. Portuense is occupied by clones—vendors selling the same selection of cheap garments, toiletries, furniture, plastic jewelry, and shoes. We're talking 2m stacks of €2 clothes. If you're not exhausted by the madhouse (reminiscent of the hustling crowds of the Vatican Museums), make it to the antiques section where cooler treasures reside: old comic books, records, jewelry, and furniture.

✚ *Bus #40 to Largo Argentina and tram #8.* ⏰ *Open Su 7am-2:30pm.*

MERCATO DI VIA SANNIO
V. Sannio

🍴♿ SOUTHERN ROME
☎06 06 08

Cheap doesn't have to mean mass-produced and homogenous. Head here early to be the first of many to dig through mostly used clothes and items. A refreshing change from the ubiquitous street merchants spattering Rome, this large market is the outdoor equivalent of a New York thrift store. Hipsters rejoice.

✚ *Ⓜ A: San Giovanni.* ⏰ *Open M-Sa 9am-1:30pm.*

CAMPO DEI FIORI
Campo dei Fiori

🍴♿ CENTRO STORICO

Thank God there's a place to buy fresh fruit and vegetables in the middle of overpriced trattorias: the lively Campo makes a great lunch spot if you don't mind the crowds. Giving as much flavor to the *piazza* during the day as bars give it at night, the market's open stalls vend cheap clothing, produce, fish, and even alcohol—no need to head to San Marino to pick up some absinthe.

✚ *Bus #116 or tram #8.* ⏰ *Open M-Sa 7am-2:30pm.*

MERCATO DELLE STAMPE

Largo della Fontanella di Borghese

The small *piazza* and academic assortment of goods keep this market more manageable than most others in Rome—after all, how rowdy can a crowd get around a stack of books? Older crowds weave through the stalls, where you can find a curious selection of used books, old prints, and other dusty articles.

🚌 *Bus #224 or 913 to P. Imperatore or bus #492, 116, or 81.* 🕐 *Open M-Sa 9:30am-6pm.*

essentials

PRACTICALITIES

- **TOURIST OFFICES: Comune di Roma** is Rome's official source for tourist information. Green **P.I.T. Info booths** are located throughout the city around most major sites. English-speaking staff provide limited information on hotel accommodations and events around the city, though plenty of free brochures and a city map are available. The booths also sell bus and Metro maps and the **Roma Pass** *(PIT booth locations include V. Giovanni Giolitti 34 in Termini, P. Sidney Sonnino in Trastevere, and V. dei Fori Imperiali ☎06 06 08 for main info center; check online for individual booth numbers 🖥www.turismoroma.it, 🖥www.060608.com* 🕐 *Most locations open daily 9:30am-7pm; Termini location open 8am-8:30pm.)* **Enjoy Rome** has only 2 offices but provides much more comprehensive services, including tour bookings, information on bike and scooter rental, city maps, accommodations advice, and general orientation tips. They also publish a free city guide, *Enjoy Rome*, which details extensive information on transportation, city monuments and museums, suggested eating and entertainment, and daytrips. *(Main branch at V. Marghera 8A; 2nd office in P. San Pietro ☎06 44 56 890 🖥www.enjoyrome.com* 🚌 *From Termini, walk down V. Marghera.* 🕐 *Both locations open M-F 8:30am-6pm, Sa 8:30am-2pm.)*

- **EMBASSIES AND/OR CONSULATES:** See **Essentials**.

- **CURRENCY EXCHANGE AND BANKS: Money exchange** services are especially abundant near Termini and major sights but tend to have high rates. **Western Unions** are also readily available. *(*🕐 *Most banks open M-F 8:30am-1:30pm and 2:30-5pm.)*

- **LUGGAGE STORAGE: Termini Luggage Deposit.** *(*☎06 47 44 777 🖥www.grandistazioni.it* 🚌 *In Termini, below Track 24 in the Ala Termini wing.* ℹ *Takes bags of up to 20kg each for 5 days max. Cash only.* 💲 *€4 for 1st 5hr., €0.60 per hr. for 6th-12th hr., €0.20 per hr. thereafter.* 🕐 *Open daily 6am-11:50pm.)*

- **LOST PROPERTY: La Polizia Municipale** holds property a few days after it is lost; check the closest branch to where you lost your item. After that point, all lost property is sent to **Oggetti Smarriti**, run by the Comune di Roma. To retrieve an item, you must present a valid form of ID, a statement describing the lost item, and a cash payment of €2.97. *(Circonvallazione Ostiense 191 ☎06 67 69 3214 🖥www.060608.it or email oggettismarriti@comune.roma.it with questions* 🚌 Ⓜ*B: Piramide or* Ⓜ*B: Garbatella.* 🕐 *Open M 8:30am-1pm, Tu 8:30am-1pm and 3-5pm, W 8:30am-1pm, Th 8:30am-5pm, F 8:30am-1pm.)* For property lost on Ⓜ**A lines:** *(P. dei Cinquecento ☎06 48 74 309* 🕐 *Open M 9:30am-12:30pm, W 9:30am-12:30pm, F 9:30am-12:30pm.)* Ⓜ**B lines:** *(Circonvallazione Ostiense 191 ☎06 67 69 32 14* 🕐 *Open M-F 9am-1pm.)*

- **GLBT RESOURCES:** The Comune di Roma publishes a free guide to gay life in Rome, *AZ Gay*, with listings for gay-friendly restaurants, hotels, clubs, and bars. Pick one up at any P.I.T. Point. **ARCI-GAY** is a resource for homosexuality awareness, offering free courses, medical, legal, and psychological counseling, and advice on gay-friendly establishments in the city. (*V. Zabaglia 14* ☎*06 64 50 11 02;* ☎*800 71 37 13 for helpline* ■*www.arcigayroma.it* Ⓜ*B: Piramide. Walk up V. Marmorata and turn right onto V. Alessandro Volta; it's at the intersection with V. Zabaglia.* **i** *ARCI-GAY cards allow access to all events and services run by the program throughout Italy; €15 (valid 1 year).* Ⓩ *Open M-Sa 4-8pm. Helpline open M 4-8pm, W-Th 4-8pm, Sa 4-8pm. Welcome Groups Th 6:15-9pm, Young People Groups F 6:30-9pm.)*

EMERGENCY!

- **POLICE: Police Headquarters.** (*V. San Vitale 15* ☎*06 46 86* ⚐ Ⓜ*A: Repubblica.*) **Carabinieri** have offices at V. Mentana 6 (☎*06 58 59 62 00* ⚐ *Near Termini.*) and P. Venezia (☎*06 67 58 28 00*). **City Police** (*P. del Collegio Romano 3* ☎*06 69 01 21*).

- **CRISIS LINES: Rape Crisis Line: Centro Anti-Violenza** provides legal, psychological, and medical counseling for women of all nationalities. (*V. di Torre Spaccata 157, V. di Villa Pamphili 100* ☎*06 23 26 90 49;* ☎*06 58 10 926* ■*www.differenzadonna. it* Ⓩ *Phone lines open 24hr.*) **Samaritans** provides psychological counseling on the phone in many languages; call for in-person guidance. (☎*800 86 00 22* ■*www. samaritansonlus.org* Ⓩ *Line operating daily 1-10pm.*)

- **LATE-NIGHT PHARMACIES: Farmacia della Stazione** is by Termini Station. (*P. dei Cinquecento 49/51* ☎*06 48 80 019* Ⓩ *Open 24hr.*) **Farmacia Internazionale** is toward the Centro Storico. (*P. Barberini 49* ☎*06 48 25 456* ⚐ Ⓜ*A: Barberini.* Ⓩ *Open 24hr.*) **Farmacia Doricchi** is toward the Villa Borghese. (*V. XX Settembre 47* ☎*06 48 73 880* Ⓩ *Open 24hr.*) **Brienza** is near the Vatican City. (*P. del Risorgimento 44* ☎*06 39 73 81 86* Ⓩ *Open 24hr.*)

- **HOSPITALS/MEDICAL SERVICES: Policlinico Umberto I** is Rome's largest public hospital. (*Vle. del Policlinico 155* ☎*06 44 62 341* ■*www.policlinicoumberto1.it* ⚐ Ⓜ*B: Policlinico or bus #649 to Policlinico.* Ⓢ *Emergency treatment free. Non-emergencies €25-50.* Ⓩ *Open 24hr.* **International Medical Center** is a private hospital and clinic. (*V. Firenze 47* ☎*06 48 82 371* ■*www.imc84.com* ⚐ Ⓜ*A: Repubblica.* **i** *Prescriptions filled. Call ahead for appointments.* Ⓩ *Open M-F 9a-8pm.*) **Rome-American Hospital.** (*V. Emilio Longoni 69* ☎*06 22 551 for emergencies,* ☎*06 22 55 290 for appointments* ■*www.rah.it* ⚐ *Well to the east of the city; consider taking a cab. To get a little closer, take bus #409 from Tiburtina to Piazzale Prenestina or tram #14 from Termini.* **i** *English-speaking. Private emergency and laboratory services include HIV testing.* Ⓩ *Call-line for appointments. open M-F 8am-8pm, Sa 8am-2pm. Hospital open 24hr. for emergency care.*)

GETTING THERE ✈

By Plane

DA VINCI INTERNATIONAL AIRPORT (FIUMICINO) (FCO)

30km southwest of the city   ☎06 65 951

Commonly known as Fiumicino, Da Vinci International Airport oversees most international flights. If you're arriving in Rome from a different continent, you'll almost certainly land here, as it's serviced by most carriers. To get from the airport—which is located right on the Mediterranean coast—to central Rome, take the **Leonardo Express** train to **Termini Station.** After leaving customs, follow signs to the **Stazione Trenitalia/Railway Station,** where you can buy a train ticket at an automated machine or from the ticket office. (Ⓢ *€14.* Ⓩ *32min., every 30min. 6:47am-11:37pm.*) The **Sabina-Fiumicino Line (FR1)** will take you to **Trastevere Station** and other Roman suburbs. (Ⓢ *€8.* Ⓩ *20-45min., every 15min. 5:57am-11:27pm.*) Visit ■www.trenitalia.it to check specific times. Don't buy a ticket from individuals who approach you, as they may be scammers. If you arrive late, you will have

essentials · getting there

to use an automated machine. Before boarding the train, make sure to validate the ticket in a yellow box on the platform; failure to do so may result in a fine of €50-100. If you need to get to or from Fiumicino before 6:30am or after 11:30pm, the easiest option is to catch a **taxi**. For destinations in Central Rome, you'll be charged a flat rate of €40, which should include baggage and up to four passengers. Check with the driver before departing.

ROME CIAMPINO AIRPORT (CIA)

15km southeast of the city   ☎06 65 951

Ciampino is the rapidly growing airport serviced by **budget airlines** like Ryanair and EasyJet. There are no trains connecting the airport to the city center, but various options for getting into Rome from Ciampino exist. The **SIT Bus Shuttle** (☎06 59 23 507 ▪www.sitbusshuttle.it Ⓢ €4. ☒ 40min., every 45-60min. 7:45am-11:15pm.) and **Terravision Shuttle** (☎06 97 61 06 32 ▪www.terravision.eu Ⓢ €4. ☒ 40min.; every 20-50min., depending on time of day, 8:15am-12:15am.) both run from the airport to V. Marsala, outside Termini Station. For easy access to the Rome Metro, the **COTRAL bus** runs to Rome's ⓂA: Anagnina station (Ⓢ €1.20. ☒ 30min., every 40min. 6am-10:40pm.)

By Train

All **Trenitalia** trains run through **Termini Station,** the main transport hub in central Rome. International and overnight trains also run to Termini. City buses #C2, H, M, 36, 38, 40 64, 86, 90, 92, 105, 170, 175, 217, 310, 714, and 910 stop outside in the P. del Cinquecento. The station is open 5:30am-midnight; if you are arriving in Rome outside of this time frame, you will likely arrive in **Stazione Tiburtina** or **Stazione Ostiense,** both of which connect to Termini by the night bus #175.

Trains run to and from **Florence** (Ⓢ €16.10-44. ☒ 1½ -4hr., 52 per day, 5:57am-8:15pm.), **Venice** (Ⓢ €42.50-73.50. ☒ 4-7hr., 17 per day, 6:45am-8pm.), **Milan** (Ⓢ €46-89. ☒ 3-8hr., 33 per day, 6:45am-11:04pm.), **Naples** (Ⓢ €10.50-44. ☒ 1-3hr., 50 per day, 4:52am-9:39pm.), and **Bologna.** (Ⓢ €36-58. ☒ 2-4 hr., 42 per day, 6:15am-8:15pm.)

GETTING AROUND

Rome's public transportation system is run by **ATAC.** (☎06 57 003 ▪www.atac.roma.it ☒ Open M-Sa 8am-8pm.) It consists of the **Metro, buses,** and **trams,** which service the city center and outskirts, as well as various **Ferrovie Urbane** and **Ferrovie metropolitane,** which service more distant suburbs including Ostia Lido, Tivoli, Fregene, and Viterbo. Transit tickets are valid for any of these lines and can be bought at *tabacherrie* throughout the city, at some bars, and from self-service machines or ticket windows at major stations including Termini, Ostiense, and Trastevere. A **BIT** (integrated time ticket; €1) is valid for 1¼hr. after validation and allows unlimited bus travel plus one Metro ride within that time frame; it is generally the most economical choice. A **BIG** (integrated daily ticket; €4) is valid until midnight on the day of validation and allows unlimited bus and Metro use. The **BTI** (integrated tourist ticket; €11) grants unrestricted access for three days after validation. The **CIS** (integrated weekly ticket; €16) grants unrestricted access for seven days after validation. Tickets **must be validated** at Metro station turnstiles and stamping machines on buses and trams.

By Bus

The best way to get around the city other than by walking is by bus: dozens of routes service the entire city center as well as outskirts. **Bus stops** are marked by yellow poles and display a route map for all lines that pass through the stop.

By Metro

Rome's **Metro** system consists of two lines: ⓂA, which runs from Battistini to Anagnina (hitting P. di Spagna and S. Giovanni), and ⓂB, which runs from Laurentina to Rebibbida (hitting the Colosseum, Ostiense, and southern Rome); they intersect only at **Termini Station.** While the Metro is fast, it does not service many regions of the city

rome bus routes

Below are some Roman bus routes that connect the sights and regions you're most likely to frequent.

- **#64:** Termini, P. Venezia, C. Vittorio Emanuele, P. Navona, Campo dei Fiori, Pantheon, Castel Sant'Angelo/St. Peter's Basilica.
- **#40:** Same as 64, but runs express.
- **H:** Termini, V. Nazionale, P. Venezia, V. Arenula, Trastevere.
- **#116:** V. Veneto, P. Barberini, P. di Spagna, C. Rinascimento, Campo dei Fiori, P. Farnese, St. Peter's.
- **#170:** Termini, V. Nazionale, P. Venezia, Testaccio, EUR.
- **#175:** Termini, V. dei Tritone, V. del Corso, Jewish Ghetto, Ostiense.
- **#492:** Tiburtina, Termini, P. Venezia, P. Cavour, P. Risorgimento.
- **#23:** P. Clodio, P. Risorgimento, Lungotevere, Punto Garibaldi, Basilica di San Paolo.

Night Buses run from 12:30-5:30am on the ½hr., mostly out of Termini and P. Venezia:

- **#78N:** Piazzale Clodio, Piazzale Flaminio, P. Venezia, Termini.
- **#40N:** Metro B route.
- **#29N:** Piazzale Ostiense, Trastevere, Vatican, San Lorenzo, Colosseo, Piazzale Ostiense.
- **#80N:** Route of train from Roma to Ostia Lido.

and is better used for getting across long distances than between neighborhoods. Stations throughout the city are underground and marked by poles with a red square and white M. Tickets are validated at turnstiles upon entering the station.

By Tram
Electric trams make many stops but are still an efficient means of getting around. A few useful lines include **tram #3** *(Trastevere, Piramide, Aventine, P. San Giovanni, Villa Borghese, P. Thorwaldsen)*, **tram #8** *(Trastevere to Largo Argentina)*, and **tram #19** *(Ottaviano, Villa Borghese, San Lorenzo, Prenestina, P. dei Gerani)*.

By Bike
ATAC runs **Bikesharing** *(☎06 57 03 💻www.bikesharing.roma.it)*. Purchase a card at any ATAC ticket office. *(🚇 [M]A: Anagnina, Spagna, Lepanto, Ottaviano, Cornelia, Battistini or [M]B: Termini, Laurentina, EUR Fermi, or Ponte Mammolo. ⏰ Open M-Sa 7am-8pm, Su 8am-8pm.)* Bikes can be parked at 19 stations around the city. Cards are rechargeable. *($ €5 initial charge, €0.50 per 30min. thereafter. ⏰ Bikes available for a max. 24hr. at a time.)* Plenty of companies also rent bikes, including **Bici and Baci** and **Eco Move Rent**.

By Scooter
Rome is truly a city of scooters. Depending on the vehicle, prices range from €35-85 per day. A helmet (required by law) and insurance are usually included. **Bici and Baci** rents bikes and scooters. *(V. del Viminale 5 ☎06 48 28 443 💻www.bicibaci.com ⏰ Open daily 8am-7pm.)* **Treno e Scooter Rent** also rents scooters with lock and chain included. *(Stazione Roma Termini ☎06 48 90 58 23 💻www.trenoescooter.com ⏰ Open daily 9am-2pm and 4-7pm.)* **Eco Move Rent** rents scooters, Vespas, and bikes, lock included. *(V. Varese 48/50*

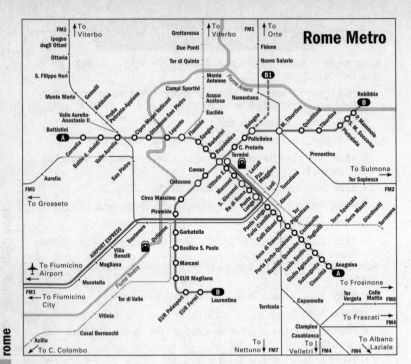

☎06 44 70 45 18 📧www.ecomoverent.com ⏰ Open daily 8:30am-7:30pm.)

By Taxi

Given the scope of Rome's bus system, taxis should only be reserved for desperate or time-sensitive affairs. Legally, you may not "hail" a cab on the street—either call **RadioTaxi** (☎06 66 45) or head to a taxi point (near most major sights) where drivers wait for customers. Ride only in yellow or white cars and look for a meter or settle on a price before the ride. **Rate 1** is charged for rides within the center. (💲 €0.78 per km.) **Rate 2** is applied to rides outside. (💲 €1.29 per km.) Though it's hard to tell what rate is being applied, write down the license number if the cost seems especially high. A tip is not expected.

VENICE

On any given day, the number of tourists in Venice—20 million annually—constitutes a larger percentage of the city's population than do locals—all 60,000 of them. This has given the city an unfairly reductive reputation as a tourist hub whose beauty and charm have been eviscerated by camera-toting yokels without an appreciation for anything outside a good photo op. Though you're certain to encounter the neon fanny pack crowd in the major squares, churches, museums, and monuments, if you let yourself escape down any one of Venice's many labyrinthine side streets, you'll discover traces of Venice's glorious past preserved in dilapidated *palazzi*, beautiful syncretic architecture hinting at Eastern influences, and street signs written in the vanishing Venetian dialect. Moreover, you'll find a vibrant and resilient local culture impervious to the tourist onslaught. Characterized by an incredible performance art and music scene, some of Italy's best seafood, bustling docks where local artisans still repair boats by hand, and numerous schools dedicated to building upon Venice's artistic legacy in the modern era, this hardy spirit makes modern Venice a joy to explore. This collection of 117 islands in a lagoon of the Adriatic Sea is famously both a difficult city to know and an easy city to love, but if you're not afraid to step off the beaten path, you'll come to appreciate the subtleties of the Venetian character that can't be discovered on a gondola ride or captured in a postcard.

greatest hits

- **MARK OF GREATNESS.** P. San Marco may be Venice's most (fanny-)packed piazza, but its awe-inspiring buildings and views fully justify braving the crowds (p. 131).

- **LOSE YOURSELF.** Wander the winding walkways of Dorsoduro. Given the city's bizarre street system, it's pretty easy to get lost anywhere. In this neighborhood, though, it's a pleasure (p. 114).

- **ESCAPE THE CITY.** Pay a visit to Lido, Venice's beach resort. Just take a vaporetto across the lagoon and you can lounge on the shore of the Adriatic (p. 144).

student life

For all its many charms, Venice is not a city with a vibrant student scene. You're far more likely to run into another tourist group than a frat party. One exception can be found in the neighborhoods of San Polo and Dorsoduro, thanks to **Ca' Foscari University,** which is located on the border between the two *sestiere* and brings in the city's most lively youth culture. Dorsoduro is home to easily the greatest concentration of bars in the city as well as Venice's only true club. That being said, this isn't really a student city, though if you look hard and get to know people, you'll find that there's plenty of entertainment to be had, and not just in churches or museums. Try heading to Lista di Spagna in Cannaregio to experience locals lounging around on a piazza drinking wine through the evening, a chilled-out but certainly pleasurable way to enjoy this city.

orientation

Venice's historical center is comprised of six main *sestieri* (neighborhoods). Often divided along vague boundaries, the neighborhoods each consist of several islands. **San Marco** is at the geographic center of the city, across the Grand Canal from **San Polo** and **Santa Croce.** Cannaregio lies to San Marco's north and **Castello** to its northeast, while **Dorsoduro** marks the city's southern edge. Outside of the city proper, a set of numerous islands including Giudecca, Lido, Murano, and Burano are not to be forgotten.

call me!

The phone code for Venice is ☎041.

SAN MARCO

While walking along the quiet canals of Venice's residential neighborhoods, it's easy to forget that on an average day the city is populated by just as many tourists as full-time residents. Cross over to San Marco, and that fact hits you with full force—dozens of museums, upscale hotels, designer stores, art galleries, and, of course, thousands upon thousands of tourists. The crisis of conscience most travelers undergo when planning their time in Venice is usually this: "How much time should I spend in San Marco." Because let's be honest—as crowded and expensive as San Marco is—the neighborhood is popular for good reason. The museums and sights here are as impressive as you'll find anywhere in Europe, and the tourist industry has brought world-class shopping, hotels, and cuisine to the area, particularly to the region closest to **Piazza San Marco.** Travelers who want to spend just a couple days in Venice but want to see all of the city's typical postcard attractions should look for a budget hotel on the fringes of the neighborhood. This won't put you more than a 10min. walk from either the Rialto Bridge or P. San Marco. Be forewarned, however, that San Marco is conspicuously less residential than any other neighborhood in Venice—if you're in a section that isn't currently overrun by tourists, it's likely to seem a bit abandoned or even post-apocalyptic.

If, as a child, you went on one of those family vacations in which one of your parents had drawn up a rigorously planned itinerary in order to hit all the main attractions, you should already have some idea of what being in San Marco feels like. Travelers who are more fearful of missing a single important sight than they are of traipsing through dozens of miles of museum corridors should love the area, but the average budget traveler would be just as content staying in another neighborhood and devoting a day to see the three or four things in this sight-heavy region that sound most interesting.

CANNAREGIO

Cannaregio is one of Venice's largest neighborhoods, and for travelers willing to step off the beaten path, it offers a great opportunity to see a less touristy side of Venice than is on display in places like San Marco. Most hotels are located on the eastern and western edges of the neighborhood (by the Rialto Bridge and train station, respectively) in areas with a fair amount of tourist traffic, but the beauty of Cannaregio is that you're never more than 10min. away from both the liveliest, most crowded *piazze* and the quiet residential neighborhoods that are more representative of typical Venetian life. Get ready to tap into your spiritual side, however, as churches comprise most of Cannaregio's notable sights. If you're the type who might accidentally mistake the baptismal font for a drinking fountain, you can still spend a day exploring Cannaregio's peaceful canals and side streets instead. Either way, both the holy and the wholly secular should check out the Ca' d'Oro (p. 136) or the Jewish Ghetto (p. 136), two of Venice's most historic spots that will interest anyone with even a passing fancy in art or architecture.

SAN POLO

San Polo is the smallest of Venice's six neighborhoods, but its location in the heart of the city makes it a prime tourist destination. The **Rialto Bridge** markets and **Frari** basilica are among San Polo's highlights. Many tourists also favor the neighborhood for shopping, both for souvenirs and upscale clothing, and dining, as San Polo's concentration of high-quality restaurants sets the city standard. Surprisingly, despite the heavy tourist traffic, there are relatively few hotels. However, those that are available tend to be reasonably priced affairs with good access to the city's points of interest. Despite the neighborhood's small size, it's surprisingly easy to get lost, especially if you think that the signs reading "San Marco" are actually leading you toward the square—in many cases, they're not. Your best bet is use a map and stick to wider streets with more tourists. If you try to take shortcuts, you'll probably end up walking in circles.

SANTA CROCE

Although a small neighborhood by Venetian standards, Santa Croce is incredibly diverse and easily accessible from western Cannaregio, San Polo, and Dorsoduro. **Piazzale Roma,** the main stop for most buses and taxis coming into Venice, is located in Santa Croce and defines the character of the neighborhood's western side. Restaurants and hotels around this transportation hub tend to be of a generic international style, so visitors to Santa Croce who see only this section of the neighborhood will leave unimpressed. The small area near San Polo, however, offers some of the best restaurants and hotels in Venice at exceptionally reasonable prices. From the main street of **Salizada San Pantalon,** the sights of Cannaregio as well as the restaurants and nightlife of Dorsoduro are easily accessible. The Rialto Bridge and P. San Marco are a ways off, but the vaporetti run frequently. For travelers willing to trek a bit in order to reach Venice's main sights, Santa Croce can serve as a budget-friendly base camp.

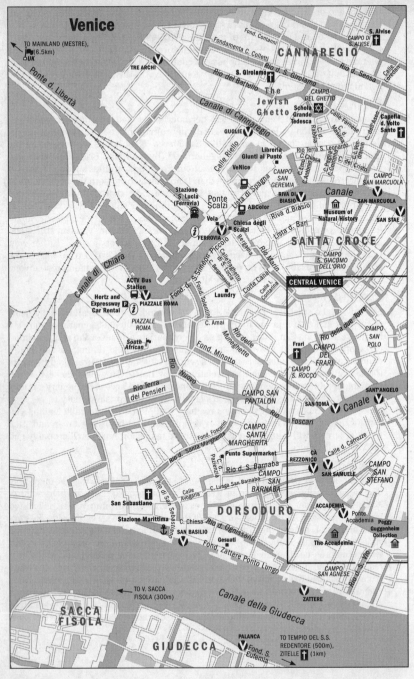

Venice

TO MAINLAND (MESTRE), (6.5km)

Ponte d. Libertà

Canale di Chiara

Canale di Cannaregio

Fond. Contanni

Fondamenta C. Colletti

TRE ARCHI

S. Girolamo
Rio del Battello

Rio d. S. Girolamo

Rio d. Sensa

CANNAREGIO

CAMPO DI S. ALVISE

S. Alvise

Calle Loredan

The Jewish Ghetto

CAMPO DEL GHETTO

Scuola Grande Tedesca

Capella d. Volto Santo

GUGLIE

Calle Riello

Libreria Giunti al Punto

VeNice

ABColor

Stazione S. Lucia (Ferrovia)

Ponte Scalzi

Vela

Chiesa degli Scalzi

FERROVIA

Lista di Spagna

CAMPO SAN GEREMIA

Rio Terra S. Leonardo

C. d. Rabbia

RIVA DI BIASIO

Riva d. Biasio

Canale

Museum of Natural History

Lista d. Bari

SAN MARCUOLA

CAMPO SAN MARCUOLA

SAN STAE

SANTA CROCE

CAMPO S. GIACOMO DELL'ORIO

ACTV Bus Station

Hertz and Expressway Car Rental

PIAZZALE ROMA

PIAZZALE ROMA

South African

Fond. di S. Simeon Piccolo

Calletagletto d. S. Lucia

C. Bergamaschi

Bergama

Rio Marin

Corte Canal

Calle L. Contarina

CENTRAL VENICE

Fond. d. S. Fond Toyentini

Laundry

C. Amai

Fond. Minotto

Rio delle Muneghette

Rio della due Torre

Frari

CAMPO DEI FRARI

CAMPO S. ROCCO

CAMPO SAN POLO

Rio Terra dei Pensieri

Rio Nuovo

CAMPO SAN PANTALON

Rio Foscari

SAN TOMA

SANT'ANGELO

Canale

Fond. Foscarini

CAMPO SANTA MARGHERITA

Rio d. Santa Margherita

Punto Supermarket

Rio d. S. Barnaba

CAMPO SAN BARNABA

Calle d. Pazienza

C. Lunga San Barnaba

Calle Avogana

Calle d. Cartoze

CÀ REZZONICO

SAN SAMUELE

CAMPO SAN STEFANO

San Sebastiano

Rio di San Sebastiano

Stazione Marittima

SAN BASILIO

C. Chiesa

Gesuati

Rio d. Ognissanti

Fond. Zattere Ponto Lungo

DORSODURO

ACCADEMIA

Ponte Accademia

The Accademia

Peggy Guggenheim Collection

CAMPO SAN AGNESE

Rio d. S. Vio

TO V. SACCA FISOLA (300m)

Canale della Giudecca

ZATTERE

SACCA FISOLA

GIUDECCA

PALANCA
Fond. S. Eufemia

TO TEMPIO DEL S.S. REDENTORE (500m), ZITELLE (1km)

venice

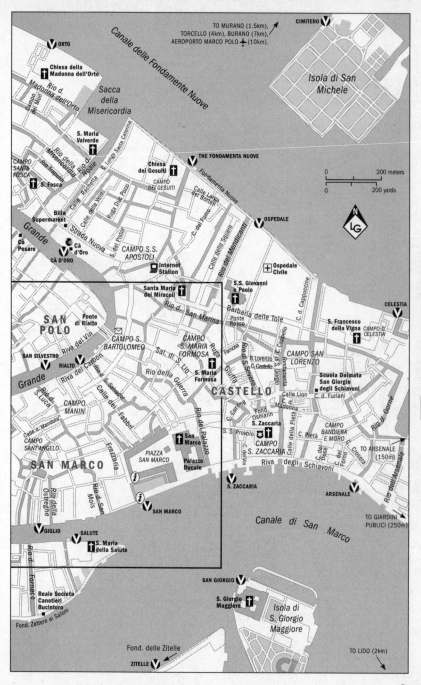

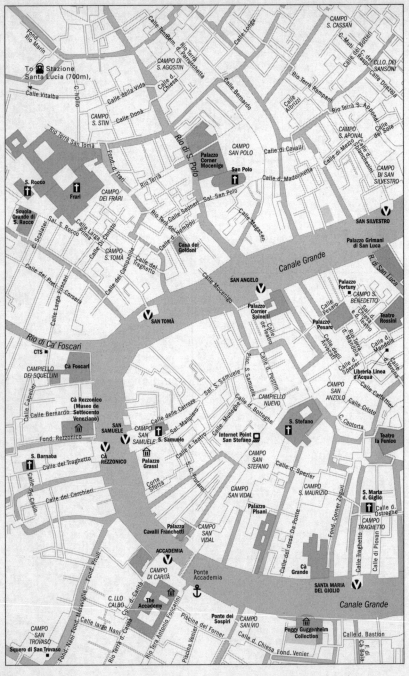

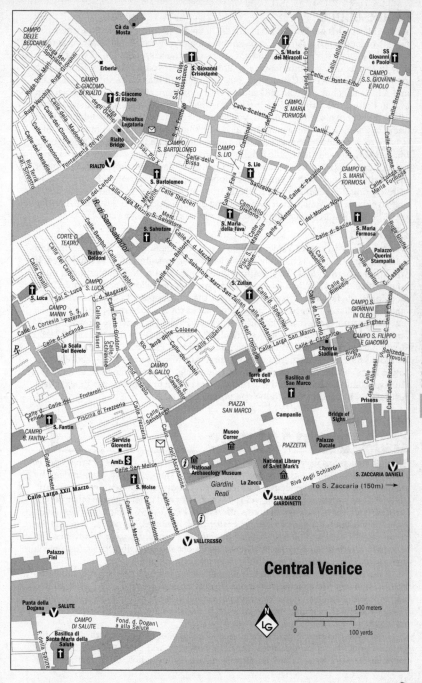

Central Venice

🏛DORSODURO

As neighborhoods go, Dorsoduro is a *Let's Go* favorite. Unlike some of the other *sestiere*, Dorsoduro possesses the ideal combination of awesome local flavor, proximity to major sights, great nightlife, and exceptional restaurants. Granted, if you want to stay in Dorsoduro, you'll probably pay 25% more than you would for a comparable room in Santa Croce or Cannaregio, but, as in most Italian cities, with a little luck and a little haggling you can still end up with a bargain. Moreover, the intersection of San Polo, Santa Croce, and Dorsoduro is the heart of Venice. From here, or just about anywhere else in Dorsoduro, you shouldn't be more than a few minutes from some of Venice's best museums. You also won't have to struggle too much to make it back to your hotel after a night out. Dorsoduro has its fill of unique side streets but remains an easily navigable neighborhood (at least by Venetian standards), with more incredible restaurants, fabulous art galleries, and cool shops than any other district in Venice. Whether you stay in Dorsoduro or not, do not make the mistake of relegating the neighborhood to the bottom of your itinerary—there is no better way to experience Venice than by wandering through Dorsoduro, *sans* map, in a day spent getting lost in the neighborhood's winding roads and alleyways.

CASTELLO

With proximity to two of Venice's prime tourist destinations, the Rialto Bridge and P. San Marco, Castello is in many ways a less expensive alternative to San Marco. If you know where to look, you can find great hotels and restaurants at much more competitive prices. While Castello tends to get a lot of spillover tourist traffic from San Marco, the farther north and east you go, the more apparent Castello's charming, quaint local character becomes. Since Venice lacks traditional streets, neighborhoods can change from block to block. This is especially evident here, where crowded, loud, and overdeveloped thoroughfares suddenly give way to quiet and scenic side streets. If you have a few days in Venice, it's certainly worth exploring this neighborhood, including its eastern portion; however, there are few notable sights, and it's easy to get lost. Though residents proudly proclaim that eastern Castello represents the true, vanishing Venice, visitors will find the west more to their liking, with excellent restaurants and easy access to the rest of the city.

accommodations

Though Venice has very few hostels, there are dozens upon dozens of great budget hotels throughout the city that are typically worth the extra cost. Save money by requesting a room with a shared bathroom. Your bedroom will be private (and typically with its own sink), but you will share a shower and toilet with the other people on your floor. Since most small hotels offering Wi-Fi, A/C, or wheelchair-accessibility only have a limited number of rooms with these features, particular requests for room selection should be made ahead by phone or email. Booking in advance can also help you find a lower rate. Nightly rates almost always include breakfast, which can range from some toast and coffee to an extravagant affair.

Even if you're trying to book last-minute during the high season, you should be able to find affordable, quality options. Hotels dot the sidewalks, so walk around and talk to the managers of a few different establishments before paying for a room. Don't be afraid to negotiate prices; offering to pay in cash sometimes helps travelers finagle a lower rate.

If you want to sleep right by Venice's major sights or in a room with views of the Grand Canal, it'll cost you. Most travelers, however, will probably find the minor inconvenience of being a few minutes removed from the hot spots worth the few dozen euro they save nightly by staying at one of Venice's numerous budget accommodations.

SAN MARCO

Unlike most other Venetian neighborhoods, which are home to primarily 1- and 2-star hotels, San Marco is packed with establishments of the 4- and 5-star variety whose luxury is exceeded only by the amount you'll have to drop to book one of their rooms. Still, there are bargains to be had, particularly if you're willing to stay on the western side of the neighborhood, farther from the **Rialto Bridge** and **Piazza San Marco.** If your main priority is proximity to these sights, you ought to consider a hotel in Castello, which can end up being both closer to the main attractions of San Marco and less expensive than a hotel that claims a San Marco address.

👍 NOVECENTO 💳🚭📶❄ HOTEL [5]

Calle del Dose 2683 ☎041 52 12 145 🖥www.novecento.biz

Incorporating South and East Asian design influences, trendy Novecento sets the standard for boutique hotels in Venice. With excellent lounge areas, top-notch rooms (each with its own unique design theme), and access to a nearby fitness club free of charge, Novecento offers amenities and a quality of service unmatched by the vast majority of budget hotels in Venice.

➤ V: Santa Maria del Giglio. Walk north approximately 45sec.; hotel is on the right. ℹ Breakfast included. $ Singles €100-130; doubles €160-260; triples €180-300.

👍 HOTEL CASANOVA 💳♿ HOTEL [5]

Frezzeria 1284 ☎041 52 06 855 🖥www.hotelcasanova.it

Approximately 1min. away from P. San Marco, Hotel Casanova is an incredible value for the area. Though you'll have to contend with chaos on the narrow street below from dawn until dusk, you can't get much closer to Venice's main attractions. With Hotel Casanova's exceptional accommodations, the largest and most comfortable you'll find anywhere in Venice in this price range, you get convenience without sacrificing quality.

➤ Exit the southwest corner of P. San Marco, opposite Basilica di San Marco, and take first right onto Frezzeria; the hotel is less than 1min. ahead on the right. ℹ Breakfast included. $ Singles €70-120; doubles €90-170; triples €120-200; quads €150-230.

HOTEL SERENISSIMA 💳🚭📶❄ HOTEL [5]

Calle Goldoni 4486 ☎041 52 00 011 🖥www.hotelserenissima.it

Close to P. San Marco yet far enough away to evade most tourist traffic, the aptly named Hotel Serenissima sits on a quiet street with great shopping and fine dining nearby. The rooms are full of white decorations, meaning that any smidge of dirt could show up tenfold. Perhaps that's why the management keeps every room strikingly clean. If you've been trudging around the canals all day, make sure to take your boots off so as not to dirty this place's immaculate interior. Despite such an uncommon appeal to the more fastidious standards of American tourists, rooms are not significantly marked-up and are often available at reasonable rates even for last-minute bookings.

➤ From P. San Marco, exit west opposite Basilica di San Marco, turn right, and continue straight for 2-3min. across 1 bridge; the hotel is on the left. ℹ Breakfast included. $ Singles €81-120; doubles €120-180; triples €150-235; quads €190-275.

RESIDENZA SAN MAURIZIO 💳🚭❄ HOTEL [4]

Campo San Maurizio 2624 ☎041 52 89 712 🖥www.residenzasanmaurizio.com

A 5-7min. walk from P. San Marco but only 3-4min. from Dorsoduro, Residenza San Mauricio is at an ideal location for travelers who want to see the museums of Dorsoduro, spend time around the P. San Marco, and see the sights of the Rialto Bridge. Located down a quiet alley off Campo San Maurizio, the hotel offers some of the lowest prices you'll find in San Marco, and it doesn't compromise the quality of its rooms. It also has a thoroughly competent website, which people looking to book online will quickly discover is uncommon among Venetian hotels.

✝ *V: Santa Maria del Giglio. Walk north, pass 1 bridge on the left, turn left onto the 2nd bridge, and cross consecutive bridges; the hotel is less than 1min. away on the right.* *i* *Breakfast included.* Ⓢ *Singles €55-85; doubles €85-110; triples €80-130; quads €100-155.*

HOTEL A LA COMMEDIA
✎ ♿ (ⁿ)❀   HOTEL ❺
Corte Del Teatro Goldoni 4596/A   ☎041 27 70 235 ▣www.commediahotel.com

One of the very few four-star accommodations *Let's Go* would even consider for inclusion in a guide to Venice, Hotel A La Commedia is the most expensive listing we have for Venice, but it is also one of the most luxurious and service-oriented hotels in the city. Located in one of San Marco's premier shopping blocks, Hotel A La Commedia is everything you'd expect from the price tag, plus it includes unexpected luxuries like the gorgeous rooftop wine bar and terrace, a great place for late-night socializing above one of San Marco's more animated squares.

✝ *From the Rialto Bridge, turn right and continue along Riva del Carbon for approximately 2min.; turn right onto Calle del Carbon, continue for 1min.; the hotel is on the right.* *i* *Breakfast included. Wi-Fi access €5 per 30min.* Ⓢ *Singles €85-399; doubles €119-399; triples €175-510; quads €295-630.*

ALBERGO SAN FANTIN
✎❀   HOTEL ❺
Campiello della Fenice 1930/A   ☎041 52 31 401 ▣www.hotelsanfantin.it

A family-owned hotel since 1957, Albergo San Fantin managed to weather the 7-year period between the 1996 burning down of **Teatro La Fenice** (p. 172) and its reconstruction in 2003 due to excellent rates, attentive service, and delightful decor that complements the style of the neighboring theater. With excellent proximity to P. San Marco and the neighborhood of Dorsoduro, Albergo San Fantin also enjoys a location in one of the few areas of San Marco that feels like a residential neighborhood rather than a tourist playground.

✝ *V: Vallaresso. Go north, take the 1st left, cross 1 bridge, take the 2nd right after the bridge, and continue across another bridge through Campo S. Fantin; the hotel is in Campiello della Fenice.* *i* *Breakfast included.* Ⓢ *Singles €65-130; doubles €100-170; triples €150-210.*

HOTEL ASTORIA
✎ ♿ (ⁿ)❀   HOTEL ❹
Calle Fiubera 951   ☎041 52 25 381 ▣www.hotelastoriavenezia.it

A small, modest hotel on a crowded street near P. San Marco, Hotel Astoria offers some of the best rates you'll find anywhere in Venice, making it a truly exceptional value for the San Marco area. Though less roomy and perhaps not as extravagantly decorated as some hotels nearby, Hotel Astoria boasts Wi-Fi included in your room cost, an elevator, and several other amenities that make it thoroughly practical.

✝ *From P. San Marco, walk beneath the St. Mark's Clock Tower and turn left onto Calle Fiubera; the hotel is less than 1min. ahead on the right.* *i* *Breakfast included. Free Wi-Fi.* Ⓢ *Singles €45-125; doubles €105-190; suites €180-280.*

CANNAREGIO

Cannaregio has some of the best budget hotels in Venice, particularly on the western islands near the train station. Luckily, the rest of the traveling world hasn't caught on yet, and even if you're arriving in Venice without a reservation during the busy season, Cannaregio has many top-notch accommodations that can be booked at reasonable rates. The neighborhood itself is mostly residential and has a more laidback vibe than other areas of Venice.

HOTEL SILVA ARIEL

HOTEL [4]

Calle della Masena 1391/A ☎041 72 93 26 www.arielsilva.it

If you're able to negotiate a good price with the manager, Hotel Silva Ariel is one of the best values you'll find in all of Venice. A couple blocks removed from the more tourist-laden area around Campo San Geremia, this beautiful and remarkably spacious hotel sits relatively close to almost anything you would want to see in Cannaregio.

Left from the train station, then 5min. walk over Guglie Bridge and left onto Calle della Masena. i Breakfast included. [$] Singles €55-75; doubles €80-100.

approximations

Enrico Fermi—physicist, quantum theorist, statistician. Italian.

Fermi had one of the greatest scientific minds of the 20th century, but spending time in Italy is enough to make you question his method of informal approximation. Basically, Fermi argued that one could accurately estimate the answers to complex problems by appropriately analyzing their necessary factors and assumptions. Fermi's theory has clearly been taken to heart by the people of Italy, because everyone here approximates. Everything. All the time. And, sadly, not always as well as Fermi did.

Directions tend to be kind of dicey approximations—we're pretty sure that over 75% of hotels in Venice claim to be within 5min. walking distance of the Rialto Bridge. Wi-Fi availability is also a source of wild estimation. If a hotel advertises wireless internet access, what they really mean is that they have some *approximation* of Wi-Fi—even if it's only in the lobby and working roughly 3hr. per day. Most restaurants and hotels boast of their A/C, which they definitely have...at least in one room. But it might not be working this week.

There are perks to this system of guesstimation as well. In the states, we tend to think of prices as set in stone, but here, they are simply estimates—estimates that can be recalculated based on how charming a shop owner finds you. The approximation of opening and closing times also tends to work out well: in Venice, you'll never have a restaurant door closed on you because you arrived 5min. after business was supposed to end. Also, if you sleep past check-out time, don't sweat it—as long as you exit your room *approximately* on time.

To strung-out, type-"A" Americans, the blurry lines of Venetian approximation can be frustrating to no end. If you, like *Let's Go* researchers, make a habit of hanging around in hotel lobbies, you'll see plenty of arguments between managers and customers over technicalities to which the customer adheres rigidly and the proprietor, well, not so much. Venice is a wonderful city with a lot to be appreciated, but to most enjoy the city, it's best to quickly learn how to chill out and take things as they come. And trust that they will turn out right...more or less.

HOTEL BERNARDI SEMENZATO

HOTEL [2]

Calle dell'Oca 4366 ☎041 52 27 257 www.hotelbernardi.com

Lots of hotels on the eastern side of Cannaregio are overpriced and poorly maintained, but Hotel Bernardi bucks the trend by offering great rooms at ridiculously low prices (well, for Venice at least). The singles without private bathrooms can get uncomfortably warm during the summer, but the free Wi-Fi more than makes up for this minor discomfort.

➡ *From Campo SS. Apostoli, head north on Salizada Pistor and take the 1st left.* **i** *Breakfast included. Free Wi-Fi.* $ *Singles €30-35; doubles €54-78.*

HOTEL ROSSI 💳🚭📶❄ HOTEL [3]

Lista di Spagna 262 ☎041 71 51 64 💻www.hotelrossi.ve.it

Just a few steps off Lista di Spagna, Hotel Rossi's peaceful setting seems miles (kilometers?) away from Cannaregio's more active center. Next to one of the neighborhood's nicest gardens, this hotel has reasonably large rooms, air conditioning, and understated classic Italian decor—all of which make it popular with middle-aged tourists, but perhaps less so with students scared away by the high Wi-Fi fee *(€14 per 24hr.)*.

➡ *Walk 3min. from the train station, then turn left down a side street immediately before Campo San Geremia.* **i** *Breakfast included.* $ *Singles €45-72; doubles €80-95.*

HOTEL STELLA ALPINA 💳♿📶❄ HOTEL [5]

Calle Priuli 99/D ☎041 52 45 274 💻www.hotel-stellaalpina.com

If you've been on the road for a while and the thought of another night spent in a sleeping sack is making you wish you'd stayed home and taken that summer job at Taco Bell, look no further than Hotel Stella Alpina, which offers budget-friendly luxury to the tired traveler. From the classic, almost formal, furnishings in the lobby to the modern decor in the dining room and bedrooms, this hotel's ambience certainly tops that of your local fast food franchise. But you'll have totally forgotten about your lost opportunity in the food service industry once you've laid yourself down in one of the hotel's air-conditioned rooms on the most comfortable bed you might ever find. Just make sure to get the job next summer to pay for this splurge . . .

➡ *From train station, turn left at the 1st st. past Calle Carmelitani and walk for about 1.5min.* **i** *Breakfast included. Discount for booking ahead online.* $ *Singles €70-90; doubles €75-105.*

ALBERGO CASA BOCCASSINI 💳♿ HOTEL [4]

Calle Volto 5295 ☎041 52 29 892 💻www.hotelboccassini.com

You could walk right past Albergo Casa Boccassini and never know it was there, nestled as it is in an unassuming residential area removed from Cannaregio's major thoroughfares. However, you'd be missing one of this neighborhood's little-known all-stars. Casa Boccassini's comfortably-sized and thoughtfully decorated rooms seem well priced (especially if you haggle down the rate), but the true standouts of this inconspicuous hotel are its gorgeous garden and the delightful indoor and outdoor seating you can enjoy while eating your complimentary breakfast.

➡ *Coming from Fondamenta Nuove along Calle del Fumo, turn right at the 1st st. past Calle Larga dei Boteri.* **i** *Breakfast included* $ *High-season singles €70, low-season €50.*

HOTEL TINTORETTO 💳♿❄ HOTEL [4]

S. Fosca 2316 ☎041 72 17 91 💻www.hoteltintoretto.com

Hotel Tintoretto is a great hotel—if you can book it for the right price. Located right off Strada Nova in a section of Cannaregio that has relatively few budget hotels but is close to everything else in the neighborhood, this is an exceptionally clean, comfortable place to stay. Call ahead to find out about prices and attempt to bargain your way to a better deal, because if you can get a room toward the lower half of Tintoretto's spectrum, especially during the busy season, you'll be taking advantage of one of Cannaregio's sweetest deals.

➡ *Strada Nova, about 12min. from train station and 10min. from Rialto Bridge.* **i** *Breakfast included.* $ *Singles €41-150; doubles €74-210.*

HOTEL SAN GEREMIA 💳♿ HOTEL [4]

Campo San Geremia 290 ☎041 52 42 342 💻www.sangeremiahotel.com

Located directly on Campo San Geremia, this is a solid pick for students looking to be as close as possible to the busier sections of Cannaregio as well as the neighborhood's most exciting nightlife. The hotel itself is fairly typical for the area; however, its exceptionally helpful staff and competitive prices set it apart from rival establishments.

From train station, follow Lista di Spagna until reaching Campo S. Geremia. i Breakfast included. $ Singles €50-70; doubles €70-90.

HOTEL AL VAGON — HOTEL ❸

Cannaregio 5619 — ☎041 52 86 861 www.hotelalvagon.com

If you have a burning desire to be on the eastern side of Cannaregio closer to Rialto Bridge, check out Hotel Al Vagon. It offers clean, spacious rooms at much better rates than most hotels in the area. As is the case with many of the hotels listed here, calling ahead and trying to figure out the logistics of your stay before you arrive could get you a significantly lower quote on your room.

Along Strada Nova eastward, cross the 1st bridge past Ca' d'Oro and turn left. i Breakfast included. $ Singles €30-70; doubles €50-120.

HOTEL MARTE E BIASIN — HOTEL ❷

Ponte delle Guglie 338 — ☎041 71 63 51 www.hotelmarteebiasin.com

Hotel Marte e Biasin, located in two separate buildings divided by a canal, has more personality than just about any other hotel you'll find in Cannaregio—maybe even in all of Venice. The managers are charmingly upfront and take pride in running a tight ship, so the rooms are always well kept. However, all the Harry Potter fans who wonder what life was like under the staircase of Number 4, Privet Drive should take a look at the hotel's tiny single bedrooms with shared bath to get a sense of the boy wizard's plight. Despite the cramped and spartan quality of some of its rooms, Hotel Marte e Biasin is a great option for travelers trying to save some money in an expensive city. Whether you're paying in Galleons or euro, this hotel's prices can't be beaten.

From train station along Lista di Spagna, turn left immediately before bridge. i Breakfast included. $ Singles €25-85; doubles €40-100. 5% student discount.

SAN POLO

Though San Polo is home to relatively few hotels and hostels, the ones that are here offer a central location at double-take rates.

ALBERGO GUERRATO — PENSIONE ❹

Calle drio la Scimia 240/A — ☎041 52 85 927 www.pensioneguerrato.it

Located in an 800-year-old *palazzo* just steps away from the Rialto Bridge, Albergo Guerrato offers competitive rates on some of the most desirable rooms in Venice. Characterized by simple but neat aesthetics that focus less on excessive decoration and more on comfort, they're perfectly suited to hard-living travelers.

From the Rialto Bridge, continue west and turn onto the 3rd street on the right; the hotel is shortly ahead on the right. i Breakfast included. $ Doubles €95-140; triples €120-155; quads €185; quints €195.

A VENICE MUSEUM — HOSTEL ❷

Calle del Traghetto 2812 — ☎340 73 57 468

The owners of A Venice Museum, one of the very few true youth hostels in Venice, are so committed to running a fun, vibrant, engaging, and social establishment that they've banned everyone over 40 (not a joke—check the age requirements). The price is unbelievable, you can do laundry on-site (an indescribably huge perk given the lack of laundromats in Venice), and the hostel hosts dinner every night for only €3. If you're the type who doesn't mind waiting for the shower and loves to party with loud music until late at night, you're sure to have a blast here.

V: San Tomà. Go straight, make the 1st right, take the next right, and then take the next right. The hostel is not conspicuously advertised; look for a dark green door with several doorbells. Ring

the one that says "Museum" for entrance to the hostel. *i* Breakfast included. Sheets €5 per night; towels €2. Dinner €3. Under 40 only. Ⓢ Dorms €28-35.

LOCANDO CA' SAN POLO

⏎⅊♿(ᵗᵖ)❄ HOTEL ❹

Calle Saoneri de la Malvasia 2697 ☎041 24 40 331 🖳www.casanpolo.it

If you want luxurious accommodations in Venice without spending all your money at once, do you (a) seduce a rich Venetian heiress, (b) sneak into Palazzo Ducale and take up residence in the Doge's Apartments, or (c) stay here? Ca' San Polo is by far the most legal, moral, and plausible of these three options. With study desks, blackout curtains, comfortable king-size beds, and beautiful views of the neighborhood from the third-floor terrace and dining area, this hotel proves that budget and luxury are not mutually exclusive.

⚶ V: San Tomà. Continue north toward Frari, turn right, continue across the bridge, turn right, and take the 1st left; the hotel is ahead on the right. Signs indicate the direction toward the hotel. *i* Breakfast included. Ⓢ Doubles €80-110; triples €100-120; quads €140-180.

HOTEL ALEX

⏎⊗ HOTEL ❸

Frari 2606 ☎041 52 31 341 🖳www.hotelalexinvenice.com

A small family hotel just across the bridge from the Frari, Hotel Alex prides itself on offering clean, quiet, and comfortable rooms. Though students may feel out of place in the family atmosphere, quads that go for €20 per person per night make hosteling look like a crummy deal. Consider booking in advance to request a room with a balcony overlooking the street.

⚶ V: San Tomà. Continue north toward Frari, turn right, continue across the bridge, turn right, and turn left; the hotel is ahead on the left. *i* Breakfast included. Ⓢ Singles €35-56; doubles €40-120; triples €60-162; quads €80-200.

LOCANDA POSTE VECIE

⏎⊗ HOTEL ❸

Pescheria Rialto 1612 ☎041 71 82 44 🖳www.locandapostevecie.com

Close to the Rialto Bridge, Locanda Poste Vecie is right in the heart of one of Venice's most crowded and lively districts, but with comfortable rooms decorated in traditional Venetian style, it manages to maintain a serene ambience. Consult its website before booking, as it offers frequent discounts and promotions online.

⚶ From the Rialto Bridge, continue straight for about 200m through Campo De Le Becarie and take the 2nd right after the Campo. The hotel is on the right. *i* Breakfast included. Ⓢ Doubles €70-130; triples €90-160; quads €110-190.

HOTEL IRIS

⏎⊗(ᵗᵖ) HOTEL ❸

V. San Polo 2910/A ☎041 52 22 882 🖳www.irishotel.com

Located right at the intersection of Dorsoduro and San Polo and just steps away from the vaporetto, Hotel Iris offers convenient access to all of Venice's neighborhoods in addition to peaceful, comfortable rooms in one of Venice's most scenic areas. Prices vary frequently and tend to spike on weekends, so be sure to book well in advance.

⚶ V: San Tomà. Walk straight until reaching a T intersection, turn left, continue to the canal, and turn right; the hotel is ahead on the right. *i* Breakfast included. Ⓢ Singles €40-100; doubles €70-120; triples €120-180; quads €160-240.

SANTA CROCE

Although Santa Croce isn't known for its budget accommodations, you can find a room at the right price to make the neighborhood your home-away-from-home. Santa Croce is centrally located, with San Marco and the Rialto Bridge just minutes away and the nightlife in Dorsoduro easily accessible. At the same time, the neighborhood enjoys wide, quiet streets that aren't overrun with tourists. It's best to stay away from its western side, as you're more likely to discover good deals in the eastern section.

ALBERGO AI TOLENTINI

HOTEL 4

Santa Croce 197/G ☎041 27 59 140 www.albergoaitolentini.com

Albergo ai Tolentini is a small hotel without many different options accommodations-wise, but what it does have is exceptional. Start with what are in all likelihood the largest double rooms you'll find for less than €100 in Venice, decorated in an elaborate Venetian style and featuring private baths. Add on the hotel's convenient location, which is about as central as you can get in Venice, and you've got the makings of one very serviceable little hotel.

Follow Piazzale Roma east, cross consecutive bridges, turn left, and continue along canal for 3-4min. before turning right away from Hotel Sofitel. Continue for 2min.; hotel is on the left. ***i*** *Breakfast included.* $ *Doubles €85-115.*

ALBERGO CASA PERON

HOTEL 3

Salizzada San Pantalon 84 ☎041 71 00 21 www.casaperon.com

A small, family-owned hotel with tons of personality, Albergo Casa Peron is worth the time to book in advance. A prime location on one of Santa Croce's main streets put this hotel in our good graces from the outset, but Albergo Casa Peron scores extra points with *Let's Go* for its supremely cool owner and the pet parrot who helps oversee the hotel from his shoulder.

Follow Piazzale Roma east, cross consecutive bridges, and continue for approximately 2min. ***i*** *Breakfast included.* $ *Singles €30-90; doubles €50-100; triples €80-130.*

PENSIONE DA IVANO

PENSIONE 3

Santa Croce 373 ☎041 52 46 648 www.daivanovenezia.it

Close to Piazzale Roma, Pensione da Ivano possesses a peaceful location, despite being a bit out of the way. The spacious, well-decorated rooms are only brightened by the friendly presence of their dedicated manager, who has owned the *pensione* and nearby Caffé Las Ramblas for the past 37 years. Feel free to chat him up, as he loves to talk with travelers about his city.

East from Piazzale Roma, turn right at the 1st canal you see and turn right onto Sestiere Santa Croce. Go to Caffé Las Ramblas, where you can be redirected to the pensione (4min. away). ***i*** *Breakfast included.* $ *Rooms €45-100.*

HOTEL FALIER

HOTEL 5

Salizada San Pantalon 130 ☎041 71 08 82 www.hotelfalier.com

Most of the hotels in the Santa Croce area are rather pricey, but Hotel Falier bridges the gap between luxury and budget fairly well. The price of a single room is as far from inexpensive as Venice is from Sicily, but the doubles are a good value compared to some of the luxury hotels in the neighborhood, without any compromise in quality. You won't be cheated the extra bucks you're shelling out: the hotel's phenomenal location is accompanied by an excellent dining room, a desk manager fluent in English, a lovely balcony, and other subtle pleasantries.

Follow Piazzale Roma east, cross consecutive bridges, and continue for approximately 2min. ***i*** *Breakfast included.* $ *Singles €100-150; doubles €120-170.*

HOTEL DALLA MORA

HOTEL 5

Salizada San Pantalon ☎041 71 07 03 www.hoteldallamora.it

A clean, simple, and modern hotel with fantastic views of the city from its terrace, Hotel Dalla Mora offers excellent rooms just removed from Santa Croce's main street. While rooms tend to be on the small side, the open terrace (under repair at the time of publication) is an ideal place to relax and watch the city go by.

Follow Piazzale Roma east, cross consecutive bridges, and continue for approximately 2min. Hotel is down a side street to the right. ***i*** *Breakfast included.* $ *Singles €70; doubles €80-100; triples €95-120; quads €105-142.*

HOTEL LOCANDA SALIERI 💳🚭📶 HOTEL [3]

Fondamenta Minotto 160 ☎041 71 00 35 💻www.hotelsalieri.com

Great views, nice (though nondescript) rooms, and an attentive staff make Hotel Locanda Salieri an excellent option. Prices are variable, so take a stab at haggling down the proposed rate. Without anything especially unique distinguishing it from the crowd, this hotel should be booked for its accessible location.

🚶 Follow Piazzale Roma east, cross consecutive bridges, continue about 30sec.; the hotel is on the left. ℹ Breakfast included. [$] Doubles €50-160.

DORSODURO

Finding a good hotel at the right price can be a bit tricky in Dorsoduro, but if you're patient and willing to put in a little bit of legwork calling places or checking their websites, you should be able to find a solid rate on a great hotel in the heart of Venice's best neighborhood.

👍 **HOTEL MESSNER** 💳♿📶❄ HOTEL [5]

Fondamenta di Cà Bala 216/217 ☎041 52 27 443 💻www.hotelmessner.it

Described by its owner as "three hotels in one," Hotel Messner offers one-, two-, and three-star accommodations—great for budget travelers who want to save money but still have the flexibility to choose their room's amenities. Regardless of star ranking, most rooms are brightened by floor-to-ceiling windows that prove a blessing in the humid Venetian summer.

🚶 V: Zattere. Turn right, walk 4-5min., turn left onto Fondamenta di Cà Bala and continue for about a min. Reception is approximately 1min. past the hotel in Ristorante Messner. ℹ Breakfast included. [$] Singles €70-105; doubles €95-160; triples €135-180; quads €150-200.

👍 **HOTEL ALLA SALUTE** 💳♿📶 HOTEL [3]

Fondamenta di Cà Bala 222 ☎041 52 35 404 💻www.hotelsalute.com

A lot of hotels in Venice overdo the whole Venetian theme, making you feel as if you're trapped in an antique dealer's storage facility. Hotel alla Salute, by contrast, presents a simple, modern take on Venetian aesthetics with some of the least cluttered and most beautiful hotel rooms in the city. Given the hotel's prime location and generous breakfast buffet, staying here is quite a deal.

🚶 V: Zattere. Turn right, walk 4-5min., turn left onto Fondamenta di Cà Bala and continue for about 2min. ℹ Breakfast included. [$] Doubles €64-95; family rooms (fit 3-5) €75-135.

HOTEL AMERICAN 💳♿📶❄ HOTEL [4]

San Vio 628 ☎041 52 04 733 💻www.hotelamerican.com

If you can book Hotel American anywhere at the bottom of their price range, we strongly advise you to do so. In addition to its old-world-hotel regal air, the American possesses all the amenities you could possibly want from a budget hotel.

🚶 V: Zattere. Turn right, walk 3-4min., turn left onto San Vio and continue for just over 1min. ℹ Breakfast included. [$] Singles €60-230; doubles €80-370; suite €150-460. Extra bed €20-70.

CA' SAN TROVASO 💳♿❄ HOTEL [5]

Fondamente delle Romite ☎041 27 71 146 💻www.casantrovaso.com

Ca' San Trovaso, one of the few hotels in Venice that is honest about how far it is from major sights, has recently undergone renovations that make it a gem of a budget hotel in Dorsoduro. One huge plus to staying at Ca' San Trovaso is access to the rooftop solarium, which provides excellent views of the city as well as space to relax.

🚶 V: Zattere. Turn right, take the 1st possible left, cross the bridge, turn left, cross the bridge immediately ahead, turn immediately right; the hotel is shortly ahead to the left. ℹ Breakfast included. [$] Singles €75-100; doubles €80-145; triples €90-160.

ANTICA LOCANDA MONTIN

⬤⊗ B AND B ❹

Fondamenta Eremite 1147   ☎041 52 25 151 ▣www.locandamontin.com

Although it is less than 2min. from each of Dorsoduro's two biggest streets, Antica Locanda Montin feels removed from these heavily trafficked areas. This is a small inn that lacks some of the conveniences available at large hotels, but it makes up for this inadequacy with a quaint small-town ambience and excellent values on exceptionally comfortable rooms.

✠ *V: Zattere. Turn right, take the first possible left, cross the bridge, turn left, turn immediately right, and the hotel is shortly ahead on the left.* ⓘ *Breakfast included.* Ⓢ *Singles €50-70; doubles €130-160.*

HOTEL GALLERIA

⬤⊗ HOTEL ❹

Campo de la Carità 878   ☎041 52 32 489 ▣www.hotelgalleria.it

A small boutique hotel located near the Accademia, this establishment replicates the Accademia's formidable, faded-glory sort of charm with gorgeous rooms that were clearly designed with an eye towards quality rather than economy. Though perhaps less meticulously run than hotels with larger tourist volume, you're unlikely to find more spectacular rooms in this price range, particularly with a location so close to San Marco and the major galleries of Dorsoduro.

✠ *From the Ponte dell'Accademia, facing the Accademia, turn right and walk for approximately 1min. The hotel is on the right.* ⓘ *Breakfast included.* Ⓢ *Singles €65-86; doubles €110-160.*

ALBERGO HOTEL ANTICO CAPON

⬤⊗⦅ʼᵖʼ⦆❄ HOTEL ❷

Campo San Margherita 3004   ☎041 52 85 292 ▣www.anticocapon.altervista.org

Hotel Antico Capon's location is both a blessing and a curse. If you're planning to hit the hay every night at 9pm to get up early and see Venice, you'll probably be frustrated with the constant din of Campo San Margherita, Dorsoduro's prime nightlife spot, echoing throughout the square. On the other hand, if you want to party every night you're in the city but don't want to navigate winding streets back to your hotel in the wee hours of the morning, Antico Capon might be your best bet. The rooms here are cheap for a reason: they're tiny.

✠ *Opposite the northeast corner of the square.* ⓘ *Breakfast included.* Ⓢ *Doubles €45-95; triples €60-75; quads €120.*

HOTEL TIVOLI

⬤⊗⦅ʼᵖʼ⦆❄ HOTEL ❸

Crosera San Pantalon 3838   ☎041 52 42 460 ▣www.hoteltivoli.it

Another great pick if you want to be close to Venetian nightlife, Hotel Tivoli is within 2min. of Campo San Margherita, Santa Croce, and San Polo. The rooms are comfortable and spacious (if a bit plain), the owner is exceptionally friendly, and there's a great open-air courtyard where you can enjoy breakfast or a late-night pizza after a long night on the town.

✠ *From Campo San Margherita, go west, cross the 1st bridge you come to, continue across the square, turn right at the cross street, continue for about 1min.; the hotel is on the right.* ⓘ *Breakfast included.* Ⓢ *Singles €30-90; doubles €40-150; triples €75-180; quads €95-210.*

PENSIONE SEGUSO

⬤♿ PENSIONE ❸

Zattere 779   ☎041 52 86 858 ▣www.pensioneseguso.com

Located right on the Zattere, Seguso is a modest *pensione* with lovely antique furniture and comfortable rooms as well as a friendly and helpful staff. The location is excellent, but it's worth calling in advance to try to book a room on one of the lower floors; since some travelers report the top floors get uncomfortably warm during the summer.

✠ *V: Zattere. Turn right; continue for 2-3min.; the hotel is on the left immediately before a bridge.* ⓘ *Breakfast included.* Ⓢ *Singles €40-160; doubles €65-190; triples €150-245; quads €170-250.*

accommodations • dorsoduro

CASTELLO

Castello is bursting at the seams with overpriced hotels looking to exploit tourists who mistakenly believe they just have to be within a 5min. walk of the Rialto Bridge and P. San Marco. Hidden among these flashy establishments, however, are a good number of hotels that are accessible to the major sights but manage to maintain the quiet neighborhood ambience that makes Venice so charming. Hotel prices tend to fluctuate more in Castello than in most neighborhoods, so it's worth calling around to see the best available rates. Keep in mind that if you stay in the northern section of Castello, you'll have a much easier time getting to Cannaregio and San Polo, whereas if you stay in the southern or western section you'll have better access to San Marco, Dorsoduro, and all vaporetto lines.

👍 LA RESIDENZA — 💳🚭📶 HOTEL [4]

Campo Bandiera e Moro 3608 ☎041 52 85 315 💻www.venicelaresidenza.com

Every hotel in Venice wants to claim that it is located in a former palace, but at La Residenza, you can tell that they aren't lying. The regal decor, stately reception area, and magnificently decorated guest rooms evoke a sense of Venice's extravagant mercantile history. Although this is far from the typical budget hotel, staying here provides a uniquely Venetian experience.

➜ From P. San Marco, walk towards the water, turn left, and cross 4 bridges; then turn left and continue to Campo Bandiera e Moro. ℹ Breakfast included. Free Wi-Fi. $ Singles €50-110; doubles €60-200. Extra bed €35.

👍 THE GUESTHOUSE TAVERNA SAN LIO — 💳🚭📶❄ B AND B [4]

Salizada San Lio 5547 ☎041 27 77 06 69 💻www.tavernasanlio.com

Staying in Venice on a budget means foregoing a lot of luxuries that might be taken for granted in American hotels, but if you book a room at the Guesthouse Taverna San Lio at the right time, you can get an incredible room that feels authentically Venetian yet still includes Wi-Fi, A/C, a private bathroom—creature comforts certainly not enjoyed by the city's Renaissance residents—and, perhaps most importantly, a mouth-watering breakfast. The hotel also boasts excellent proximity to both the Rialto Bridge and P. San Marco in an area that is lively with local color.

➜ From Rialto Bridge, go east along Salizada San Lio for 3-4min.; hotel is on the right. ℹ Breakfast included. Free Wi-Fi. $ Doubles €70-150; triples €100-180; quads €130-200.

FORESTERIA VALDESE — 💳♿ HOSTEL, HOTEL [2]

Palazzo Cavagnis 5170 ☎041 52 86 797 💻www.foresteriavenezia.it

One of the few places in Venice to get a shared dormitory room more typical of a hostel, Foresteria Valdese is an oasis of value in a sea of €90-per-person, one-star hotels. The hotel is run by a Protestant church that maintains the house in which the hotel is located. While the reservation system can be tricky, especially for dorms, Foresteria Valdese offers both a unique experience and a great deal in Venice.

➜ From Campo Santa Maria Formosa, take Calle Larga Santa Maria Forma; Foresteria Valdese is immediately across the 1st bridge. ℹ Breakfast included. $ Dorms €23-29; doubles €78-96; triples €90-111; quads €114-144.

ALBERGO DONI — 💳🚭 HOTEL [4]

Calle del Vin 4656 ☎041 52 25 267 💻www.albergodoni.it

Rooms at the low end of the price range here are an absolute steal. Although you'll pay for proximity to P. San Marco with heavy tourist traffic and some street noise, the hotel's 17th-century building features spacious rooms, excellent antique furniture, and even some breathtaking ceiling frescoes.

➜ From P. San Marco, walk toward the water, turn left, and cross 2 bridges; take the 1st left and walk 30sec. ℹ Breakfast included. $ Singles €50-65; doubles €60-120.

CASA QUERINI

Campo San Giovanni Novo 4388   ☎041 24 11 294 📧www.locandaquerini.com

HOTEL ❺

Situated in a quiet square apart from the madding crowds of P. San Marco, this hotel is an excellent choice for anyone who wants to be near Venice's tourist center but still enjoy a tranquil stay in a hotel with all the amenities. The decor is a bit minimalist and lacks the same Venetian touch of most other hotels in the area, but with private bathrooms, Wi-Fi, and A/C, this hotel's comfort-inducing features present a good trade-off for a lot of exhausted travelers.

🚶 *From P. San Marco, walk toward the water, turn left, cross Ponte della Paglia, turn left onto Calle dei Albanesi, walk 2min., and turn left at Campo San Giovanni Novo.* *i* *Breakfast included. Wi-Fi €6 per hr.* Ⓢ *Doubles €110-150; triples €135-175.*

under the sea

Traveling to Venice is a wayfarer's dream: great food, incredible history, and beautiful architecture. But sometimes visiting the city can feel a bit like being a boatswain on the post-iceberg Titanic because, like the Titanic, Venice is sinking. Over the past century, Venice has sunk about 1 ft. and is predicted to sink by as much as another 20 in. during the next 50 years. That might not sound like much, but seeing P. San Marco, the most famous landmark in Venice, underwater during the highest tides of the year has the locals feeling a bit seasick. The evidence of the city's watery fate is evident everywhere—stairways that a couple centuries ago led to perfectly functional docks are now covered by several ft. of water.

Novel solutions ranging from constructing moveable dams to pumping water into the foundations of the city have been proposed, but Venetians are far from reaching consensus. A $4 billion project to construct mobile inflatable flood barriers is underway, but it has met with opposition from some who contend it will destroy the natural ecology of the lagoon and actually make flooding worse. Whether a radical solution is achieved or the city continues to rely on the duct-tape approach of fixings things as they break, you'll likely share the locals' concern when you realize that the street you're walking on right now could be the place you bring your kids for a swim in 20 years' time.

HOTEL CANADA VENEZIA

Salizada San Lio   ☎041 52 29 912 📧www.canadavenice.com

HOTEL ❹

Set back a bit from the more hectic and heavily trafficked areas of Castello, Hotel Canada Venezia, situated in an area far from the cacophony of tourists that echoes throughout the area around P. San Marco, might be more popular with older travelers than students. It does, however, merit a look from anyone desiring one of the more upscale budget hotels in Castello.

🚶 *From Rialto Bridge, walk east across Campo S. Bartolomeo, cross a bridge, and then continue for less than 1min.; the hotel is on the left.* *i* *Breakfast included. Free Wi-Fi.* Ⓢ *Singles €65-129; doubles €85-165; triples €110-199; quads €140-254.*

HOTEL AL PIAVE

Ruga Giuffa 4838   ☎041 52 85 174 📧www.hotelalpiave.com

HOTEL ❺

The perfect place for pastel or antique aficionados, Hotel Al Piave is on the expensive side but still offers a good value, especially if you're looking for a multi-person room. A classically Venetian hotel with touches of northern European influence, Hotel Al Piave offers all the amenities you could want from a hotel in the City of Water.

⇟ From Campo Santa Maria Formosa, go directly southeast past Calle dei Orbi, cross 1 bridge, and continue for less than 1min. ℹ Breakfast included. Free Wi-Fi. $ Singles €130-150; doubles €160-190; triples €160-220.

LOCANDA SILVA HOTEL ❸

Fondamenta del Remedio 4423 ☎041 52 27 643 🖥www.locandasilva.it

With some of the most picturesque canal views you'll find in Venice and the best rates in Castello, Locanda Silva is an excellent value for budget travelers. The rooms are great for the price, and the hotel provides a superb point from which to explore both P. San Marco and the Rialto Bridge area.

⇟ From P. San Marco, go north and then turn right onto Calle Larga San Marco; continue until Calle de Angelo, turn left, turn right onto Calle de Remedio, continue until end, and then turn left. ℹ Breakfast included. $ Singles €40-80; doubles €50-135; triples €90-180.

ALBERGO AL NUOVO TESON HOTEL ❺

Calle Pescaria 3980/81 ☎041 52 29 929 🖥www.hotelalnuovoteson.com

In several places, the business cards for Albergo al Nuovo Teson boast of the hotel's presence on everyone's favorite procrastination tool, Facebook. While the walls are decorated with vignettes from Venetian history and the interior is filled with antiques, the hotel's web presence demonstrates its determination to meet the demands of modern tourists. You'll have to pay for the privilege of becoming a "fan," though—as in most Venetian hotels, they charge you for Wi-Fi.

⇟ From P. San Marco, walk south toward water, turn left, cross 2 bridges, and then make a left on last street before 3rd bridge. ℹ Breakfast included. Wi-Fi €1 per hr., €4 per 8hr. $ Singles €75-145; doubles €85-170; triples €110-160; quads €120-170.

HOTEL CANEVA HOTEL ❸

Ramo Dietro La Fava 5515 ☎041 52 28 118 🖥www.hotelcaneva.com

An excellent option for any budget travelers who want to stay in the postcard-perfect, quiet Venetian hotel located right at the intersection of two canals with easy access to both the Rialto Bridge and P. San Marco. The rooms are well-maintained and comfortable, but the beautiful location and building are really what distinguish Hotel Caneva from similar establishments in Castello.

⇟ From the Rialto Bridge, cross Campo San Bartolomeo; continue to Calle Stagneri, cross a bridge, and continue; the hotel is on the right. ℹ Breakfast included. $ Singles €40-80; doubles €40-120; triples €70-140; quads €80-180.

OUTSKIRTS

By staying in the outskirts, you can upgrade your digs on the cheap or go even more bargain-basement than is possible in the *centro*. Lido is loaded with hotels that are less expensive than their Venetian counterparts, and **camping** on the islands or the Italian mainland is a popular alternative for even more saving. While camping might conjure up images of improvised tents and fishing for dinner, Italians campsites offer RV-park luxury, with fully furnished trailers or at least fairly decent permanent tents.

OSTELLO DI VENEZIA (HI) HOSTEL ❷

Fondamenta Zitelle 86 ☎041 52 38 211 🖥www.hostelvenice.com

Ostello Venezia sets the standard for hostels in Venice. With 260 beds, a restaurant, common room, bar, and state-of-the-art facilities, it's an incredible value. Located in Giudecca, it's not too far from Dorsoduro or San Marco. Groups can often book rooms in advance, but outside of those cases, dorms are strictly divided by gender. For those apprehensive about leaving their belongings unattended in a room with a dozen other people, the hostel provides free private lockers with keys and padlocks. Though having to use the vaporetto system can be a bit of a hassle, the hostel's great facilities and efficient and helpful staff more than make up for any inconvenience caused by its out-of-the-way location.

꩜ *V: Zitelle, turn right and continue for less than 1min. The hostel is on the left.* ⓘ *Breakfast included. €3 daily surcharge for those without YHA membership. Wi-Fi €2.50 per 12hr., internet terminals €3 per hr.* Ⓢ *Dorms €22.* 🕐 *Lockout 10am-1:30pm.*

CAMPEGGIO SAN NICOLÒ
꩜♿ CAMPING ❶

V. dei Sanmichieli 14 ☎041 52 67 415 ▧www.campingsannicolo.com

Lido's only major camping site, Campeggio San Nicolò is a great budget option. Though the site is removed from Lido's major vaporetto stops, bike rentals make the island extremely accessible. Tents offer reasonable short-term accommodations, and campers are surprisingly nice given the cost per person. This kind of camping is an interesting and uniquely European experience—something worth trying before you leave Italy (though not cool enough to be attempted when rain is in the forecast).

꩜ *From dock Lido San Nicolò, turn right, and continue north for about 5min. There will be signs indicating the direction of the camp site.* ⓘ *Laundry €3. Parking €2. Bike rental €7.* Ⓢ *Prices vary depending on what exactly you're looking for, but will probably cost about €18 per person per night.*

CAMPING JOLLY
꩜♿✳ CAMPING ❶

V. Giuseppe de Marchi 7 ☎041 92 03 12 ▧www.ecvacanze.it

This is a place to stay if you want to *say* you came to Venice but actually spend your whole trip partying on the Italian mainland. It takes about 45min. to get from Camping Jolly to Venice proper, so don't pop your tent here if you want to be in the city. Instead, come here for the nice pool, awesome bar, tons of backpackers, and a DJ who seems to love Kanye West. Lots of people think that traveling is a lost art in the age of the internet, but dancing to ▧Thriller with backpackers from Japan, some hair-metal fans from Germany, and a pair of Italian bartenders is a great reminder of what it can be when done right.

꩜ *There are several ways to get to Camping Jolly. The best route from Venice is to take bus #6 from the train station toward Marghera, get off at V. Paleocapa, turn onto V. Beccaria, and continue for about 10min. until you reach V. Della Fonte. Turn right onto V. Della Fonte and continue until the street ends. You'll see an outdoor park/sports complex. Follow the walkway along the park until you reach an underpass. Go through the underpass, and you will emerge at Camping Jolly.* Ⓢ *1- to 3-person tents €12.50; bungalows (up to 3 people) €39-58.50; casa mobile (up to 4 people) €60-79; chalet (up to 5 people) €84-116.*

LOCANDA AL SOFFIADOR
꩜⊗Ⓧ⦙✳ HOTEL ❹

Vle. Bressagio 1 ☎041 73 94 30 ▧www.venicehotel.it

For those who want a traditional hotel with relatively easy access to Venice but also hope to spend more time exploring the islands of the northern lagoon, Locanda Al Soffiador offers an ideal location. In a great spot on Murano, an island with enough shopping, studios, and history to keep glass aficionados occupied for days, the hotel is just over 20min. from the Venetian "mainland" (if it's possible to apply that term to a collection of islands). It boasts great proximity to the rest of the northern lagoon as well. The hotel itself is beautiful, well-maintained, and much less expensive than comparable hotels in Venice.

꩜ *V: Faro, walk straight ahead along the island's main street; the hotel is about 3min. ahead on the right.* ⓘ *Breakfast included.* Ⓢ *Singles €50-60; doubles €60-90; triples €80-130.*

accommodations · outskirts

sights

a chorus of churches

For a small city, Venice sure has a lot of churches—a lot of very memorable ones that are worth your time, too. Most of them charge €3 for entry, though, which might make you ask if they're worth your money. Eliminate this calculation, however, with the Chorus Pass, which can be purchased for €10 and grants unlimited entry to participating churches (there are 18 of them) for a year. Buy it at participating churches and then feel free to wander in and out as much as you wish: it won't cost you another cent (unless the collection plate comes around).

An incredible number of churches, museums, palaces, and historic sights line Venice's canals—you could easily spend a month in the city and still be stumbling across new places to check out on a daily basis. If you're planning to spend any time sightseeing here, you should seriously consider purchasing the **Rolling Venice Card** (available at any IAT/VAT Tourist office for €4), a tourist pass for visitors to the city between the ages of 14 and 29 which provides unlimited use of ACTV public transit, free admission to the Civic Museums of Venice, free admission to the churches that are a member of the Chorus Pass collective, reduced admission at any number of other sights, and discounts at various hotels and restaurants.

SAN MARCO

It's easy to be overwhelmed by the number of sights in San Marco. In fact, before you even head out into the wider neighborhood, it's easy to be overwhelmed by the number of sights in **Piazza San Marco** alone. In the *piazza*, the two main attractions, **Basilica di San Marco** and **Palazzo Ducale,** are found easily enough, but several other sights of great interest are often overlooked by visitors. In the wider *sestiere* closer to **Rialto Bridge,** for example, attractions like the excellent **Palazzo Grassi** await. Perhaps most importantly, before braving this area be sure to meditate for a couple of minutes, have a glass of Venetian wine, pop a couple of Xanax, or do whatever else is necessary to prepare yourself for the jostling, shoving, elbowing, shouting, and general rudeness that crops up as inevitably in the heart of *La Serenissima* as it does in any overcrowded tourist area. Once you've done that, you'll be ready to experience one of the densest concentrations of spectacular sights in the whole of Europe.

◙ PALAZZO DUCALE
● ♿ PALAZZO, MUSEUM

P. San Marco 1 ☎041 27 15 911 ▣www.museicivicveneziani.it

This massive palace that served as the residence of Venice's pseudo-monarchical mayor and the seat of his government throughout most of Venetian history is, perhaps, the best showcase of Venetian history, art, and architecture you'll find in a single building. Unfortunately, it has lost much of its character in recent years as it has increasingly sought to traffic as many visitors as possible through its exhibits with the most minimal inconvenience. Unlike the serene **Accademia** or **Peggy Guggenheim Collection**, where it's possible to move leisurely through the galleries and follow no particular path, the Palazzo Ducale poses challenges to those who would like to meander through its halls, as numerous guided tours block hallways and crowd some of the museum's most famous attractions. For the best way to see the Palazzo, rent a handheld audio tour *(€5)* or stop by the the museum shop to purchase a guide before you enter. Then, proceed at your

venice

Around Piazza San Marco

0   200 meters

0   200 yards

own pace. While there are many bottlenecks in some of the more famous rooms, where guides tend to linger, if you time things well, you should be able to evade clusters of tourists while still managing to see everything. And there is a remarkable amount to see, from Sansovino's statues in the courtyard to Veronese's *Rape of Europa.*

Every room open to the public is worth visiting, and *Let's Go* recommends allowing yourself to wander through the Palazzo, spending more time in the rooms that are of particular interest to you. If you decide to go all-in and read about the history of every room, you could easily spend 4hr. in the place, but in any case, budget at least 90min. for your visit. No visit to the Palazzo Ducale can be complete without seeing Tintoretto's *Paradise,* an impossibly massive oil painting with strongly religious themes that gives the **Great Council Room** an ominous, foreboding air. The numerous exhibitions in the **Doge's Apartments,** including the Doge's private libraries and dining room, should prove fascinating to anyone with an interest in Venetian history or high culture. Surprisingly, one of the least crowded sections of the palace is the area containing the **Bridge of Sighs** and prisons, which constitute an extensive labyrinth throughout the lower eastern side of the palace and provide stark contrast to the opulence and majesty of the floors above.

Entrance to the Palazzo Ducale is along the waterfront. $ Apr 1-Oct 31 €13, EU citizens ages 18-25, ages 6-14, over 65, and holders of the Rolling Venice card €7.50; Nov 1-Mar 31 €12/6.50. Open daily June-Oct 8:30am-6:30pm; Nov-March 9am-6pm; Apr-May 9am-7pm. Ticket office closes 1hr. before museum.

BASILICA DI SAN MARCO — CHURCH

P. San Marco ☎041 27 08 311 www.basilicasanmarco.it

This basilica is maybe the top "can't miss" sight in all of Venice, and not just because admission is free. Lines to the Basilica are often long, but don't be deterred. Visitors rarely spend more than 15min. inside the Basilica, so even if you're behind a few hundred people, it shouldn't take more than a wait of 20min. or so for you to enter what is universally considered the most impressive church in Venice. If you're planning a day in P. San Marco, either go to the Basilica first thing in the morning before it is crowded or mid-afternoon when light streams in through the windows and provides some of the most striking natural illumination you'll find anywhere in the world.

Even before you enter the church, you cannot help but be struck by its size and intricate design. Spend a few minutes admiring the basilica's facade, overlooked by far too many visitors. It is every bit as impressive as the inside's soaring domes, marble inlay, and gorgeous golden mosaics that acquire an eerie life-like quality in the proper lighting. The majesty of the church is a testament to the history of Venice, as the Basilica di San Marco dates back to the origins of the city. Founded in the ninth century by two Venetian merchants who daringly stole St. Mark's remains from the city of Alexandria and smuggled them past Arab officials by hiding them in a case of pork meat, the church was originally a much smaller, more modest wooden building that suffered serious damage during a fire in the 11th century. Venice, emerging as a powerful city state, dedicated substantial time, effort, and funding to the construction of the new Basilica di San Marco, which was further embellished as the Republic of Venice rose in stature. Today, it stands more or less as it was completed in the 17th century. The church's interior is clearly the product of the various cultural influences that have affected the Venetian identity, seamlessly incorporating Byzantine, Roman, and Northern European influences into an interior that is simultaneously ostentatious in its gilded excess and mysterious in the dark, rich detail of its altars and mosaics.

Though admission to the Basilica is free, those interested in further exploration of the remarkable building's history will have to pay extra to see its three affiliated sights: the Pala d'Oro, treasury, and St. Mark's Museum. Anyone intrigued by the Byzantine influences in the Basilica should take a few minutes to appreciate the **Pala d'Oro,** an altar retable that is widely regarded as one of the most spectacular intact examples of Byzantine artwork. A visual history of the life of Saint Mark, the Pala d'Oro was meticulously designed with thousands of precious gemstones adorning what is certainly one of the most breathtaking pieces of religious artwork you'll see anywhere in Italy. The **treasury** houses various precious objects of religious significance, a collection that anyone with an interest in the history of the Basilica will enjoy exploring even if it includes a small fraction of the number of artifacts it featured prior to the Napoleonic invasions. **St. Mark's Museum** helps to contextualize the Basilica and is a great primer in Venetian history for anyone with a short stop in Venice. Nevertheless, visiting the museum isn't essential to appreciating the astounding beauty of the

Basilica, which is the main attraction here.

⚜ *Entrance on east side of P. San Marco, north of Palazzo Ducale.* ℹ *Modest dress required—no bare shoulders or revealing skirts or shorts.* ⓢ *Basilica free. St. Mark's Museum €4. Pala d'Oro €2. Treasury €3. All prices reduced 50% for groups of 15 or more.* ⌚ *Basilica open Easter-Nov M-Sa 9:45am-5pm, Su 2-5pm; Nov-Easter M-Sa 9:45am-5pm, Su 2-4pm. Pala d'Oro and treasury open Easter-Nov M-Sa 9:45am-5pm, Su 2-5pm; Nov-Easter M-Sa 9:45am-4pm, Su 2-4pm. Museum open daily 9:45am-4:45pm.*

▨ PALAZZO GRASSI
MUSEUM

Campo San Samuele 3231   ☎041 52 31 680 ▢www.palazzograssi.it

A highbrow museum of contemporary art that's not afraid to laugh at itself, Palazzo Grassi is at once entertaining and refreshing. Sponsored by François Pinault and affiliated with the **Punta della Dogana** museum in Dorsoduro, Palazzo Grassi features artwork in numerous media from prominent contemporary artists such as **Matthew Day Jackson, Cy Twobly,** and **Jeff Koons.** The Palazzo's signature piece is a series of canvases that constitute a visual interpretation of events in Japanese history. Created by Takashi Murakami over the course of six years, the work was initiated at the behest of Pinault for installation specifically in this gallery. Even if you aren't familiar with modern art, there are enough pieces in enough media here that something is bound to interest, challenge, or even just amuse you. Unlike other sights in Venice, Palazzo Grassi doesn't shy away from self-parody. This is exemplified in Rob Pruitt's "101 Artistic Ideas," a work featured in the Mapping the Studio exhibition. Some of Pruitt's ideas have been put into practice throughout the museum. You might think you've seen every imaginable take on the Renaissance fresco after a few days in Venice, but until you've seen Idea #72 ("Put ◉googly eyes on things") put in practice on a priceless 17th-century mural, you really don't know what you're missing. Palazzo Grassi's sense of humor makes its collections more accessible to those with a casual interest in artwork, as do the frequent events that the museum hosts to introduce visitors to prominent artists and the artistic process. Such events seek to contradict, defy, and critique notions about art while maintaining a certain levity that gives the museum its welcoming, cheeky character.

⚜ *Follow the signs to Palazzo Grassi/Palazzo Fortuny from anywhere in San Marco. If coming from the Rialto Bridge, continue along the streets running parallel to the Grand Canal, staying near the Canal, until you see signs directing you toward Palazzo Grassi. Palazzo Grassi is also immediately adjacent to vaporetto stops S. Samuele (line 2) and S. Angelo (line 1).* ⓢ *€15, with affiliated Punta della Dogana in Dorsoduro €20.* ⌚ *Open M 10am-7pm, W-Su 10am-7pm. Last entry 1hr. before close.*

PIAZZA SAN MARCO
PIAZZA

P. San Marco

Indisputably the most important square in Venice and home to many of the city's most important historical and cultural attractions, P. San Marco is a study in contrasts. Chaotic despite its spectacular views of Venice's serene lagoon, this dignified, historical home of Venetian government is now overrun by tour groups of texting teenagers and foreigners who chase pigeons for amusement. In this way, P. San Marco encapsulates both the best and worst of Venice. When you stand in the square, you're only moments from the **Basilica di San Marco,** the **Campanile,** the **Palazzo Ducale, Saint Mark's Clock Tower,** and almost half a dozen notable museums. You're also just a few steps away from Venice's most upscale shopping and dining establishments, which draw visitors from all over the world. Though not without its high-end attractions, the Piazza has mass appeal as well, with occasional street performers, numerous salesmen offering knock-off designer goods, gelato galore, and the infamous pigeons who have given rise to an industry of their own. Shrewd locals sell stale bread to tourists who want to feed the birds. The

boldest (or dumbest) of these avian-loving visitors cover themselves in bread so as to attract dozens of the flying scourge to roost on them. (Why anyone would want pigeons sitting on their shoulders is a mystery.) It takes a rare disposition to appreciate the Piazza at its chaotic midsummer peak—particularly after the arduous trip into the city, the square's crush of people can be quite overwhelming. It is best to visit early in the morning or late at night, when the Piazza evokes memories of a time before Venice had become one of the world's tourist capitals. In recent years, the Piazza has been known to flood at high tide, so when you are ready to soak up San Marco's old-world glamour, make sure to leave those new Ferragamo pumps you just bought at home.

This is possibly the only place in Venice that isn't hard to find. $ Free.

CAMPANILE — TOWER

P. San Marco ☎041 27 08 311 www.basilicasanmarco.it

One of the most prominent buildings in P. San Marco, the Campanile is undeniably the dominant fixture of the Venetian skyline—so much so that in 1997, a group of separatists advocating the political division of Italy decided to storm the tower to proclaim their message from its heights. The incident, which marked the 200-year anniversary of the end of the Venetian Republic, is one of the tower's few claims to legitimate historical significance, since the original (completed in 1514) spontaneously collapsed in 1902. Remarkably, given the size and central location of the tower, no one was killed during the collapse, and the reconstruction of the tower was completed a decade later. The Campanile has a fully functioning elevator capable of taking over two dozen people to the top of the tower, from which you can enjoy fantastic views of the city. Unfortunately, it's a complete tourist trap, since access to the lift costs €8 and usually requires a substantial wait. Most visitors, at least those without a political message to proclaim from the heights of the tower, will likely be content to admire the simple brick structure of the Campanile from ground level.

In P. San Marco. $ Entrance and lift access €8. Open daily July-Sept 9am-9pm; Oct 9am-7pm; Nov-Easter 9:30am-3:45pm; Easter-June 9am-7pm.

FONDAZIONE DI VENEZIA: FOTOGRAFIA ITALIANA — MUSEUM

P. San Marco 71/C ☎041 22 01 215 www.fondazionedivenezia.org

A small photography museum featuring seasonal exhibits that change frequently, the Fondazione di Venezia's museum of Italian photography is a great addition to P. San Marco. Unlike the other museums in the square, which can become frustratingly expansive and unapproachable after several hours of staring at the similar-looking artifacts that fill each of them, the Italian Photography museum is distinguished by a smaller, selective collection of works presented in an engaging and informative manner. As the name of the museum implies, the Fondazione di Venezia has set up a retrospective on the history of Italian photography, from its late 19th-century influences to its more modern forms. The museum can be thoroughly explored in under an hour and offers greater context and perspective within which to consider the works featured in Venice's other art museums, including both of François Pinault's museums and **The Peggy Guggenheim Collection** in Dorsoduro.

The southwest corner of P. San Marco, opposite the entrance to Museo Correr. $ €5, under 14 and over 65 free. Open M 10am-6pm, W-Su 10am-6pm.

CALLE LARGA XXII MARZO — SHOPPING

Calle Larga XXII Marzo

Venice's premier shopping street might not be as over-the-top ostentatious as those in larger Italian cities such as Rome and Milan, but it features an unrivaled selection of stores featuring the wares of Italy's elite design houses, including Bulgari, Gucci, and Ferragamo. A majority of Italian designers and several internationally prominent brands are interspersed among luxury hotels and fashionable restaurants along this street that manages to reconcile Venice's characteristically modest, understated, neighborhood architecture with world-class shopping surprisingly well. In this way, Calle Larga XXII Marzo escapes the generic international feel that plagues so many premier shopping districts. Though you're unlikely to find anything here that could be considered budget shopping by any stretch of the imagination, the street is still one of San Marco's most scenic locales and an excellent place to browse even if you're not planning to buy anything. For further information, see **Designer Stores**.

Exit the southwest corner of P. San Marco, continue west across a bridge, and you will arrive at Calle Larga XXII Marzo. ⏰ Most stores open daily 10am-7:30pm.

TEATRO LA FENICE ♿ 🍸 THEATRE

Campo S. Fantin 1965 ☎041 78 65 11 💻www.teatrolafenice.it

This theater, formerly known as San Benedetto, was christened *La Fenice* ("The Phoenix") following its reconstruction after a 1773 fire that decimated its original, the heart of Venice's performing arts scene. The star-crossed theater was to burn to the ground twice more, once in 1836 and again in 1996, before being rebuilt in its present form. Each disaster granted the theater's ownership an opportunity to further elaborate on the original design and prove the building worthy of its name. La Fenice continues to host concerts on a nightly basis and remains one of Venice's most prominent and popular centers of the performing arts. The theater's extensive and problematic history makes it exceptionally intriguing to visitors who come for tours before a show or merely to see the inside of one of Europe's most storied theaters. The tour grants visitors access to several levels of seating, including the exclusive box seats reserved during performances for the Italian elite and the famous salons where the theater's esteemed patrons mingle. Though the tour is likely of most interest to those with a background in opera or music, the reconstructed building is marvelous in its rich detail and refined opulence, and the 45min. tour is still a fascinating introduction to one of the centerpieces of Venetian culture. For more information on performances see **Theater**.

Exit the southwest corner of P. San Marco, opposite Basilica di San Marco and take 1st right onto Frezzeria; continue for 3-4min., following the turn left in Frezzeria as the road becomes Calle del Frutariol; turn left at Calle de la Verona; the theater is shortly ahead on the right. $ €7, students under 26, over 65, and holders of the Rolling Venice Card €5. ⏰ Open daily 9:30am-6pm.

TORRE DELL'OROLOGIO-ST. MARK'S CLOCK TOWER CLOCKTOWER

P. San Marco ☎848 08 20 00 💻www.museicivicivenezianі.it

Also known as the Moors' Clock Tower, the Torre dell'Orologio was constructed as a symbol of Venice's wealth, scientific prowess, and artistic skill when the Republic of Venice was near the height of its power. The clock tower, which has undergone little alteration since the beginning of the 16th century, is less impressive than the nearby **Basilica di San Marco** and **Campanile** in terms of sheer size, but its expert artistry rivals any of Venice's more famous sights. Thousands of tourists pass beneath the clock tower each day without knowing that tours of the structure are available. These are run through the Civic Museums of Venice, though visits require prior booking. Many rave about the tour, which features a history of the building as well as views of the clock tower's inner workings, but during peak months, tours may fill up weeks in advance. In addition to a reservation, you'll have to be in good physical condition to navigate the tower's narrow corridors.

*The north end of P. San Marco. **i** Prior booking required. $ €12, ages 6-14 and over 65, students 15-25, and holders of the Rolling Venice card or Museum Pass from the Venice Civic Museums €7. ⏰ Tours available in English M-W at 10am and 11am, Th-Su at 2pm and 3pm.*

MUSEO CORRER

♿⛪☸❄ MUSEUM

P. San Marco 52   ☎041 24 05 211 🖳www.museiciviciveneziani.it

The largest and most impressive of the three museums affiliated with the **Palazzo Ducale**, the Museo Correr exhibits artifacts from the history of Venice in an informative and compelling presentation that offers a refreshing change of pace from the rest of P. San Marco. Though the museum is one of Venice's finest, it's rarely crowded, especially in comparison with the nearby **Basilica** and Palazzo Ducale. Designed to entertain both serious history buffs and tourists seeking shelter from Venice's midsummer heat, the Museo Correr features a different theme relating to the history of Venice in each room, resulting in a surprisingly novel and effective presentation. For the visitor who has no particular interest in ▓medieval coinage, for example, it's easy to bypass the exhibit on that particular subject and continue on to rooms focused on cartography, military history, or any other aspect of Venice's illustrious past. The museum's second floor contains a substantial gallery of medieval and early Renaissance artwork, a boon for sightseers on a tight schedule who would like to visit the **Accademia** but might not have sufficient time to do so. If you're planning to visit the Palazzo Ducale, carve out some time for the Museo Correr, as it offers perhaps the most engaging history of Venice you'll find anywhere in the city.

✣ *Entrance in southwest corner of P. San Marco.* Ⓢ *May-Sept €13, students and seniors €7.50; Nov-Apr €12/€6.50. Free admission with a ticket from the Palazzo Ducale. Pass to all Civic Museums €18/€12.* 🕒 *Open daily Apr-Oct 9am-7pm; Nov-Mar 9am-5pm. Last entry 1hr. before close.*

NATIONAL ARCHAEOLOGY MUSEUM

♿⛪♿ MUSEUM

P. San Marco 52   ☎041 24 05 211 🖳www.museiciviciveneziani.it

Founded in the mid-16th century, the National Archaeology Museum features mostly ancient Roman and Greek artifacts that were regarded as historically significant even at the time of the museum's founding. Unlike most other museums in Venice, which rarely contain any objects predating the city's founding, the National Archaeology Museum has numerous objects in its collection that are over two millennia old. Though the Archaeology Museum is not as well organized as the **Museo Correr**, and many of the artifacts are presented without information to help put them in a historical context, there are still a few items that make the museum well worth a visit. Several Rosetta Stone-esque tablets engraved in Latin and Greek script and fragments of huge statues erected at the height of the Roman Empire's power throughout the Mediterranean are of especial interest.

✣ *Entrance in southwest corner of P. San Marco.* Ⓢ *May-Sept €13, students and seniors €7.50; Nov-Apr €12/€6.50. Free admission with a ticket from the Palazzo Ducale. Pass to all Civic Museums €18/€12.* 🕒 *Open daily Apr-Oct 9am-7pm; Nov-Mar 9am-5pm. Last entry 1hr. before close.*

NATIONAL LIBRARY OF SAINT MARK'S

♿⛪♿ MUSEUM, LIBRARY

P. San Marco 52   ☎041 24 05 211 🖳www.museiciviciveneziani.ite

Also known as the Marciana Library, the National Library of Saint Mark's was founded in the mid-16th century and moved to the western wing of the Palazzo Ducale after the fall of Napoleon. One of the best-preserved collections of original texts and manuscripts from the early Renaissance period, the Marciana Library currently houses over one million books, including tens of thousands of manuscripts and original texts, several drafts of Cavalli's operas, and foundational translations of the Bible. Though the section of the library open to public viewing is relatively small, its incredible design, a testament to the importance of the library for the Venetian state, and the thousands of books shelved within the main section of the library will awe both bibliophiles and the barely literate.

✣ *Entrance in southwest corner of P. San Marco.* Ⓢ *May-Sept €13, students and seniors €7.50; Nov-Apr €12/€6.50. Free admission with a ticket from the Palazzo Ducale. Pass to all Civic Museums €18/€12.* 🕒 *Open daily Apr-Oct 9am-7pm; Nov-Mar 9am-5pm. Last entry 1hr. before close.*

English every Su (except the 4th Su of each month) at 10am,

MUSEUM

☎041 52 00 995 www.museicivicivenezian.it

zo Grassi and Palazzo Fortuny as fairly comparable prominent foundations and featuring exhibitions nately, this perceived similarity doesn't hold up Fortuny is not nearly as impressive or engaging as ce both museums change exhibitions fairly often, either museum might vary according to what is ld be noted that Palazzo Fortuny is a significantly have become a significantly lower priority for the ms of Venice than the more prominent **Palazzo Du-** o. Nonetheless, for the connoisseur of modern art al interest, the museum features exhibitions that ertainly make great use of the gorgeous *palazzo* example, the curators frequently find interesting in the darkness of the *palazzo*'s interior rooms or with the moving water of the small canal adjacent to from the ground floor of the museum. Exhibitions also emes of construction and decline, which are already ripe in that results from placing a modern museum within an ancient te the museum's unique setting, the collection of art displayed on any given day can be relatively small, causing you to regret parting with €6-9 for such a short visit.

From the Rialto Bridge, turn right, walk along the waterfront, continue until you have to turn left, and make the 2nd right onto a street that continues onto a bridge; cross the bridge, continue straight, and make the 1st right possible; the museum is at the end of the street. Signs indicating the direction toward the museum are posted throughout central San Marco. $ €9, students ages 15-25, ages 6-14 and over 65, holders of the Rolling Venice Card, and those with tickets from the Palazzo Ducale or Civic Museums of Piazza San Marco €6. Open M 10am-6pm, W-Su 10am-6pm. Last entry 1hr. before close.

PALAZZO CAVALLI FRANCHETTI PALAZZO, MUSEUM

Campo Santo Stefano 2842 ☎041 53 34 420 www.vivaticket.it

Right across the bridge from the **Accademia** in the Instituto Veneto di Scienze Lettere ed Arti, Palazzo Cavalli Franchetti hosts frequent art exhibitions often featuring the work of 19th- and 20th-century Venetian artists. Exhibitions typically run for several months at a time, and though the artists, movements, and artistic forms vary, the quality of the exhibits remains consistently excellent. Exhibitions tend to be relatively small and rarely feature more than a few dozen works, so a visit to Palazzo Cavalli Franchetti doesn't take an inordinate amount of time. Nonetheless, a visit will often provide greater insight into the work of a particular artist or movement featured in other Venetian museums. The Palazzo, though located in San Marco, is just moments away from the Accademia and an excellent place to visit as part of an art museum day featuring the three major Dorsoduro collections. When visiting the museum, be sure to dedicate at least a few minutes to admiring the *palazzo* itself, which is impressively maintained and features gorgeous frescoes as well as statuary that is almost as impressive as the artwork you'll find in the museum.

Across the Ponte dell'Accademia from the Accademia. $ €9. Open daily 10am-6pm. Last entry 30min. before close. Hours may vary depending on exhibitions featured.

CANNAREGIO

To get the most out of Cannaregio, take the locals' advice and treat your stay here as an opportunity to experience the real Venetian lifestyle rather than as a time for sight-seeing. Most of the notable attractions in the neighborhood are churches which hold architectural as well as religious interest, but the two can't-miss destinations in Cannaregio are the Ca' d'Oro and the Jewish Ghetto.

◪ CA' D'ORO
◆& MUSEUM

Strada Nova 3932   ☎041 52 00 345 ▣www.cadoro.org

A truly Venetian institution, this palace of a few centuries ago now houses one of the most impressive art collections in the region. Comprised of works dating from the city's earliest days, the museum's assortment of art is surprisingly extensive, easily meriting a visit of 2 or 3hr. The ex-*palazzo*'s architecture rivals the art for splendor, as do the views of Venice (perhaps the best you'll find) from the museum's balconies. All of these aesthetic delights make the somewhat pricey tickets *(€6.50)* well worth the expense, even if you're not that into art. Plus, you'll be able to tell your parents of at least one high-culture experience you had while you were in Italy. Ah, *la dolce vita*.

✠ Going east on Strada Nova, find the Ca' d'Oro on the right immediately before reaching Calle della Testa. *i* Bookshop and Loggias only accessible by staircase. ⑤ €6.50, EU citizens 18-25 €3.25, EU citizens under 18 and over 65 free. ② Open M 8:15am-2pm, Tu-Su 8:15am-7:15pm. Last entry 30min. before close.

THE JEWISH GHETTO
& NEIGHBORHOOD

Around Campo di Ghetto Nuovo   ☎041 71 50 12 ▣www.moked.it/jewishvenice

Stepping into Venice's Jewish Ghetto, the first neighborhood in the world to bear a title that has now become so ubiquitous that suburban teens questionably use it to describe their two-year-old cell phones, will give you a taste of what this part of the city was like a few centuries ago. Much of the ghetto's original architecture has been preserved, including several **synagogues**. Although you'll be able to see the buildings of Venice's past, don't expect to witness any Shylock-ian angst—unlike residents who lived here in the 16th century, today's inhabitants of the ghetto are not forced here by government edict. The area remains uniquely Jewish, however, with strong Israeli and Italian-Jewish influences. Many of the signs in this section of Cannaregio are written in Hebrew as well as Italian.

✠ Across the Guglie Bridge going northeast, turn left onto Fondamenta Pescheria, walk 1 block and turn onto Ghetto Vecchio.

CHIESA DEI GESUITI
⊗ CHURCH

Campo dei Gesuiti

Duck into Chiesa dei Gesuiti and be rewarded by the impressive art it contains, including an original work by Titian. Gesuiti was built later (by Venetian standards) than many other churches in Cannaregio, so a visit here will give you a sense of what was hip and happenin' back in the 18th century. Cannaregio's streets are dotted with churches, but if you only have time for one holy encounter, make a beeline for Gesuiti.

✠ From Sestiere Cannaregio, going east, turn right onto Campo del Gesuiti. ② Open M-Sa 10am-noon and 4-6pm.

THE FONDAMENTA NUOVE
& STREET

Northeast Cannaregio

If the tourist hordes of Strada Nova turn you off from Venice's longest street, the broad walkways and cool sea breezes of Fondamenta Nuove should provide a refreshing respite to enjoy excellent views of neighboring islands, most prominently San Michele. The street runs along the northernmost part of Cannaregio, and with several vaporetto stops scattered along its path, Fondamenta Nuove is

venice

always busily trafficked, though never excessively. The Fondamenta Nuove is lined by excellent and sometimes expensive restaurants as well as some of the best gelato shops in Cannaregio, so consider treating your stomach and psyche to this pleasant promenade.

⇨ *Take Calle Larga from Strada Nova to Fondamenta Nuove.*

SANTA MARIA DEI MIRACOLI 🚫♿ CHURCH

Campo dei Miracoli 6075

Unless you have the Chorus Pass (which gets you free admission), it might not be worth the €3 to enter Santa Maria dei Miracoli, but it doesn't cost anything (except a few minutes of your time) to admire the red, white, blue, and gray marble patterns of the church's exterior. Although Santa Maria isn't as imposing as Cannaregio's other churches, some consider it to be one of the city's most beautiful.

⇨ *Follow Calle Castelli west from Teatro Fondamenta Nuove.* $ *€3, with Chorus Pass free.* ⏰ *Open M-Sa 10am-5pm, Su 1-5pm.*

CHIESA DELLA MADONNA DELL'ORTO 🚫♿ CHURCH

Calle Larga Piave 3505/D ☎041 71 99 33 💻www.madonnadellorto.org

Remarkably impressive from the exterior, Madonna dell'Orto has a dimly-lit interior and may not be worth the price of admission *(€3)*. Although a bit of a trek from anywhere else you're likely to be in Cannaregio, it's worth the 5-10min. side-trip if you're interested in architecture.

⇨ *Walk north from Campo dei Mori toward the northernmost part of Cannaregio.* $ *€3, with Chorus Pass free.* ⏰ *Open M-Sa 10am-5pm, Su 1-5pm.*

CHIESA DEGLI SCALZI ♿ CHURCH

Corner of Fondamenta Santa Lucia and Calle Carmalitani

Just steps away from the train station, breathtaking church Scalzi provides backpackers arriving in the city with their first glimpse of Venice's beauty. Its lovely, intricately carved facade should certainly be admired, particularly from the nearby bridge, but avoid eating by the church, where restaurants are generally mediocre and overpriced.

⇨ *From train station, turn left and walk 30sec.* ⏰ *Open daily 7am-noon and 4-7pm.*

SAN POLO

Though a small neighborhood, San Polo has several sights that are well worth visiting. In addition to the **Rialto Bridge** and the area immediately surrounding it, several nearby churches and museums count among Venice's most rewarding destinations.

👍 RIALTO BRIDGE ♿ BRIDGE

Over the Grand Canal

Even before the Rialto Bridge, or *Ponte di Rialto*, was built in 1591, its site at the intersection of four of Venice's six *sestiere* (San Marco, Cannaregio, San Polo, and Castello, to be precise) served as a major point of transfer among Venice's islands. In the 12th century, construction began on a series of bridges to accommodate pedestrian traffic across the **Grand Canal,** but as trade in the Republic of Venice continued to expand, the need for a permanent structure that wouldn't interfere with boat traffic became apparent. Though numerous famous Italian artists of the day were considered, ultimately **Antonio da Ponte** directed the project, deciding on the controversial stone construction that has become a Venetian trademark. The bridge today stands in essentially the same form in which da Ponte designed it, with three lanes of pedestrian traffic divided by two narrow lanes of shops, and it continues to be a center of shopping and dining for Venetian locals and tourists. With glass shops, stores stocked with souvenirs, athletic apparel sellers, trendy boutiques, and *haute couture*, the shopping options on the Rialto Bridge offer something for almost anyone. Those

the grand canal

The best introduction to the city of Venice may be a ride along the Grand Canal, the 4km waterway that is the main thoroughfare for most of Venice's boat traffic. Though many tourists opt to experience the canal via gondola ride, most budget travelers making their way through Italy in smaller groups will find the cost of such a trip, even with the most reasonably priced gondoliers, a bit steep. A much-overlooked option is to hop on the vaporetto Line 2 (*€6.50 per ride*) with a guidebook and take in some of the major sights of Venice from there. Granted, your watery carriage can get a bit crowded, and locals making their way to and from work aren't likely to be enthusiastic about conspicuous tourists in their presence, but if you get on mid-morning when it's not too busy, you'll be able to both admire the facades of Venice's gorgeous *palazzi* with ease and familiarize yourself with the city, for a fraction of what it would cost you to do so on a gondola ride. Whatever transport you opt for, you shouldn't miss an opportunity to see the city from its unique waterways. Since most of Venice's main attractions are located either along the banks of the Grand Canal or the lagoon, standing on *terra firma*, you just can't gain the same appreciation for the majesty of this maritime city as you can when floating on its waters.

venice

who grow tired of browsing should enjoy the vantage point from the bridge's high point, which affords the city's best view of the Grand Canal. Facing north, you'll be able to see some of Venice's best-preserved *palazzi*, while facing south you're sure to be graced with breathtaking visions of the San Marco and San Polo waterfront and gondolas docked along the canal. Those seeking the perfect picture of the bridge should head south on San Marco from the Rialto Bridge, cross two smaller waterfront bridges, and then take a snapshot that captures Rialto's entire span.

✤ *From anywhere in the city, follow the bright yellow signs that say Per Rialto and you will eventually make it to the bridge.*

⬛ FRARI ✦♿ CHURCH
Campo dei Frari 3072   ☎041 52 22 637 ▣www.basilicadeifrari.it

From the outside, Basilica di Santa Maria Gloriosa dei Frari might look like it belongs more in the industrial section of **Giudecca** than in the pantheon of Venice's great churches, but if you make it inside this rough, foreboding brick structure you'll be awestruck by one of the city's largest and most spectacular churches. Second only to the **Basilica di San Marco** in size, the Frari houses numerous notable works by famous artists such as **Bellini** and **Titian** as well as remarkably well-preserved wooden seating that once cradled the bottoms of Venetian nobility and several spectacular mausoleums dedicated to the church's early patrons. The church is large enough to have several smaller rooms that function as museums of the church history and house frescoes, stonework, and historical golden artifacts. Unlike most churches in Venice, which can take just a couple of minutes for the typical tourist to enjoy, it can take an hour to fully appreciate the artistic subtleties of the Frari. The numerous altars are all masterpieces in their own rights, while the mausoleums are a spectacular display of Venice's artistic prowess as well as the egotism and incredible wealth that characterized the city's elite throughout most of its history. Though the church is a spectacular sight to visit at any time of day, try to make it near opening or closing, when there are fewer tour groups around. At these times, every footstep that hits the church's stone floor can be heard echoing under its towering arches, and its serene beauty can be best appreciated.

V: Campo San Tomà. Proceed straight until you reach a T intersection, turn right, make the 1st left, and continue to the square; the entrance to the church is immediately ahead. $ €2.50, with Chorus Pass free. Audio tour €2. ⏰ Open M-Sa 9am-6pm, Su 1-6pm.

SCUOLA GRANDE DI SAN ROCCO — MUSEUM

Campo di San Rocco 3054 ☎041 52 34 864 💻www.scuolagrandesanrocco.it

Home to some of Tintoretto's greatest works as well as canvases by **Titian,** Scuola Grande di San Rocco is not as extensive as many other galleries in Venice, but its works are every bit as impressive. The Scuola Grande was originally designed as a place for laypersons of the Catholic faith to meet and promote various acts of religious piety. In keeping with the purpose of the organization, the canvases here address primarily religious themes, though there's still an interesting contrast between the Scuola's opulence and its intended purpose as a center of charitable giving. Today, the Scuola has been preserved primarily as an art museum, and though the displays are small, the collection is well-organized and quite accessible to visitors. Anyone who has spent hours craning their necks to admire paintings on the ceilings of Venetian museums, *palazzi*, and churches will appreciate the mirrors provided for examining Tintoretto's magnificent religious scenes painted on the second-floor ceiling. As the home of both this spectacle and two beautifully preserved smaller rooms nearby, the second floor is the clear highlight of the museum. Smaller temporary exhibitions are often housed on the first floor, but they generally pale in comparison to the permanent collection.

From Campo dei Frari, walk to the west end of the church, turn right, and follow the signs north toward San Rocco. The school is on the left. $ €7, students €5, under 18 €3. ⏰ Open daily 9:30am-5:30pm. Last entry 30min. before close.

CHIESA DI SAN GIACOMO DI RIALTO — ♿ CHURCH

Campo San Giacomo

Whereas most churches in Venice offer only endless Baroque masterpieces that, while stunning at first, all tend to look pretty similar after the 12th time, Chiesa di San Giacomo di Rialto stands as a remnant of an older Venice. This plain piece of the city's history is rendered all the more poignant by the church's location in the heart of one of Venice's most hectic shopping and nightlife centers. The church, which was consecrated in 421 CE, is as old as the city itself and stands today as a much simpler, more modest edifice than the many other spectacular churches that have filled *La Serenissima.* Covered in dark, faded brick, San Giacomo's exterior evidences its years of history, while its interior tends to focus less on lighting, soaring arches, and breathtaking canvases than most other churches that you'll see. Nevertheless, it feels more authentically Venetian, as it is representative of a local style that was less influenced by Renaissance developments in art and architecture. With drunken teens stumbling about the bars around Rialto, huge TVs blaring soccer matches from around the world, and the perpetually rising tide of Venice almost reaching the northern end of Chiesa di San Giacomo, this stout sanctuary stands as a bit of an anachronism. Yet, in doing so, it encapsulates a great deal of what defines Venice, both past and present.

Immediately before the steps leading up to Rialto Bridge. ⏰ Open M-Sa 10am-6pm.

CAMPO SAN POLO — ♿ PIAZZA

Campo San Polo

As Venice's second-largest public square—you may have heard of the largest, **Piazza San Marco**—Campo San Polo is the default winner of the award for largest Venetian square that doesn't spend half its time under a flood of seawater or tourist traffic. It's also home to some of the city's most important events, including outdoor concerts, screenings for the **Venice Film Festival**, and numerous pre-Lenten festivities during Carnevale. During major events, the square is transformed from a quiet, open space housing a few street vendors and gelato stands into the Venetian equivalent of an amphitheater, packed with tourists and locals enjoying some of the best partying Venice has to offer. Events hosted in Campo San Polo tend to be well-publicized and draw crowds from the Veneto mainland as well as many international arrivals.

Even if there aren't any major events going on in Campo San Polo while you're visiting Venice, this historic square deserves a visit. Formerly the site of bullfights and religious services, the square is now quiet most days and home to several small restaurants and cafes. It's worth spending some time looking at San Polo's historic buildings, including the **Palazzo Tiepolo Passi,** a 16th-century palace that has been converted into a hotel, and the **Chiesa di San Polo,** which houses several works by **Giovanni Tiepolo.**

From the Rialto Bridge, walk through the markets along Ruga dei Oresi, turn left onto Rughetta del Ravano, continue for approximately 4min., and you'll arrive at Campo San Polo.

SANTA CROCE

MUSEUM OF NATURAL HISTORY — MUSEUM

Santa Croce 1730 ☎041 27 50 206 www.museicivicivenezani.it

Venice's Museum of Natural History is one of those rare museums that can be as much fun for adults as it is for children. Unlike many Venetian museums, which house great collections that are presented devoid of context in empty *palazzi*, the Museum of Natural History almost seems like a museum of modern art when you first enter. Fossils hewn into simulated archeological sites rather than housed in glass cases successfully draw the visitor more into the museum experience. Rooms detailing the history of earlier life forms build up the ambience with judicious use of theatrical lighting, while the quiet primordial soundtrack is as entertaining on its own as anything the museum houses. Toward the end of the collection, the artifacts become a bit less impressive, and the last couple of rooms begin to replicate the Museo Correr's bland presentation style. Stay awake for the taxidermy room, though, which is beyond bizarre and should either frighten visitors, entertain them, or do a little bit of both. A full visit to the museum takes 30-60min. and may take even less time for visitors who aren't able to read Italian, since information about the exhibits is displayed in only the one language.

V: San Stae. Continue down Salizada San Stae, make the 1st right that leads to a bridge, continue straight across 2 bridges, then make the 2nd possible right, and continue until you reach the museum. It will be difficult to find, but if you follow the signs to Fontego dei Turchi, you will get there. $ €4.50, students ages 15-25, ages 6-14, over 65, and holders of the Rolling Venice Card €3, under 6 and holders of the Civic Museums pass free. Open W 9am-5pm, Sa-Su 10am-6pm. Last entry 1hr. before close.

CA' PESARO — MUSEUM

Santa Croce 2070 ☎041 72 11 27 www.museicivicivenezani.it

Though in most cities Ca' Pesaro would be deserving of a **thumbpick,** the otherwise spectacular museum is just one of many impressive modern and contemporary art collections in Venice. This museum features an interesting mix of paintings and sculpture—mostly from the late 19th and early 20th centuries—that chronicles the development of modern art as a transnational movement. As one of Venice's more famous art museums, Ca' Pesaro has the added advantage of hosting frequent temporary exhibitions, which generally feature pieces from

venice

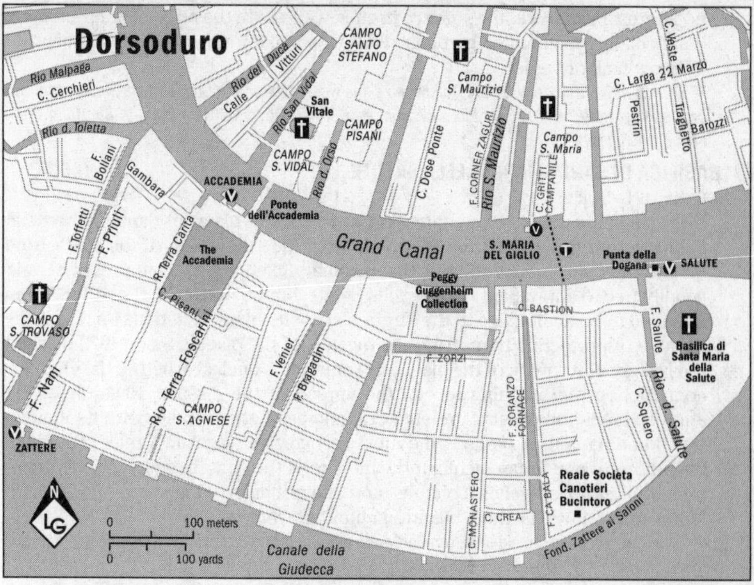

the mid- to late 19th century and tend to be more lowbrow, general-interest affairs than the more esoteric exhibits in its permanent collection. Even those left unimpressed by the art can still marvel at the *palazzo*'s intact ceilings, which far too many visitors miss completely. Others may explore the second floor's gallery of East Asian artwork. Though this exhibit is not nearly as well-presented as the first floor's modern art gallery, the assemblage of Japanese ornamental weaponry accompanied by informational videos about the extensive decorating process is far different from anything else you'll find in Venice.

🧭 V: San Stae. Exit the church square left (facing away from the Grand Canal), cross the 1st bridge possible, continue straight, make the 1st possible left, and you should see the entrance to the museum. There will also be signs indicating the direction toward the museum. $ €6.50, students ages 15-25, ages 6-14, over 65, and holders of the Rolling Venice Card €4, under 6 and holders of the Civic Museums pass free. 🕐 Open Tu-Su Apr-Oct 10am-6pm; Nov-Mar 10am-5pm. Last entry 1hr. before close.

DORSODURO

👍 THE PEGGY GUGGENHEIM COLLECTION 💳♿ MUSEUM

Dorsoduro 704 ☎041 24 05 411 💻www.guggenheim.org

When you walk into a museum and the first room features works by Miró, Picasso, Dalí, and Magritte, you know it's exceptional. The Peggy Guggenheim Collection is a great museum to visit, both for art aficionados and for those who think of karate-kicking turtles when they hear the names of Leonardo, Michelangelo, Donatello, and Raphael. The collection is a relatively small one that includes notable works from almost every major movement of the late 19th and early 20th centuries. It is comprised of works that notable traveler Guggenheim collected during her lifetime, and thus contains pieces that hail from all over Europe and the Americas. Her assortment of artwork emphasizes the international character of art produced during this period while retaining a certain Venetian flair: a substantial number of works are by Venetian and Italian artists. Even if you have no interest in artwork, the *palazzo* itself is well worth the price of admission. Its immaculately maintained gardens and house make it one of the most beautiful *palazzi* in all of Venice.

🧭 From Santa Maria della Salute, follow the signs west towards the Guggenheim Museum for approximately 4min. $ €12, students €7, seniors €10. ⏰ Open M 10am-6pm, W-Su 10am-6pm. Last entry 5:45pm.

👍 BASILICA DI SANTA MARIA DELLA SALUTE — ⊘ CHURCH

Campo della Salute ☎041 52 25 558

Don't make the mistake of contenting yourself with views of Santa Maria della Salute across the water from P. San Marco. While the vision of the sun setting behind the church is incredible, the sanctuary itself is just as impressive—and equally free to enjoy. Santa Maria della Salute, built between 1631 and 1687, was intended to be an homage to the Virgin Mary, who many Venetians believed was capable of protecting them from the ravages of the plague. Since 1629 marked the last great outbreak of the plague in Venice, it is unclear whether the church's construction did anything to end the spread of the disease. Regardless, the church stands today as an architectural and aesthetic wonder, with its innovative dome remaining perhaps the most recognizable sight in Venice. Paintings by Tintoretto and Titian highlight the interior of the church, which also features numerous statues, arches, columns, and altars that have led some to call Santa Maria della Salute the most beautiful church in Venice.

🧭 From the Ponte dell'Accademia, turn left and continue to the eastern tip of Dorsoduro (approximately 6-8min.). ⏰ Open daily 9am-noon and 3-5:30pm.

PUNTA DELLA DOGANA — 🎫♿❄ MUSEUM

Fondamenta della Dogana alla Salute 2 ☎041 52 31 680 💻www.palazzograssi.it

A new museum by the über-chic François Pinault, the Punta della Dogana-Palazzo Grassi complex is an absolute must-see for anyone with an interest in contemporary art. Simultaneously more interactive, more accessible, and more intimidating than any conventional art museum, Punta della Dogana features artwork that is visceral, graphic, and that blurs the distinctions between low and high art—even in a country famed for its Renaissance celebration of the human form, you'd be hard-pressed to find a museum with more phallic representations. A great complement to the collection of earlier works found in the Accademia and the assortment of modernist art featured in the Guggenheim, Punta della Dogana's collection of contemporary art is one of the most impressive in Italy. Due to the combined entry fee, it is especially worth seeing if you also plan to check out the Palazzo Grassi in San Marco.

🧭 From the Ponte dell'Accademia, turn left and continue to the eastern tip of Dorsoduro for 6-8min. $ €15, with affiliated Palazzo Grassi in San Marco €20. ⏰ Open M 10am-7pm, W-Su 10am-7pm. Last entry 1hr. before close.

THE ACCADEMIA — 🎫♿ MUSEUM

Campo della Carità ☎041 52 00 345 💻www.gallerieaccademia.org

Venice's premier museum for pre-19th-century art, the Accademia is currently undergoing extensive renovations that limit the number of visitors it can accommodate daily. These renovations have also changed the museum layout, but the Accademia still remains chock-full of important Italian art. Unlike the **Peggy Guggenheim Collection** or **Punta della Dogana**, which feature relatively few works, the Accademia is home to a substantial collection that will likely leave most casual visitors overwhelmed. Nonetheless, there are several truly awe-inspiring works to be found in its hallways, and there is perhaps no better place than the Accademia to enjoy Venice from an artistic perspective, as many of the works featured represent scenes and sights that will be familiar to travelers who have already spent a few days in the city.

🧭 Immediately across the Ponte dell'Accademia from San Marco. $ €6.50, EU citizens 18-25 €3.25, EU citizens under 18 and over 65 free. ⏰ Open M 8:15am-2pm, Tu-Su 8:15am-7:15pm.

GESUATI
⊗ CHURCH

Fondamenta delle Zattere ai Gesuati 917 ☎041 27 50 462 💻www.chorusvenezia.org

One of Venice's more modern churches, the Gesuati church (also known as Santa Maria del Rosario) was not completed until 1755 and thus reflects a more modern, majestic style than many others within the city. The altars, ceilings, and beautiful natural lighting distinguish Gesuati from other Venetian churches. Its highlights include paintings by Tintoretto and Tiepolo, which make spending a half hour or longer wandering Gesuati's nave very easy to do. You spent enough money to make it to Venice—don't get miserly over the €2.50 entrance fee like so many other tourists. There's no need to resign yourself to pressing your face against the entryway window for 20sec.—drop the cash and enjoy one of Venice's most beautiful churches.

🧭 V: Zattere. Directly across from stop. $ €2.50, with Chorus Pass free. ⏰ Open M-Sa 10am-5pm, Su 1-5pm.

FONDAMENTA ZATTERE
♿ STREET

Fondamenta Zattere

Along with **Fondamenta Nuove**, this is one of Venice's best waterfront streets along which to stroll and enjoy the views. From Fondamenta Zattere you can see Giudecca, which many people believe is best appreciated from across the lagoon. One of the broadest streets in Venice, Fondamenta Zattere is also a prime location to find street performers, cafes, and great docks on which to sit while watching boats go by. Strolling down Zattere, you're sure to see Gesuati, the Accademia, and, if you make it all the way to the end, Punta della Dogana and Santa Maria della Salute, along with many other smaller museums and historic *palazzi*. When in Dorsoduro, don't pick out a couple of prime sights and make a beeline for them—part of what made the neighborhood so appealing to expats and artists in the mid-20th century was the breathtaking views of Venice that are best appreciated from Fondamenta Zattere, so make like Emilio Vedova and soak in the scene.

🧭 Along the southern edge of Dorsoduro. $ Free.

REALE SOCIETA CANOTTIERI BUCINTORO
◉⊗ MUSEUM

Fondamenta Zattere ai Saloni 263 ☎041 52 05 630 💻www.bucintoro.org

A museum perfectly suited for the Queen of the Adriatic, the Reale Societa Canottieri Bucintoro [L]**boating** museum features trophies, articles, banners, designs, and much more paraphernalia from the history of competitive rowing in Venice. It's not a particularly large museum, and a thorough visit can be done in under an hour. You wouldn't guess the size, however, based on the enthusiasm of the people working at the museum, all of whom are members of the boating society and are well-versed in the history of their organization. If you get to the museum at the right time, you might have the good fortune to see a boat brought into the attached workshop for repairs. A uniquely Venetian experience, indeed.

🧭 V: Zattere. Turn right and continue for 3-5min. The museum is on the left. $ €1. ⏰ Open Tu-Sa 9am-6pm, Su 8:30am-1pm.

PONTE DELL'ACCADEMIA
⊗ BRIDGE

Over the Grand Canal

Perhaps the most underappreciated bridge in Venice, the Ponte dell'Accademia, though quaint when compared with the Rialto Bridge's grandeur, is not without its own unique charm. While many locals would have preferred a stone bridge over the Ponte's wooden construction, this design choice has made it a less conspicuous (and therefore less-touristed) sight—a welcome step back from the mercantile overcrowding that makes the Rialto nearly impossible to navigate on busy days. With better views of the Grand Canal than perhaps any other bridge in the city, access to **San Marco** that avoids its busy eponymous *piazza*, and quieter cafes, Ponte dell'Accademia is absolutely worth seeing.

V: Zattere. Turn right, make the 1st possible left, and continue past the Accademia to the end of the street at the Grand Canal, where the bridge is located. $ Free.

islands of the lagoon

The islands in the lagoon surrounding Venice are often given short shrift by travelers on tight schedules, but they have played a vital role in Venetian history and remain fascinating to this day. If you have a couple of hours of free time and the foresight to plot a good vaporetto route from island to island, you can visit a half-dozen of them with relative ease. The one thing shared by the islands is their ability to retain distinct identities. The major islands remain strikingly different from one another and proud of their independent cultural and historical legacies. Some are strongly provincial and have generally eschewed economic diversification, while others have maintained a strong sense of local community despite being subject to change and turmoil. Many are still virtually uninhabited. Visitors tend to have mixed feeling about the islands of the Venetian Lagoon, some considering them not worth the time or trouble, others maintaining that the islands are the main reason to visit the city. If you want a complete overview of the city of Venice, get on a boat and explore the myriad opportunities the lagoon offers.

SAN SEBASTIANO — CHURCH

Campo San Sebastiano ☎041 27 50 462 www.chorusvenezia.org

Before you visit Venice, it might be a good idea to make a long list of churches you want to see. There are a lot. If you are an art aficionado, put this one, perhaps the city's brightest and most colorful, pretty high up. San Sebastiano is home to *History of Esther*, one of Paolo Veronese's most famous works. Despite maintaining the monochromatic, plain facade typical of most Venetian churches, San Sebastiano has an interior decked out with beautiful and historically significant paintings which are as much of a draw as the building itself. In other respects, the edifice is quite similar to the other churches that populate nearly every street corner of the floating city.

Walk east along Fondamenta delle Zattere until it ends; go right, continue past 1 bridge, and turn left onto the 2nd bridge. $ €2.50, with Chorus Pass free. Open M-Sa 10am-5pm, Su 1-5pm.

LIDO

Once the world's most popular beach resort, Lido is largely forgotten by the 20 million travelers who visit Venice annually. Though the island's beautiful and historic hotels still fill up each summer, it's now a quiet counterpart to the city center rather than the main draw for international travelers. As a result, visitors to the island can enjoy scenic bike rides along the coastline, strolls along gorgeous tree-lined streets, and sun-bathing spots on one of its eastern coast's pristine (if occasionally crowded) beaches—all without too much trouble. Since the vaporetto #1 line regularly makes stops at the island, and frequent ferries run from Piazzale Roma, the seeming wall between Lido and the city center is more of a psychological barrier than anything else. If you're in San Marco or eastern Castello, you can easily make a quick 3hr. trip to Lido and see a lot of the island without difficulty.

GRAND VIALE ♿ PROMENADE

Grand Vle.

This famous promenade cuts from eastern Lido—with its majestic hotels and fine restaurants—to the western portion of the island, where you'll find miles of sandy shoreline, gorgeous beach resorts, and the glamorous theaters and hotels that support Lido's annual film festival. A walk along the Grand Viale can take as little as 15min. or as long as several hours, depending on how intent you are on enjoying the sights. Since Lido was largely uninhabited until the 20th century, it lacks the grandly historic character that distinguishes Venice, but you'd never mistake it for a Hawaiian or Caribbean resort community. Walking along the Grand Viale, you'll experience Lido as a resort town worthy of an F. Scott Fitzgerald novel, with beautiful hotels that feature towering columns, breathtaking mosaic facades, and a spectacularly anachronistic sense of Old World aristocracy. If you make it to the eastern side of the island and turn right onto Lungomare Gabriele D'Annuzio, you'll see what may be Lido's most impressive sight, the grandiose and slightly preposterous **Grand Hotel des Bains** (the setting of Thomas Mann's novella *Death in Venice*), which still annually hosts the most impressive gathering of celebrities this side of Cannes during Venice's own film festival.

➜ *From dock Santa Maria Elizabetta, walk straight ahead. The Grand Viale runs east-west.*

SPIAGGE DI VENEZIA 💳♿🍸 BEACH

Piazzale Ravà ☎041 52 61 249 🖥www.veneziaspiagge.it

With hotels limiting access to a lot of the prime stretches of **beach** in Lido, just spending a day on the shore can end up costing over €50 per person simply for chairs, umbrellas, and towels. Spiagge di Venezia—which manages two popular stretches of beach in Lido—is the more budget-conscious option if you want to soak up the sun without spending too much cash. You could certainly rack up the charges with food, drinks, a changing room, and umbrella and chair, but none of these are necessary to enjoy Lido's magnificent sandy expanses and pristine waters.

➜ *From dock Lido San Nicolò, go east on V. Giannantonio Selva for 6-8min. and you'll reach the Spiagge.* $ *Beach free. Umbrella and chair €12. Private changing room €23.* 🕐 *Open daily 9am-7pm.*

GIUDECCA

Giudecca, technically a part of Dorsoduro but separated from the neighborhood by the Giudecca Canal, is the most easily accessible of the lagoon islands, as the vaporetto #2 line zigzags the Giudecca Canal and makes several stops on the island. A €2 ticket for crossing the Giudecca canal supposedly exists, but the vaporetto operators *Let's Go* spoke with said they didn't care if we hopped on for one stop free of charge. Thanks guys! In recent years there has been talk of constructing a tunnel between Dorsoduro and Giudecca, but it appears no such plans will be implemented in the foreseeable future. Giudecca seems to have a rather cyclical history. It was first inhabited by wealthy families who claimed a preference for large estates with gardens but were really being pressured to leave the city due to political controversy. The lack of large-scale residential development on the island later made Giudecca the center of the city's early 20th-century industrial boom, and for a time, the island produced the vast majority of commercial boats used in the city. After WWII, Giudecca lacked viable industry and fell into disrepair but is completing the cycle again with the development of upscale housing and hotels. Though Giudecca is coming back into fashion, its industrial history remains an influence: the island's most prominent landmark and one of Venice's most prestigious hotels, **The Molino Stucky Hilton,** is located in a former granary and flourmill which retains a sternly industrial exterior despite its interior's refinement and elegance.

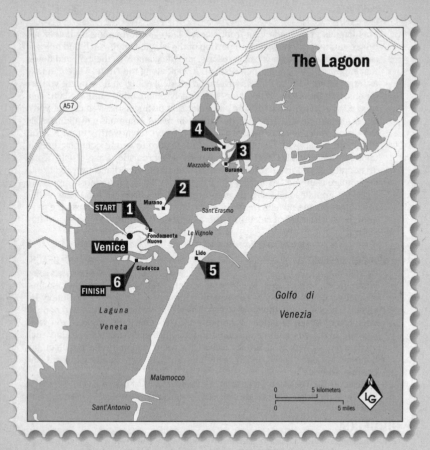

lagoon

1. FONDAMENTA NUOVE. Your starting point for a tour around the lagoon islands of Venice is in the city itself. When we talk about the islands in the lagoon, it's easy to forget that the island lagoons aren't on the periphery of the city—they *are* the city. The islands that make up what we think of as "Venice" just happen to be the closest bunched. Anyhow, the vaporetto stops along the Fondamenta Nuove in northern Cannaregio are the most convenient places from which to access the northern lagoon islands. Before you depart, take a few minutes to appreciate the sea breezes and fantastic views out over the water. It might be a good idea to pack a picnic for the trip, since restaurants on some islands are few and far between, and many are just out to hook in tourists wandering aimlessly and hungrily around the islands. Alternatively, just fill up in the top-quality gelato stores that line the Fondamenta Nuove, although you'd have to eat a lot to last you all day. Once you're ready to leave your landlubber ways behind, hop on the vaporetto line LN towards the first island, Murano.

2. MURANO. Murano is often called "The Glass Island," and that's the main thing it's got going on. Murano is around the same size as the *sestiere* in Venice, and, like them, is crisscrossed by a number of canals and connected by many bridges. Though it isn't the most charming of Venice's islands, this first stop makes a nice transition to the more beautiful treats still to come. Once you've had your fill of glass workshops (and maybe bought a little something to take home, if you can afford it), get back on the LN vaporetto and continue on your way,

3. BURANO. For all you fans of artisan goods, Burano will be the perfect stop after Murano. To complement your transparent glassware, pick up some classy white lace. If you couldn't care less about lace and find the color white boring, then Burano is still a great place to visit. Admire the colorful houses lining the docks here; they certainly offer a very different kind of waterfront housing from the *palazzi* lining the Grand Canal. To get to Torcello, take the T or N vaporetto line.

4. TORCELLO. Probably the strangest of all the lagoon islands, Torcello offers the biggest contrast from anything else you'll find in Venice. Largely deserted today, it offers few remnants of the days when 20,000 people lived here—most buildings were torn down and had their materials recycled over the last several centuries. Torcello makes the perfect continuation from Burano, since both offer plenty of greenery and open space in which to reflect and get away from the tourist masses of Venice proper. Once you've gotten all the reflection time you need, take the N vaporetto back to Burano and switch to the LN to head to the most famous island in the Venetian Lagoon: Lido.

5. LIDO. Rather like Torcello, Lido has fallen somewhat from its former prosperity. It certainly hasn't fallen quite as far, though. Unlike in its northern counterpart, plenty of people do still live here, and a fairly strong tourist economy survives. If all the walking all morning has tired you out, now would be a great time to plop yourself down on the sandy beach and eat that picnic you packed. If you happen to be here in early September (or were intelligent enough to plan it that way), you can sample the style and spectacle of the Venice Film Festival. If here at any other time, much of the style remains (the island is packed with luxury hotels), although the spectacle might be a little reduced. Take as long as you want lounging or strolling on the glorious Grand Viale promenade; you're experiencing the undoubted crown jewel of the Venetian Lagoon. After a few hours—or sooner if you're the kind of person who hates sand—you can head back to the big city, or continue to the final major lagoon island.

6. GIUDECCA. La Giudecca is technically part of Venice proper, in the Dorsoduro *sestiere*. However, some kind of water transportation is required to get there and it certainly feels very different from the rest of the city. To get here from Lido, you'll need to head back to the main city itself first: take vaporetto line 1 and switch at San Zaccaria to the Giudecca-bound line 2. That boat zig-zags up the island, so you have the choice of getting off at Giudecca's eastern or western end (or you can get off in the middle, of course). Getting off at Redentore will put you right Il Redentore, Andrea Palladio's spectacular church that, despite some hefty competition, is one of the architectural highlights of Venice. Take a break from all the Byzantine influence that permeates the city and enjoy the elegant Classical designm although even Palladio incorporated a few Eastern elements. Try to guess what they are! (Hint: look at the towers.) After appreciating that (and heading inside to view some magnificent artwork by the likes of Tintoretto and Veronese), take some time to explore Giudecca, an industrial but increasingly fashionable part of Venice. To get back to the city, hop back on the vaporetto 2. We hope you enjoyed touring the Venetian lagoon, one of Venice's foremost but most forgotten attractions.

WALKING TOUR

LET'S GO www.letsgo.com ✦✦✦

IL REDENTORE — CHURCH

Campo S.S. Redentore 195 ☎041 27 50 462 💻www.chorusvenezia.org

One of Venice's most celebrated churches, Il Redentore is by far the biggest attraction on Giudecca. The church, which was constructed to give thanks for divine deliverance from the plague (perhaps a bit prematurely) in 1577, is considered one of **Andrea Palladio's** greatest works, displaying his acute awareness of proportion in architectural design. Inside the church, paintings from some of the city's greatest artists, including **Saraceni, Veronese,** and **Tintoretto** hang, underscoring the prominence of the church in Venetian society. So highly regarded was Palladio's masterpiece that it gave rise to its own festival, the **Festa del Redentore,** which began as an annual political procession from the **Doge's Palace** to the church and, though now largely devoid of religious sentiment, continues to be celebrated every third weekend in July.

 # Take vaporetto line #2 to Redentore; the church is immediately ahead. $ €2.50, with Chorus Pass free. Elevator to campanile €4. ⏰ Open M-Sa 10am-5pm. Last entry 15min. before close.

MURANO

Known colloquially as "The Glass Island," Murano is one of the largest lagoon islands and has been the center of Venice's glass industry since the 13th century, when concerns about the possibility of fires in the city center led politicians to ban glass production. Of course, safety concerns never stopped enterprising Venetians from *selling* the glass anywhere, and buyers of the stuff are everywhere. Nevertheless, Murano remains the glass headquarters of Venice. Though the large brick buildings, open kilns, and occasional abandoned workshops give the island a slightly gritty industrial feel, it also features a few beautiful tree-shaded streets with glass shops displaying the work of the island's top artisans. If you spend more than a few minutes exploring Murano, you're almost certain to find a *fornace* in operation where you can see some of the world's most talented artisans practicing their craft. If you're lucky, you might even find a studio that lets visitors try their hand at glass blowing. Travel times to Murano vary, but expect to spend at least 30min. getting there by vaporetto lines #41, 42, or LN, which are generally the most accessible options.

MUSEO DEL VETRO — MUSEUM

Fondamenta Giustinian 8 ☎041 73 95 86 💻www.museiciviciveneziani.it

Anyone with enough interest in artisan glass to visit Murano shouldn't leave without checking out the Museo del Vetro, which traces the development of Murano's glass industry from its earliest stages to the present day. The museum features several exceptional pieces, both contemporary and historical, that reflect the ways in which glass has been historically used both practically and aesthetically. Though the collection is impressive, the real draw is the wing dedicated to glass production that gives an overview of how different glasses are made and the minerals that are used to give the material its different colors and textures. Don't miss the museum garden and its fascinating artifacts.

 # V: Museo (accessible by lines R, 41, 42, N, and DM). Follow the signs to the museum. $ €6.50, students ages 15-25, ages 4-14 and over 65, and Rolling Venice Card holders €4. Admission included in Civic Museums Pass. ⏰ Open daily Apr-Oct 10am-6pm; Nov-Mar 10am-5pm. Last entry 30min. before close.

BASILICA DI SANTA MARIA E SAN DONATO — ♿ CHURCH

Calle San Donato 11 ☎041 73 90 56

A unique church, Murano's Basilica contrasts sharply with the Renaissance architecture that you'll find throughout Venice and Italy as a whole. With distinct Byzantine influences in its exterior, elaborate arches, and strong geometric patterns, the Basilica embodies Eastern influences that have profoundly shaped the development of Venetian culture and society. The floors within the church, comprised of thousands upon thousands of jewel-like tiles, are incredibly intricate and some of the city's most breathtaking mosaics. What really sets the church apart, though, are the two displays near the altar. The first, a giant glass cross that symbolizes Murano's pride in its local industry, outshines practically every other glass trinket you'll find on the island. The second, probably Venice's most unusual church display, is a collection of bones reputed to be the remains of a **dragon** killed by the church's namesake, Saint Donatus of Arezzo. The bones, which are over 1m long each, have never been definitively identified and remain a source of wild speculation.

V: Museo (accessible by lines R, 41, 42, N, and DM). Walk past the museum along the canal for about 2min.; the church is ahead on the left. $ Free. Open daily 8am-7pm.

BURANO

Burano—about an hour away from Venice by vaporetto lines LN and N—is a relatively small island best known for its handmade lace production and fishing industry. Visitors to Burano almost inevitably stop in Murano first, since that island is on the way from Venice, and are consistently surprised at the contrast between the two. Whereas Murano is populated by brick and stone buildings and is almost as devoid of vegetation as Venice, Burano boasts several large parks, lots of open space, and famously colorful houses. Originally, at least according to legend, the fishermen of the island painted their homes ostentatious shades of blue, pink, red, green, yellow, and orange so that each could readily identify his home from a distance when returning to the island, and the fantastically colorful homes have evolved into a Burano trademark. While this tradition is now somewhat obsolete given technological improvements in nautical navigation, lace production in Burano continues in much the same fashion that it has for centuries. Though you can shop for Burano-style lace in Venice, Burano itself is the best place to find a wide selection of lace goods that are guaranteed to be handmade. Be forewarned, however, that the lace production process is labor-intensive, and that labor will be reflected in the price of pretty much anything you buy. Even if you're not shopping for lace, it's still absolutely worth paying a visit to Burano. An hour or two of wandering will bring you to the beautiful **Church of San Martino** and its infamous leaning campanile; the **Lace Museum** *(P. Galuppi 187 ☎041 73 00 34)*, which is returning in 2011 after an almost year-long sabbatical; and some of the most beautiful and whimsical buildings in all of Venice.

TORCELLO

Accessible by vaporetto line N and a ferry (T) from Burano, Torcello isn't the easiest island to get to but definitely rewards those who make the effort. Though the island—the first settlement in the lagoon—was once home to over 20,000 people, from the 12th to the 15th centuries it was largely abandoned as the lagoon surrounding it became a swamp. Torcello is now home to only a few dozen people managing a couple of restaurants, a hotel, and the scant attractions that bring tourists to the island. Walking around this bit of land can be a surreal experience; it's hard to comprehend that this largely abandoned and overgrown island once was home to the largest population center of the Venetian Republic. So few relics remain.

CATHEDRAL OF SANTA MARIA ASSUNTA — CHURCH

Isola di Torcello ☎041 27 02 464

Founded over 13 centuries ago, the Cathedral of Santa Maria Assunta offers a strong reminder of the thriving community that once existed on Torcello. It's definitely not worth making the trip all the way out to Torcello just for this small church, but as an example of the eclecticism in Venice's early places of worship, its mosaics and incredible rendering of the Last Judgment are engaging. The campanile, once abandoned, is again in operation and affords the best view of the northern lagoon you'll find anywhere. Also affiliated with the cathedral are the smaller churches of **Santa Fosca** and **Museo di Torcello,** both of which are sure to fascinate any visitors intrigued by the strange history of Venice's abandoned island.

➡ From the island's only vaporetto stop, follow the path to the island's only substantial settlement. It's a 7-10min. walk; just look for the tower in the distance. $ Church €4. Campanile €4. Both €7.50. ⏰ Open daily Mar-Oct 10:30am-6pm; Nov-Feb 10am-5pm.

SAN GIORGIO MAGGIORE

A small island adjacent to Giudecca, San Giorgio Maggiore is notable mostly for its eponymous church and the adjacent monastery. The island is accessible by vaporetto lines #2, N, LN, 20, and CL.

BASILICA DI SAN GIORGIO MAGGIORE — 👍♿ CHURCH

Isola di Giorgio Maggiore — ☎041 52 27 827

Basilica di San Giorgio, in addition to being the subject of one of Monet's most spectacular works (*San Giorgio Maggiore at Dusk*, the painting stolen in the 1999 remake of 🎬**The Thomas Crown Affair**), is considered one of the crowning achievements of Venice's Classical Renaissance architecture. Constructed in a style reminiscent of a Roman temple, the church is second only to the nearer **Santa Maria della Salute** in the hierarchy of remarkable sights that can be seen from P. San Marco. The church's interior houses large, strikingly lifelike and vivid canvases painted by **Ricci** and **Tintoretto,** which are in proportion with the awesome majesty of the whole place. Though the church itself ranks among Venice's best, perhaps the main attraction is the *campanile*, which provides incredible views north to the neighborhood of San Marco. Attached to the church, a former monastery is now occupied by the **Cini Foundation,** a cultural organization that manages the **Teatro Verde** and frequently hosts exhibitions that are among the best in Venice.

➡ From the island's only vaporetto stop, the church is about 30m directly ahead. $ Free. Ride to the top of the campanile €3, students €2. ⏰ Open daily May-Sept 9:30am-noon and 2-5:30pm; Oct-Apr 9:30am-noon and 2-5:30pm.

food

As you might expect in a city visited by over 20,000,000 tourists each year, Venice has no shortage of restaurants. Almost all are receptive to international travelers and offer English-language menus and service, particularly those where the tourist industry is centered.

Since visitors to Venice range from international celebrities to student backpackers, most restaurants try to accommodate all tastes and budgets. Even in the most upscale Venetian restaurants, you should typically be able to get a pizza for less than €10. That being said, a few restaurants in prime locations bank on being able to overcharge hungry tourists who don't have the energy to look beyond the first place they see. Avoid suffering a less-than-memorable *and* expensive meal and do a bit of comparison shopping before settling on an eatery. Also take note of whether you should expect a service charge. These should be written on the menu of most establishments that have one. While common, the service charge can come as an unpleasant surprise.

Most restaurants in Venice serve food typical of the Veneto region, which shouldn't offer any particular surprises for travelers familiar with the basics of Italian cuisine. Risotto, beans, and polenta are particularly popular here. Menus tend to be rather seafood-heavy, but pasta, chicken, and steak are also fairly standard offerings. Pizza, of course, is a staple of almost every dining establishment. Since the tradition of eating cat in Northern Italy has been banned, there shouldn't be anything too troubling on the menu for English-speaking tourists, with the possible exceptions of squid-ink pasta *(nero di seppia)* and **horse** meat *(cavallo)*, which aren't too common. For students really looking to save time and money, sandwich shops, snack bars, kebab shops, and small pizzerias often offer decent and reasonably filling meals, including drink, for less than €6.

grocery greatness: part 1

Since pretty much every hotel in Venice is "breakfast included," but most are about as liberal with croissants and cereal as they are with Wi-Fi, expect your morning sustenance to consist of little more than a roll with Nutella (maybe some orange juice if the management is feeling magnanimous). At a grocery store, however, you can get fresh fruit and bread, both more substantial than what most hotels offer for breakfast. Plus, purchasing them at the grocery store means you don't have to get up at 8:30am.

When grocery shopping in Venice, you have two options: supermarkets or smaller local stores. Here are the pros and cons of supermarkets.

PROS

1) Supermarkets tend to have a greater selection. Back home, this probably means more choice and better value. In Venice, this means getting to laugh at absurd products like Durex Jeans, a brand of condom whose marketers apparently failed to consider the uncomfortable implications of comparing their particular product to another with the texture of denim.

2) The music. America brought the world Isis, MC Hammer, and Michael Jackson, but you have to travel halfway around the world to hear music of that quality blasting in a supermarket.

3) Many Italian supermarkets stock incredible fresh baked goods, Italian cheeses, and more kinds of sliced deli meat than you knew existed. This can quickly become a "con" if going home looking like Marlon Brando in the mid-'90s isn't part of your travel plans.

CONS

1) Really, really long check-out lines. If you're buying a six-pack of Birra Moretti, expect it to be a three-pack, at best, by the time you get out.

2) You shouldn't even try to speak English with the check-out-counter employees, who don't appreciate delays while trying to keep lines manageable. If you do make the attempt, they will probably look at you with about as much contempt as they would if you had just propositioned them with a box of Durex Jeans.

3) Familiar brands aren't always what they seem. You might think you can guess what the Italian on your box of soap means, but you'll be playing with fire. Don't make the mistake of one *Let's Go* researcher, who spent two weeks washing his hair with what turned out to be women's body wash. You, too, could reap the benefits of delightful added volume, but the extra scent might be a bit overbearing...

food

SAN MARCO

Like most things in San Marco, dining tends to be expensive and upscale. You'll find some of Venice's best restaurants here, but they tend to be some of the priciest as well. Despite this trend, there are a surprising number of restaurants that offer great values, particularly if you're willing to trek a couple blocks away from P. San Marco and the Rialto Bridge.

👍 TRATTORIA PIZZERIA AI FABBRI — 💳♿🍸❄ TRATTORIA, PIZZERIA [3]

Calle dei Fabbri 4717 ☎041 52 08 085

An eclectic pizzeria that cooks up more than just your conventional *margherita* and *quattro formaggi* varieties, Pizzeria Ai Fabbri is distinguished by a high degree of culinary creativity, evident in their unusual appetizers (including sumptuous duck dumplings) and wide selection of side dishes that wouldn't find their way onto a typical Venetian menu. Though a flatscreen TV by the entrance tuned into news or soccer matches gives the restaurant a bit of a bar-ish feel, those who would prefer a quiet meal in the back dining room can enjoy the same excellent menu in a more serene setting.

➡ Go through the St. Mark's Clock Tower, turn left, continue to Calle dei Fabbri, and continue for 2-3min.; the restaurant is on the right. [$] Entrees €7.50-23. ⏰ Open daily 11am-midnight.

👍 BISTROT DE VENISE — 💳♿🍸❄🌳 RISTORANTE [4]

Calle dei Fabbri ☎041 52 36 651 💻www.bistrotdevenise.com

With an innovative menu that features historic recipes citing origins in the 16th century (which appears to be when the restaurant won its first award, given the incredible number of honors it has since racked up), Bistrot de Venise specializes in traditional Venetian food prepared to the absolute highest standard. Though the sticker shock might dissuade some budget travelers, if you want a world-class meal in San Marco, you won't find anything nearly this good for anything less.

➡ Go through the St. Mark's Clock Tower, turn left, continue to Calle dei Fabbri, and continue for about 2min.; the restaurant is on the right. [$] Entrees €18-28. ⏰ Open M-Th noon-3pm and 7pm-midnight, F-Sa noon-3pm and 7pm-1am, Su noon-3pm and 7pm-midnight.

RISTORANTE NOEMI — 💳♿🍸❄🌳 RISTORANTE [5]

Calle dei Fabbri 912 ☎041 52 25 238 💻www.ristorantenoemi.com

For those of you craving a steak or some veal after weeks spent subsisting on a carb-heavy Italian diet, Ristorante Noemi should make its way onto your radar, as it is reputed to serve up some of the best grilled food in Venice. Affiliated with the upscale Hotel Noemi but catering to a clientele that goes beyond the hotel's guests, this restaurant offers high-quality traditional Venetian food at respectable prices, especially if you manage to avoid the temptation to order the menu's highest-priced items.

➡ Go through the St. Mark's Clock Tower, turn left, continue to Calle dei Fabbri, and continue 2min.; the restaurant is on the right. [$] Entrees €8-34. ⏰ Open daily 11:30am-midnight.

ACQUA PAZZA — 💳♿🍸❄🌳 SEAFOOD [5]

Campo San Angelo 3808 ☎041 27 70 688 💻www.veniceacquapazza.it

Acqua Pazza, roughly translated as "Crazy Waters," is both the name and the motif of this fine restaurant near San Marco's two modern art museums. Featuring excellent seafood and bizarre, though amusing, aquatically inspired decor—Acqua Pazza is just as sweet as it is salty—its €12 house desserts are some of the best confections Venice has to offer.

➡ From Teatro La Fenice, continue northwest on Calle de la Verona for less than 2min., take the 1st left after crossing a bridge, take the next right, and take the next left; the restaurant is in Campo San Angelo. ℹ Men are required to wear long pants to dinner. [$] Entrees €18-35. ⏰ Open daily noon-3pm and 7pm-11pm.

BAR MIO 💳♿🍸 SNACK BAR ❶

Frezzeria 1176

If you're feeling bold, try to claim a spot at Venice's most heavily trafficked snack bar. You'll be rewarded with a sandwich crisped to perfection—though never overheated—at a pleasantly low price. You're unlikely to see any other tourists in Bar Mio, but that doesn't mean the place is starving for business. The incredibly efficient employees don't have a moment's rest from opening to close, as locals constantly stream in for first-class coffee and sandwiches.

➜ Exit the southwest corner of P. San Marco, opposite Basilica di San Marco, and take 1st right onto Frezzeria; the restaurant is less than 1min. ahead on the right. $ Sandwiches €4.50-7. ⏰ Open daily 6:30am-9pm.

RISTORANTE ANIMA BELLA 💳♿🍸 RISTORANTE ❸

Calle Fiubera 956 ☎041 52 27 486

A quirky and small restaurant that bills itself as a combination *ristorante*, pizzeria, and grill, Anima Bella is more reminiscent of the dining room in a typical Italian villa than a tourist-filled restaurant in San Marco. Since Anima Bella tends to focus on relatively few dishes prepared exceptionally well, you could order anything off the menu without regretting it. However, while everything here is prepared with care, you could eat ravioli for weeks in Venice and find none that match the quality you'll get at Anima Bella.

➜ Exit P. San Marco beneath St. Mark's Clock Tower, take 1st possible left onto a street with a bridge and cross the bridge; the restaurant is on the right. $ Entrees €8-20. ⏰ Open daily 11am-10pm.

RISTORANTE AL COLOMBO 💳♿🍸❄️🌳 RISTORANTE ❺

Corte del Teatro 4619 ☎041 52 22 627 💻www.alcolombo.com

Many upscale restaurants in San Marco offer similar menu items at equal prices, but none can match Ristorante Al Colombo's excellent patio, jovial service, and delightful Chateaubriand. Unlike many fine restaurants in San Marco whose excessive formality pushes them to the point of dourness, Ristorante Al Colombo isn't afraid to have a bit of fun. Case in point: the spectacular centerpieces arranged around national team soccer balls that one *Let's Go* researcher witnessed while visiting at the peak of World Cup fever.

➜ From the Rialto Bridge, turn right and continue along Riva del Carbon for approximately 2min.; turn right onto Calle del Carbona and continue for 1min.; the restaurant is in the square. $ Entrees €16-45. ⏰ Open daily noon-midnight.

HOSTARIA AI CORISTI 💳♿🍸❄️🌳 RISTORANTE ❸

Calle delle Veste 1995 ☎041 52 26 677 💻www.hostariaaicoristi.com

A phenomenal place to take a date out for dinner before a romantic night at the opera, Coristi is one of the few truly upscale restaurants in San Marco where you can enjoy an excellent meal without spending too much coin. Featuring traditional Venetian seafood, pizzas, and pasta, Hostaria complements its delectable cuisine with subtle lighting, exceptional woodwork, and refined traditional Venetian decor that should get you ready for an elegant evening.

➜ Exit the southwest corner of P. San Marco, opposite Basilica di San Marco, take 1st right onto Frezzeria and continue for 3-4min., following the turn left in Frezzeria as the road becomes Calle del Frutariol; turn left at Calle de la Verona and continue past the theater; the restaurant is on the left. $ Entrees €7-23. ⏰ Open M-Tu, Th-Su noon-11pm.

RISTORANTE AI DUE VESCOVI 💳♿🍸❄️🌳 RISTORANTE ❸

Calle Fiubera 812A-813 ☎041 52 36 990 💻www.aiduevescovi.com

Ristorante Ai Due Vescovi is perfect for a group of people who can't agree on whether to hit up a sit-down restaurant for some fine dining or grab a quick bite at the pizzeria. Ai Due Vescovi is a little bit of both. While the classic standby of crusty fresh-baked pizza is definitely on deck, the menu also offers an exceptional selection of risottos and local cheeses.

➜ Exit P. San Marco beneath St. Mark's Clock Tower; take 1st possible left onto a street with a bridge, and cross the bridge; the restaurant is on the left. $ Entrees €6.50-32. ⏰ Open daily noon-3pm and 6-10pm.

RISTORANTE LA FELUCA 💳♿🍸❄ RISTORANTE [3]

Calle della Mandola 3648 ☎041 24 12 785 💻www.ristorantelafeluca.com

This seems like a thoroughly decent though unremarkable Venetian restaurant—until you dig into the 🍰**dessert,** that is. These over-the-top cakes, pastries, tiramisu, and other Venetian sweet treats, are so irresistible that if VH1 left Biz Markie and Kevin Federline alone with it for about 10min., *Celebrity Fit Club* wouldn't have to worry about finding new contestants for the show's next three seasons.

➜ Go through the St. Mark's Clock Tower, turn left, continue to Calle dei Fabbri, continue for 2min., and turn left at the 2nd left after the 2nd bridge you cross; continue through Campo S. Luca, then through Campo Manin. The restaurant is on Calle della Mandola on the left. $ Entrees €8-23. ⏰ Open daily 10am-11pm.

TRATTORIA-PIZZERIA AL GALLO D'ORO 💳♿🍸❄⛅ PIZZERIA [3]

Calle dei Fabbri 1075 ☎041 52 30 624

Offering more substantial entrees than many other comparable restaurants that want you to order numerous courses, Gallo D'Oro also distinguishes itself with great pastas, delicious gnocchi, and a superb selection of desserts. Its outdoor seating is pleasantly tucked away down a less frequented side street.

➜ Go through the St. Mark's Clock Tower, turn left, and continue to Calle dei Fabbri; the restaurant is immediately ahead on the left. $ Entrees €6.50-22. ⏰ Open daily noon-11pm.

CANNAREGIO

As many great places as there are to eat in Cannaregio, there are just as many mediocre and touristy options. Stay away from the main streets and menus targeting out-of-towners, and you'll find some of the best cuisine Venice has to offer.

👍 **RISTORANTE CASA BONITA** 💳♿🍸⛅ RISTORANTE [3]

Fondamenta S. Giobbe 492 ☎041 52 46 164

One of the trickiest things about eating in Venice is that almost every restaurant claims to be authentically Venetian and displays a mouth-watering menu—then you walk in and realize that there are more Germans than Italians in the house. Casa Bonita is the rare Venetian restaurant that is both accessible from the main thoroughfares and genuinely Venetian. Often packed throughout the day, this restaurant caters to local tastes with excellent food in generous portions for a reasonable price. The canal-side outdoor seating is excellent, and the bar gives you any number of excuses to stay at your table and people-watch after your meal.

➜ From the train station, turn left and walk 5min. down Lista de Spagna. Immediately before Guglie Bridge, turn left and continue for 4min. $ Entrees €12-18. ⏰ Open Tu-Su 10am-3pm and 5:30pm-1am.

OSTERIA BOCCADORO VENEZIA 💳♿🍸⛅ RISTORANTE [5]

Campo Widmann 5405/A ☎041 52 11 021 💻www.boccadorovenezia.it

Unlike your typical Venetian restaurant, Osteria Boccadoro Venezia offers an haute-cuisine reinterpretation of the region's traditional foods. Although Osteria Boccadoro's prices may seem excessive, rest assured that its food merits the cost. The restaurant's minimalist, modern aesthetic might not match up to your standard idea of what a fine Venetian restaurant looks like, but in sacrificing a bit of tradition, this *osteria* has foregone nothing in terms of stomach-pleasing fare, winning over discerning locals and tourists alike with its quality dishes.

⇟ Halfway along Calle Widmann. $ Entrees €20-28. ⏰ Open Tu-Su noon-2:30pm and 7-10:30pm.

grocery greatness: part 2

Since we've unloaded all our cheap jokes at the expense of supermarkets, it's now time to do exactly the same for local grocery stores. These are everywhere and range from small convenience stores to bakeries and *gelaterie* that also stock basic grocery items.

CONS

1) They're never open. You thought supermarkets had limited hours? Getting an audience with your local grocer is about as difficult as getting one with the pope.

2) Expiration dates can be dicey. Definitely remember that they're marked the European way–Day/Month/Year, not Month/Day/Year. You don't want to forget that when you're getting milk for your cereal, as some of us have found out the hard way.

3) These stores are small, and Italian customer service involves much more observation of customers than actual servicing of them. Expect uncomfortable moments.

PROS

1) Whereas chain stores tend to have set selections to keep up with their competitors, local stores are able to feature more variety in accordance with their owners' tastes. In most cases, this means more absinthe–a lot more.

2) They're a surprisingly good place to watch soccer matches. Sure, it might take 45min. to find someone willing to ring up your bottle of water and croissant, but if you're here, you're probably on vacation anyway–just enjoy the snapshot of Italian culture.

3) The owners tend to be really friendly, and if you're willing to chat, you're sure to get tips on some hidden Venetian gems, such as restaurants and cafes you would otherwise never visit. This can be problematic if one of these "hidden gems" happens to be a grandniece who just so happens to be your age ("You are about 30 years?"), speaks English "very good," and the owner would just love to introduce her to you.

TRATTORIA STORICA 🍴♿🍸 RISTORANTE [3]

Ponte dei Gesuiti 4858 ☎041 52 85 266 💻www.trattoriastorica.it

Trattoria Storica is an upscale, family-operated Venetian restaurant with exceptionally friendly service and great food. An excellent choice for anyone looking to savor a longer meal in a quieter section of Cannaregio, Storica offers generous portions that make for a very filling dinner, though you might consider splitting one of their dishes for lunch with a fellow traveler. With a helpful English-language menu, the restaurant does a great job welcoming foreigners without compromising its Venetian character.

⇟ Exiting the Gesuiti to Campo dei Gesuiti, turn left and cross the bridge; Storica is on the left. $ Entrees €16-22 . ⏰ Open daily 11am-4pm and 7pm-midnight.

GAM GAM ♿ KOSHER [3]

Canale di Cannaregio 1122 ☎041 71 52 84

Perhaps the premier kosher restaurant for the more-than 1000 Jewish residents of Venice, Gam Gam brings together traditional Italian kosher cooking (and if that phrase sounds like an oxymoron to you, you really should try out Gam Gam), Venetian cuisine, and newer Israeli culinary influences in a menu unlike any other you'll find in Venice. Although almost all of Gam Gam's patrons are Orthodox or Conservative Jews, this restaurant is also a great place for gentiles to experience Venice's small but remarkably vibrant Jewish community. Just make sure to call in advance, since the restaurant occasionally hosts private functions. That's not necessarily a reason to avoid the place, however, since if you look Jewish, you might just get invited in to sample some free food, as was one *Let's Go* Researcher-Writer. Also worth checking out is the affiliated dessert shop just a couple storefronts north.

 # From Campo S. Geremia, cross the Guglie Bridge and turn left. $ Entrees €8-15. ⏰ Open M-Th noon-10pm, F noon-4pm, Su noon-10pm.

PASTICCERIA MARTINI BAKERY [1]

Rio Terà San Leonardo 1302 ☎041 71 73 75

At first glance, Pasticceria Martini is a lot like other pastry shops in Cannaregio, but once you try one of their croissants, you'll realize why so many residents pass by a half-dozen other pastry shops on their way here. The pastries (made fresh several times daily) are excellent, and several of their coffee options (including coffee with ginseng) are wildly popular. You can stop in here for a quick and tasty breakfast or lunch, but just try to resist walking away with a fat sack of Martini's mini-pastries, all sold by weight.

 # Just past the Guglie Bridge going North. $ Pastries €1. Coffee €1.50. ⏰ Open daily 6am-9pm.

TRATTORIA DA'A MARISA ♿ RISTORANTE [3]

Fondamenta San Giobe, Cannaregio 652 ☎041 72 02 11

Though the hours are extremely limited, it's worth visiting Trattoria da'a Marisa while it's open: you'll experience some of the best cuisine Cannaregio has to offer. The restaurant's cuisine is perfectly complemented by its cheerful ambience, and musicians sometimes visit the patio to serenade diners, many of whom are locals enjoying their meals by the canal in a scene that feels quintessentially Venetian.

 # From Campo S. Geremia, walk toward the Guglie Bridge and turn left immediately before the bridge. Continue for 3-4 min. The restaurant is on the left. $ Entrees €13-20. ⏰ Open M noon-2pm, Tu noon-2pm and 8pm, W noon-2pm, Th-Sa noon-2pm and 8pm. One serving time in the evenings.

OSTERIA L'ORTO DEI MORI ♿🍷 RISTORANTE [4]

Campo dei Mori ☎041 52 43 677

The best dining option near **Madonna dell'Orto** (p. 137), Osteria L'Orto Dei Mori combines classic and modern aspects of Venetian identity remarkably well with its trendy-yet-traditional style. Its patio on the Campo dei Mori offers great views of one of the most architecturally fascinating squares in Cannaregio, and the tasteful, earth-tone colors of the dining room make eating inside an appealing option as well. An excellent choice for dinner, this restaurant is the perfect place a leisurely meal—at least, you'll feel that way until the check arrives.

 # Directly across the bridge from the Church Madonna dell'Orto. $ Entrees €14-23. ⏰ Open M 12:30-3:30pm and 7pm-midnight, W-Su 12:30-3:30pm and 7pm-midnight.

NAVE DE ORO ♿🍷 ENOTECA [1]

Rio Terà San Leonardo 1370 ☎041 71 96 95

Essential for any traveler seeking lots of alcohol for little money, the Nave De Oro in Cannaregio is one of six locations in Venice where wine is sold by the liter and "BYOB" stands for bring your own (empty) bottle. Provided you have €2 and an empty bottle of any kind (yes, even an old water bottle will do), you can get a liter of one of the surprisingly good regional wines offered by the friendly and knowledgeable staff. Welcome to Venice—you know you're in Europe when the wine is less expensive than the water.

✦ East of the Guglie Bridge along Rio Terà San Leonardo. ⑤ Wine €1.70-2.20 per L. ⏰ Open M-Sa 8am-1pm and 4:30-7:30pm.

RISTORANTE AL BRINDISI
Campo San Geremia 307

✦♿♁♈⛱ RISTORANTE ❹
☎041 71 69 68 ▣www.albrindisi.it

A contender for the title of best restaurant in Campo San Geremia, Ristorante Al Brindisi offers a great vantage point for people-watching in the square as well as tasty food to flavor the experience. The wall-length mirror at the back of the restaurant brings together the patio and the indoor seating, giving the restaurant an open vibe that often keeps it buzzing for up to an hour after its official 11pm closing time.

✦ From train station, turn left and walk about 4-5min. along Lista di Spagna. ⑤ Entrees €12-18. 2-course menu €20; menu completo €25. ⏰ Open daily 9am-11pm

FRULALA
Strada Nova 2235 and Campiello R. Selvatico 5620

●♿♈ SMOOTHIE BAR ❷
☎038 02 67 02 77 ▣www.frulala.com

With two locations in Cannaregio separated by a 5-10min. walk, Frulala offers multiple opportunities to take a break and slurp on a frosty, all-fruit smoothie. If it's been a rough travel day, Frulala also offers some strong but equally delicious and refreshing cocktails that won't make your wallet cry. The pop music blasting from the restaurant doesn't really match Cannaregio's more staid vibe, but it does reflect the sunny disposition of the smoothie-serving staff.

✦ Strada Nova: From the Ca' d'Oro, walk northeast along Strada Nova for 3min.; the stand is on the right shortly before a large bridge. Campiello R. Selvatico: From Chiesa di Santa Maria dei Miracoli, continue along the side of the church opposite the canal and turn left; the restaurant is in a sq. shortly ahead. ⑤ Smoothies €2.50-7.50. ⏰ Open daily 9am-midnight.

SAN POLO

Along the Grand Canal, San Polo suffers from the same generic tourist cuisine that you'll find near all of Venice's sightseeing destinations, but if you manage to get away from the main drag around the Rialto a little bit, you'll be rewarded with the unique specialties and terrific ambience of Venice's best small restaurants.

▨ ANTICO FORNO
Ruga Rialto 970/973

●♿♈ PIZZERIA ❷
☎041 52 04 110

Let's Go's top recommendation for pizza in Venice, Antico Forno makes standard pies with top-quality ingredients as well as adventurous vegetarian options (olives, a variety of peppers, feta cheese, etc.) and deep-dish pizza that will put anything from Chicago to shame. The price might seem a bit high for single slices, but a large piece of their perfectly crisped and seasoned deep-dish pizza is substantial enough to serve as a meal.

✦ From Rialto Bridge, go straight ahead to Ruga Rialto and turn left onto Ruga Rialto; Antico Forno is ahead on the right. ⑤ Slices €2-3.50. ⏰ Open daily 11am-10pm.

▨ CIOCCOLATERIA VIZIOVIRTÙ
Calle Balbi 2898

✦♿ CIOCCOLATERIA ❶
☎041 27 50 149 ▣www.viziovirtu.com

Venice's premiere chocolatier, Cioccolateria VizioVirtù crafts an incredible selection of creative, delicious, and (unfortunately) expensive chocolates in-house daily. While VizioVirtù does an excellent job with staples such as pralines, truffles, and baked goods, its mastery of the fine art of confectionery is best on display in its unconventional chocolates, including ones spiced up with red pepper, and replica Venetian masks that make great, site-specific gifts.

food · san polo

⚲ *V: San Tomà. Walk straight until you reach a T intersection and turn left; the shop is on the right.* Ⓢ *Various chocolate creations €1-2.50.* 🕐 *Open daily 10am-7:30pm.*

OSTERIA NARANZARIA

♥♿🍴❄ RISTORANTE ❹

Naranzaria 130   ☎041 72 41 035 💻www.naranzaria.it

Osteria Naranzaria is a trendy, international-style restaurant and lounge with a menu as diverse as its clientele. Without completely abandoning its Venetian roots, the restaurant takes risks, dishing up unusual items such as fresh sushi, supposedly the best of its kind available in the city. Naranzaria also tends to serve smaller portions, so it's a great place to have a light lunch by Rialto Bridge or enjoy some sushi and drinks before heading out for the night.

⚲ *From Rialto Bridge, walk past San Giacomo, turn right, and cross the square; the restaurant is directly ahead.* Ⓢ *Entrees €7-18. Sushi 10 pieces for €15.* 🕐 *Open Tu-Su noon-2am.*

BIRRARIA LA CORTE

♥♿🍴❄🍺 RISTORANTE ❸

Campo San Polo 2168   ☎041 27 50 570 💻www.birrarialacorte.it

The top restaurant in Campo San Polo, Birraria la Corte boasts a pretty adventurous repertoire without abandoning the staples of every Italian menu. Two unconventional entrees it has perfected include buffalo steaks and chicken curry, both of which go great with any number of the imported beers the restaurant has on tap.

⚲ *From the Rialto Bridge, walk through the markets along Ruga dei Oresi, turn left onto Rughetta del Ravano, continue for approximately 4min., and cross the square; the restaurant is in the northwest corner.* Ⓢ *Entrees €6.50-19.* 🕐 *Open daily noon-2:30pm and 7-10:30pm.*

MURO VENEZIA FRARI

♥♿🍴❄🍺 RISTORANTE ❹

Rio Terà dei Frari 2604   ☎041 52 45 310 💻www.murovenezia.com

Muro Venezia eschews the dry, regal ambience typical of most fine Venetian restaurants in favor of a more cutting-edge aesthetic. This preference for the avant-garde is also on display in the restaurant's creative interpretations of classic Venetian recipes, including one of the most incredible vegetable risottos you'll ever have. If you like the feel here, you should check out the bar owned and operated by the same people near the Rialto Bridge, **Muro Venezia Rialto**.

⚲ *From Campo dei Frari, cross a bridge to the east, turn right, continue for 30sec. to the end of the street, and turn left.* Ⓢ *Entrees €7-25.* 🕐 *Open M-W 11am-1am, F-Su 11am-1am. Kitchen open noon-3pm and 7-10:30pm.*

RISTORANTE DA SANDRO

♥♿🍴 RISTORANTE ❸

Campiello dei Meloni 1473   ☎041 52 34 964

A small, traditional restaurant near the Rialto Bridge that focuses on a few Italian classics rather than cosmopolitan cuisine, Ristorante da Sandro is a great place to get a delicious, authentic Italian meal that won't break the bank. Try the homemade lasagna: it's Garfield-approved.

⚲ *From Rialto Bridge, continue straight to Ruga Rialto and turn left onto Ruga Rialto; the restaurant is ahead on the right.* Ⓢ *Entrees €6-22.* 🕐 *Open M-Th 11:30am-11:30pm, Sa-Su 11:30am-11:30pm.*

AL GIARDINETTO

♥♿🍴❄🍺 RISTORANTE ❸

San Tomà 2910   ☎041 79 57 67 💻www.algiardinetto.com

Jovial staff, excellent food, and reasonable prices. You really can't go wrong with that combination. You also can't go wrong with house-recommended scallop risotto or grilled chicken, potatoes, and wine for €9. This quaint canal-side restaurant on the border with Dorsoduro offers 'em all.

⚲ *V: San Tomà. Continue straight until you reach a T intersection, turn left, continue to the canal, and turn right; the restaurant is ahead on the right.* Ⓢ *Entrees €6-13.* 🕐 *Open Tu-Su 10am-3pm and 6:30-11:30pm.*

ANTICA OSTERIA GIORGIONE

San Polo 1022/B

●&♥❀❄ RISTORANTE ❹

☎041 24 12 124 ▣www.anticogiorgione.com

Though perhaps a bit up-market for most budget travelers, Antica Osteria Giorgione is the place to go for a splurge-worthy, phenomenal meal in San Polo. The historic restaurant, which has been in operation for over 120 years but is fully updated with a state-of-the-art kitchen, combines traditional and modern influences in its cuisine to devise menu items you won't find in many other places, including incredible swordfish steaks and delicious artichoke salad.

☞ *From the Rialto Bridge, immediately turn left, continue along the Grand Canal for 3-4min., take the 7th possible right, walk straight for 30sec., and make the 1st possible left; the restaurant is shortly ahead.* Ⓢ *Lunch €10-24. Dinner €16-24.* Ⓣ *Open daily noon-3pm and 7:30-10pm.*

PIZZERIA DUE COLONNE

Calle della Chiesa 2343

●&♥ PIZZERIA ❸

☎041 52 40 685

Pint-sized Pizzeria Due Colonne features a menu with great seafood, pastas, and pretty much every kind of pizza you could imagine. The portions are a whopping size for the low prices, which should save you enough that you don't feel too bad about spending a bit extra on their famous fried calamari.

☞ *From Campo dei Frari, exit the square east, cross a bridge, turn left, cross another bridge, continue right along Calle Dona, and cross another bridge; the restaurant is ahead on the right.* Ⓢ *Entrees €6.50-15.* Ⓣ *Open daily noon-2:30pm (3pm for pizza) and 7-10:30pm.*

SANTA CROCE

If you're looking to get a meal in Santa Croce, stay toward the east side of the neighborhood. You can walk around the western end for half an hour without finding anything worthwhile, but if you stick to the eastern side, especially immediately southeast of Piazzale Roma, you'll discover a lot of small, personality-filled neighborhood restaurants that offer great values for budget travelers.

▨ RISTORANTE RIBOT

Fondamenta Minotto 158

●&♥❄ RISTORANTE ❸

☎041 52 42 486

Venice is an incredible culinary city, but Ristorante Ribot manages to stand out, with exceptional food at real-world prices. The restaurant pays tribute to the best of traditional Venice—regional cuisine, excellent Italian wines, and a beautiful patio garden—but keeps it fresh with an innovative kitchen, modern design, and live music three to four times a week. It's tough to find better food anywhere in Venice, let alone at comparable prices.

☞ *Follow Piazzale Roma east, cross consecutive bridges, and continue for approximately 2min.* Ⓢ *Entrees €8-14.* Ⓣ *Open daily noon-2:30pm and 7-10:30pm.*

▨ PANIFICO BAROZZI

Salizada San Pantalon 86/A

●& BAKERY, GROCERY STORE ❶

☎041 71 02 33

One of the trickiest things about Venetian pastries is that, from a window shopper's perspective, every store's baked goods look practically identical. Sadly, looks can be deceiving, meaning that identical-looking cookies can in fact vary in quality from barely palatable to incredibly delicious. Panifico Barozzi's pastries, however, taste as scrumptious as they appear. With an impressive number of different delicacies to sample and the added bonus of a small grocery store (surprisingly tough to find in most neighborhoods) stocked with inexpensive and convenient snacks, this is a one-stop shopping experience you can't miss.

☞ *Follow Piazzale Roma east, cross consecutive bridges, and continue for approximately 3min.* Ⓢ *Pastries €1-2.* Ⓣ *Open daily 6am-7:30pm*

ANTICO GAFARO

Salizada San Pantalon 116/A

●&♥❄ RISTORANTE, PIZZERIA ❸

☎041 52 42 823

A traditional restaurant with excellent pastas (especially lasagna) and serviceable pizzas, Antico Garafo is so perfectly Venetian that it could pass for a movie set. With the gorgeous backdrop of a canal frequented by quiet boats and some of the neighborhood's most beautiful buildings, this restaurant is a great place to relax and enjoy a long meal.

🚶 Follow Piazzale Roma east, cross consecutive bridges, and continue for approximately 3min. $ Entrees €8-22. 🕐 Open daily 11:30am-11:30pm.

AGLI AMICI 💳♿🍸⛅ SNACK BAR, RISTORANTE [3]

Sestiere Santa Croce 189 ☎041 52 41 309

With impressive omelettes and a great selection of cheeses, Agli Amici is a welcome anomaly in Venice, where breakfast usually consists of nothing more than tea and toast. Although the seafood options are a bit expensive, everything else here is of solid value, making this restaurant a quick but hearty lunch stop.

🚶 Follow Piazzale Roma east, cross consecutive bridges, immediately turn left, and continue for 90sec. $ Entrees €6-20. 🕐 Open daily 8am-7:30pm.

LAS RAMBLAS 💳♿🍸⛅ CAFE [3]

Santa Croce 373 ☎041 52 46 648

Inspired by Barcelona's famous pedestrian street, Las Ramblas does not quite recreate the famous Catalan circus feel: its tranquil atmosphere is a far cry from the street-performing madness of its namesake. Nevertheless, the restaurant serves delicious food at reasonable prices that are, rain or shine, far better than most restaurants you'll find around Piazzale Roma. It's worth waiting for a sunny day, however, to appreciate the restaurant's beautiful patio.

🚶 Following Piazzale Roma east, turn right at the 1st bridge you see; continue for 30sec.; turn right again and continue for 30sec. $ Entrees €8-20. 🕐 Open daily 9:30am-11pm.

TRATTORIA ALLE BURCHIELLE 💳♿🍸⛅ SNACK BAR [2]

Fondamenta delle Burchielle 393 ☎041 71 03 42

Close to Piazzale Roma, Trattoria alle Burchielle offers authentic Venetian food at exceptional prices. The outdoor seating by the canal is wonderful, and given the prices, you can enjoy several courses without breaking the bank.

🚶 Following Piazzale Roma east, cross the 1st bridge you see and turn right immediately; the restaurant is on the right. $ Entrees €7.50-15. 🕐 Open daily noon-10pm.

TRATTORIA IN CAMPIEO 💳♿🍸⛅ RISTORANTE [3]

Campieo Mosca 24 ☎041 71 10 61

A step back from Salizada San Pantalon, Trattoria in Campieo has Campieo Mosca almost entirely to itself and uses this space to full effect, offering a great outdoor setting in which to enjoy a tasty Venetian meal. Although the food is excellent, be forewarned that portions tend to run on the small side. Consider stopping here for a light lunch unless you don't mind lightening your wallet considerably.

🚶 Follow Piazzale Roma east, cross consecutive bridges, continue for approximately 3min., and turn right into Campieo Mosca. $ Entrees €10-22. 🕐 Open daily noon-3pm and 6-10:30pm.

ALIBABA KEBAB 💳♿ KEBAB, PIZZERIA [1]

Salizada San Pantalon ☎041 52 45 272

Anyone staying in Venice for an extended period of time should seriously consider trying some sort of kebab, one of Venice's major ethnic foods. Alibaba Kebab offers pretty exceptional and authentic kebab at a reasonable price and in one of the nicest kebab restaurants you'll find in the city. Also serves pizzas, but seeing how there's a pizzeria on every corner, you might as well take the opportunity to try something a little different.

🚶 Follow Piazzale Roma east, cross consecutive bridges, and continue for approximately 5min. $ Pizza €1.50. Kebab €4. 🕐 Open daily 11am-3pm and 5:30-9:30pm.

AL BACCO FELICE 💳♿🍸⛱ RISTORANTE, PIZZERIA [2]

Campo Tolentini 197 ☎041 52 87 794

Out of the way in a quieter section of Santa Croce, Al Bacco Felice is one of the best places off of Salizada San Pantalon to enjoy a longer meal. The food is exceptionally good for the prices, and the restaurant has a secluded garden that takes advantage of Venice's beautiful weather.

➜ Follow Piazzale Roma east, cross consecutive bridges, turn left, and continue along canal for 3-4min. before turning right, away from Hotel Sofitel. Continue for 2min.; the restaurant is on the left. $ Entrees €7-13. ⏰ Open daily 11am-4pm and 6:30-11pm.

FRITTO AND FRUTTA 🥗♿ SNACK BAR, SMOOTHIE BAR [2]

Fondamenta dei Tolentini 220 ☎041 52 46 852

A truly unique establishment, Fritto and Frutta (translation: Fried and Fruit) specializes in various fried foods and delicious fruit smoothies. Though the latter is likely better for your health than the former, the temptation of mixing and matching among fried cheeses, olives, chicken wings, and pizza will likely prove irresistible to anyone who sets foot in the store. The prices of Fritto and Frutta's snackable foods are also irresistibly reasonable.

➜ Follow Piazzale Roma east, cross consecutive bridges, turn left, and continue along canal for 2min. Fritto and Frutta is on the right. $ €3.50 per serving. ⏰ Open M-Sa noon-8pm.

OSTERIA AE CRAVATE 💳♿🍸 RISTORANTE [4]

Salizada San Pantalon ☎041 52 87 912

Although the dozens of ties hanging from the walls and ceiling might give you the impression that Osteria ae Cravate has strict dress standards, this snug Venetian restaurant actually is pretty relaxed. Even with Osteria ae Cravate's congenial, social atmosphere, you get the sense that things are much more serious in the kitchen, which dishes up the food so that your meal's presentation will rival its flavor.

➜ Follow Piazzale Roma east, cross consecutive bridges, and continue for approximately 4min. $ Entrees €8-19. ⏰ Open daily noon-10:30pm.

DORSODURO

Most of the nice restaurants in Dorsoduro tend toward the expensive side, but the neighborhood also offers some of the best cafes and pizzerias in the city, which makes the area appealing to travelers on a budget.

👍 RISTORANTE LINEADOMBRA 💳♿🍸⛱ RISTORANTE [5]

Ponte dell'Umiltà ☎041 24 11 881 💻www.ristorantelineadombra.com

Probably not the type of restaurant most budget travelers can afford to eat at more than once a trip, but if you're prepared to spring for an expensive meal, you won't find a restaurant that takes its work more seriously than Ristorante Lineadombra. The food is reputed to be some of Venice's best and is served in a beautiful, modern restaurant aesthetically similar to the nearby **Punta della Dogana** in its minimalist sensibility. Since you're going to pay a premium anywhere you eat along Zattere, you might as well go all-out and enjoy a truly excellent meal.

➜ V: Zattere. Turn right and continue for 6-7min. The restaurant is on the left, with patio seating on the right. $ Entrees €21-35. ⏰ Open daily noon-3pm and 7-10:30pm.

👍 SUZIE CAFE 💳♿🍸 CAFE [2]

Dorsoduro 1527 ☎041 52 27 502 💻www.suziecafevenice.com

With tons of classic-rock memorabilia, highlighted by a sweet guitar boasting half a dozen signatures on its body, Suzie Cafe distinguishes itself from other snack bars and cafes with both great food and high-personality decor. You could spend weeks in Venice without finding a better place to sit down and enjoy an €8 meal.

➜ V: Zattere. Turn left; walk 5-7min. to end of Zattere, turn right, and continue for 2-3min.; the snack bar is in the corner of a square. $ Sandwiches and light meals €4-11. ⏰ Open M-Th 7am-8pm, F 7am-1am.

RISTORANTE AI GONDOLIERI 💳🚫🍸 RISTORANTE [4]

San Vio 366 ☎041 52 86 396 🖥www.aigondolieri.com

An upscale restaurant that is famous for its catering, having hosted multiple events for the nearby Guggenheim Museum, Ristorante Ai Gondolieri is a great place to take a date after a day of visiting art galleries. Although Ai Gondolieri can be expensive, especially if you order a bottle off of their extensive wine list, the quality is proportionate to the price.

➜ From Santa Maria della Salute, walk east towards the Guggenheim, past the museum; when you reach the bend in the canal, the restaurant will be immediately across the water. $ Entrees €11.50-32. ⏰ Open M noon-3:30pm and 7-10:30pm, W-Su noon-3:30pm and 7-10:30pm.

IL DOGE ⊛♿ GELATERIA [2]

Campo San Margherita 3058 ☎041 52 34 607

Sure, there are gelato places on pretty much every street corner in Venice, but Il Doge is unique. It doesn't use syrups or artificial flavors in its ice cream, opting instead for fresh ingredients that make for a better taste and texture. And, although the quality is high, the prices are among the lowest you'll find in a Venetian *gelateria*. With a few unique flavors that defy description, Il Doge has quickly helped at least one *Let's Go* researcher fatten up.

➜ The southwest corner of Campo San Margherita. $ 1 scoop €1.20, 2 scoops €2, 3 scoops €2.80. ⏰ Open daily noon-11pm.

PIZZA AL TAGLIO 💳♿🍸 PIZZERIA [2]

Sacca de la Toletta 1309 ☎041 52 36 518

The Pizza Academy diploma on the wall doesn't lie—the owner of this shop knows how to cook up some serious pizzas and sandwiches. Unlike the bland, flat, lukewarm stuff you'll find at many pizzerias, Pizza Al Taglio's pizza and sandwiches are fresh, filling, and delicious. The nutella calzones *(€1.50)* are sure to make your day but ruin your diet.

➜ From the Accademia, go east, turn left at the 1st canal you meet, and turn right at the 1st bridge ahead on the left; continue straight for 2-3min. $ Slices of pizza €2. Sandwiches €3. Calzones €3. ⏰ Open daily 10:30am-10:30pm.

RISTORANTE CANTINONE STORICO 💳♿🍸⛅ RISTORANTE [3]

Fondamenta di Ca' Bragadin 660/661 ☎041 52 39 577

Situated between the Guggenheim and Accademia, Ristorante Cantinone Storico is the rare Dorsoduro restaurant that offers great Venetian cuisine in a relaxed setting at prices more commonly seen in the back roads of Cannaregio and the eastern reaches of Castello. Stop here for a long lunch break between visits to the neighborhood's museums.

➜ V: Zattere. Turn right, walk 3-4min., and turn left onto Fondamenta Bragadin. Continue for 2-3min.; the restaurant is on the right. $ Entrees €10-24. ⏰ Open daily 12:30-5:30pm and 7:30-10:30pm.

RISTORANTE MESSNER 💳♿🍸❄⛅ RISTORANTE [3]

Fondamenta di Cà Bala 217 ☎041 29 60 695 🖥www.hotelmessner.it

A great restaurant that you might unknowingly walk right past, Ristorante Messner serves great internationally influenced Venetian food in some of Dorsoduro's nicest garden seating. The prices are exceptional for the area, and the staff has the same excellent attention to detail and dedication to service that makes **Hotel Messner** (p. 122) a thumbpicked accommodation in Dorsoduro.

➜ V: Zattere. Turn right, walk 4-5min., turn left onto Fondamenta di Cà Bala, and continue for about 2min. $ Entrees €6-15. ⏰ Open daily noon-3:30pm and 5:30-11pm.

TRATTORIA DONA ONESTA 💳♿🍸❄ RISTORANTE [3]

Calle Larga Foscari 3922 ☎041 71 05 86 🖥www.donaonesta.com

Just across a bridge from Santa Croce, Trattoria Dona Onesta is a fantastic

Venetian restaurant that's one quiet side street away from the overpriced and overcrowded restaurants of Campo San Margherita. Customers rave about the food, and thanks to the menu's pricing, you can get a couple courses without breaking the bank. If you go to Trattoria Dona Onesta, be sure to budget some time to enjoy the leisurely dining atmosphere that makes the restaurant a favorite among locals.

From Campo San Margherita, go west, cross the 1st bridge you come to, and continue across the sq.; turn right at the cross st., continue until you reach an open sq., turn left; the restaurant is immediately before the bridge. $ Entrees €6.50-13. ⏰ Open daily 12:30-3:30pm and 5:30-10:30pm.

RISTORANTE PIZZERIA AL PROFETA RISTORANTE, PIZZERIA 3

Calle Lunga San Barnaba ☎041 52 37 466

If you walk past Al Profeta on a summer afternoon, you might wonder why the place is nearly empty. The impressive menu of pizzas and vegetarian cuisine combined with the building's novel interior adorned with dozens, if not hundreds, of mid-century movie-star mug shots, make this look like exactly the sort of place that should be packed. If you step inside, however, you'll see that Al Profeta's real draw is the gorgeous shaded patio, which stays comfortably cool despite the summer heat and is packed whenever the restaurant is open. Boasting great proximity to some of the major sights around Campo San Margherita in combination with a quiet, calmer ambience afforded by a private garden, Al Profeta is an excellent option for lunch or dinner in Dorsoduro.

From Campo San Barnaba, walk east for 3-4min. along Calle Lunga San Barnaba; the restaurant is on the left. $ Entrees €8-20. ⏰ Open daily noon-2:30pm and 6:30-10:30pm.

CASTELLO

Since Castello is so close to P. San Marco, it gets a lot of tourist traffic, and restaurants with well-priced cuisine tend to be few and far between. There are quite a few good restaurants in Castello, but they're typically a bit pricier than comparable restaurants in other neighborhoods. In a lot of cases, you're going to have to compromise either on quality (and opt for a cheap restaurant) or convenience (and trek out to Cannaregio or eastern Castello), or just be prepared to pay a bit more than you otherwise might.

TAVERNA SAN LIO RISTORANTE 4

Salizada San Lio 5547 ☎041 27 70 669 www.tavernasanlio.com

One of the best restaurants you'll find in all of Venice, Taverna San Lio serves an incredible Venetian menu with a bit of international flair. Reflecting the owner's eclectic taste, both the decor and the cuisine are strongly Venetian but reflect the city's increasingly cosmopolitan identity. If the quality of the food isn't enough to turn heads, the bright colors of the walls will catch your attention.

From Rialto Bridge, go east along Salizada San Lio for 3-4min.; restaurant is on the right. $ Entrees €12-26. ⏰ Open M noon-11pm, W-Su noon-11pm.

RISTORANTE AI BARBACANI RISTORANTE 3

Calle del Paradiso 5746 ☎041 52 10 234 www.ristoranteaibarbacani.com

Far and away the most impressive restaurant in the area around Santa Maria Formosa, Ristorante ai Barbacani boasts an excellent Venetian menu, extensive wine list, subtle, yet elegant Venetian decor, and gorgeous floor to ceiling windows that open on to a canal trafficked by gondoliers and kayakers. If you're looking to impress a date, consider calling ahead to reserve the table for two closest to the window near the bridge.

From Campo Santa Maria Formosa, immediately across westernmost bridge off the square. $ Entrees €9-20. ⏰ Open daily noon-2:30pm and 6-10:30pm.

CIP CIAP
⊗⊗🍸 PIZZERIA ❶

Calle del Mondo Novo 5799/A ☎041 52 36 621

You'll be hard pressed to find pizza of this quality for a better price in Venice. The calzones and pizza are made fresh several times daily and then cooked to order. Budget travelers weary of the sensibly-sized portions found in most Venetian restaurants may find themselves suffering a stomachache after gorging themselves on Cip Ciap's cheap pies.

⇆ Immediately across bridge to Calle del Mondo Novo from S. Maria Formosa. $ Calzones €3. Pizza €1.50 per slice. ⏰ Open M 9am-9pm, W-Su 9am-9pm.

RISTORANTE AL COVO
💳♿🍸☁ RISTORANTE ❹

Campiello della Pescaria 3968 ☎041 52 23 812 💻www.ristorantealcovo.com

From the outside, there isn't anything too striking about Ristorante al Covo, but this modest restaurant offers the most incredible Venetian cuisine in Castello, if not the entire city. Though pricey for budget travelers, a €25 meal here is an absolute steal when compared to other restaurants of comparable quality.

⇆ East from P. San Marco, cross 4 bridges and turn left onto the last street before the 5th bridge going east. $ Main Courses €16-29. ⏰ Open daily 12:45-3:30pm and 7:30-midnight.

RISTORANTE PIZZERIA SAN PROVOLO
💳♿🍸☁ RISTORANTE ❸

Campo San Provolo 4713 ☎041 52 85 085

If you're looking to get a meal around San Marco at a good restaurant that caters to tourists, Ristorante Pizzeria San Provolo is a great choice. The staff is very friendly and speaks English well, the menu has many options in various price ranges, and the patio seating is exceptional.

⇆ From P. San Marco, walk south toward water, turn left, cross 2 bridges, make the 1st left, and continue through Campo San Provolo; the restaurant is on the left. $ Entrees €9-29. ⏰ Open M-Th 11:30am-10:30pm, Sa-Su 11:30am-10:30pm.

TRATTORIA DA NINO
💳♿🍸☁ RISTORANTE ❸

San Zaccaria 4668 ☎041 52 35 886 💻www.trattoriadanino.com

Though Trattoria da Nino doesn't exactly give off a traditional Venetian vibe, the menu is authentic Italian done well. The patio seating is excellent, and the restaurant itself has a great, relaxed ambience and exceptionally friendly staff.

⇆ From P. San Marco, walk south toward water, turn left, cross 2 bridges, make the 1st left, and walk about 1min.; the restaurant is on the left. $ Entrees €10-22. ⏰ Open daily 11:30am-10:30pm.

RISTORANTE LA NUOVA GROTTA
💳♿🍸☁ RISTORANTE ❹

Calle delle Rasse 358 ☎041 72 41 018

One of the best places in Castello to sit down and enjoy a long, peaceful meal, La Nuova Grotta does a great job of shutting out the chaos of nearby P. San Marco and channeling Castello's charming neighborhood atmosphere. The menu is typical Venetian cuisine but much more authentic and of higher quality than most restaurants in this section of the neighborhood.

⇆ From P. San Marco, walk south toward water, turn left, cross 1 bridge, take 2nd left onto Calle delle Rasse, and continue for 2min.; the restaurant is on the left. $ Entrees €8-22. ⏰ Open daily 10:30am-11:30pm.

nightlife

For all of its fascinating history, awe-inspiring architecture, and delightful cuisine, the one thing that Venice desperately lacks is nightlife. Whereas the ubiquity of historic *palazzi*, excellent seafood, and lovely hotels in Venice means you could find them while blindfolded, if you head out in search of a random bar you'll likely end up heading home an hour later with nothing more than a kebab to show for it. Stick to the major hot spots listed here, and you'll have a lot more success. Additionally, be prepared for a much more laid-back bar scene than that of most major Italian cities. You're not going to find much dancing or serious partying, but there are a couple great places to sit back, enjoy a few drinks, and appreciate Venice at night. **Campo San Margherita** in Dorsoduro is the city's biggest nightlife hub, and that whole neighborhood is the place to be after 9pm. Crime in Venice is less of a concern than it is almost anywhere else in Italy, but use common sense: don't carry too much cash or walk alone at night, and you will probably be fine.

SAN MARCO

After tourists head out for dinner at around 7pm, the bells of the Campanile stop chiming every few minutes, and pigeons and seagulls are left to drift aimlessly in the sky as the tourists who fed them bread during the day disappear. It is at this time of day that P. San Marco is at its finest.

After the beauty of the early evening, things get slower and duller. Dozens of places market themselves as"bars," but that term is more likely to denote a light-fare restaurant that serves alcohol than a nightlife hotspot. There are certainly a couple of places worth visiting, but since San Marco caters to the city's typical tourist, expect to see a lot more middle-aged couples holding hands and a lot fewer students downing body shots.

BACARO LOUNGE BAR

♨ & ♈ ✿ BAR

Sestiere San Marco 1345   ☎041 29 60 687

An ultra-chic minimalist bar just steps away from P. San Marco, Bacaro Lounge is one of the few establishments in San Marco that caters to the young and fashionable post-dinner crowd. Whereas most bars here are filled with middle-aged tourists rocking fanny packs and visors, Bacaro Lounge recalls the scene at an exclusive club in Manhattan or LA. With an understated playlist, sleek lounge set-up conducive to free conversation and mingling, and an extensive list of wine and cocktails, Bacaro Lounge is clearly the hottest place to be after dark in San Marco.

  ☈ *Exit the southwest corner of P. San Marco, opposite Basilica di San Marco; the bar is shortly ahead on the left.* ⑤ *Drinks €3.50-13.* ⌚ *Open daily until 2am.*

RISTORANTE GRAN CAFFÉ QUADRI

♨ & ♈ ☺ CAFE

P. San Marco 121   ☎041 52 22 105 ▣www.quadrivenice.com

Caffé Quadri isn't a bar or club, and the tone tends more toward refinement than debauchery, with a string quartet dressed in formalwear setting the soundtrack. Sipping one of their excellent drinks (the wine list is unbeatable, and the coffee is reputedly some of Venice's best) to the tune of the strings playing in the background, you'll experience P. San Marco as it ought to be, showcased in the lovely setting provided by this cafe.

  ☈ *In the northwest corner of P. San Marco.* ⑤ *Drinks €3-8. Dessert €3-7.* ⌚ *Open daily until 12:30am.*

GRAND CANAL RESTAURANT AND BAR

♨ & ♈ ☺ HOTEL BAR

Calle Vallaresso 1332   ☎041 52 00 211 ▣www.hotelmonaco.it

A welcoming hotel bar, the Grand Canal Restaurant and Bar in upscale Hotel

Monaco manages to avoid pretension and cultivate a clientele that stretches beyond the hotel's guest list. The wine list is exceptionally good, the bar has comfortable seating, and the dock opens into a nice summer breeze and excellent views across the water to **Basilica di Santa Maria della Salute**.

� *From P. San Marco, walk towards the water, turn right, and continue for 2min.; Hotel Monaco is at the end of the street.* ⑤ *Drinks €4-10.* ☼ *Open daily until midnight.*

CANNAREGIO

People don't travel to Cannaregio for its nightlife, but anyone can enjoy sitting outside with a good bottle of wine or a couple scoops of gelato while taking in this low-key neighborhood's nighttime scene. The natives here are generally more receptive to out-of-town visitors than are the residents of Venice's more popular destinations, probably because Cannaregio remains free of the floods of gondola-searching tourists that fill places like P. San Marco. Cannaregio's decidedly more intimate Campo San Marco on Lista di Spagna is a particularly pleasant place to while away the night hours, as Venetian locals and tourists socialize in restaurants and on benches well into the evening.

CASINO MUNICIPALE DI VENEZIA: CA' VENDRAMIN CALERGI ✦♿♀✳ CASINO

Cannaregio 2040 ☎041 52 97 111 🖳www.casinovenezia.it

One of the first things you might notice after getting off the plane at VCE is that Venice takes its gambling seriously—even the baggage carousels have a roulette-wheel theme, sponsored by the (in)famous Venetian Municipal Casino. While serious gamblers might want to head straight to Lido where the historic casino's main branch still operates, the Cannaregio location should be fun for anyone who just wants to play (or count) some cards and have a few drinks.

✦ *Going east on Strada Nova, take the 1st left past Calle Vendramin.* *i Male guests should wear formal jackets.* ⑤ *Entry €5, guests at some hotels get in free. Ask at your reception desk.* ☼ *Open M-Th 3pm-2:30am, F-Sa 3pm-3am, Su 3pm-2:30am.*

THE IRISH PUB VENEZIA ✦♿♀ BAR

Cannaregio 3847 ☎041 52 81 439 🖳www.theirishpubvenezia.com

A friendly crowd of boisterous locals and rowdy tourists brings The Irish Pub Venezia some of the best nightlife in the neighborhood. The drinks are strong and the bar is crowded, but patrons tend to be jovial and are happy to strike up a conversation on Venice, politics, or just about any other subject at the drop of a hat. Loud music and the pub's proximity to the late-night restaurant Neapolis Kebab keep it hopping long into the evening, even on weekdays.

✦ *Just off Strada Nova, on the left going east.* ⑤ *Drinks €3-6. Snacks €6-12.* ☼ *Open daily until 1:30am.*

SAN POLO

Nightlife-wise, San Polo is second only to Dorsoduro. The area around the **Rialto Bridge** in particular is home to some of Venice's best bars, popular with both Venetian locals and tourists.

🔲 JAZZ CLUB 900 ✦♿♀♨ JAZZ CLUB

San Polo 900 ☎041 52 26 565 🖳www.jazz900.com

Just down Ruga Rialto from the bars near the Rialto Bridge, Jazz Club 900 is a live-music hot spot. With shows up to several times each week, top-notch pizza, and reasonable prices on bottles, glasses, and pitchers of beer, this venue can be a chill hangout or a lively music bar, depending on what groups the club is hosting.

✦ *From the Rialto Bridge, continue straight, turn left onto Ruga Rialto, continue for 2min., and turn right: it's ahead on the left. Signs lead to the jazz club.* ⑤ *Drinks €2.50-5. Pizza €6-11.* ☼ *Open Tu-Su 11:30am-4pm and 7pm-2am.*

MURO VENEZIA RIALTO
💳♿🍸❄☁ BAR

Campo Bella Vienna Rialto 222 ☎041 24 12 339 💻www.murovenezia.com

With chic metal-and-dark-leather decor reminiscent of trendy bars in downtown Manhattan, Muro Venezia Rialto is one of Venice's most popular drinking spots for travelers and locals in their mid-20s. A bit more upscale than most other bars around the Rialto Bridge, Muro Venezia keeps the music low and emphasizes its lounge ambience.

➡ From Rialto Bridge, continue straight ahead for less than 2min., and turn right; the bar is on the left. $ Drinks €3-7. ⏰ Open M-Sa 9am-3:30pm and 4pm-1:30am, Su 4pm-1:30am.

ANCÒRA VENEZIA
💳♿🍸❄ BAR

Rialto 120 ☎041 52 07 066 💻www.ancoravenezia.it

One of Venice's most popular (and crowded) bars, Ancòra complements the subtle Asian and modernist aesthetics of its decor with some of the most universally lauded bartenders in the city. If the bar is overly crowded, grab a drink to enjoy outside in Campo di San Giacometto.

➡ From the Rialto Bridge, continue straight; Ancòra is the last bar on the right side of the Campo di San Giacometto. $ Drinks €3-6.50. ⏰ Open M-Sa 9:30am-2am.

BAR AI 10 SAVI
💳♿🍸 BAR

Rialto 55 ☎041 52 38 005 💻www.ai10savi.com

A popular hangout for local teens and groups of tourists alike, Bar Ai 10 Savi lacks the pretense of some other Rialto nightspots and sticks to the basics: 👍**strong drinks** at great prices. The bar is crowded enough that patrons spill out onto the street in chatting groups to enjoy a cold one and the Campo di San Giacometto.

➡ From Rialto Bridge, continue straight; the bar is on the left side of Campo di San Giacometto. $ Drinks €2.50-5.50. ⏰ Open daily 8:30am-1am.

SANTA CROCE

In a city not known for its nightlife, Santa Croce is about the last place you'd want to go for an evening out. Unlike some other neighborhoods with at least a few bars and restaurants open late, Santa Croce offers only a couple of places that keep the home-fires burning after midnight.

BAR AL CARCAN
💳♿🍸☁ BAR [3]

Salizada San Pantalon ☎041 71 32 36

While most of Santa Croce shuts down around 11pm (even on weekends), Bar Al Carcan stays crowded well into the night with tourists and locals alike looking to get a quick nightcap or enjoy a few drinks on the patio. The bar is small and fairly popular, though never overcrowded, and offers cheap drinks and good music.

➡ Follow Piazzale Roma east, cross consecutive bridges, and continue for approximately 2min. $ Drinks €3-6. ⏰ Open until 1am most days during the summer.

👍 DORSODURO

Dorsoduro has far and away the best nightlife of any neighborhood in Venice. Though there are dozens of bars and clubs, the vast majority of them are concentrated around **Campo San Margherita,** which is located just minutes away from Santa Croce and San Polo. As there isn't any action to be found on the island's western and southern edges, your best bet is to barhop near this vibrant campo. "Night"life in Dorsoduro begins before sunset during the summer, and the infamous **Club Piccolo Mondo** keeps it going almost until daybreak. So if you're looking for some bacchanalian revelry in the surprisingly sober city of Venice, Dorsoduro is the place to go.

👍 CLUB PICCOLO MONDO
💳♿🍸☁ CLUB

Accademia Dorsoduro 1056 ☎041 52 00 371 💻www.piccolomondo.biz

The definitive epicenter of Venetian nightlife, Club Piccolo Mondo puts most other bars in the city to shame. Small and down a dark side street near the Accademia, it might not impress from the outside, but if its world-class bar, excellent music, chill lounge areas, and awesome dance floor are enough to draw Mick Jagger and Naomi Campbell, they should be able to earn your patronage, even with the steep cover charge *(€10)*. The club prides itself on the diversity of its clientele, which ranges from students to middle-aged patrons and includes locals as well as tourists, so anyone should feel welcome here. A lot of visitors opt to start the night at another bar before coming to Club Piccolo Mondo, due to the place's expensive drinks. As a result, things usually don't get too crazy until after midnight.

⇟ From Ponte Accademia, facing the Accademia, turn right; continue onto the 1st street directly ahead (running parallel to the Grand Canal); continue for approximately 2min.; club is on the right. $ Cover €10. Drinks €9-12. ⏰ Open daily 11pm-4am.

🏆 VENICE JAZZ CLUB 💳🚭🍸 JAZZ CLUB

Ponte dei Pugni/Fondamenta del Squero 3102 ☎041 52 32 056 💻www.venicejazzclub.com

The Venice Jazz Club is a great place to begin a night out in Dorsoduro. While most bars are still in restaurant mode, this club is serving drinks to the tune of excellent music. It tends to attract an international crowd of 20-somethings and empty out once concerts end, despite technically remaining open. Given that it's the premier spot for live jazz music in Venice, perhaps this focus on the jams is to be expected.

⇟ From Campo San Margherita, walk towards Campo San Barnaba; turn right immediately before the bridge; the club is just ahead on the right. $ Cover €20; includes one drink. Drinks €5-10. Appetizers €5-15. ⏰ Opens daily at 7pm. Concerts start at 9pm and usually last about 2hr.

MADIGAN'S PUB 💳♿🍸⛱ IRISH PUB

Campo San Margherita 3053/A

Madigan's Pub seeks to replicate the ambience of an Irish pub and does so to great effect, creating the loudest, rowdiest bar in Campo San Margherita and maybe in all of Venice. On weekend nights, the pub is packed, both inside and on the patio, with international patrons drinking beers, taking shots, and shouting to old (and new) friends over the bar's deafening music.

⇟ At the southwest end of the Campo San Margherita. $ Drinks €4-8. ⏰ Open daily until 1:30am.

MARGARET DUCHAMP 💳♿🍸⛱ BAR

Campo San Margherita 3019 ☎041 52 86 255

One of the biggest bars in Venice and a Dorsoduro institution, Margaret Duchamp is the most prominent watering hole in Campo San Margherita. Though the bar typically plays jazz or pop, the music isn't overwhelmingly loud, making this an excellent place for a few hours of chill time spent enjoying some of the best mixed drinks in Venice.

⇟ At the southwest end of the Campo San Margherita. $ Drinks €3.50-9. ⏰ Open daily 9am-2am.

ORANGE RESTAURANT AND CHAMPAGNE LOUNGE 💳♿🍸⛱ BAR

Campo Santa Margherita 3054/A ☎041 52 34 740 💻www.orangebar.it

With an excellent patio, comfortable lounge furniture, and an awesome terrace looking out over Campo San Margherita, Orange Restaurant and Champagne Lounge has a more refined ambience than other Venetian bars. It might not get as crazy as some Dorsoduro hotspots, but make no mistake: with a wine list featuring over 60 Italian vintages and 20 imports, mega-screen TVs, and a top-notch bartender, Orange is a choice place for a night out.

⇟ At the southwest end of the Campo San Margherita. $ Drinks €4.50-12. ⏰ Open daily 10am-2am.

BISTROT AI DO DRAGHI

⌖♿♀♨ BAR

Campo San Margherita

☎041 52 89 731

More bohemian than most bars in Campo San Margherita, Bistrot Ai Do ◨Draghi tends to draw grungier travelers than the other bars in the square. In fact, this place is so full of such when-did-you-last-shower travelers that it's a surprise there isn't a stack of backpacks in the corner. The bar itself has an exceptionally relaxed and social character, with conversation rather than music constituting the dominant background noise.

⌖ *The northeast corner of Campo San Margherita.* Ⓢ *Drinks €1.50-6.* ☼ *Open M-Tu 7:30am-2-am, Th-Su 7:30am-2am.*

BLUES CAFE

⌖♿♀ BAR

Crosera San Pantalon

☎348 24 06 444

Like most bars east of Campo San Margherita, Blues Cafe has a calm, sophisticated vibe that draws patrons in their late 20s and early 30s. Unlike a lot of other bars, Blues Cafe keeps the good times rolling well into the evening every night of the week, especially when there is live music. *Let's Go* gives Blues Café bonus points for musical diversity, as it spins jazz, pop, and the best old-school hip hop playlist this side of the South Bronx.

⌖ *From Campo San Margherita, go west, and cross the 1st bridge you come to; continue across the square; the bar is on the 1st cross street you come to.* Ⓢ *Drinks €4-10.* ☼ *Open M-F 10am-2am, Sa-Su 3pm-2am.*

IMAGINA CAFE

⌖♿♀♨ CAFE, BAR

Campo San Margherita 3126

☎041 24 10 625 ▤www.imaginacafe.it

Part art gallery, part cafe, and part bar, Imagina Cafe is a favorite hangout of the Venetian *intelligentsia*. With awesome white, leather couches, consistently changing artwork, and sophisticated drinks, Imagina Cafe is a great place for stimulating conversation about the latest exhibit in François Pinault's **Punta della Dogana** contemporary art museum, but probably not the best bar if you want to get crunk or hear Miley Cyrus's latest hit.

⌖ *The southwest end of the Campo San Margherita, near Ponte dei Pugni.* Ⓢ *Drinks €2-8.* ☼ *Open Tu-Su 8am-2am.*

CAFFE BAR AI ARTISTI

⌖♿♀♨ CAFE, BAR

Campo San Barnaba 2771

☎39 68 01 35

If you want to grab a bite to eat before calling it a night or heading to **Club Piccolo Mondo**, but don't want to be the one person eating a full meal in a bar with 200 people sipping on mixed drinks, Caffe Bar Ai Artisti is a great stop. With exceptionally good food, a strong drink selection, a bumping playlist, and proximity to both Campo San Margherita and Club Piccolo Mondo, Caffe Bar Ai Artisti is an excellent place to hang out, for 20min.—or 4hr.

⌖ *From Campo San Margherita, continue along Rio Terà Canal, cross the bridge, and enter Campo San Barnaba.* Ⓢ *Drinks €3.50-8. Food €8-16.* ☼ *Open M-F 7am-2am, Sa 8am-2am, Su 9am-2am.*

IMPRONTA CAFE

⌖♿♀ CAFE, BAR

Crosera San Pantalon 3815

☎041 27 50 386

Whether you go earlier in the evening, when the cafe is almost always packed, or late at night, when it has a much quieter, intimate atmosphere, you're sure to appreciate Impronta Cafe's sleek aesthetics, extensive bar options, and nifty dessert menu. A great place to take a date after a night out or to cool down after some serious barhopping, this bar and cafe offers a serene and more sensible alternative to much of Dorsoduro's nighttime action.

⌖ *From Campo San Margherita, go west, and cross the 1st bridge you come to; continue across the square; the club is on the 1st cross street you come to.* Ⓢ *Drinks €2.50-6. Snacks and desserts €3-8.* ☼ *Open M-Sa 7am-2am.*

CASTELLO

A great place to sit outside at a cafe and relax well into the night, Castello isn't particularly notable for its nightclub scene. However, its good number of bars and cafes still draw large crowds during the summer. Most nightlife hotspots are along the waterfront that marks the southern boundary of the neighborhood, but there are a couple of places worth checking out further north close to the Rialto Bridge as well as on the eastern side of Castello.

TAVERNA L'OLANDESE VOLANTE — BAR

Castello 5658 ☎041 52 89 349

Blasting reggae beats until 2am, Taverna L'Olandese Volante is one of the most popular bars in the neighborhood. It seems to have wide appeal, drawing tourists, locals, students, and middle-aged customers to its great selection of beers on tap, prime location in one of Castello's best squares, and thoroughly impressive (and surprising) reggae playlist. Excellent, mahn.

From Rialto Bridge, walk east toward Salizada San Lio; continue along Salizada San Lio, then turn left at T-intersection at end of street; the bar is shortly before the 1st canal. $ Drinks €2.50-6. Snacks €5-12. Open Sa-Su until 2am in high season.

BAR VERDE — SNACK BAR

Calle de le Rasse 4525 ☎041 52 37 094

Bar Verde isn't an overwhelmingly unique establishment, but it's a great place to grab a couple of drinks and something quick to eat late at night near P. San Marco in Castello. The bar is frequented mainly by tourists staying at hotels in the area, so your neighbor at the bar may run the gamut from a budget traveler sipping inexpensive beer to a middle-aged couple stepping out for some late-night gelato.

From P. San Marco, walk south toward water, turn left, cross 1 bridge, turn left onto 2nd street on the left, and continue for about 2min. $ Drinks €3-6. Gelato €1.50-4. Snacks €6-12. Open Sa-Su until 2am in high season.

CAFFE INTERNAZIONALE — CAFE, BAR

Riva degli Schiavoni 4183 ☎041 52 36 047

A great place to grab a coffee or beer and maybe a quick snack right along the water, Caffe Internazionale is distinguished by an excellent patio with incredible views of the canals. This is a convenient stop at which to refuel before catching the vaporetto home after a long night in Castello or San Marco, and the nearby docks serve as an intriguing vantage point for people-watching the party boats and luxurious yachts that constantly drift past.

From P. San Marco, walk south toward water; turn left and continue for 2-3min., crossing 2 bridges; the bar is on the left. $ Drinks €2-5. Snacks €5-10. Open Sa-Su until 1:30am in high season.

BAR METROPOLE — HOTEL BAR

Riva degli Schiavoni 4149 ☎041 52 05 044

Probably as close as most budget travelers will get to the opulent hotel in which this establishment is housed, the elegant yet intimate bar at the Metropole is a great place to get some of the most expertly mixed drinks in Venice. While you might be breaking the bank (there are particularly tempting options for doing so on their wine list), you're paying for quality. The high-class ambience is also well worth the cost.

From P. San Marco, walk south toward water; turn left and continue for 3-4min., crossing 3 bridges; the bar is on the left. $ Drinks €5-12. Open Sa-Su until 2am in high season.

ARCO BALENTO — SNACK BAR

Castello 3977 ☎041 52 29 940

Popular with locals, Arco Balento is a great bar for grabbing a table and splitting a few rounds with friends. (Even) quieter and less flashy than the rest of Castello's nightlife, Arco Balento remains a good destination due to its strong

venice

drink selection and neighborhood vibe.

🚶 From P. San Marco, walk south toward water, turn left, and walk 5-6min., crossing 4 bridges. Then turn left on 3rd street after 4th bridge. $ Drinks €3-6. Snacks €6-14. ⏰ Open until 2am.

OSTERIA AL GARANGHÈLO 💳♿🍸⛱ RISTORANTE

V. Giuseppe Garibaldi 1621 ☎041 52 04 967 💻www.garanghelo.com

The restaurant officially closes at midnight, but this is Italy, where no one cares about such technicalities. On summer nights, especially weekends, Osteria al Garanghèlo has customers coming in well into the night. The restaurant feels more like a nighttime destination than other late-night restaurants in Castello, with loud Italian music, enthusiastic conversation, and a lot of energy.

🚶 From P. San Marco, walk south toward water, turn left, and continue for 7-10min. $ Drinks €4-6. Entrees €7-13. ⏰ Open M until midnight, W-Su until midnight.

arts and culture

At the height of its power during the Italian Renaissance, the Venetian Republic was one of the centers of artistic and cultural innovation, and the profound legacy of the Renaissance is evident in the architecture, music, painting, and theater that so many tourists flock to Venice to enjoy. Things have been changing quickly, though, and particularly in recent years, Venice has begun to incorporate more contemporary and modern influences in its creative scene. As a result, you'll find an incredible diversity of artistic and cultural experiences here, from the classical to the avant-garde and from the expensive to the remarkably affordable.

ORCHESTRAL MUSIC

INTERPRETI VENEZIANI - CHIESA DI SAN VIDAL 💳♿ SAN MARCO

Campo San Vidal 2862/B ☎041 27 70 561 💻www.interpretiveneziani.com

Held in the beautiful San Vidal Church in San Marco, Interpreti Veneziani's concert series has garnered the acclaim of the most discerning critics and is regarded by many as the best orchestral music in Venice. While many churches host concerts that are more casual and better suited for those who feel like they should listen to this kind of music but don't really understand it, Interpreti Veneziani caters to serious aficionados, and their concerts are much more akin to a performance at La Fenice than your typical church choir.

🚶 Immediately across the bridge from the Ponte dell'Accademia. $ Tickets are usually €40.

FRARI CONCERT SEASON - BASILICA DEI FRARI 💳♿ SAN POLO

Campo dei Frari 3072 ☎041 52 22 637

Famous for its organ, which serves as the centerpiece of many concerts, Basilica dei Frari keeps things a bit less formal than some of the other orchestral events in the city but no less praiseworthy. Concerts here tend to be less predictable than those at other venues, since the church often welcomes guest choirs (and offers reduced ticket prices for the occasion), but the venue is in high demand, meaning that performances are invariably of the highest quality.

🚶 V: Campo San Tomà. Proceed straight until you reach a T intersection; turn right, make the 1st left, and continue to the square; the entrance to the church is immediately ahead. $ Tickets €18.

CHIESA DI SANTA MARIA FORMOSA - COLLEGIUM DUCALE 💳♿ CASTELLO

Campo Santa Maria Formosa ☎041 98 81 55 💻www.collegiumducale.com

With the benefit of the marvelous acoustics of one of Venice's smaller churches, Collegium Ducale produces some of the most highly regarded opera and Baroque music performances in the city, at a pretty decent price. Santa Maria Formosa, a favorite church among many visitors to Venice, is a more intimate venue than

most others in the city and an excellent place to experience a concert.
⚐ *From Rialto Bridge, continue straight on Salizada San Lio until you reach a T-intersection; turn left; the church is immediately ahead.* ⓢ *Tickets €25, students and over 65 €20.* ☑ *Concerts typically begin at 9pm.*

ENSEMBLE ANTONIO VIVALDI - SAN GIACOMO DI RIALTO   ⚑ᕦ SAN POLO

Campo San Giacometto   ☎041 42 66 559 ▣www.ensembleantoniovivaldi.com

The ultimate historical experience of classical music in Venice, Ensemble Antonio Vivaldi (named for Venice's most famous classical musician) plays concerts in the city's oldest church, San Giacomo di Rialto. Located in a central square, the church enjoys not only an excellent historical ambience but also proximity to restaurants and nightlife, allowing concertgoers to indulge in dinner, a show, then cocktails afterward—all without having to leave Campo San Giacometto.

⚐ *Northern side of the Rialto markets, immediately before the steps leading up to the Rialto bridge.* ⓢ *Tickets €25, students and over 65 €20.* ☑ *Box office open daily 10am-6pm, until 8:45pm on the day of performances. Shows begin at 8:45pm.*

THEATER

▩ TEATRO LA FENICE   ⚑ᕦᵞ SAN MARCO

Campo San Fantin 1965   ☎041 78 65 11 ▣www.teatrolafenice.it

Venice's most versatile and prestigious venue, Teatro La Fenice is the place to go if you can only see one musical or theatrical performance during your stay. The theater itself is a remarkable building, having earned its name (The Phoenix) after rising from the ashes of three separate fires, and it's worth the price of admission just to experience the space on the night of a show. However, La Fenice is more than just a beautiful building. Its world-class acoustics draw some of the globe's top musical and theatrical talent. If you opt for the least expensive seats, you might find your view obscured, but regardless of where you're sitting, the performances here are unforgettable.

⚐ *Exit the southwest corner of P. San Marco, take the 1st right onto Frezzeria, continue for 3-4min., following the turn left in Frezzeria as the road becomes Calle del Frutariol, and turn left at Calle de la Verona; the theater is shortly ahead on the right.* ⓢ *Ticket prices depend on quality of seats and type of show. Opera €10-180, concerts €10-60, ballet €10-100.* ☑ *Show times vary, with performances most weekday evenings and weekend afternoons and evenings.*

TEATRO SAN GALLO   ⚑ᕦᵞ❀ SAN MARCO

Campo San Gallo   ☎041 24 12 002 ▣www.teatrosangallo.net

Teatro San Gallo has established a niche market with its nightly performances of *Venezia*, a show performed in English with seven different language translations available. This makes it a perfect place for readers of this book to experience the city's theater scene. In addition to hosting a phenomenal show, Teatro San Gallo partners with an adjacent trattoria to offer package deals that allow visitors to purchase a cheap yet elaborate dinner along with their ticket.

⚐ *Exit P. San Marco north onto Calle dei Fabbri and make the 2nd left after the bridge; the theater is shortly ahead in Campo San Gallo.* ⓢ *€39, students €25, ages over 65 €30, 10-14 €15, under 10 free.* ☑ *Performances daily at 7pm.*

TEATRO GOLDONI   ⚑ᕦᵞ SAN MARCO

Calle dei Fabbri 4650   ☎041 24 02 011 ▣www.teatrostabileveneto.it

Named after **Carlo Goldoni,** one of Venice's most influential playwrights, the Teatro Goldoni offers perhaps a greater variety of theatrical performances than any other venue in the city. The theater hosts numerous different performances over the course of a season, ranging from conventional European dramas to more contemporary works that present new and challenging perspectives on the art of theater. With its notable acoustics, Teatro Goldoni is also a fine place to take in musical performances.

venice

✈ From Rialto Bridge, turn right onto Riva del Carbon, continue for 3-4min., and turn right onto Calle dei Fabbri; the theater is shortly ahead on the left. [$] Prices vary according to seating and shows; contact box office for up-to-date information.

gondolas

Probably the most recognizable (and cliché) symbol of Venice, the gondola once filled the city's canals, serving as the city's main mode of water transportation. They were decorated with brilliant colors and designs that rivaled the extravagance of the famed Venetian Carnevale masks, but the city put the kibosh on the artistic arms race in the 16th century and mandated black as the standard color. In the centuries that followed, the gondola eventually fell out of favor as more efficient means of aquatic transportation became available, but several hundred still remain for the enjoyment of tourists. To prevent unsanctioned price-gouging, legal standard rates *(€80 for 40min. and up to 6 people, €40 for each additional 20min., 25% price increase for night tours)* have been established for gondola rides. Some gondoliers manage to circumvent these by charging for add-ons such as tours, singing, or other amusements. The gondola is certainly a Venetian novelty and many travelers will feel that their trip is incomplete without a ride in one, but budget travelers unwilling to shell out more for a 40min. ride than they're spending on the night's accommodations can hop on the *traghetti* for a much abbreviated, more goal-oriented (getting from one side of the Grand Canal to the other) version of the same experience. It's €0.50, and comes without the funny hats and singing (usually).

TEATRO FONDAMENTA NUOVE — 🎟♿ CANNAREGIO

Fondamenta Nuove 5013 ☎041 52 24 498 🖥www.teatrofondamentanuove.it

A smaller venue that often hosts less conventional and more avant-garde performances than Venice's best-known theaters, Teatro Fondamenta Nuove is the favorite of many locals and quickly endears itself to tourists who see its shows. Visitors who want to see artistically innovative performances with challenging content would be wise to check out Fondamenta Nuove's programming. The theater also hosts frequent musical performances, so be sure to look up their website for the upcoming schedule.

*✈ From Ca' d'Oro, turn left onto Strada Nova, then right onto Corte Longa Santa Caterina; continue for 5-7min., then turn left onto Fondamenta Nuove. **i** Tickets can be purchased online or by telephone and picked up at the theater before the show begins, or purchased at Venice tourism offices. [$] Prices vary according to seatings and shows; contact box office for up-to-date information.*

CINEMA

GIORGIONE MOVIE D'ESSAI — 🎟♿❄ CANNAREGIO

Cannaregio 4612 ☎041 52 26 298

Though Venice is famous for hosting the world's oldest film festival and frequently screens films in various museums and civic centers, the historic center has only one cinema open on a daily basis. Giorgione Movie D'Essai usually screens two different films each day and often shows English-language films with Italian subtitles. Though the theater tends to favor art house films, it hosts some popular American films as well.

*✈ V: Fondamenta Nuove. Go east until you reach Calle del Squero; turn right, continue until dead end, and turn right again. **i** Tickets are available up to a week before screenings, and ticket windows open 30min. before show time. [$] €7.50, students €5.50. ⏰ Typically, each of the 2 rooms*

screens a film twice daily, usually around 5pm and 8pm.

FESTIVALS

Venice is home to two of the premier arts festivals in Europe, the Venice Biennale and the Venice Film Festival. Although Venice is a popular tourist destination year-round, the number of visitors spikes during these two events as art and film aficionados flock to the city.

LA BIENNALE DI VENEZIA

Ca' Giustinian, San Marco 1364/A ☎041 52 18 711 🖳www.labiennale.org

First held as a relatively small art exhibition in 1895, the Venice Biennale has sky-rocketed into one of the world's most celebrated festivals of contemporary artwork. Though war, politics, and changes in the artistic community intervened to dramatically restructure the festival several times during the 20th century, it continues to attract some of the world's most talented and original artists. The festival is organized around 30 national pavilions that display contemporary artwork from the sponsor countries but also incorporates various special exhibitions. Critics laud the national pavilion format of presentation, which encourages expression of each participating nation's unique perspectives on contemporary artwork and makes visiting the Biennale as culturally informative as it is aesthetically challenging. While the Biennale is held only once every two years (that is, after all, what the name boils down to), it has become such a popular event that it has given rise to other festivals including the **International Architecture Exhibition** and **International Festival of Contemporary Music,** which have run for 12 and 54 years, respectively. The Biennale is held in years ending with an odd number (so 2011 is in luck), while the other festivals are typically held during years ending in an even number.

♯ *In the Giarddini Pubblici in Castello. Get there via vaporetto line #1, 2, 41, 42, 51, 52, or N.* ⌚ *June 4-Nov 27 2011. Odd-numbered years only.*

VENICE FILM FESTIVAL

Ca' Giustinian, San Marco 1364/A ☎041 52 18 711 🖳www.labiennale.org

Venice is home to the world's oldest film festival, which was first held in 1932 and continues to draw thousands of artists, actors, directors, and film critics to the city each fall for film screenings and celebrations of Italian and international cinema. The festival, held on Lido, has endured political turmoil (which saw Mussolini Cups awarded as the festival's top prize) and its home island's gradual decline as a popular tourist destination, yet it hasn't waned in popularity. Famous actors from all over the world, including popular Hollywood stars, continue to come to the festival each year, bringing extra verve to the peaceful beaches of eastern Lido. At this time of the year, members of the film industry, along with the journalists, fans, and paparazzi they attract, fill 1000-seat auditoriums for showings of both popular and smaller-market films.

i Contact information above is for La Biennale di Venezia offices, which operate the administration of the Venice Film Festival. ⌚ *Early Sept.*

shopping

With innumerable designer stores, clothing boutiques, Murano glass shops, Burano lace vendors, Carnival mask workshops, and other stores operated by local artisans, Venice is a shopper's paradise. Every neighborhood has something to offer, but the best places can be found along the main streets of San Marco, Cannaregio, and San Polo as well as the areas adjacent to the Rialto Bridge. Though there are a fair number of shops with generic, overpriced merchandise who prey on tourists who haven't done sufficient comparison shopping, there are also a lot of great stores with incredible deals, especially for the shrewd negotiator. While the amount of English that shop owners speak is usually inversely proportional to how hard you press for a discount, prices can often be talked down. Failing that, tax refunds are often offered by stores that specialize in high-priced goods. If you're spending more than a few euro, it's worth asking about every possible discount, including those affiliated with *Let's Go* and **Rolling Venice** (if you have the card) as well as those that come from paying in cash. Some owners will deduct as much as 10% if any of these apply.

VENETIAN ARTISAN GOODS

Of the top three artisan goods made in Venice—glass, masks, and lace—only the masks are typically produced in the city itself. Glass is produced in the northern lagoon island of **Murano**, which has been a world capital for high-quality artisan glass goods since Venice's glass furnaces were banished from the city center in 1291, while lace is generally produced in **Burano**, a quiet island to the north of Murano whose economy is based primarily on fishing and the production of handmade lace. Though the islands offer numerous stores and the most extensive selection of glass and lace, there's no need to make a trip to the northern lagoon just to go shopping. Venice has a solid number of reputable stores and has lately been seriously cracking down on counterfeit goods. Glass and masks tend to make great and affordable presents or souvenirs, but be cautious when shopping for Burano lace. Making elaborate lace by hand is an exhausting and time-consuming process, so many stores sell Burano-style lace that is actually machine-made. There isn't a whole lot of difference between the two styles, but if getting the real deal matters to you, pay special attention to the price. If the price you're paying doesn't seem outrageously expensive, you can be pretty sure what you're getting isn't handmade.

👍 CA' MACANA — 💳♿ DORSODURO

Dorsoduro 3172 — ☎041 27 76 142 💻www.camacana.com

Venice is overrun with mask shops, but Ca' Macana is one of the few places that focuses exclusively on Carnival masks and regards its work as a serious art form. Though the shop has an unmatched selection of masks, it's Ca' Macana's workshops, where you can see masks being made by hand, that truly set it apart. The masks are great souvenirs, but keep in mind that the larger ones can be tough to transport: shipping a mask overseas will likely set you back twice the cost of the mask itself.

‡ From Campo San Barnaba go south; the store is ahead on the left. The showroom and mask-making courses are in 2 different storefronts just north of Campo San Barnaba. $ Masks €15-60. ⏰ Open daily 10am-7pm.

MA.RE — 💳♿ SAN MARCO

V. XXII Marco 2088 — ☎041 52 31 191 💻www.mareglass.com

MA.RE is stylish and cutting-edge without being jarringly avant-garde and offers pieces that are practical and functional rather than just glass for glass's sake. Unlike other stores specializing in kitsch and easily mass-produced artifacts, MA.RE makes sensible yet innovatively designed products. This is particularly evident in the beautiful wine, cocktail, and drinking glasses that manifest the talent of their Murano artists—without stretching the artistry to the point that it overwhelms the product.

‡ Exit the southwest corner of P. San Marco, continue west across a bridge, and keep walking for less than 2min.; the store is ahead on the right. $ Prices vary depending on quality of glass and product. ⏰ Open daily 10:30am-7pm.

DUE ZETA — 💳 SAN MARCO

Calle Larga San Marco 368-371 — ☎041 63 17 79 💻www.duezeta.net

A lot of the glass sellers around San Marco greet tourists with a smile and a

50% markup, but the manager of Due Zeta is much more likely to introduce himself with a sneer and offers of steep discounts. The expansive store—which fills its three storefronts with an incredible selection—offers everything from inexpensive glass jewelry and souvenirs to gorgeous high-end glass artwork that is worth taking some time to admire, even if you're not in the market for a €2500 chandelier.

🪧 From P. San Marco, 2nd street to the north. $ Earrings and other jewelry as little as €3. Chandeliers up to €2500. ⏰ Open daily 9am-11pm.

P. SCARPA 💳♿ SAN POLO

Campo Frari 3007 ☎041 52 38 681

One of the few lace shops outside of Burano that sells high-quality handmade products from the island, P. Scarpa captures the atmosphere of Burano perhaps better than any other store in Venice proper. If you care about your product being handmade, make sure to check with the staff. Because it's almost impossible to tell just by looking.

🪧 Along the southern edge of the square opposite the church. $ Prices vary. A lot. ⏰ Open daily 10:30am-7pm.

DESIGNER STORES

Most major Italian design houses and internationally recognized brands have outposts in Venice, the vast majority of which are just west of **Piazza San Marco.** Shopping for designer clothing and accessories is entirely different from shopping for most other local goods, since haggling over prices won't be well-received, and discounts are unlikely to apply. Purchases will be prohibitively expensive for a lot of budget travelers, but the shopping experience itself should be enjoyable. If you do purchase anything pricey, be sure to inquire about the possibility of a **Value Added Tax refund.**

👍 SALVATORE FERRAGAMO 💳♿ SAN MARCO

Calle Larga XXII Marzo 2098 ☎041 27 78 509 💻www.ferragamo.com

Ferragamo, a design group originally based in Florence that now owns hundreds of stores all over the world, has earned a reputation over the years for making exceptionally high-quality products that never go out of style. Though perhaps most famous for their shoes and leather goods, Ferragamo's clothing, fragrances, and accessories have all garnered high praise from the fashion world. If you only bother to visit one designer store in Venice, make it this one, where you can experience Ferragamo's world-class customer service and see products by the design group that aren't available in North America.

🪧 Exit the southwest corner of P. San Marco and continue west for 2-3min.; the store is ahead on the left. ⏰ Open daily 10am-7:30pm.

ERMENEGILDO ZEGNA 💳♿ SAN MARCO

Bocca di P. San Marco 1242 ☎041 52 21 204 💻www.zegna.com

Though top-quality men's suits continue to be Zegna's hallmark, the internationally acclaimed fashion house is by no means limited to men's formalwear. With perhaps more square footage than any other designer store in Venice, Zegna offers an incredible selection of men's and women's fashion and is the place to go for everything from swimwear to Venetian high society garb.

🪧 Exit the southwest corner of P. San Marco and turn right; the store is shortly ahead. ⏰ Open M-Sa 10am-7:30pm, Su 10am-7pm.

EMILIO PUCCI 💳♿ SAN MARCO

Calle Vallaresso 1318 ☎041 52 05 733 💻www.emiliopucci.com

Distinguished by its trademark outrageous (and distinctively Italian) use of bright colors and bold patterns, Pucci is the ideal place to shop for a dress and matching handbag that are sure to turn heads. Though the store is rather small and the men's section is limited to a few ties, the service is second to none. If you're the type who favors audacious fashion and can pull it off, you'd be remiss to leave Italy without at least checking out one Pucci store.

➜ *Exit the southwest corner of P. San Marco and take the 2nd left; the store is about 1min. away on the left side of the street.* ⏰ *Open daily 10am-7pm.*

GUCCI 💳♿ SAN MARCO

Calle Larga XXII Marzo 2101 ☎041 24 13 968 💻www.gucci.com

The best-known and best-selling Italian designer internationally, Gucci has something for everyone, whether it be Wall-Street-ready suits or worn and ripped jeans. The Venice store has a great selection, but be forewarned that Gucci's international fame makes it a common destination for most tourists passing through the San Marco fashion district, causing it to be pretty overcrowded. If you successfully wagered €50 on double zero at a roulette table in Casino di Venezia and have decided to go for a total wardrobe makeover, check out the other Gucci store at San Marco 258 near the St. Mark's Clocktower, which specializes in shoes, watches, jewelry, and the luggage you'll need to take it all back home.

➜ *Exit the southwest corner of P. San Marco and continue west for about 3min.; the store is ahead on the left.* ⏰ *Open daily 10am-7:30pm.*

PRADA 💳♿ SAN MARCO

Salizada San Moisè ☎041 52 83 966 💻www.prada.com

Prada has made a name for itself by challenging the norms of the fashion world, and if you visit their Venice location, you'll see it is no exception to this philosophy. With strong colors, innovative and suggestive fabric cuts, and strikingly original combinations of different design influences, Prada continues to be a label charting its own course in the fashion world. Even if you don't stop in, it's worth spending a while admiring the window displays, which are the most creative and amusing you'll find in any of the city's stores.

➜ *Exit the southwest corner of P. San Marco and continue west; the store is on the right shortly before the bridge.* ⏰ *Open daily 10am-7:30pm.*

MARKETS

Though Venice has relatively few open spaces and streets, it is the setting for a number of respectable outdoor markets selling fresh fruit, vegetables, and seafood. Though the markets can be a bit intimidating to the timid traveler—you might be surprised by the vendors' brusque manners—if you're assertive, you'll find excellent values on the freshest and most delicious produce in the city. Prices are typically posted, so you don't have to worry about getting overcharged. Do make sure you're paying for produce that isn't blemished or bruised, though, since some vendors try to pass the damaged wares off on tourists who are less likely to complain.

👍 **RIALTO MARKET** 🚫💳♿ SAN POLO

San Polo

Once the biggest market in the Mediterranean, the Rialto Market still does business largely the way it has for nearly the past millennium. With wholesalers, retailers, restaurateurs, local shoppers, and tourists, things can get kind of crazy, but the spectacle of the market is part of what makes it great. If you scour for long enough, you should be able to find almost anything you want, including imported delicacies that most local supermarkets don't stock. The Rialto Market is more than a mere relic in Venice. Indeed, it remains a vital piece of the city's culinary scene—most locals will tell you to avoid ordering fish in a restaurant on Mondays because the Rialto fish market isn't open Sunday or Monday, meaning the city's entire stock is less likely to be fresh.

➜ *On the San Polo side of the Rialto Bridge, walk toward the Grand Canal and continue west.* Ⓢ *Prices are variable but cheap.* ⏰ *Open M-Sa 8am-noon. Fish available Tu-Sa 8am-noon.*

MARKETS OF RIO TERÀ SAN LEONARDO ⊛♿ CANNAREGIO

Rio Terà San Leonardo 1300-1500

When traffic starts to pick up in Cannaregio and the streets become crowded with pedestrians, the middle part of Rio Terà San Leonardo becomes one of Venice's best outdoor markets. With an excellent selection of fresh fruits, both from within Italy and around the world, the markets on this street are a delightful place to chat with local shoppers while getting a quick and delicious snack at an exceptional price.

➜ From the west, just across Guglie bridge. From the east, along Strada Nova. $ Fruit €1-10 per kg. ⏰ Open daily about 8:30am-sunset, depending on weather.

TRADITIONAL BOAT MARKET ⊛♿ DORSODURO

Campo San Barnaba

A relic from Venice's past without a fixed name or address, the 👍**boat** market docked near Campo San Barnaba is the best remaining example of Venice's answer to the supermarket. If you want to actually buy things, go to one of the markets listed. If you want a cool experience, come here. In theory, it's a market run out of a boat, but it's actually so popular that it also occupies a storefront opposite the boat's moorings.

➜ Exit Campo San Margherita in the southwest corner and continue west until you reach the bridge; the market is on the water. $ Prices are variable but quite cheap. ⏰ Open M-Sa 8am-6pm. Hours may vary, especially during winter.

essentials

PRACTICALITIES

venice

- **TOURIST OFFICES: APT Tourist Office** provides information, maps, tours, the Rolling Venice Card, and theater and concert tickets. Outposts are located throughout the city. *(Main Office: P. Rom ☎041 24 11 499 💻www.turismovenezia.it ℹ Additional offices near P. San Marco (San Marco 71) and on Lido (Gran Viale 6/A). ⏰ Open daily 9:30am-1pm and 1:30-4:30pm.)*
- **LUGGAGE STORAGE: Stazione Santa Lucia.** *(☎041 78 55 31 💻www.grandistazioni.it ➜ At the train station. ℹ Cash only. $ First 5hr. €4, €0.60 per hr. up to 12, €0.20 per hr. thereafter. ⏰ Open daily 6am-midnight.)*
- **DISABILITY SERVICES: Informahandicap** provides information to physically disabled travelers in Venice, which, given the city's crazy design, is potentially a very useful thing. *(San Marco 4136 ☎041 27 48 144 💻www.comune.venezia.it ➜ Nearest vaporetto stop is Rialto. On Riva del Carbon, 2-3min. southwest of Rialto Bridge. ⏰ Open Th 9am-1pm.)*
- **PUBLIC TOILETS: AMAV W.C.** provides public toilets in various locations throughout the city, indicated by blue and white signs that read "W.C." *(⊛ $ €1.50. ⏰ Open daily 8:30am-8:45pm.)*
- **POST OFFICES: Poste Venezia Centrale.** *(Main office at San Marco 5554, with branches all over the city ☎041 24 04 158 💻www.poste.it ➜ Nearest vaporetto stop Rialto. The post office is off of Campo San Bartolomeo, directly in front of the Rialto Bridge. ⏰ Open M-Sa 8am-7pm.)*

EMERGENCY!

- **POLICE:** There are police stations all over the city, but the main one is the **Carabinieri** office. *(Campo San Zaccaria, Castello 4693/A ☎041 27 411 ⚓ Walk straight and follow the signs from vaporetto San Zaccaria.)*

- **HOSPITALS/MEDICAL SERVICES: Ospedale Civile.** *(Campo Giovanni e Paolo Santissimi, Castello 6777 ☎041 52 94 111 ▣www.ulss12.ve.it ⚓ Walk east from vaporetto Fondamenta Nuove and turn right after 1st bridge. i Be forewarned: the hospital has limited hours and is likely to redirect you elsewhere for further treatment.)*

GETTING THERE

By Plane

As many tourists are crestfallen to discover, though **Aeroporto Marco Polo (VCE)** *(☎041 26 09 260 ▣www.veniceairport.it)* is billed as Venice's airport, once you've made it there, the journey to Venice's historic center has only just begun. You could opt to take a water taxi to reach the *centro*, which would cost about €100, but there are several more economical ways to make it to Venice from the airport. **Alilaguna** *(☎041 24 01 701 ▣www.alilaguna.it)* offers transport directly from VCE to the city center at €12 per passenger, but the service isn't necessarily the most expedient option. The ultimate budget solution is to take any one of a number of bus lines to **Piazzale Roma,** located near the Calatrava Bridge just minutes away from **Stazione Santa Lucia.** The buses, which offer convenient transportation throughout the region, are operated by **ACTV** *(☎041 24 24 ▣www.hellovenezia.it)* and cost as little as €2.50. This is comparable to the **ATVO Shuttle** bus, which also stops at Piazzale Roma and costs €3 for a one-way trip. Regardless of how you plan to get from Aeroporto Marco Polo to the city, be sure to get your ticket before leaving the airport—tickets for transportation services are most easily purchased at the windows there.

By Train

Most travelers who are already in Italy will either reach Venice by bus or by train. The extra-urban line operated by ACTV runs several buses per hour between Venice and the two nearest major cities, Padua and Treviso. However, each trip takes about an hour, and the consensus is that train travel is more economical and convenient, particularly for those traveling with luggage. Several train lines run through **Stazione Santa Lucia** *(☎041 26 09 260 ▣www.veneziasantalucia.it),* in the east of the city, bringing people from **Bologna** *(Ⓢ €8.90. ⏰ 2hr., 30 per day.),* **Florence** *(Ⓢ €22.50. ⏰ 2-3hr., 20 per day.),* **Milan** *(Ⓢ €14.55. ⏰ 2½-3½hr.),* **Padua** *(Ⓢ €2.90. ⏰ 26-50min., 80 per day.),* **Rome** *(Ⓢ €42.50. ⏰ 3½-6hr., 20 per day.),* and numerous local destinations.

GETTING AROUND

On Foot

Though Venice is a wonderful city with many great things to offer visitors, convenience of transportation isn't one of them. Within the city's six *sestiere*, there are absolutely no cars, buses, or trains, and the occasional skateboard or pushcart is about the only thing you'll see with wheels. While poets, musicians, and various members of the literati have waxed nostalgic about the beauty of Venice's romantic, tangled streets, those same winding walkways are likely to provoke less lyrical outbursts from those unfamiliar with the city. Even experienced travelers will likely find themselves frustrated when navigating the city, since maps struggle to provide adequate detailing of the city's smaller thoroughfares. Additionally, streets are often nameless or change names unexpectedly, and street numbers organized by neighborhood give only a general indication of where particular addresses are to be found. Your best bet is to memorize a few major landmarks, know the vaporetto stop nearest your hotel, know at least one *campo* near your hotel or hostel, and keep the cardinal directions in mind.

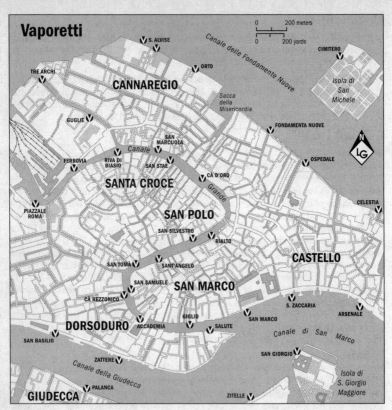

Vaporetti

0 ... 200 meters

0 ... 200 yards

S. ALVISE

Canale delle Fondamente Nuove

CIMITERO

ORTO

TRE ARCHI

CANNAREGIO

Sacca della Misericordia

Isola di San Michele

GUGLIE

FONDAMENTA NUOVE

SAN MARCUOLA

Canale

FERROVIA

RIVA DI BIASIO

SAN STAE

CA D'ORO

OSPEDALE

SANTA CROCE

Grande

CELESTIA

PIAZZALE ROMA

SAN POLO

SAN SILVESTRO

RIALTO

CASTELLO

SAN TOMA

SANT'ANGELO

SAN SAMUELE

CA REZZONICO

SAN MARCO

S. ZACCARIA

ARSENALE

GIGLIO

SAN MARCO

DORSODURO

ACCADEMIA

SALUTE

SAN BASILIO

Canale di San Marco

ZATTERE

SAN GIORGIO

Canale della Giudecca

PALANCA

Isola di S. Giorgio Maggiore

GIUDECCA

ZITELLE

venice

By Boat

In some cases, particularly when bridges are scarce, travelers will find it more convenient to get to their destination by boat. Before you spend a lot of money on an expensive vaporetto ticket, consider whether a **traghetto** might get you to your destination more quickly. There are several major stops in the city where you can catch these small ferries, essentially gondolas without the kitsch, that will take you across the Grand Canal for only €0.50. Signs toward *traghetti* stops tend to be clearly indicated, and odds are, wherever you are, there will be one nearby. *Traghetti* hours vary and are limited during the winter, but in general, they remain an excellent means of transport around Venice. The vaporetti offer more extensive service throughout the city and operate 24hr. per day but are also more expensive. A single vaporetto ride costs €6.50 and longer-term passes which offer unlimited service are also available *(☎ 12hr. pass €16; 24hr. €18; 3-day €21; 4-day €28; 7-day €50)*, but the best option for students visiting in the short-term may be to purchase a three-day pass *(€22)* that includes unlimited transport via vaporetti and mainland-connecting buses as well as the benefits of the **Rolling Venice Card.**

FLORENCE

With Michelangelos crammed into every corner and Botticellis stacked clear to the sky, Florence isn't quite a real city—it's more like a storage facility for the Renaissance. Race through the Tuscan capital in three to five days, consuming masterpieces like a fresco-eating Pac-Man, and you're bound to remember Florence as a beautiful—if blurry—delight. Look too closely, though, and the seams begin to show. A large portion of the city's seemingly 16th-century buildings and frescoes are actually 19th-century reproductions, sometimes making it feel as if you're in a chase scene out a cheap cartoon where the same handful of background cells have been reused over and over again. Add in the overwhelming tourist crush and the lack of any local industry aside from the manufacture of plaster *Davids*, and it can all start to seem a bit Disney World.

So don't stretch out your stay. With little green space, performance art, or night-life, Florence is the place for concentrated sightseeing at its best. In the end, you'll find it's better to give the city just a few days of intense museum- and church-going and leave feeling as though you've seen only the tip of a remarkable iceberg than overstay and never want to visit another gloriously frescoed cathedral again. Because really, they truly are glorious.

greatest hits

- **LINES BE DAMNED.** There's a reason people wait in 4hr. lines to get into the Uffizi. See possibly the world's greatest collection of Renaissance art, and follow our guide to understanding the art and avoiding the lines (p. 197).

- **BOBOLI TOP.** The luscious Boboli Gardens south of the Arno River offer views and rare greenery (p. 211).

- **GELATO GIANTS.** Where is it better, Rome or Florence? Head to Grom (p. 215) or Gelateria dei Neri (p. 221) to find out where you stand in the eternal ice cream debate.

- **THE JOYS OF ACCADEMIA.** Michelangelo's *David* is the centerpiece of the Galleria dell'Accademia in San Marco. There are numerous replicas all over the city (Florentines like to remind you of why they're great), but this is the real thing (p. 206).

orientation

Our coverage of Florence is divided into neighborhoods that roughly correspond to the major church districts. These distinctions are mostly for convenience's sake, to divide the city into more manageable chunks. In a short visit, you are unlikely to notice any significant variation from one area to the next, but here are some rules of thumb. Near the Uffizi is expensive. The eastern third of the city is student-y and contains some bright patches of nightlife. The train station has the cheaper eats, sleeps, and shopping. The other side of the river is home to more locals and trees. Everything is very quiet near the city walls. All roads lead to the Duomo.

THE DUOMO

In a city where the streets were lain with 15th-century logic and everything looks pretty much the same, you'll find the Duomo an invaluable navigational aid. No matter how lost you get, you'll probably be able to find your way back here, so learn to get to your hostel from the Duomo and you're all set. Likewise, it makes a handy meeting point when you're trying to coordinate plans without a cell phone.

PIAZZA DELLA SIGNORIA

Near the **Uffizi** and river, this *piazza* is where the well-heeled and the honeymooning spend their time and money. With cheaper food and lodging options to the immediate east and north, you'll come here mostly to hang out in the spacious *piazze* and see some of the city's most famous sights.

SANTA MARIA NOVELLA

Santa Maria Novella train station will likely be your first introduction to Florence, and whether you first venture east or south will color your earliest impressions of the city. To the east of the train station you'll find the cheap accommodations and casual food joints you'd expect of a neighborhood that serves as a transport hub. To the south await the church that gives the station its name, a pastoral *piazza*, and streets filled with folks hanging out late into the evening. Don't bother venturing north or west, as you'll be leaving Florence's historic center before you've even set foot in the heart of the city.

SAN LORENZO

Slightly east of the train station is this land of budget accommodations and 99 cent stores. San Lorenzo's vendors and the fresh food market of **Mercato Centrale** make this part of Florence an excellent base, even if staying here means you'll be a bit removed from the city's nightlife.

SAN MARCO

By "San Marco," we mean pretty much everything from **Piazza San Marco** itself north up to the edge of the old city. The defining characteristic of this area is the sheer number of museums and bus stops per sq. ft. Stick to the south edge late at night, though—north of the *piazza* is one of the quietest areas of the old city, and once the buses stop running, it can be unsafe. Travel with a friend if you're passing through this part of San Marco late at night.

SANTA CROCE

Wander eastward from the Duomo and you'll likely find yourself in Santa Croce. The neighborhood runs east along the Arno away from central Florence. With few big-name tourist attractions and a lot of university students, this part of town is where you'll primarily find cheap lunches and evening entertainment—or perhaps just a lot of English speaking students clutching copies of this book and asking where the party's at: Florentine nightlife is more about hanging around outside and drinking with friends than pumping bass and exclusive clubs. It'd be a pretty cool trick if we turned some *piazza* into nightlife central just by sending you all there, but really, why mess up a good thing?

WEST OLTRARNO

This is the cool part of the Oltrarnos—the area on the south side of the Arno. It feels more authentic and lived-in than the other side of the river but still has a high density of hostels and museums. All-in-all a nice scene, and worthy of a visit if you're in town for more than a day or two.

EAST OLTRARNO

Aside from the **Piazzale Michelangelo,** there probably isn't much to bring you here. We've set the Oltrarnos' east-west dividing line at the **Ponte Vecchio,** but you'll find a large residential stretch between the immediate Ponte Vecchio area and the nightlife of **Ponte San Niccolo.** Head uphill for views.

accommodations

Travel in a small group to get your money's worth in Florence, particularly during the low season. Two to four people can score gorgeous rooms in three-star hotels for a lower per-person rate than you'll find at a hostel. Although most hotel rooms are doubles, it is not difficult to find triples, quads, and even family suites. For the solo traveler, options are a little more limited. Florence is home to only a few good hostels, and most otherwise affordable accommodations charge a pretty penny for singles. However, if you're only in town for a few days, there are plenty of acceptable options in central locations. If you're sticking around a little longer, consider commuting from a hostel outside the city, where you'll find better deals, cleaner air, and more adventurous travelers. Whatever your situation, keep in mind that low season is called "low" for a reason: nightly room rates can drop by €10-20 when the city is less flooded with out-of-towners seeking beds. In our listings, we've stuck to high-season rates, so those of you traveling to Florence in February can silently gloat every time you read a price estimate and think about how much lower your rate will be.

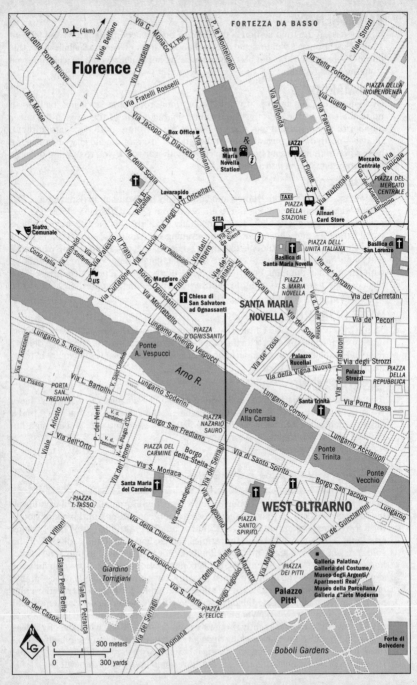

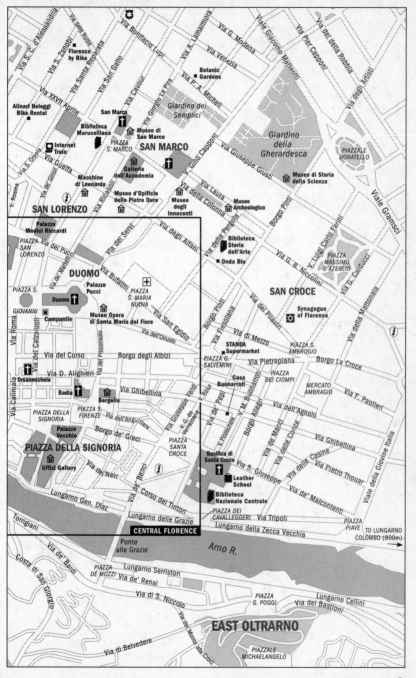

accommodations

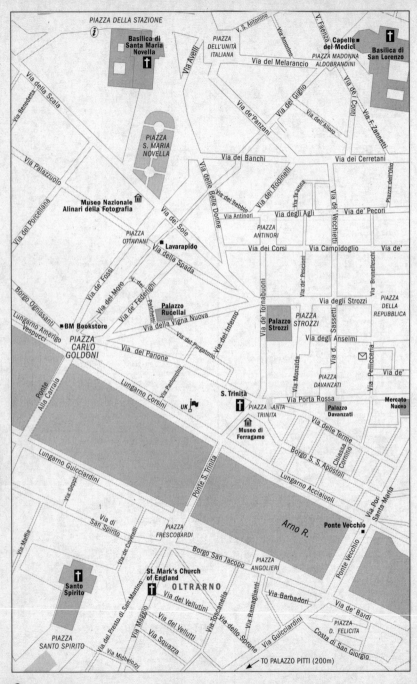

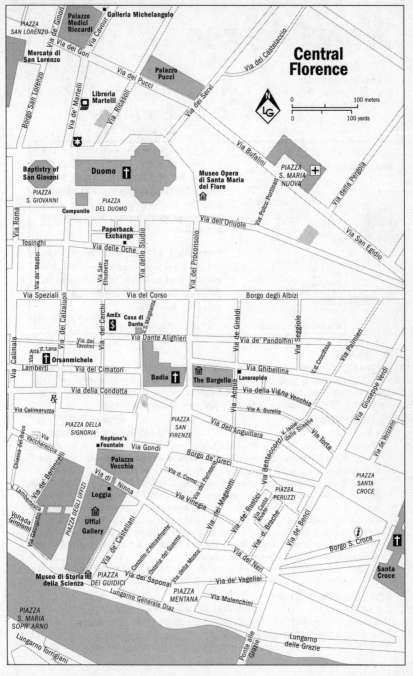

Central Florence

PIAZZA SAN LORENZO

Palazzo Medici Riccardi

Galleria Michelangelo

Mercato di San Lorenzo

Via de' Ginori

Via dei Gori

Via Cavour

Via dei Pucci

Palazzo Pucci

Via del Servi

Via del Castelaccio

Via di Martelli

Libreria Martelli

Via Ricasoli

Borgo San Lorenzo

Via de' Medici

Via Bufalini

PIAZZA S. MARIA NUOVA

Via della Pergola

Baptistry of San Giovani

Duomo

Museo Opera di Santa Maria del Fiore

Via Porta Portinari

PIAZZA S. GIOVANNI

PIAZZA DEL DUOMO

Campanile

Via dell'Oriuole

Via San Egidio

Via Roma

Tosinghi

Paperback Exchange

Via delle Oche

Via San Elisabetta

Via dello Studio

Via del Proconsolo

Via Speziali

Via del Corso

Borgo degli Albizi

Via del Calzaiuoli

Via de' Cerchi

AmEx

Casa di Dante

S. Margherita

Via de' Giraldi

Via de' Pandolfini

Via delle Seggiole

Vc. Crocifisso

Via Palmieri

Calimala

Arte d. Lana

Orsanmichele

Via dei Tavolini

Via Dante Alighieri

Via della Condotta

Lamberti

Via del Cimatori

Badia

The Bargello

Via Ghibellina

Lavarapido

Via della Vigna Vecchia

Via Giuseppe Verdi

Via Acqua

Via A. Burella

Via de' Bentaccordi

V. Isole delle Stinche

Via Torta

Via Verzano

Via Calimaruzza

PIAZZA DELLA SIGNORIA

Neptune's Fountain

Via Gondi

PIAZZA SAN FIRENZE

Via dell'Anguillara

PIAZZA PERUZZI

Chiasso del Bucco

Via Vacchereccia

Palazzo Vecchio

Borgo de' Greci

Via d. Corno

Via del Pardescio

Via Canto Rivolo

Via de' Rustici

PIAZZA SANTA CROCE

Via de' Baroncelli

Via di Ninna

Loggia

Via Vinegia

Via dei Magalotti

Via d. Brache

Borgo S. Croce

V. Lambertesca

Uffizi Gallery

PIAZZA DEGLI UFFIZI

Castello d'Altrafronte

Osteria del Guanto

Via della Mosca

Via de' Neri

Via de' Benci

(i)

Voltada Giroiami

Via Giorgofili

Castellani

Santa Croce

Museo di Storia della Scienza

PIAZZA DEI GUIDICI

Via dei Saponai

PIAZZA MENTANA

Via de' Vagellai

Via Malenchini

PIAZZA S. MARIA SOPR' ARNO

Lungarno Generale Diaz

Lungarno Torrigiani

Ponte alle Grazie

Lungarno delle Grazie

accommodations

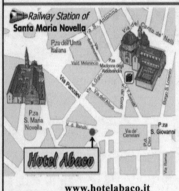
THE DUOMO

There are a lot of options in the most central part of the city, though none are super
cheap. The Academy is your best bet, particularly if you can book in advance. To go
up a notch, check out the many nice small hotels, mostly found to the east and north
of the Duomo. While Florence *is* tiny, it's still nice to be at its center.

ACADEMY HOSTEL   ◉ & (ᵗ) ※ HOSTEL ❷

V. Ricasoli 9   ☎055 23 98 665 ▧www.academyhostels.com
This is the poshest hostel in Florence, and if you're planning ahead, it is the place
to stay. For a few euro more than **Ostello Archi Rossi** and **Hostel Plus**—the other good
hostel options in town—you get free pasta and wine every evening at 6:30pm as
well as towels, privacy screens, bedside tables, and no bunk beds. Academy is
also far smaller than the other options, sleeping only 30 people at a time. For
better or for worse, the price keeps away the hordes of drunk teenagers and the
more adventurous backpackers, so the Academy mostly attracts middle-ground
types who book in advance. The uncommonly helpful day staff learn names and,
like the ritziest of concierges, know the city inside and out. Lockout may seem
inconvenient, but it keeps the place spotless.
*❖ Less than a block north of the Duomo, on the left. **i** Breakfast and dinner included. Credit card
min. €150. Free Wi-Fi. ⓢ Dorms €29-34. ⓩ Reception 24hr. Lockout 11am-2pm.*

HOTEL LOCANDA ORCHIDEA   ◆ & (ᵗ) HOTEL ❸

V. Borgo Degli Albizi   ☎055 24 80 346 ▧www.hotelorchideaflorence.it/history.html
A lovely, homey little place, with tile floors, leather couches, and a narrow terrace that's overgrown in a romantic sort of way. It's charmingly cluttered and
den-like in most of the common space, but the shared bathrooms are large and
clean.

florence

➔ V. Borgo Degli Albizi leads from the southeast of the Duomo piazza. i Tea and coffee all day. Good ceiling fans. $ Singles €30-55; doubles €50-75; quads €80-120. ⏰ Reception 8am-10pm.

HOTEL CASCI
💳♿📶 HOTEL [4]

V. Cavour, 13 ☎055 21 16 86 💻www.hotelcasci.com

Twenty-four rooms of varying sizes each have wood shutters, cable on actually new-ish TVs, and big ol' bathtubs. A very large breakfast room hosts a very large, American-style breakfast buffet (gluten-free upon request). Flexible triples and larger family rooms make this a good option for a small group traveling together.

➔ North of the Duomo, on the right. i Breakfast included. Free Wi-Fi. $ Doubles €80-150; quads €150-230. 10% discount for paying cash. ⏰ Reception 24hr.

RESIDENZA DEI PUCCI
💳🚭📶 B AND B [4]

V. dei Pucci 9 ☎055 26 43 14 💻www.residenzadeipucci.com

Each of the 12 double rooms (and one panoramic suite) of this classy little bed and breakfast is different, but four-poster beds, glass-fronted armoires, and little balconies are frequent features. A nice Italian breakfast is included.

➔ Northeast of the Duomo. i Wi-Fi available for a fee. $ Doubles €80-150, superior €105-170; suite €120-250. €15 discount for single person in double room. ⏰ Reception 9am-8pm.

HOTEL DALÍ
💳♿📶 HOTEL [3]

V. Dell' Oriuolo 17 ☎055 23 40 706 💻www.hoteldali.com

Despite the name, there's nothing particularly surreal about this sunny little hotel. Simple rooms with stenciled walls and rugs on the floor are made more pleasant by ceiling fans and windows looking onto a small, verdant courtyard. Dalí also offers free parking, which is kind of a big deal—this is quite possibly the only hotel in its price range to offer such a perk.

➔ About a 5min. walk down Oriuolo from the Duomo, on the right. i Breakfast only included when checking out. $ Singles without bath €35-40; doubles €50-65, with bath €60-80. ⏰ Reception 24hr.

PIAZZA DELLA SIGNORIA

This is the area where your parents would stay, so the budget options are limited and usually shady. However, among all the posh hotels are a few that would make excellent splurges.

☑ HOTEL BRETAGNA
💳♿📶🍸 HOTEL [4]

Lungarno Corsini 6 ☎055 28 96 18 💻www.hotelbretagna.net

Beautiful historic suites with frescoed ceilings merit a price tag that's twice as high, and even this hotel's standard rooms are lovely. A tiny balcony off the lobby looks out on the Arno—at sunset, it's a fine place for a coffee or smoke. Breakfast is served in a hall lined with antique porcelain adjacent to a banquet hall that would not be out of place in one of the city's major *palazzi*.

➔ Facing the river, it's 2 blocks right of Ponte Vecchio. i Breakfast included. $ Doubles €90-110; historic rooms €110-140. Several larger suites available. ⏰ Reception 24hr.

HOSTEL VERONIQUE / ALEKIN HOSTEL
💳♿📶 HOSTEL [2]

V. Porta Rossa 6, 2nd and 4th fl. ☎055 26 08 332

These are two barebones hostels on two floors of the same building, run by mother and son. Rooms are all private and sleep two to four. The bathroom on the hall is shared. The place could use a better paint job, but otherwise it's clean and serviceable.

➔ Just north of Mercato Nuovo. i Free Wi-Fi. Cash preferred. $ Beds around €25. ⏰ Alekin (he of the title) will sleep in the hostel if there are any late arrivals expected.

RELAIS CAVALCANTI HOTEL ❹

V. Pellicceria 2 ☎055 21 09 62 www.relaiscavalcanti.com

Antique photographs line the pastel hall off of which you'll find airy rooms named after artists. Painted armoires and, in some cases, bathtubs are room highlights. Complimentary coffee and pastries all day.

V. Pellicceria is off of P. della Signoria. *i* *Free Wi-Fi.* $ *High-season standard rooms €90; doubles €110.* *Reception 9am-1pm, and they're around in the afternoon if there are check-ins coming. Will give a key to guests.*

SANTA MARIA NOVELLA

As in almost any city, there are plenty of budget hotels located right next to the train station. If you roll into town late and are just looking for somewhere to crash, head straight to **Via Fiume,** which is lined with hotels. The area between the station and river offers some posher options. Whatever you're looking for, make sure to ignore the monstrous Majestic Hotel that is very visible from the train station—despite the building's valuable real estate, it is empty and abandoned.

PENSIONE LA SCALA PENSIONE ❹

V. della Scala 21 ☎055 21 26 29

Don't be scared off by the name of the building in which Pensione La Scala is situated—Residence Bellevue. This place may be a bit mental, but it's no institution. Rather, it's a comfy, personal bed and breakfast with a stuffed crocodile, frescoed ceilings, a nifty vintage radio that sometimes works, and a dining room table full of books and papers. It will be cleared for breakfast only if you're able to get on avuncular proprietor Gabriel's good side. Gabriel lives on premises and describes himself as Santa Claus—especially to those who are quick to flash a smile, or show up on an under-booked night., or pay cash.

Down from the train station, on the left. *i* *Cash preferred.* $ *Doubles €80-90; triples €120-135; quads €160-180.* *Reception 24hr., but Gabriel would rather not be woken up at odd hours.*

HOTEL CONSIGLI HOTEL ❸

Lungarno Amerigo Vespucci 50 ☎055 21 41 72 www.hotelconsigli.com

If you are traveling in a small group, this gorgeous hotel on the Arno is a no-brainer. The grand staircase of the 16th-century building leads to airy rooms with original frescoes on the ceilings: the family-size suites are an especially impressive option for a well-behaved group of four. Brave a narrow spiral staircase to have a glass of wine on the enormous terrace overlooking the river. And with the American consulate right next door, you're sure to be first in line for the airlift if Florence is invaded by zombies.

Follow the river west, up past the consulate. *i* *Breakfast included. Remodeling project underway in 2010, prices (and quality) may rise thereafter.* $ *Doubles €90; triples €120; family suite €130.*

DESIREE HOTEL HOTEL ❸

V. Fiume 20 ☎055 23 82 382 www.desireehotel.com

All the hotels in this old, palatial building have attractive stained glass—but Desiree gets the lion's share, with stained glass plentiful in both the lobby and in some of the 18 unique rooms. Other rooms have little balconies, chandeliers, or big antique armoires, and even the plainer rooms have flowers painted on the bathroom tiling. Sip your coffee on the sunny, small balcony off the breakfast room when the weather's nice.

V. Fiume is parallel to the train station. $ *Singles €75; doubles €100; quads €140.* *Reception 24hr.*

HOTEL SERENA

👜♿❋ HOTEL ❷

V. Fiume 20

☎055 21 36 43 🖳www.albergoserena.it

The most notable characteristic of this simple little hotel is the Yorkshire terrier. Florence isn't much of a dog town, so if you're starved for some canine affection, the sweet Yorkie might be the thing to distinguish this otherwise standard option from the many similar hotels in its price range. There's also some nice stained-glass doors and stuff. But a Yorkie, really!

🍴 *From train station, left onto V. Nazionale then left onto V. Fiume.* 𝒊 *Breakfast included.* Ⓢ *Singles €35-50; doubles €50-60; triples €75; quads €90-100.* 🕐 *Reception 24hr.*

STELLA MARY

👜♿❋ HOTEL ❸

V. Fiume 17

☎055 27 41 599 🖳www.hotelstellamary.it

The seven rooms of this understated little hotel have white walls and simple decor, ideal if you need a palate cleanser after the sensory overload of Florentine decorative art. Rooms have big windows, but many of them face the train station.

🍴 *V. Fiume is parallel to train station.* 𝒊 *Breakfast included.* Ⓢ *Singles €50-85; doubles €60-98; quads €85-145.* 🕐 *Reception 24hr.*

SAN LORENZO

Most of the budget accommodations in San Lorenzo are clustered around **Via Nazionale** and **Via Faenza,** with good proximity to the train station and the cheap food of **Mercato Centrale.** There's a fine Roman-style drinking fountain at the corner of Nazionale and Faenza as well, so fill your bottles.

🏨 OSTELLO ARCHI ROSSI

👜♿(ᵖ) HOSTEL ❷

V. Faenza 94r

☎055 29 08 04 🖳www.hostelarchirossi.com

The large garden courtyard might be the only green space you'll see in Florence outside of church cloisters. The quirky garden is charming enough that you will forget you are in a massive 100+ bed hostel, and the walls packed with notes, drawings, and signatures from previous guests will give you something new to look at every time you walk up the stairs. Trying to find a familiar face while balancing a tray full of American-style breakfast *(included),* however, might remind you uncomfortably of your freshman-year dining hall. Excellent dinner options are also available most nights *(€2.50 for pizza and pasta),* but those with a culinary streak may lament the lack of a kitchen. Pay a little extra for an ensuite room, because the communal bathrooms are shared by too many. On the plus side, this hostel has more computers than most American public schools. Despite some trade-offs, this is the best hostel in Florence. Good luck trying to find somewhere to scrawl your own name—look for *Let's Go* across from the water cooler.

🍴 *From the train station, take V. Nazionale and then a left onto V. Faenza.* 𝒊 *Beer on sale at desk.* Ⓢ *Dorms €21-27.* 🕐 *Reception 6:30am-2am.*

🏨 HOSTEL PLUS

👜♿(ᵖ) HOSTEL ❷

V. Santa Caterina D'Alessandria 15

☎055 46 28 934 🖳www.plushostels.com

It's a chain hostel, sure, but it's the nicest darn chain hostel our *Let's Go* researchers have ever seen. With so many rooms, it can feel a little empty when there aren't nine million tourists around, but that just means more space for you on the spacious terrace bar. Climb up another level to the flat roof, which sports some folding chairs, a guard rail, and, the best panoramic 🌄view of Florence you'll find outside Giotto's tower. Down in the basement is a restaurant *(€10 for breakfast, pasta dinner, or a bottle of wine),* another full bar, a disco complete with ball, a sauna, a Turkish bath, and a heavily chlorinated swimming pool flooded with colored lights. Rooms themselves are standard dorms—avoid the nauseating Pepto-pink walls of the all-female floor—but otherwise it's chain-hostel standard. Security is a little iffy—this researcher just waltzed right in and hung out on the roof for an hour.

➡ Follow V. Nazionale way up until it changes names. ℹ Breakfast €10. $ Dorms €20-25. 🕒 Reception 24hr.

👍 SOGGIORNO ANNAMARIA / KATTI HOUSE — 💳♿📶 B AND B [3]

V. Faenza 21 ☎055 21 34 10 💻www.kattihouse.com

If you are traveling with a small group and don't mind sharing queen-size beds, stay here. This lovely B and B feels more like a flat that you're borrowing from some posh aunt. Wood-beamed ceilings, grandfather clocks, and comfortable living rooms characterize these suites of rooms. On the second floor, four bedrooms share a big, sunny living room with a built-in bar. Each bedroom sports a TV and a tea kettle (as we said, posh aunt).

➡ On V. Faenza, look for the doorway with all the Let's Go stickers. ℹ Breakfast included. $ Singles €70; doubles €85; quads €130.

HOTEL ESTER — 💳♿📶 HOTEL [3]

V. Largo Alinari 15 ☎055 23 02 185 💻www.roominflorence.com

Down the block from the train station, the two levels of Hotel Ester boast an array of private rooms with flatscreen TVs, mini-fridges, and overhead fans. The longer the hike, the better the view—the third story rooms boast a lovely prospect, while the larger rooms across the street at sister hotel Luna Rossa are a good deal for groups *(quad €120).*

➡ From train station, turn left at the McDonald's; Hotel Ester is about 1 block down on the right. Luna Rossa and Maison de Charme are across the street and adjacent, respectively, but share Hotel Ester's reception. $ Mar-Oct doubles €75, with bath €90; Nov-Feb €55/60.

HOLIDAY ROOMS — 💳🚭📶❄ HOTEL [3]

V. Nazionale 22 ☎055 28 50 84

Good luck navigating the byzantine V. Nazionale numbering system to find this simple hotel, but once you arrive, you'll agree that its convenient location makes it a gem. Attractive, small rooms adorned with art prints and shuttered windows are complemented by flatscreen TVs, wooden armoires, and computers ensuite. The colorful communal kitchen sports a full set of appliances and a shelf of books that provides ample entertainment alternatives to watching the water boil.

➡ From the train station, walk down V. Nazionale for about 5min.; no point watching the building numbers, just look for the name on the right. You'll hit it after you pass V. Chiara. $ Doubles €60-70.

OSTELLO CENTRALE EURO STUDENTS — 💳♿ HOSTEL [2]

V. Faenza 46r ☎055 41 44 54

Pass through a driveway lined with EU flags to enter the half-hearted patio at the center of this no-frills hostel. The laundry hanging from the lines overhead provides a bit of old world charm, but it's also a little drippy. The dorms are twins instead of bunk beds, but what you gain in comfort you lose in floor space. Note that it's sometimes called Hostel Central on internet booking sites.

➡ Coming from the train station on V. Nazionale, take a right onto V. Faenza and look for the driveway with flags. $ Dorms €20-22.

SAN MARCO

This is not a great neighborhood for accommodations: the cheaper options can't compete with the ones you'll find in neighboring San Lorenzo. If you plan to go out late at night on weekends, don't stay here. It's a little too deserted after midnight for comfort.

DAVID INN — 👥🚭📶 HOSTEL [2]

V. Ricasoli 31 ☎055 21 37 07 💻hostelfirenze.splinder.com

One of the few small hostels in Florence, David Inn sits on the top floor of an otherwise residential building, and is the sort of place that provides you with somewhere to sleep—and not much else. No common space except for a couple squashy couches against an orange wall. The dorms are your basic bunk-bed situation, and the kitchen is tiny. But the small hostel scene in town is fairly dire, so if Academy is full or too posh for your hosteling tastes, then try here.

➡ About a 5min. walk north of the Duomo, on the right. ***i*** *Luggage storage. $ Dorms €24-26. ⏰ Reception 24hr.*

OSTELLO GALLO D'ORO 💳🚭📶 HOSTEL ❷

V. Cavour 104 ☎055 55 22 964 💻www.ostellogallodoro.com

San Marco's other small proper hostel option calls a quieter location on the other side of the neighborhood its home. The building's big shared entryway is a little confusing, but you want the stairs on the right. The place has a college dorm feel, with rooms that line a single hallway. It's small, friendly, and clean, and has its own tiny balcony for a coffee or a smoke.

➡ 5min. up V. Cavour from San Marco, on right. ***i*** *Breakfast included. $ Beds €28-30. ⏰ Reception 24hr.*

HOTEL GIOIA 💳♿📶❄ HOTEL ❸

V. Cavour 25 ☎055 28 28 04 💻www.hotelgioia.it

The 28 rooms here are reminiscent of an American chain hotel—they must've ordered the bedspreads from Holiday Inn's supplier—but if you're skeeved out by all these hotels with no proper entrance of their own, then this hotel's video-monitored, dedicated entry from the street will provide a pleasant surprise. Inside, four couches are arranged in a square around a television, which makes for a somewhat greater socializing potential than what's to be found at other hotels.

➡ Easy to find–has its own door! ***i*** *Breakfast included. $ Doubles €65-90. ⏰ Reception 24hr.*

HOTEL SAN MARCO 🍴🚭📶❄ HOTEL ❸

V. Cavour 50 ☎055 28 18 51 💻www.hotelsanmarcofirenze.it

The white walls of this little hotel are far cleaner than their scuffed counterparts in the entryway. The guest kitchen is fully equipped and the breakfast tables are small and relatively private, although the TV is frequently blasting Italian soap operas.

➡ Just past the Gran Caffe from the piazza. $ Singles €40-50; doubles €70. ⏰ Reception 24hr.

HOTEL BENEVUTI 💳♿❄ HOTEL ❸

V. Cavour 112 ☎055 57 21 41 💻www.benvenutihotel.it

The wood paneling on the walls lends a sort of Brady Bunch aesthetic, but the 20 rooms are clean, simple, and recently renovated. Ask for a room with A/C or one that faces the courtyard for a quiet evening.

➡ North of San Marco on V. Cavour, about 5min. ***i*** *Breakfast included. Elevator possibly too small for many wheelchairs. $ Doubles €60-75; triples €70-90. ⏰ Reception 2pm-midnight.*

SANTA CROCE

Looking to minimize the stumble home after a night out? Unfortunately, you are probably out of luck, because affordable accommodations in Santa Croce are difficult to come by. Check out places in the adjacent Duomo area, or perhaps try shacking up with a student at the university...

HOTEL ARIZONA 💳♿📶 HOTEL ❺

V. Luigi Carlo Farini 2 ☎055 24 53 21 💻www.arizonahotel.it

If you're studying at the university and your parents come to visit, this might be a good place to put them; otherwise, you'll do better in another neighborhood. The small reception area has squishy armchairs, an upright piano, and a generous stack of magazines (mostly Italian fashion and, oddly, *Smithsonian*). The sedate rooms are a bit cramped, but some compensate with little balconies looking on to the street. All the rooms are more or less the same.

⇨ To the right of the synagogue. ℹ Minibar ensuite. Wi-Fi €4 per hr. $ High-season singles €130; quads €179. ⏰ Reception 24hr.

HOTEL ARISTON 💳🚭📶 HOTEL [3]

V. Fiesolana 40 ☎055 247 6980 💻www.hotelaristonfirenze.it

Sad gray hallways lead to characterless but spacious rooms with big closets and ceiling fans. The lobby has a small bar, an array of breakfast tables, and a plaster *David.* Windows face either the street or an air shaft.

⇨ You can see the neon hotel sign from the intersection at Pietrapiana. ℹ Breakfast included. Free Wi-Fi. $ High-season doubles €65-70. ⏰ Reception 24hr.

WEST OLTRARNO

This side of the river has a decent concentration of good hostels, but they aren't significantly cheaper than the more centrally located places. You have to really want to be in West Oltrarno to stay here.

👍 OSPITALE DELLE RIFIORENZE 🍴♿📶 HOSTEL [1]

P. Piattellina 1 ☎055 21 67 98 💻www.firenzeospitale.it

Carved out of an old monastery, this socially aware hostel still feels like a religious escape. Live like a monk in a little pre-fab cell for two or three and hang out in the cavernous common space, featuring an ornate but decaying 15th-century ceiling that looks like something off the Titanic. All kinds of classes are run here including yoga, capoeira, and ceramics. Some of them are free, others are free for your first session. The folks at this nonprofit, co-operative hostel are a special sort—take one of their booklets providing walking tours of the people's Florence, which shift the historical perspective from the Medici to the Medici's handmaids.

⇨ From P. Santo Spirito, the "ostello" signs direct you to this one. ℹ Free Wi-Fi. $ 3- to 4-bed dorms €15; doubles €40; triples €45. ⏰ Reception 7am-noon and 3pm-2am. Curfew 2am.

HOSTEL SANTA MONACA 💳🚭📶 HOSTEL [1]

V. Santa Monaca 6 ☎055 26 83 38 💻www.ostello.it

This former monastery has all the charm of a local community center, despite the occasional cast-iron gate or vaulted ceiling. Rooms are simple, bathrooms are shared, and everything is kept clean during a strict 10am-2pm lockout. A nice large mess hall lined with picnic tables and a digital projector for sporting events are the few perks. A small grocery store is next door, but the "kitchen" is poorly equipped and overcrowded at meal times. You'll reap the benefits of Santa Monaca's proximity to the P. di Santo Spirito after-dinner scene—as long as you're back for the 2am curfew.

⇨ From P. Santo Spirito, take a right onto V. Sant'Agostino and then a left onto V. Santa Monaca. ℹ Free Wi-Fi. $ Dorms €17.50-20.50. ⏰ Reception 7am-2am. Curfew 2am. Lockout 10am-2pm.

SOGGIORNO PITTI 🍴🚭📶 HOSTEL, HOTEL [2]

P. Pitti 8 ☎329 06 40 765 💻www.soggiornopitti.com

This is a sort of a hotel-hostel combo—the feel is hostel, with a big comfy common space, but most of the rooms are private, with double beds and twins. The bathrooms are clean but not terribly plentiful. That being said, it is a serviceable hostel and benefits from the best location of the three in West Oltrarno. But if you look elsewhere in Florence you'll find nicer options than this.

⇨ Across the street from Palazzo Pitti. $ Dorms €20; doubles with bath €70; quads €92. ⏰ Reception 8am-11pm.

EAST OLTRARNO

Unless you have a reason to stay here, you might as well book a room at a nice bed and breakfast another few kilometers away in Bagno a Ripoli. Either way, you'll still have to take a bus to reach the sights.

PLUS CAMPING MICHELANGELO
💳⊗📶 CAMPING [1]

Vle. Michelangelo 80 ☎055 68 11 977 💻www.camping.it

Camping sure sounds nice, doesn't it? A bit of the **great outdoors,** some greenery, roughing it a little? Don't be fooled. Whether you're packing a tent or renting a bungalow, this campsite has all the appeal of the neighboring Piazzale Michelangelo—which is to say, of a parking lot. The bungalows sleep two or three in bunk beds. You have to share a key, and there's no locker in the tent, so we don't recommend going halvsies on one with a stranger. Bathrooms are in a facility at the top of the hill akin to the locker room at a large gym. Wi-Fi is expensive and limited. The cafe is your only option for food that doesn't require a good walk, though at least the view is nice from its seating area.

➡ To the left of Piazzale Michelangelo, or take the #12 bus to the Camping stop. $ 2-bed tents €29; 3-bed €36. ⏰ Reception 24hr.

HOTEL DAVID
💳♿❄ HOTEL [5]

Vle. Michelangelo 1 ☎055 68 11 695 💻www.davidhotel.com

A large, standard sort of hotel right over the Ponte San Niccolo—the bridge that marks the very eastern edge of the city center. If you have a reason to be this far east, then it's a good—if expensive—option.

➡ On the south end of Ponte San Niccolo. i Buffet breakfast included. $ Doubles €150. ⏰ Reception 24hr.

sights

Hope you like the Renaissance! Seriously, that's the big game in town here. If you search really hard you can find museums or attractions that don't have their roots in the 16th century, but there aren't many. If you do like the Renaissance, this is literally the best place in the world for you. Options abound, so it's best to take your time and appreciate things rather than letting them become a devalued mush of crucifixes and portraits of semi-attractive women.

THE DUOMO

Your Duomo-related sights are pretty much the main event for this neighborhood—the church itself, and the other bits and pieces of the Duomo complex.

DUOMO
♿ CHURCH

P. del Duomo 1 ☎055 23 02 885 💻www.operaduomo.firenze.it

Honestly, it's better on the outside. The Duomo complex is enormous and distinctive, looming over every other Florentine building. All roads seem to lead to the Duomo and its shockingly colorful facade, capped with that giant red gelato-cone of a dome. It's famous, it's old, and it's free: clearly it must be the greatest tourist attraction known to humanity.

Well, it's all right. There are a lot of really great churches in Florence, and the Duomo just happens to be the biggest. It truly is enormous, but once you've stood in line behind half a dozen cruise-ship excursion groups to file your way inside the mighty cathedral, you might find yourself wondering—"is that all there is?"

Fortunately, it's not. Unfortunately, all the good parts have been divvied up, so you can only sample a bit at a time. All the statues, paintings, and other adornments have been moved into the Museo across the street, and you have to pay separately to climb the dome or the tower. For free, you get a rather empty, cavernous church.

There are certainly highlights. The inside of the vast dome is ornately frescoed and extremely impressive, even from ground level. On the opposite side of the nave a 24hr. clock by **Paolo Uccello** oxymoronically runs counter-clockwise. If you take the stairs in the middle of the church's floor down to the basement, you can pay €3 to see the archeological remnants of the Duomo's previous incarnations, which is cool if you like that sort of thing.

And in a bit of irony, that notable green-white-and-pink marble facade that's so impressive from the outside—well, it's a fake. Or rather, it's not contemporary to the cathedral itself. The Duomo's facade was left unfinished in the 16th century and was eventually removed completely, leaving the great cathedral buck naked. Only in the late 19th century—last Thursday by Florentine standards—did the Duomo receive its famous decoration. Like much of Florence, it's not actually from the Renaissance—it's the Victorian equivalent of a Renaissance Faire.

Still really pretty, though.

⚲ *Come on, you can't miss it.* ℹ *Audio tour available in English.* Ⓢ *Free. Archeological site €3. Audio tour €5, students and under 18 €3.50.* 🕗 *Open M-F 10am-5pm, Sa 10am-4:45pm, Su 1:30-3:30pm. 1st Sa each month only open 10am-3:30pm.*

a man with a plan

After 100 years of construction, the Duomo still had a gaping hole. The architects found themselves stumped—during construction, they had not realized that the dome the design called for would have to be larger than anything previously built or even considered possible. After several decades of leaving the church open to the elements, the commission for the construction was awarded to an unlikely candidate: **Filippo Brunelleschi,** who had been trained as a goldsmith, not an architect. How did Brunelleschi end up gaining the commission for the largest dome of his age? Legend states that he proposed a competition: whichever architect could make an egg stand up on a slab of marble would take over the dome's construction. When everyone else attempted and failed, Brunelleschi cracked the egg at the bottom and placed the newly flat edge on the marble. Fortunately, he was as talented at architecture as he was at rule-bending, and his ingenuity led to the spectacular dome that is still the most stunning sight on Florence's skyline.

CAMPANILE AND DOME
P. del Duomo

♦⊗ CHURCH

☎055 23 02 885 💻www.operaduomo.firenze.it

Normal travel not tiring enough for you? Try climbing 400+ stone steps! These two sights are combined into one review here because, well, there's no reason to split them up. Both involve climbing a heck of a lot of stairs to see an extremely rewarding view. The major distinction is which you would rather see up close: the inside or the outside of Brunelleschi's dome.

If you would rather see the inside, then climb his architectural miracle. You'll ascend a lot of twisty, narrow stairs for a long time. Halfway to the top, you can step out on a platform at the base of the cupola for a closer look at the Duomo's vast fresco through murky anti-suicide plexiglass. Then it's back to the stairwell for the last couple hundred stairs before emerging to a truly worthwhile view of Florence and the surrounding hills.

The Campanile is much the same, but when you reach the summit, you get a perfect next-door view of the dome. Relatedly, if you're going to do that corny thing from the movies and meet your lover on top of the Duomo, make sure you settle on whether to meet at the dome or the tower. Otherwise, you might be staging your reunion via shouting and semaphore flags.

Enter the dome from the north side of the rounded part of the Duomo. Enter the Campanile at the base of the big tower thing. ***i*** *Not for the out-of-shape.* $ *Dome €8. Campanile €6. Tour of the dome and the cathedral's terraces €15.* ⏰ *Dome open M-F 8:30am-7pm, Sa 8:30am-5:40pm. Campanile open daily 8:30am-7:30pm.*

MUSEO OPERA DI SANTA MARIA DEL FIORE — ♿ MUSEUM

P. Duomo 9 ☎055 22 02 885 💻www.operaduomo.firenze.it

If the Duomo seems a little empty compared to the other big name churches, that's because all the good stuff got moved here. Preservation concerns over the years led the cathedral to be stripped of its statues, paintings, and other shiny objects. They remain on display, if not in their proper context, in this winding little museum where you can escape the Duomo complex's crowds and get up-close and personal with the goods. There's a *pieta* that Michelangelo originally intended for his own tomb, some nifty trios of statues in the courtyard, and the incredibly creepy **Mary of the Glass Eyes** (you'll know it when you see it).

On the second floor, models and sketches of the Duomo detail the long genesis of its 19th-century facade. And if you like the mechanics of this sort of thing more than the pretty pictures, there's a great display of the fixed pulleys and hoists used to construct Brunelleschi's dome.

Behind the Cupola. ***i*** *Most texts in Italian, but the more important ones are also in English.* $ *€6. Audio tour €3.50.* ⏰ *Open M-Sa 9am-7:30pm, Su 9am-1:40pm.*

BAPTISTERY OF SAN GIOVANNI — ♿ MUSEUM

P. Duomo ☎055 22 02 885 💻www.operaduomo.firenze.it

The octagonal building beside the Duomo is the Baptistery, and nearly all Florentines until the 19th century were baptized here, including big names like **Dante.** It features an incredible mosaic ceiling and some highly intricate ornamentation—but if you're feeling cheap and churched out, you can pretty much get the idea from looking in through the exit. In fact, the outer doors of the Baptistery are as much a big deal as the inside. Ghiberti's splendid golden eastern doors (facing the cathedral steps) were dubbed the **"Gates of Paradise"** by Michelangelo, and if we trust anyone to prescribe aesthetic judgment on a work of art, it's him.

The octagonal building next to the Duomo. $ *€4.* ⏰ *Open in summer M-W 12:15-6:30pm, Th-Sa 12:15-10:30pm, Su 8:30am-1:30pm; in winter M-Sa 12:15-6:30pm, Su 8:30am-1:30pm. In both seasons open 1st Sa of the month 8:30am-1:30pm.*

PIAZZA DELLA SIGNORIA

UFFIZI GALLERY — ♿ ❄ MUSEUM

Piazzale degli Uffizi 6 ☎055 238 8651 💻www.firenzemusei.it

Welcome to the Uffizi. The first thing you should know about this museum is that the *David* is not here—he's on the other side of town, in the Accademia. Also, the *Mona Lisa* is in France, and de Nile ain't just a river in Egypt.

If you're looking for an art history lesson, don't expect to find one in this listing. You won't find one in the galleries' texts either: although the explanatory panels are in both Italian and English, they are not hugely informative. Your best bet is to take an audio tour *(€5.50)* or to stick with *Let's Go*. We'll do our best to point out some things you might not notice on your own.

The Uffizi's rooms are numbered. Look to the lintel of the doorway to figure out what room you're in. Our instructions will assume that you are going through the galleries sequentially.

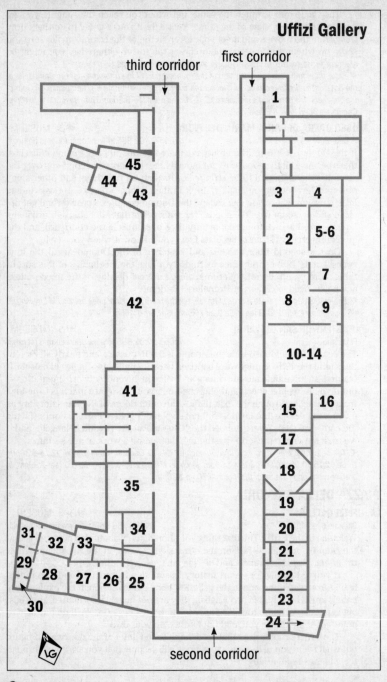

Uffizi Gallery

third corridor

first corridor

1

3   4

5-6

2

7

8   9

10-14

15   16

17

18

19

20

21

22

23

24

45

44

43

42

41

35

34

31   32   33

29

28   27   26   25

30

second corridor

Start the Uffizi from the top. Don't crumple up your ticket at the bottom of your bag (or paste it directly into your notebook like we did) because, after climbing two flights of the Uffizi's grand staircase, you'll be asked to flash your ticket once more. At this point, you're standing in an enormous hallway lined with statues and frescoed to within an inch of its life.

Room 1 is on your right, but you can't enter. Instead, peer at some nice marble figures from the doorway, and then continue in the opposite direction. **Room 2** begins the long parade of Jesuses that you'll be visiting today. Check out the amazingly expressive and contemporary-looking crucifix on the wall to your immediate left as you enter.

Rooms 3-4 are particularly gilded. In Martini's *Annunciation*, Gabriel literally spits some Latin at Mary, who responds with the mother of all icy stares.

Things get less golden and a little more colorful in **Room 5**. In **Room 6**, take some time with Beato Angelico's fun *Scenes From the Lives of Hermits*. Who knew hermits were so social? If you're with a friend, try narrating some of the little vignettes or see if you can identify which clusters of hermits match the following titles:

"Not dead yet!"

"It rubs the lotion on its skin."

"The lion sleeps tonight."

"Psychiatric advice, five cents please."

"Questionably Appropriate Activities With Animals"

Room 8 is all about Filippino Lippi. In the center of the room, his two-sided panel of a rather homely couple staring longingly at one another gives confirmation that even ugly people can find love.

Our second big-name artist is in **Room 9**. On your left are seven panels portraying the Virtues—which woman is which?—all painted by Piero del Pollalol. Well, all except for *Fortitude*, on the left. She is one of the earliest documented works by his student, a fellow by the name of **Botticelli**.

Rooms 10-14 are the main event. Where there be crowds and benches, there be the postcard works. Not that you need us to tell you this, but Botticelli's *Birth of Venus* is on the left—that's right, behind all those people. Push your way to the front to enjoy all the little details that don't come across in the coffee mug and mousepad reproductions, like the gold trim on the trees, the detail of the fabrics, and Venus's rather poor haircut. It's like she tried to get the Rachel but left on an extra 4ft.

Look to the opposite side of the room for a big triptych with some seriously wonky perspective courtesy of Van Der Goes. On the right-hand panel are Mary Magdalene, St. Margaret, and—holy crap, ⚡what IS that thing?!

Room 15 is another example of the student surpassing the teacher. Examine the painting by Verrochio across the room on the right. Several of the painting's figures—it is still contested which specifically—were painted by his student, Leonardo da Vinci. Maybe you've heard of him? The two paintings to the left are fully Leonardo's. If you guessed it in advance, give yourself a pat on the back for being a good art historian.

Odds are, you're going to start speeding up at this point, so to keep pace, you might want to take a break at the **Cafeteria**—go out into the main hallway and follow the signs.

In a city full of museums, this is one of very few proper museum cafeterias. Unfortunately, it's not very good. It opens onto a really lovely balcony—the roof of the Loggia you observed while down below in P. Della Signoria—but the only seating is for pricey waiter service. Take some snacks with you or buy an espresso at the bar and stand outside to enjoy the up-close view of the Palazzo

Vecchio while refreshing your brain.

Right then, where were we? **Room 19** has Pietro di Cosimo's depiction of Perseus tackling Andromeda, a monster with a serious under-bite. In the bottom right, check out those twisted musical instruments. They're imaginary, but they don't look too far off from what you might find in the Accademia's instruments gallery, do they?

If you're getting sick of Catholicism, skedaddle to **Room 20** to view a couple rare portraits of Martin Luther. Ninety-five theses, three chins. In the rear left, take a gander at the really nifty painting of a book open mid-skim. **Room 22** has a Mantegna triptych on the right with a curved center panel that makes it seem almost 3D. **Room 25** varies the Jesus-ness with some scenes from Joseph's story in Exodus on the right. Directly in front, there's a sweet frame with a bunch of saints' heads sticking out of it, Brady Bunch style.

In **Room 28,** the same cute spaniel makes a cameo in two different works by Vecellio on the right-hand wall. To their right is—merciful Zeus, that thing again! Hope it's not trying to eat the spaniel...

There's a seriously ginormous baby in **Room 29's** Parmigianino painting, which is called *Madonna of the Long Neck* for reasons that will be obvious.

A really interestingly composed painting of a woman bathing hangs on the near-right wall of **Room 31**. What do you look at first? Don't be shy, we know you're eyeing her luscious breasts. And then you probably look at her legs and thighs, and perhaps the rest of her. And then, if you haven't yet turned away, maybe you will notice King David in the top left corner. The woman is Bathsheba, and Brusasorci's painting is remarkable for making you, the viewer, mimic the intensity of David's ogling gaze.

Room 33 is more of a corridor, but don't skip the left-hand part, which has a nice *Pyramus and Thisbe* and an evocative *St. Sebastian*. (That's the guy with all the ⚔arrows, of whom you'll be seeing quite a lot.) On the left in **Room 35** is a *Massacre of the Innocents* by Daniele Ricciarelli. Though feminists might be excited about the painter's vaguely female name, sadly, Daniele was a dude like every other artist in the Uffizi. Despite the pile of dead babies in this painting, *Let's Go* does not condone the making of 🔄dead baby jokes.

Finally you'll reach the **Room of Niobe,** an impressive palatial space full of statues posed as if frozen while cowering in horror, not unlike the poses of the ash corpses in Pompeii. These statues were discovered in the Villa Medici gardens and are supposed to be the unfortunate children of Niobe about to be slain by the gods as revenge for their mother's pride in her progeny.

The last couple of rooms have some 18th-century stuff. But you don't care about that. You waited in line for 3hr. and then proceeded through an endless line of rooms filled with Renaissance art, so maybe it's time to just go home. 🔄**Congratulations** on finishing the Uffizi; now you can go act like a Botticelli expert among all your friends, even if the only thing you remember is Venus's terrible haircut.

✤ *It's the long narrow part of P. della Signoria. Enter (or stand in line) on the left, reserve tickets on the right. To avoid the lines without paying for a reservation, try arriving late in the day, when your time in the museum will be limited by closing.* **i** *2-3hr. wait in line is average.* Ⓢ *€10, EU citizens ages 18-25 €5, EU citizens under 18 and over 65 and the disabled free. €4 reservation fee. Audio tour €5.50.* 🕐 *Open Tu-Su 8:50am-6:50pm.*

🖼 THE BARGELLO ⓢ♿❋ MUSEUM

V. del Proconsolo 4 ☎055 23 88 606 🖥 www.firenzemusei.it

For a change of pace, the Bargello offers a nice dose of 19th-century eclecticism: it's a bit like London's Victoria and Albert Museum, with objects organized by function and material. The building was once a brutal prison, but fortunately

friends in high places

If you know you want to hit a lot of the museums in Florence, consider becoming their friend first. You'll receive a single entrance to all the state museums, including the Uffizi, the Accademia, the Boboli Gardens, the Museo di San Marco, and the Bargello, among others (though not the various churches and church-related sights). It costs €60, or €40 for those under 26, but paying the entrance for all the above museums will cost you a lot more. Become a member at 💻www.amicidegliuffizi.it or visit the Welcome Desk in Sala delle Reali Poste, inside the Uffizi museum complex. *(☎055 52 13 560 ⏰ Open Tu-Sa 10am-5pm.)*

for visitors, there's no trace of this original purpose left in the architecture. The courtyard, once the site of public executions, is now adorned with terra-cotta coats of arms and family crests. Several statues remain from what must have been an extremely suggestive fountain. Look for the water spigots located in such charming locations as between a lady's legs. There's also an enormous cast cannon bearing the head of St. Paul, a devoted disciple of the prince of peace who probably wouldn't be too happy about having his face emblazoned on heavy artillery. Pass the pair of great stone lions wearing iron crowns—very *Narnia*—to find a hall full of pagan (not so *Narnia*) sculptures such as Adonis, Bacchus, and a 1565 work celebrating Florence's victory over Pisa.

The courtyard stairs bring you to some stone fowl and a series of numbered galleries. Minutely carved ivories, from tiny portraits to hair combs to a giant chess board are in **room 4.** The variety of objects that people have thought to carve from elephant tusk is astounding.

Room 6 holds a huge collection of Maiolica, an earthenware pottery that is decorated before being glazed. **Room 8** will introduce you to the Ninja Turtle you know least well. This *Salone Di Donatello* was designed for his 500th birthday in 1887, and has remained unchanged since.

Room 9 contains probably the only Arabic script you'll see in Tuscany. This chamber is devoted to Islamic art and has some very interesting ceramics and fabrics.

Room 10 is a true Victorian *wunderkammer* (or wonder-cabinet). There's the case of pipes, the case of bottles, and the collection of keys and locks. There are even table settings, scientific instruments, metalwork, jewelry, and that 17th-century spork you've been missing.

On the third floor, check out the fantastic tiny bronzes in **Room 15. Room 13's** glazed terra cotta in blues, greens, and yellows creates a color scheme that will make you feel as if you've been sucked into a game of old-school Oregon Trail.

⇟ Behind the Palazzo Vecchio. $ €4, EU citizens ages 18-25 €2, EU citizens under 18 and over 65 free. ⏰ Open daily 8:15am-5pm. Closed 1st, 3rd, and 5th Su each month, and 2nd and 4th M.

PIAZZA DELLA SIGNORIA ♿ PIAZZA

P. della Signoria

Don't be fooled by the *David* in front of the **Palazzo Vecchio**—the real deal is in the **Accademia**. The reproduction in the *piazza* fills David's original location and stands just as proud as his original did when he (allegedly) was installed facing Pisa to celebrate Florence's dominance over the Tuscan region. To the left of the statue is a giant fountain which Michelangelo despised so much that he called it a waste of perfectly good marble. To the big guy's right you'll find the **Loggia,** a portico full of statues that's as legit as any room in the Uffizi. Hang out amid the art students sketching, listen to the street musicians, and enjoy the free outdoor art. Don't miss Giambologna's spiraling *Rape of the Sabines.*

🚶 This is the main piazza around the Uffizi. $ Free.

PONTE VECCHIO ♿ BRIDGE

Ponte Vecchio

This is Florence's famous shop-covered bridge. It has been called the "old" bridge for, oh, 400 years or so, ever since the Florentines first built a second bridge over the Arno and had to find a way to distinguish this one from their new *ponte.* When the Nazis evacuated Florence, Ponte Vecchio was the only bridge they didn't destroy. Now it is full of gold and jewelry shops—more like kiosks, in many cases—as well as shadier street vendors and buskers. Come on a weekend afternoon, and you are guaranteed to be in the wedding photos of at least half a dozen bridal parties. Come at night for a romantic view of the river—and of other couples seeking the same.

🚶 From the Uffizi, walk to the river. It's the one with the shops on it. $ Free.

PIAZZA DELLA REPUBBLICA ♿ PIAZZA

P. della Repubblica

For hundreds of years, this was the sight of the walled Jewish Ghetto, but when Florence's Jewish population was finally permitted to live and work elsewhere in 1888, the Ghetto was razed and paved over to create this spacious *piazza.* Now it's just another central place to hang out, featuring a carousel *(€2)* and, in the evenings, some high quality street performers. The restaurants surrounding the square are pricey, but their live music spills into the open space for all to enjoy. Head to the northwest corner of the *piazza,* where there is a large raised map of the city with streets labeled in Braille.

🚶 From P. della Signoria walk north up V. del Calzaioli then turn left on V. Speziali $ Free.

PALAZZO VECCHIO ⊛♿ MUSEUM

In P. della Signoria ☎055 276 8465

The real draw here is that it's the only museum you can visit post-*aperitivo.* In addition, the place has got some pretty impressive architecture and views. The vast and ornate **Room of the 500's** gilded ceiling is divided into panels that frame truly massive paintings. On the second floor, the **Salon of Leo X,** a terrace with an incredible view of the city and the surrounding hills, provides a great photo op. There's a lot of repetition in this *palazzo,* though, and it can all begin to look the same. That's until you reach the **Sala dei Gigli,** which boasts a pretty rocking view of the Duomo as well as a fantastic map room that's worth all the chintz before it.

🚶 The huge one in P. della Signoria. $ €6, ages 18-25 and over 65 €4.50. Tours free if requested at time of ticket purchase. ⏰ Open M-W 9am-midnight, Th 9am-2pm, F-Su 9am-midnight. Activities and tours with costumed reenactors, skits, etc. available; call for times.

CASA DI DANTE ⊛♿ MUSEUM

V. Santa Margherita 4 ☎055 21 94 16 💻www.museocasadidante.it

Don't go here. Normally we only list sights that we do recommend, but we wouldn't want you to think our omission an oversight. We really do think you should skip the Casa di Dante. It isn't really Dante's house. It isn't even really a reproduction. It's just a building sadly lacking in artifacts. Whether you're an expert Dantista or you don't know your *Paradiso* from your *Purgatorio,* there's nothing for you here. Instead, try our alternate **Dante itinerary.**

🚶 On the corner of V. Dante Alighieri and V. Santa Margherita; it's very well sign-posted. $ €4. ⏰ Open Apr-Sept daily 10am-6pm; Oct-Mar Tu-Su 10am-5pm.

alternative dante route

If you want to pay your respects to Dante without suffering through the Casa di Dante, consider this alternative route. Follow the signs to Casa Di Dante until you find yourself in a little alleyway, V. Santa Margherita. Start by observing the outside of the Casa di Dante. It's a reproduction of a Florentine home of Dante's time, when families lived in vertical fortresses crammed within the city walls. In a pre-modern version of suburban neighborhood association rules, families that came to power often required that no other home be taller than theirs, resulting in a lot of lopped-off towers. The facade you're examining is a fair rendering of such towers. Now turn right and enter the **Chiesa di Dante,** the church where our favorite epic poet worshiped and where he may or may not have first spied his beloved Beatrice. Look to the building's walls to spy some illustrations of that event. Just outside the church, stop at fine little sandwich shop, 👍**Da Vinattieri**. As you eat, sit on the stools in the alley, imagining that you are a pining Dante waiting for Beatrice to walk past. Finally, return to Casa di Dante and go inside to satisfy all your urges for Dante kitsch at the first-floor gift shop. Because what trip to Florence is complete without getting the entire Divine Comedy printed on a shower curtain?

SANTA MARIA NOVELLA

For an additional off-beat option, check out the **Farmaceutica di Santa Maria Novella**.

👍 MUSEO DI FERRAGAMO

🎟♿ MUSEUM

P. Santa Trinita 5r ☎055 33 60 456 💻www.museoferragamo.it

That's right, the shoe guy. This small but excellently designed museum celebrates the work of the great cobbler to the stars, whose eloquent and anecdotal memoirs are liberally quoted in the museum's display text. Exhibits rotate every two years; a new installation arrived in late 2010, focusing on footwear in the second half of the 20th century. We know you may have a skeptical look on your face right now, but you don't have to be Carrie Bradshaw to appreciate a fashion and culture exhibit as thoughtfully assembled as this one. The gift shop is surprisingly tiny, but check out the real Ferragamo store upstairs to ogle shoes you can't possibly afford.

‡ Enter at P. Santa Trinita, the side of the building facing away from the river. ℹ Ticket proceeds fund scholarships for young shoe designers. $ €5, under 10 and over 65 free. ⏰ Open M 10am-6pm, W-Su 10am-6pm.

PALAZZO STROZZI

🎟♿ MUSEUM, PALAZZO

P. degli Strozzi ☎055 27 76 461 💻www.palazzostrozzi.org

While this may seem like yet another old palace, impressive like all the others, it isn't the seen-one-seen-'em-all Renaissance decor that makes Palazzo Strozzi worth visiting. The Center for Contemporary Culture Strozzina, which produces shows of recent and contemporary art in the palace's exhibit halls, is the main draw here. Recent shows have included an exhibit of De Chirico, Ernst, and Magritte as well as a series of interactive installations tracing the effect of media on modern living. The programming changes regularly, so check the website or stop by if you want to shake a little 21st century into Florence's 15th-century aesthetic.

‡ West of P. della Repubblica. $ Prices and hours vary; check website for details.

BASILICA DI SANTA MARIA NOVELLA

🍴♿ CHURCH

P. di Santa Maria Novella ☎055 21 59 18 🖥www.chiesasantamarianovella.it

If you're only going to bother with one of the non-Duomo churches, consider making it this one. The cavernous church features some glorious stained glass which, due to the church's north-south orientation, reflects beautifully on to the floors in the morning and late afternoon. The Filippino-Lippi-designed chapel to the right of the altar is almost cartoonish in the drama and action of its panels. Cappella Strozzi on the left has a sadly faded fresco of Purgatory, inspired by Dante. Try to make out the goblins, centaurs, and less familiar mythological figures like the man-dove. The basilica also features an impossibly handsome gift shop in a room dominated by a gold-trimmed reliquary cabinet and a red and blue ceiling so bright it must have been restored yesterday.

🚏 Just south of the train station; can't miss it. ℹ Audio tour stations in the middle of the sanctuary for €1; some travelers wait around for others to pay up the euro and get bored, then finish their turn. $ €3.50, over 65, travelers with disabilities, and priests free. ⏰ Open M-Th 9-5:30pm, F 11am-5:30pm, Sa 9am-5pm, Su 1-5pm.

MUSEO NAZIONALE ALINARI DELLA FOTOGRAFIA

🎟♿ MUSEUM

P. Santa Maria Novella 14a ☎055 21 63 10 🖥www.alinarifondazione.it

Can't wait to upload your own travel photos? Come here to see negatives of Italian sights that were taken in the 19th century. Despite the somewhat ambiguous name, this is not a museum *of* photography, but a museum *about* photography. It considers its topic expansively, covering not only the history of photography but the associated cultural paraphernalia, like 19th-century photo albums, that developed (get it?) alongside. One of the museum's most remarkable features is its accessibility. For obvious but unfortunate reasons, most of the art in Florence is not capable of being enjoyed by the blind. The photography museum not only provides Braille texts and audio guides specifically tailored for the blind, but also raised, touchable reproductions of important images and artifacts. The deaf are accommodated with sign language tour guides available on request as well.

🚏 Across the piazza from Santa Maria Novella. ℹ Audio tour €4. $ €9, groups of 10 or more, students, families, over 65 €7.50. M €6 for all. ⏰ Open M 3-7pm, Tu 10am-3pm, Th 3-7pm, F-Su 10am-7pm.

CHIESA DI SAN SALVATORE AD OGNISSANTI

♿ CHURCH

P. Ognissanti 42 ☎055 23 96 802

Stop in this mid-size church to pay your respects to **Botticelli**—his tomb is to the right of the altar. His portrait of St. Augustine can also be found here. There is a great deal of imaginary architecture in this church, with decorative "molding" painted directly on the walls and a fairly convincing balcony level painted on the ceiling. And of course, the 2-D balcony also has a fresco, presenting you with a ceiling painting of a ceiling painting. Try to wrap your head around that one.

🚏 1 block north of the river. $ Free. ⏰ Open daily 7am-12:30pm and 4-8pm.

SAN LORENZO

Two of the best experiences in San Lorenzo are its open-air markets, one eponymous and the other named **Mercato Centrale.**

PALAZZO MEDICI RICARDI

🎟♿ MUSEUM

V. Camillo Cavour 1 ☎055 27 60 340 🖥www.palazzo-medici.it

After innumerable treks through the detritus of the Medici's public life, you may be wondering what they were like at home. Answer: more of the same. The Medici palace sports another lovely garden, another fine chapel, and yet another pile of fantastic art. Just try to keep up with *these* Joneses.

Start with the tiny chapel. The frescoes are so cluttered with faces of generations of Medici attending the Adoration of the Magi that you'll find just as much to look at as you would in a grander commission. Then head downstairs to the interactive explanatory exhibit. Motion sensor technology lets you point at a projection of the chapel's frescoes and, without touching anything, cue explanations in Italian, French, or English. It's a neat way to learn more, but if you're excessively tall or short, be prepared to flail unsuccessfully until the guard adjusts the camera.

The palace also plays a working role in provincial government today. The **Quattro Stagioni** hall hosts the provincial council, and the gold-on-white stucco panels of the **Sala Luca Giordana,** flanked by painted mirrors and frolicking cherubim, are incongruously complemented by a projection screen, a conference table, and rows of plexiglass chairs. If nothing else, be happy for the members of the provincial council who get to gaze at fleshy angels when they zone out during dull meetings.

✚ *From San Lorenzo you can see the back of the huge brown palace. Enter from the reverse side, on V. Cavour.* ⓢ *€7, groups of 15 or more and ages 6-12 €4.* ⌚ *Open M-Tu 9am-7pm, Th-Su 9am-7pm.*

keeping up with the medici

It's impossible to tour Florence without hearing about the Medici, the family that ran the show here between the 15th and 18th centuries. While the Medici are best known for their banking skills, political prowess, and patronage to the arts and sciences, no family is without its eccentricities. Here's a crib sheet that'll help you keep the multi-faceted Medici men straight:

1) The first Medici to make it big was **Cosimo the Elder.** He was incredibly wealthy due to his father (Giovanni di Bicci) having founded the Medici Bank. He established his famliy's de facto rule in Florence by appealing to the working class, buying favors, and raising taxes on the wealthy. The players may change, but politics stays the same.

2) Cosimo had a son who was nicknamed **Piero the Gouty** because of the infection in his foot. He found it difficult to rule Florence with a swollen big toe, so he didn't last very long.

3) Despite their power, the Medici weren't always the coolest kids in the cafeteria. Rival families and a priest conspired to "sacrifice" Piero's son **Lorenzo** during a church service. After a brief period of expulsion (it's a long story), the Medici made a comeback in the early 1500s, helping to patronize artists like Leonardo da Vinci and Raphael.

4) Cosimo I de Medici is famous for establishing the Uffizi and Pitti Palace, ruling Florence, and patronizing the arts. He also deserves props, though, for embodying the "work hard, play harder" motto. In his free time he managed to father 15 children with four different women.

5) Cosimo II established the Medici family as patrons of science and technology. Cosimo *numero due* was Galileo's sugar daddy, supporting his research, giving him a place to stay, and offering him the chance to schmooze with the upper classes. In return, Galileo dedicated his books to the Medici, named some stars after them, and allowed the family first dibs on his new inventions, like the telescope.

sights · san lorenzo

MEDICI CHAPELS ✎♿ MUSEUM

P. Madonna degli Aldobrandini 6 ☎055 23 88 602 🖥www.firenzemusei.it

Ah, the Medici. If you thought they were opulent alive, wait until you see them dead! The **Cappella Principe,** an octagonal chapel that's the final home of a handful of Medici, is the grander of the two on display in this museum, despite being unfinished. Some of the Medici were smart enough to commission their own statues, and they're doing swell. Others went with the popular trend of having sons commission honorary statues after their fathers' death. This, of course, led to lots of empty statue slots. There are other late additions as well—the frescoes may look the part, but they were painted in the 1870s. As some tour guide quipped while we were eavesdropping, while the French were inventing Impressionism, the Florentines were still in the Renaissance. The **New Sacristy** is smaller and less colorful, but given its design by Michelangelo, it's nothing to sniff at. And not to be crude, but, goodness, someone should give the statue of *Night* a sweater because she's clearly finding it a bit nippy, if you know what we mean.

🧭 The roundish building to the right of San Lorenzo. ℹ Likely visit length: half hour tops. $ €6, EU citizens 18-25 €3, EU citizens under 18 and over 65 free. ⏰ Open fairly daily 8:15am-4:50pm. Closed 1st, 3rd, 5th M and 2nd and 4th Su each month.

BASILICA DI SAN LORENZO ✎♿ CHURCH

P. San Lorenzo ☎055 26 45 184 🖥www.sanlorenzo.firenze.it

The Basilica di San Lorenzo was consecrated in 393 CE: this is why Europeans scoff at Americans who think of 19th-century churches as old. The austere basilica is grey and white, but the cupola by the altar is a bit more glam. In the old sacristy is a small cupola painted with gold constellations on a midnight blue background that represent the sky over Florence on July 4th, 1442. Cool if you care about that sort of thing, but otherwise, spend your €3.50 on a big gelato and take it to the cloister on the left side of the basilica. The cloister is free and peaceful and has some of those rare Florentine trees. The domes and towers of nearby attractions peek out over the walls of the courtyard, making for a nice panorama.

🧭 In P. San Lorenzo, which is just a little north of the Duomo. $ €3.50. ⏰ Open M-Sa 10am-5-pm, Su 1:30-5pm.

SAN MARCO

There is a very high museum density around this square, second only to the Uffizi area. You could easily lose days visiting all the museums, so choose wisely.

👍 GALLERIA DELL'ACCADEMIA ★♿ MUSEUM

V. Ricasoli 60 ☎055 23 88 612 🖥www.firenzemusei.it/accademia

Sometimes tourist attractions gain their reputation for a reason. The *David* is pretty legit. Do you see those veins on his hand? The guy's a beast.

Four other statues by Michelangelo share *David*'s hall. They're unfinished, with figures that appear to be trapped in the remaining block of marble, like Han Solo encased in carbonite. You may understand on an intellectual level that the master's statues are carved from a single piece of marble, but seeing these unfinished works drives it home. One big damn rock. One man. A bunch of chisels. It's kind of miraculous, really.

Beyond its main event, the Accademia is a small museum, albeit a good one. The musical instruments gallery, to the right when you enter, is surprisingly informational. The collection itself contains the typical array of ancient instruments such as 🔍**serpents** and trumpet marines, but there are some excellent interactive elements, like models that help you understand the mechanical difference between a harpsichord and a piano. On one of a half dozen computers provided, you can also hear samples of the collection's instruments in action—believe it or not, this is not standard for major musical instrument galleries, so take advantage of the opportunity to hear a **hurdy-gurdy.** Yes, that's a real thing. Skip trying the water spring bowl, though, unless you want to be stuck with seriously grimy hands until you find a bathroom.

Past the *David* gallery on the left is a 19th-century workroom overflowing with sculpted heads and busts. Notice the little black dots freckling the pieces? They hark back to the Accademia's days as an actual academy. These are plaster casts were created for teaching, and the black dots are nails that students used as reference points as they made copies for practice. Gorgeous crucifixes and Russian Orthodox stuff make a quick spin through the upstairs worthwhile.

🈂Note: At your most contemplative pace, the Accademia won't take more than an hour. Bear that in mind when weighing the choice between paying extra for a reservation or waiting in a line that lasts far longer than you'll spend in the actual museum.

♯ *Line for entrance is on Ricasoli, off of San Marco proper.* ℹ *Make reservations at the Museo Archeologico, the Museo di San Marco, or the Museo del'Oficio. The non-reservation line is shortest at the beginning of the day. Try to avoid the midday cruise ship excursion groups.* ⑤ *€6.50, EU citizens ages 18-25 €3.25, EU citizens under 18 and over 65, and art students free. €4 reservation fee applies to all.* ⌚ *Open Tu-Su 8:15am-6:50pm. Last entrance 30min. before close. .*

will the real david please stand up?

You've heard about the *David*. You've read about the *David*. You've seen coffee mugs and aprons and boxer shorts emblazoned with the *David*. And now you're ready to see the real deal.

So you're making your way through Florence and wow! There he is! In all his naked *contrapposto* glory, chilling in the P. della Signoria. Not quite as impressive as the hype made him out to be, but then few tourist traps are. You snap a few pictures, pretend to grab *David*'s well-sculpted posterior, and congratulate yourself—you saw the statue. Your work here is done.

Think again. Do you really believe they'd keep the world's most famous statue outdoors? You can be forgiven for being fooled, though—that replica in the *piazza* rests right where the real statue originally stood before it migrated indoors in the 19th century. The replica is far from the only copy of the *David*—the world is swarming with models of the Michelangelo masterwork. Head up to the Piazzale Michelangelo to see another replica—and you haven't even left Florence yet. There's a replica at Caesar's Palace in Las Vegas and one at Ripley's Believe It or Not in Florida. The campus of California State University, Fullerton, has one whose buttocks are traditionally rubbed by students seeking good luck. At the Victoria and Albert Museum in London, a strategically placed fig leaf was once hung for visits from Queen Victoria and other delicate ladies.

So who needs to see the original, if replicas are a dime a dozen? Head to the Accademia (p. 206) and see the difference for yourself. Can't see it? At least you can feel superior to the amateurs who were tricked by the statue outside.

sights · san marco

MUSEO DI SAN MARCO
P. San Marco 3

🖐♿ MUSEUM

☎055 23 88 608 ▪www.firenzemusei.it

The first floor of this museum is divided into small cubbies the size of West Village studios. These are the cells of old monks, and each one has a different painting on the wall. Pop inside and imagine spending four decades copying manuscripts by hand in here. Then imagine what it would be like if an angel arrived to announce that you were about to experience an unplanned pregnancy—twice—by looking at Fra Angelico's two **Annunciation** frescoes. The most famous, which you'll probably recognize from postcards, is at the top of the staircase, while a less popular incarnation is on the wall of one of the cells.

The more traditional gallery space has a nice collection of illuminated manuscripts and Gregorian chants. If the graduals inspire you to do some singing yourself, we recommend finding an empty cell, shutting the door behind you, and having at it. The resonance is lovely. If you don't know any chants, don't worry. Try singing The Beatles' "Yesterday" slowly. It should do the trick.

🏃 *The north side of the piazza.* *i* *Approximate visit time: 30min.* Ⓢ *€4, EU citizens age 16-25 €2.* ⏰ *Open M-F 8:15am-1:50pm, Sa 8:15am-6:50pm, Su 8:15am-7pm.*

BOTANIC GARDENS
●♿ GARDENS

V. Micheli 3 ☎055 23 46 70 ✉msn.unifi.it

Listen. There are way more impressive botanical gardens in the world. Don't come here to learn about horticulture or to feel transported to a Chinese bamboo forest, but just to sit somewhere green and relax. It is probably the best smelling place in historic Florence outside the **Boboli Gardens**, especially so after the rain. Grab a bench to rest both your feet and your nostrils. The Botanic Gardens are also a fine place to sneak a siesta, if you don't mind getting poked on the shoulder when a guard reluctantly decides to enforce the anti-vagrancy rules.

🏃 *Continue past San Marco; gardens are on the right and kind of obvious.* *i* *Info text also in Braille.* Ⓢ *€6.* ⏰ *Open Apr-Oct M-Tu 10am-7pm, Th-Su 10am-7pm; Oct-Mar M 10am-5pm, Sa-Su 10am-5pm.*

MUSEO D'OPIFICIO DELLE PIETRE DURE
●♿ MUSEUM

V. Degli Alfani 78 ☎055 26 51 11 ✉www.opificiodellepietredure.it

That name is a mouthful, but it boils down to a whole lot of mosaics. And when you've been staring at paintings for days, it is fun to mix it up with some truly excellent examples of a surprisingly different medium that's distinct from other visual arts. By the staircase, a series of paintings paired with mosaics based on the original work allows you to examine places where the opportunity for detail is greater in mosaics (masonry) versus painting (faces). On the balcony, the workbenches of the mosaic artists are preserved so that you can marvel at how these intricate objects were created with such crude tools. Mosaics were assembled by teams in a workshop, piece by piece, in a collaborative process closer to modern animation than other forms of visual art. The vast display cases contain samples of the stone used for the work as well.

🏃 *From San Marco, 1 block down Ricasoli then left on Alfani.* Ⓢ *€4, EU citizens age 18-25 €2, EU citizens under 18 and over 65, and art students free.* ⏰ *Open M-Sa 8:15am-2pm.*

MUSEO DEGLI INNOCENTI
●⊗ MUSEUM

P. della Santissima Annunziata 12 ☎055 20 37 323 ✉www.istitutodeglinnocenti.it

The old foundlings hospital has terra-cotta babies on panels all along the outside—it's kind of hard to miss. Inside is an entire complex containing the museum and a UNICEF study center. The museum has history panels explaining the hospital, where dozens of wet nurses were once employed for the hundreds of children abandoned on the portico every year—in the 19th century, unwed mothers could give birth here in exchange for a year of service as a wet nurse. The exhibits themselves include a bunch of paintings of babies and some colorful wooden Jesus dioramas that would fit better in a *Dia de los Muertos* context than in a Catholic orphanage. This gallery is worth 15min. at most. However, there is a cavernous basement off the courtyard that is sometimes used as an exhibit space for contemporary art. It is a very atmospheric space, well-suited to site-specific work, and this museum becomes worth your time when there are exhibits installed here, so ask at the desk before you pony up €4.

➡ On the right in P. di San Marco. $ €4, children and seniors €2.50. ⏰ Open daily 10am-7pm. Last entry 30min. before close.

MACCHINE DI LEONARDO
♿ MUSEUM

V. Cavour 21 ☎055 29 52 64 💻www.macchinedileonardo.com

Itchy fingers? This little storefront exhibit is packed with wooden models of da Vinci's mechanical, aerial, and anatomical innovations. It's like taking freshman physics and skipping everything but the hands-on demos. You'll be skipping the readings too—the placards here are rather sparse. But even if you don't remember anything about friction and haven't the darndest idea how an Archimedes Screw works, it's still fun to play with pulleys and levers for a spell.

➡ 5min. up Cavour from the Duomo, on the left. $ €7. ⏰ Open daily 9:30am-7:30pm.

MUSEO ARCHEOLOGICO
♿ MUSEUM

P. Santissima Annunziata n. 9b ☎055 23 575 💻www.archeotoscana.beniculturali.it

Do you like Greek pottery? Do you *really* like Greek pottery? Then have we got the museum for you! For the rest of us, it's a clearly important collection that is sadly displayed in a way that'll make you feel as if you're zoning out in history class all over again. Come here if you want to be depressed by an underfunded museum! Hopefully some day a nice fan of *sarcophagi* will commission new panels and cough up the dough to get some fresh paint on the walls.

➡ Facing Santissima Annuziata, it's on the right. $ €4, EU citizens age 18-25 €2, EU citizens under 16 and over 65 free. ⏰ Open Tu-F 8:30am-7pm, Sa-Su 8:30am-2pm.

SANTA CROCE

Although plaques marking the water line of the 1966 Arno flood can be found all over Florence, the Santa Croce area was the hardest hit. Be on the lookout for the watermarks—some of which will be well over your head—and imagine the incredible efforts it took to save and restore Santa Croce's art from the floodwaters.

👍 SYNAGOGUE OF FLORENCE
♿ SYNAGOGUE, MUSEUM

V. Luigi Carlo Farini 4 ☎055 21 07 63 💻www.firenzehebraica.net

It may not be Renaissance vintage, but this is one Florentine house of worship that is well worth a visit. Florence is mum when it comes to the history of its working class, minority, or otherwise non-Medici population, and the synagogue is one of the only sites where average citizens get the spotlight. The story of the Jewish community and Italy's role in WWII is every bit as vital to your understanding of the city of Florence as a stack of Botticellis.

Quick history lesson: for hundreds of years, Florence's Jews lived in a walled ghetto in the center of the city. In 1868, 20 years before the ghetto was finally razed, the president of Hebrew University bequeathed money to the Jewish community of Florence to build a synagogue worthy of this fine city. The result was the exotic, Moorish structure that today stands apart from the surrounding buildings both physically and stylistically—a bold choice, especially since many contemporary synagogues were designed to blend in to avoid drawing attention to the community.

The synagogue is gorgeous and fresh in its distinctness from all the other houses of worship in town. Its warm earth tones, abstract and geometric decoration on every surface, and properly Mosaic mosaics make it a perfect example of Moorish influence. (It is also, sentiments being what they are, the only one that requires metal detectors and an armed guard). Yet despite its relative youthfulness, the fact that it still stands is semi-miraculous. The Nazis used the synagogue as a headquarters during their occupation of Florence, and when they evacuated, the temple was rigged to explode. Amazingly, all but one of the bombs failed to detonate, saving the building from total destruction.

Prior to WWII, there were 40,000 Jews in Italy, 2400 living in Florence. The synagogue contains a memorial to the Florentines killed in the camps; although the list is relatively short, the number of shared surnames indicates that a handful of large families were wiped out completely. This kind of decimation is truly devastating, especially considering that modern Italy has not yet recovered its Jewish population. There are around 28,000 Jews in Italy, more than half of them in Rome, and a mere 900 congregants support the vast Florentine synagogue.

The museum inside the synagogue is, unlike most Jewish museums in places where there aren't many Jews, not a dull "What is Shabbat?" affair but a decent historical exhibit tracing the story of Florence's Jewish population over the last half millennium. The docents get very excited when you bother asking them questions.

From the Basilica di Santa Croce, head north on V. dei Pepi for 7 blocks. Take a right onto Pilastri and an immediate left onto V. Luigi Carlo Farini. i Yarmulkes required and provided. Check bags and cameras at lockers before entering. $ €5, students €3. Open Apr-Sept M-Th 10am-6pm, F 10am-2pm; Oct-Mar M-Th 10am-3pm, F 10am-2pm. Closed Jewish holidays. The 1st fl. of the museum is open during the 2nd half of every hr.

BASILICA DI SANTA CROCE ♿ CHURCH

P. Santa Croce ☎055 24 66 105

This basilica is an enormous complex worthy of costing more than the other big churches in town, though really it's the dead celebrities buried here that jack up the price of admission. Fork over the dough and pay your respects to Florence's greats. Rossini's tomb is subtly decorated with treble clefs and violin bridges. Galileo gets a globe and an etching of the solar system (*his* solar system) to mark his grave. Machiavelli is just sort of chilling. Dante's tomb is probably cool, but it was blocked with scaffolding when we visited. Michelangelo, all things considered, really should have a grander place of burial, but since he didn't design it, we take what we can get. Even Marconi is here—that's right, the guy who invented the radio.

Aside from the famous graves, this basilica's got things going for it. The Egyptian vibe of the basilica's interior is distinctive. Plus, the very cowl and girdle worn by St. Francis are on display, looking exactly as you'd expect. To the left of the altar are some cloisters and gardens, all quite lovely and full of more dead people of the slightly less famous variety. To the right, the Santa Croce leather school is ready to instruct you in the ways of leatherworking or sell you its students' handicraft. *Let's Go* doesn't recommend trying to cheat Jesus, but some travelers report that it's not difficult to sneak in to the basilica through the leather school's entrance at V. San Giuseppe 5r.

Take Borgo de' Greci east from P. della Signoria. $ €5, ages 11-17 €3, disabled free. Combined with Casa Michelangelo €8. Audio tour €5. Open M-F 9:30am-3:30pm, Sa-Su 1-5:30pm.

CASA BUONARROTI ♿ MUSEUM

V. Ghibellina 70 ☎055 24 17 52 www.casabuonarroti.it

When Michelangelo hit it big, he did what any new celebrity would do—he bought a bunch of houses and then never lived in them. Unlike the completely fabricated Casa di Dante, Casa Buonarroti is not a reproduction. It was, in fact, home to several generations of the big guy's descendents, making it a good destination for Miche-*fan*-gelos. The museum's collection includes Etruscan archeological fragments, rare sketches and models by Michelangelo himself, and a set of 19th-century Michelangelo-themed tourist kitsch produced during a Victorian burst of Mich-mania. Our favorite curiosity is the small model of the wooden contraption used to transport *David* from P. della Signoria to the Accademia.

From Santa Croce, walk a block to the left to find V. Ghibellina. $ €6.50, students and seniors €4.50. Open M 9:30am-2pm, W-Su 9:30am-2pm.

PIAZZA DEI CIOMPI MARKET

P. dei Ciompi

It's just a *piazza* with an arch, but the antique market that runs here during the day is worth a visit.

From the basilica, go north on Borgo Allegri until you see the arches.

WEST OLTRARNO

Palazzo Pitti

The major sights of West Oltrarno are all helpfully condensed into the enormous Palazzo Pitti. It's not hard to find the complex: just cross the Ponte Vecchio and continue along the same street until you reach the very obvious *palazzo*. The Palazzo Pitti museums are batched under two ticket combos: **Ticket One** gets you into Galleria Palatina, Galleria d'Arte Moderna, and Apartamenti Reali. **Ticket Two** is for the Boboli Gardens, Museo degli Argenti, Galleria del Costume, and Museo della Porcellana. Overall, if you're choosing one ticket combo over the other, we recommend **Ticket Two.**

BOBOLI GARDENS GARDENS

Palazzo Pitti Complex

The Boboli Gardens feels a little like a cross between Central Park and Versailles, which means it's really wonderful. Imagine you're a 17th-century Medici strolling through your gardens—but don't imagine your way into a corset, ladies, because the gardens are raked at a surprising incline. They're also easily large enough for you to lose yourself here for an entire afternoon. For the best vantage point climb further up and further in. Head uphill from the palace, past several large and attractive fountains. When you feel as if you've climbed the Campanile and reached the top level, you aren't done yet. Follow the path to the right behind a wall, and you'll emerge onto the peak of the hill. This is the very edge of Florence. Immediately below, a verdant green valley rolls into the distance and the packed red buildings of the city give way to sprawling monasteries and thickset trees. It's a stunning view. Don't forget to turn around; the view of Florence behind you ain't too shabby either. As with any gardens, Boboli is most fragrant and lovely right after the rain, but make sure the downpour is really finished or you'll be spending a lot longer in the porcelain museum than any person ever should.

i Ticket 2. $ €10, EU citizens ages 18-25 €5, EU citizens under 18 and over 65 free. Open daily June-Aug 8:15am-7:30pm; Sept 8:15am-6:30pm; Oct 8:15am-5:30pm; Nov-Feb 8:15am-4:30pm; Mar-May 8:15am-6:30pm. Closed 1st and last M of each month.

GALLERIA PALATINA MUSEUM

Palazzo Pitti Complex

This enormous gallery would be more of a draw in a city that didn't also include the Uffizi. The two museums sometimes offer joint exhibits, despite being on opposite sides of town—at the time of writing, the Uffizi's mysteriously Caravaggio-less Caravaggio show only made sense upon a visit to the Palatina's Caravaggio-filled version of the same show. The permanent collection is housed in rooms named not for the art, but for the ceilings. We are still in a *palazzo*, remember, so the organizational logic is still that of a rich royal wanting to clutter his brocaded walls with all the big-ticket masterpieces he could commission. The quirkiest object in the collection sits alone in a small chamber between the Education of Jupiter and Ulysses rooms. It is Napoleon's **bathtub.** That's right: *The* Napoleon. *His* bathtub. Your entire vacation was just made worthwhile, wasn't it?

i Ticket 1. $ €12, EU citizens age 18-25 €6, EU citizens under 18 and over 65 free. Open Tu-Su 8:15am-6:50pm.

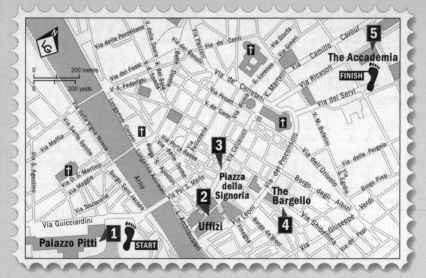

paint the town

1. PALAZZO PITTI. In a city full of museums, Palazzo Pitti is the most expansive and possibly the most luxurious. If you're here for just a short time, a visit to the Boboli Gardens is always a pleasure, although you can easily spend several hours meandering through the beautiful flora and gravel pathways. Having spent as long as you want at Pitti, begin walking down V. de' Guicciardini, crossing the Arno on the famed Ponte Vecchio.

2. UFFIZI. Florence's premier museum, the Uffizi can compete with absolutely any other in the world. Take a stroll through its cloister and witness the huge lines waiting to go in. If you're smart enough to get here shortly before the museum closes and make a reservation for the next day—you'll then be able to walk right in without having to line up.

3. PIAZZA DELLA SIGNORIA. A little north of the Uffizi, this grand L-shaped piazza lets you admire a great piece of art without even stepping inside a museum: Michelangelo's *David*. Of course, it isn't the real version, just a replica. But if you'd been here 150 years ago you'd have seen the real thing, as this is where it used to stand.

4. THE BARGELLO. Exit the piazza to the east, then head north through P. San Firenze to reach the Bargello. Though it may be the least famous of Florence's top museums, the Bargello still has its fair share of names like Michelangelo and Donatello in its collection, so it's hardly to be scoffed at.

5. THE ACCADEMIA. Unlike most important museums that receive a huge number of visitors (The Uffizi, the Louvre, the Vatican, the list goes on), the Accademia is not famous for its extensive collections. It is simply known for one work: Michelangelo's *David*. Come rain or shine, there will be huge lines stretching outside as people wait to see the sculptural miracle. If you want to end the tour with one of the art world's most celebrated masterpieces, join the line.

GALLERIA DEL COSTUME
🎟♿ MUSEUM

Palazzo Pitti Complex

If you like the costume gallery at the Met, you'll love Palazzo Pitti's Galleria del Costume. The galleria's fashion collection isn't just Medici-era vintage—it stretches all the way into the modern day. A true Italian knows that clothes are every bit as sacred as paintings of angels, so the couture is presented engagingly and thematically. Pieces from the collection rotate, but the current exhibit categorizes styles not by chronology, but by gimmick—one display includes classically-inspired sheath dresses from 1890, 1923, 1971, and 1993. It's fascinating to see the same basic ideas get reinterpreted every other generation and fun to play the "guess the decade" game before reading the title cards—you'll be surprised how easy it is to confuse the 1920s for the 1980s. The one permanent display is for the true Medici completist. Here, the actual burial clothes of several dead Medici, torn from their rotting corpses for your viewing pleasure, have been preserved. You're welcome.

i Ticket 2. $ €10, EU citizens ages 18-25 €5, EU citizens under 18 and over 65 free. ⏰ Open daily June-Aug 8:15am-7:30pm; Sept 8:15am-6:30pm; Oct 8:15am-5:30pm; Nov-Feb 8:15am-4:30pm; Mar-May 8:15am-6:30pm. Closed 1st and last M of each month.

MUSEO DEGLI ARGENTI
🎟♿ MUSEUM

Palazzo Pitti Complex

In this treasure museum, you will be overwhelmed with the abundance of riches, quite literally. If the museum were a 10th of its size, it might be the greatest thing ever. As it is, it's just a little too much sensory overload. The collection includes incredible minute ivories, precious jewels with portraits engraved on the surface, dazzling crowns, Chinese porcelain, jade mosaics, sterling silver bedpans, and a wide array of chalices from the palaces. And don't forget to look around—the collection is housed in some of the most impressively and elaborately frescoed rooms of any palace in Florence.

i Ticket 2. $ €10, EU citizens ages 18-25 €5, EU citizens under 18 and over 65 free. ⏰ Open daily June-Aug 8:15am-7:30pm; Sept 8:15am-6:30pm; Oct 8:15am-5:30pm; Nov-Feb 8:15am-4-:30pm; Mar-May 8:15am-6:30pm. Closed 1st and last M each month.

APARTAMENTI REALI
🎟♿ MUSEUM

Palazzo Pitti Complex

The back end of the Galleria Palatina gets it right by doing away with the pesky art and sticking to the rich people's bedrooms. Take a quick stroll through the apartments of the great and pick out tapestries, tassels, and toilettes for your own palace.

i Ticket 1. $ €12, EU citizens ages 18-25 €6, EU citizens under 18 and over 65 free. ⏰ Open Tu-Su 8:15am-6:50pm.

MUSEO DELLA PORCELLANA
🎟⊗ MUSEUM

Palazzo Pitti Complex

The top of that hill in the gardens is home to a porcelain museum. Sounds dull, right? Turns out, whoever spent the centuries amassing this collection of dishware really knew what he or she was doing. Play the Imaginary Wedding Registry game and plan future dinner parties in your Tuscan villa.

✥ At the highest point of the Boboli Gardens. Just keep walking up. i Ticket 2. $ €10, EU citizens ages 18-25 €5, EU citizens under 18 and over 65 free. ⏰ Open daily June-Aug 8:15am-7:30pm; Sept 8:15am-6:30pm; Oct 8:15am-5:30pm; Nov-Feb 8:15am-4:30pm; Mar-May 8:15am-6:30pm. Closed 1st and last M of each month.

GALLERIA D'ARTE MODERNA
🎟♿ MUSEUM

Palazzo Pitti Complex
☎055 23 88 616

Only in Florence could people define "modern art" as stuff that predates the

French Revolution. This gallery contains works from the 1780s onwards, but it is mostly mired in 19th-century Naturalism. The good parts of 19th-century art are pretty much left out or squashed into a single room on "Pointillism, Symbolism, and Social Themes." In an entire city devoted to the Renaissance, "social themes" gets one wall. The best part is the exit. That's not meant to be (entirely) derogatory—the staircase is actually really beautiful.

i Ticket 1. $ €12, EU citizens ages 18-25 €6, EU citizens under 18 and over 65 free. ⏰ Open Tu-Su 8:15am-6:50pm.

EAST OLTRARNO

There's not much here except the Piazzale Michelangelo and, uphill, a bit more green space than you'll find in the rest of the city center.

PIAZZALE MICHELANGELO ♿ PANORAMIC VIEWS

Piazzale Michelangelo

It's a parking lot. Still, it's the most scenic damn parking lot you'll ever see. Cross the river and bear east until you reach the base of the steps. It's about a 10min. walk uphill to the *piazzale*—a walk both cheaper and more pleasant than the one up the Campanile, but still requiring decent shoes. You can take the #12 or 13 bus if you're lazy, but the short **hike** is rather pleasant itself. At the summit, you'll be rewarded with a broad cement *piazza* upon which an oxidized reproduction of the *David* and a whole lot of parked cars enjoy a killer view. Ignore everything behind you and watch the sun set over the city.

 # From pretty much any bridge, walk left along the river until P. Guiseppe Poggi, where you will find the base of the steps. It's up from there. i Wheelchair-accessible only by bus. $ Free. ⏰ Open 24hr.

food

While Florence isn't a culinarily distinct city, it remains a great place to find good food. There are trattorias everywhere, and almost every one of them is tasty. The only major variance between them all will be in cover charge and distance from a major *piazza*. If they begin to feel a bit too similar to one another, head to smaller places: the markets, the hole-in-the-walls, the local favorites. Whatever you do, you can't go wrong.

a gelato primer

There is some truly brilliant **gelato** in Florence, and the best thing about gelato is that quality seems to have an inverse relationship with price. The range for a small cone (with two scoops) is €1-2. If you are paying more, you are probably being ripped off. Think carefully about your flavor selection. Even the smallest sizes allow for multiple flavors, so plan for good combinations–mixing banana and mint, for instance, is not a great idea. And unlike ice cream, where strawberry and strawberry-flavored are two completely different tastes, gelato actually tastes like what it's supposed to taste like. The strawberry tastes like strawberry. The coffee tastes like coffee. The snozzberry tastes like...well, you get the idea. There are great *gelaterie* all over the city; read the listings below to see what our favorites are in each neighborhood. We by no means offer an exhaustive list, but we hope to help you quickly locate the *LG*-approved *gelateria* nearest to wherever you happen to be standing.

THE DUOMO

The places along the **Piazza del Duomo** all seem to have been cast from the same mold. They cost about the same, they offer similar fare, and they all have a rockin' view of the Duomo. For slightly more variety, venture a couple blocks from the main *piazza*.

GROM

☎☿ GELATERIA ❶

V. del Campanile ☎055 21 61 58 www.grom.it

Grom is a high-end *gelateria*, which means it has a posh location right off the Duomo, a branch in New York City, and a slightly higher starting price than the city's other top-notch *gelateria*. Nevertheless, it's the best of the sweet stuff in the Duomo area. Sure, you'll find it mentioned in every guidebook and, if you catch it at the wrong time of day, you'll be waiting in line for 15min. Just come back later. The gelato will still be delicious.

⌗ Just south of the Duomo. Ⓢ Starting at €2. 🕒 Open daily Apr-Sept 10:30am-midnight; Oct-Mar 10:30am-11pm.

VESTRI CIOCCOLATO D'ANTOIE

GELATERIA ❶

Borgo degli Albizi 11r ☎055 23 40 374 www.vestri.it

Another brilliant gelato place, this one featuring the best pistachio in town, according to our very scientific research that consisted of eating too much pistachio gelato. The prices are a little higher than others, but it's gelato, so we're talking a difference of a few nickels. Plus, top-notch combo flavors like the *cioccolata fondente* with mint make it worth the pennies. There's a bit of a boutique feel to the place, the only seating is a bench right outside, and sometimes the line is long, but no matter. This is the best gelato within a half-mile radius.

⌗ Coming from the Duomo, it's on the right after Borgo degli Albizi opens up into a piazza. Ⓢ Starting at €1.80. 🕒 Open daily 10:30am-8pm.

CAFFE DUOMO

RISTORANTE ❷

P. del Duomo 29-30r ☎055 21 13 48

There are a number of nice trattorias all in a row here, staring up at the Duomo. They're all roughly equivalent and offer specials, so browse them all and decide which you like best. We prefer this one for its lighter lunch specials, particularly the cheese and cold cut platter with a glass of Chianti *(€12 for 2 people)*. The young staff have also been known to dance to Justin Bieber when business is slow.

⌗ In the shadow of the Duomo. Ⓢ Entree and a glass of wine for €9. 🕒 Open daily noon-11pm.

TRATTORIA LA MADIA

RISTORANTE ❷

V. del Giglio 14 ☎055 21 85 63

If you are tired of salt-less Tuscan bread, come here for a welcome dose of sodium. The bruschetta is especially good, as are the seafood specialties, and all are pleasantly salty compared to the same dishes in every other identical trattoria.

⌗ Off V. dei Banchi, toward Santa Maria Novella. Ⓢ Primi €10; secondi €10-18. 🕒 Open Tu-Su 1-10pm.

BUCA NICCOLINI

RISTORANTE ❶

V. Ricasoli 5-7r ☎055 29 21 24 www.bucaniccolini.it

"Make food, not war" proclaim the placemats at this trattoria, and after a big lunch, it's hard to disagree. It's inches off P. del Duomo, but every inch is another penny less for a pizza and a beer—here, they'll set you back €8. You can still see the Campanile, if you crane your neck a little.

⌗ Immediately north of the Duomo, on left. Ⓢ Pizza and beer €8. Pasta and beer €9.50. 🕒 Open daily 11am-3pm and 5pm-midnight.

food . the duomo

LITTLE DAVID 💳♿📶🍸🥡 RISTORANTE ❶

V. De' Martelli 14r ☎055 23 02 695

This spot compensates for being the littler David by offering real big pizzas. Hang out all afternoon with the free Wi-Fi, munching on the student special—pizza or pasta and a soft drink for €6.

🧭 Just north of the Duomo, on the right. $ Pizza €5.50-8. 0.5L wine €4.90. ⏰ Open daily noon-1am.

LE BOTTEGHE DI DONATELLO 💳♿🍸🥡 RISTORANTE ❷

P. del Duomo 28r ☎055 21 66 78

One of many trattorias in the Duomo piazza, but boasting an extensive gluten-free menu. The inside seating is surprisingly extensive and Tuscan-rustic, so it's a fine option in cooler weather.

🧭 Northeast side of the Duomo. $ Pizza €6.50-12. Pastas €7-12. ⏰ Open daily 11am-11pm.

PIAZZA DELLA SIGNORIA

Considering that this area teems with tourists of the well-heeled variety, there are still a surprising number of budget-friendly eateries. Good rule of thumb—the farther north or east you are of the Uffizi, the better off you are.

👍 **DA VINATTIERI** 💳♿🥡 SANDWICHES ❶

V. Santa Margherita 4r ☎055 29 47 03

This is a literal hole-in-the-wall that's well worth tracking down. Unlike most of the panini in town, these are actually made to order. As in, the guy picks up the leg of ham and cuts off a slice for your sandwich. You can step into the tiny shop or just order a quick *lampridotto (€3.50)* from the alley through the counter window. Choose from the long menu of sandwich suggestions or invent your own—they all cost the same anyway. The stools in the alley make for a fine perch while polishing off your lunch. The proprietor sometimes pops out for a smoke or a chat, but give it a minute. He'll be back.

🧭 Across the alley from Casa di Dante, so just follow the signs for that attraction. Shares a corner with Lush, which you can smell from 2 blocks away. $ Panini €3-3.50. ⏰ Open daily 10am-8pm.

👍 **FESTIVAL DEL GELATO** 💳♿ GELATERIA ❶

V. Del Corso 75r ☎055 29 43 86

We had dismissed this tacky, neon-flooded gelateria as a certain tourist trap, but when a local recommended it, we caved and gave the disco gelato a try. At our first bite of *cioccolata fondente*, the garish fluorescence melted into warm candlelight and fireflies and a violinist in white tie began to...OK, no, the place still looked ridiculous, but hot damn, that be good gelato.

🧭 Look for the neon. You seriously can't miss it. $ Gelato from €1.80. ⏰ Open daily noon-midnight.

OSTERIA DELL PORCELLINO 💳♿🍸🥡 RISTORANTE ❸

V. Val di Lamona 7r ☎055 26 41 48 💻www.osteriadelporcellino.com

This beautiful osteria has an alleyway to itself which it fills with wrought-iron tables and colored lights. Don't come for lunch, when the adjacent Mercato Nuovo is bustling. Instead, wait until the evenings when the *piazza* clears out and the space is well worth the €2 cover.

🧭 Right off Mercato Nuovo. ℹ Vegetarian menu. $ Cover €2. Primi €7-10; secondi €14-22. ⏰ Open daily noon-3pm and 5-11pm.

CORONAS CAFE 💳♿🍸🥡 CAFE ❶

V. Calzaiuoli 72r ☎055 239 6139

Cheap sandwiches and pastries *(€1-3.50)* as well as an open layout on the corner make this cafe a good spot for eating alone and people-watching. The excellent gelato is available in enormous American-appetite-sized cones if you want to be *that* guy.

☗ *Just north of P. della Signoria, on the corner.* Ⓢ *Pastries €1-3.50. Panini €3.50.* ◷ *Open daily 10am-1am.*

CANTINETTA DEI VERRAZANO
☕♿ CAFE ❶

V. Dei Tavolini 18/20r
☎055 26 85 90

The pizzas *(from €1.80)* here are cheaper and better than what you'll find at similar places. They're also tiny, but what do you expect at the price? Offers a wide variety of biscotti and cakes as well.

☗ *Off V. Calzaluioli, north of P. della Signoria.* Ⓢ *Pizzas from €1.80.* ◷ *Open daily 8am-9pm.*

OSTERIA GANINO
☕♿🍴 RISTORANTE ❷

P. de' Cimatori 4r
☎055 21 41 25

Hide from the sun under big umbrellas and a hedge of leafy green plants at this pleasant *osteria* in a low-traffic *piazza*. Sample the wide variety of desserts (€4-5) or one of the many vegetarian options.

☗ *Across from the American Express office.* Ⓢ *Primi €7-11.* ◷ *Open M-Sa noon-11pm.*

GUSTO LEO
☕♿🍸🍴 PIZZERIA ❷

V. del Proconsolo 8-10r
☎055 28 52 17 🖥www.gustoleo.com

Come to this friendly, brick restaurant near the major sights for its enormous calzones *(€7.60)* and pizzas *(€5.40-8.90)*. Wide selection of large salads and a cute little lion cartoon as a logo.

☗ *Coming from P. Della Signoria, it's on the right.* Ⓢ *Pizzas €5.40-8.90. Calzones €7.60.* ◷ *Open daily 8am-1am.*

SANTA MARIA NOVELLA

Pizzerias, cafes, and kebab shops abound near the train station and church. This is a good neighborhood to find a generic, cheap, quick eat but not a destination if you're looking for a sit-down meal.

CAFFE GIACOSA
☕♿🍸🍴 CAFE ❶

Inside Palazzo Strozzi
☎055 42 65 04 86

Backpacking is murder on your lower lumbar, and the curved wooden wall at Caffe Giacosa fits just right in the small of your back. Lean back with a cappuccino *(€1.30)*, and it's as good as ibuprofen. The prices triple for table seating, but who cares? The nice wooden wall in the self-serve area is the point of the visit. The pots of tea *(€2)* are made of fancy bagged stuff—a lot better than nothing for tea-drinkers stranded in coffee country.

☗ *Inside Palazzo Strozzi, which is west of P. della Repubblica. Has a 2nd location down the street at V. della Spada 10.* Ⓢ *Cappuccino €1.30. Pot of tea €2.* ◷ *Open daily 10am-10pm.*

OPERA ET GUSTO
☕♿🍸❋ RISTORANTE, CONCERT VENUE ❸

V. Della Scala 17r
☎055 28 81 90 🖥www.operaetgusto.com

This sleek joint is a little-black-dress sort of place, with black and red decor and limited lighting. The draw is the live performances most nights, which tend towards jazz combos and light world music but sometimes encompass diverse theatrical art forms. Considering the entertainment, the cover *(€2)* is a steal.

☗ *Coming from Santa Maria Novella, on the left.* ℹ *Show 9-10:30pm.* Ⓢ *Cover €2. Primi €10-12; secondi €11-22.* ◷ *Open daily 8:30pm-2am.*

OSTERIA E PIZZERIA CENTROPOVERI
☕♿🍸❋ PIZZERIA, RISTORANTE ❷

V. Palazzuolo 31r
☎055 21 88 46 🖥www.icentopoveri.it

Two adjacent restaurants with the same name but different menus. The long dining rooms with curved ceilings will make you feel like you're eating in a tunnel, but the light at the end is the excellent pizza *(€4-9)* on the pizzeria side, and the Tuscan specialties in the osteria, with a *prix-fixe* menu *(€35)* featuring *bistecca alla fiorentina*.

⚓ Corner of Porcellana. Ⓢ Cover €2 in osteria. Pizza €4-9. Primi €7-10; secondi €9-19. ⏰ Open daily noon-3pm and 7pm-midnight.

50 ROSSO
⊛&▾⌂ CAFE ❶

V. Panzani 50r
☎055 28 35 85

A lovely open-walled cafe with a takeaway happy hour and no surcharge for sitting. Open during basically all reasonable eating hours. Nutella crepes are divine.

⚓ From P. Santa Maria Novella, you'll find the start of V. Panzani in the northeast corner of the piazza, nearer the train station. Ⓢ Panini €2.50. Cappuccino €1.20. ⏰ Open daily 6:30am-12:30am.

TRATTORIA IL CONTADINO
⊛&▾ RISTORANTE ❷

V. Palazzuolo 69/71r
☎055 23 82 673

This weekday-only trattoria has wine racks on the wall and lazy ceiling fans—the good deal is a lovely *prix-fixe* menu of *primo*, *secondo*, veggie, and wine (lunch €11, dinner €13).

⚓ From P. Santa Maria Novella, take a right onto V. Palazzuolo. Ⓢ Prix-fixe menu €11-13. ⏰ Open M-F noon-9:40pm.

LA GROTTA DI LEO
⊛&▾ RISTORANTE ❶

V. Della Scala 41/43r
☎055 21 92 65

This brick-walled trattoria is bigger than it looks, with two grotto-esque dining rooms and a couple outdoor tables. Try the house specialty, tiramisu (€4).

⚓ Coming from P. Santa Maria Novella, take a right onto V. della Scala. Ⓢ Pizza €5-8. Primi €5-8. ⏰ Open daily 11am-1am.

SAN LORENZO

Honestly, if you're around here during the day, you should be getting your food at Mercato Centrale. But Trattoria Mario is the choice if you get to Mercato after the stalls close up. Other food options vary widely in this crowded, lively area.

▨ TRATTORIA MARIO
⊛⊗▾ RISTORANTE ❷

V. Rosina 2r
☎055 21 85 50 🖳www.trattoriamario.com

If you're starting to wonder where all the Italians are hiding, show up late for lunch at Trattoria Mario. Diners are packed into tables with strangers, and regulars will flag the waitress if they want a newcomer to be seated at their table. And then perhaps they will buy you wine. Lots and lots of wine. The food is pretty good too, with the day's offerings written on brown paper by the kitchen.

⚓ Just off Mercato Centrale, on the right. Ⓢ Daily specials €6-9. ⏰ Open M-Sa noon-3:30pm.

▨ NEGRONE
⊛&▾ RISTORANTE ❶

P. del Mercato Centrale
☎055 21 99 49

Mercato Centrale isn't just for groceries. The edges are lined with cafes, cafeterias, and panini stands that cater to workers and wise visitors. Negrone stands out as both the oldest, dating back to 1872, and the best. Crowd around the counter to order whatever happens to be on offer, take your tray, and squeeze in somewhere at the picnic tables along the wall. The food is fantastic and dirt-cheap, plus the atmosphere is far livelier than any cookie-cutter trattoria. Don't forget to bus your tray when you're done!

⚓ Along the wall of the Mercato. Ⓢ Primi and secondi €4-7. Cup of house wine €1. ⏰ Open M-Sa 7am-2pm.

▨ ANTICA GELATERIA FIORENTINA
⊛& GELATERIA ❶

V. Faenza 2a
☎388 05 80 399 🖳www.gelateriafiorentina.com

Off-beat flavors like rosewater, cheesecake, and green tea will add some variety to your gelato diet, and although the peanut butter chocolate was probably concocted to please Americans starved of their lunchbox staple, it at least succeeds in its goal. Antica is super cheap too, with cones starting at a single flavor for €1. If you want to go whole-hog American, there's a ginormo cone *(€15)* in which you can try every flavor on tap. Don't mix the cheesecake and green tea. Also, don't look too closely at the **Torture Museum** across the street.

➔ Toward the far end of V. Faenza, on the left. $ Cones from €1. ⏰ Open daily noon-midnight.

TRATTORIA ZAZA 💳♿🍸☀ RISTORANTE [2]

P. del Mercato Centrale 26r ☎055 21 54 11 💻www.trattoriazaza.it

The tented alfresco seating is typical for a *piazza ristorante*, but the quirky logo on the menu—a naked child being stung on the buttocks by a bee—should give you a clue to the offbeat glamour of the inside dining rooms. Lurid frescoes coat the vaulted ceilings, while staid dead white men watch you devour fresh pasta from gilded portraits. For those not inclined to the bloody *bistecca alla fiorentina*, there are abundant creative salad options—try Zaza's, with chicory lettuce, walnuts, brie, and Roquefort dressing.

➔ Behind Mercato Centrale. $ Cover €2.50. Primi €7-11. ⏰ Open daily 11am-11pm.

BAR CABRAS 💳♿🍸 CAFE [1]

V. dei Panzani 12r ☎055 21 20 32

Italy takes its regional specialties seriously, so you're hard pressed to find a decent cannoli outside its southern home turf. But for the best cannoli between Sicily and Boston's North End, go no further than this tiny cafe by the train station. Not looking for regionally misplaced pastries? It's also a full bar. We were going to add a cheesy Godfather pun here too, but the pastry is looking so tempting that we're gonna leave the pun and take the cannoli.

➔ Just down the street from the train station. $ Cannoli €2.50. ⏰ Open daily 8am-8pm.

RISTORANTE LE FONTICINE 💳♿🍸 RISTORANTE [2]

V. Nazionale 79r ☎055 28 21 06 💻www.lefonticine.com

While it appears deceptively small from the front dining room, a walk deeper inside this restaurant past the open kitchen reveals a beautiful lantern-lit dining room cluttered with framed paintings. Poke your head into the adjacent wine cellar and select a bottle to accompany the *prix-fixe menu dello chef (€25).*

➔ To the right of the V. Nazionale fountain, hence the name. $ Primi €6-13; secondi €8-16. ⏰ Open daily noon-2:30pm and 7-10:30pm.

OSTERIA ALL'ANTICO MERCATO 💳♿🍸☀ RISTORANTE [2]

V. Nazionale 78r ☎055 28 41 82 💻www.anticomercatofirenze.it

The €10 combo meals are the draw here—try the *bruschetta e spaghetti bolognese.* Those sick of carbs will be happy to find that "Big Salads" get their own section of the menu, and gluten-free lasagna and pasta are also prominently offered. You get the same view whether you're dining inside or out—the dining room features a mural of the street outside sans noisy cars and mopeds.

➔ Toward San Lorenzo. $ Combo meals €10. ⏰ Open daily noon-11pm.

IL PIRATA 💳♿🍸 RISTORANTE [1]

V. de' Ginori 56r ☎055 21 86 25

How could we not review the pirate cafe? Unfortunately, the place is sort of phoning in the pirate theme, but it's nevertheless refreshing to see a cafe mural that trades in knock-off Botticelli for knock-off Captain Hook. The dinner buffet *(all you can eat and a bottle of wine; €10)* is better and more varied than the other buffets in the area, with dozens of dishes available for the hungry landlubber.

*➔ From P. San Lorenzo, walk north up V. de' Ginori for a few minutes. **i** Takeout available. $ Lunch specials €5.50-7.50. Buffet €7.50, with wine €10. ⏰ Open daily 11am-11pm.*

have a nice *trippa*

If you find yourself tired of pizza, prosciutto, and other street fare, maybe it's time to learn if you're the type that likes tripe. Now, this next bit may be hard to stomach: tripe meat comes from the belly of a cow. While the gastro-intestinally gutsy can order it at many restaurants, those who want to make a little less financial commitment to a potentially sickening meal should head to the *trippaio* (tripe seller). At one of these stalls found around the city, you can try a tripe sandwich for a few euro. Ask for a *panini con il lampredotto* (also called a *pane di trippa*)—a sandwich made with slowly-stewed tripe. It's cooked with hot red chili or a garlic parsley sauce and served in a sandwich. If they ask whether you want it *bagnato,* we advise you to say yes to the broth-soaked bun you're being offered.

SAN MARCO

This is a poorly defined neighborhood, so it is hard to generalize. Odds are, you're looking for somewhere to eat after hitting up one of the many museums. Get something from Gran Caffe to go and enjoy it in the botanical garden. Via San Gallo, which runs parallel to the garden, is a bit livelier in the evening.

GRAN CAFFE SAN MARCO — CAFE 1

P. San Marco 11r ☎055 21 58 33 www.grancaffesanmarco.it

This place just keeps getting bigger. Enter from the main *piazza*, and it's a gelateria. Enter from the side street, and it's a pizzeria. Walk further in, and it's a cafeteria, coffee bar, and garden cafe. Make your way to the tented garden for a bit of quiet. It's a bit chintzy but cheap. The enormous gooey bowls of lasagna *(€4.50)* are reheated, but since when has a bit of reheating hurt lasagna?

The south end of the piazza. $ Huge variety of options, but meal-type food will run you from €3 panini to €7 secondi. Open daily 8am-10pm.

RISTORANTE PIZZERIA DA ZEUS — PIZZERIA 1

V. Santa Reparata 17r ☎328 86 44 704

Dodge a bank-account lightning bolt with Zeus's student special—pizza and a soft drink *(€5).* The large rear dining hall is air-conditioned, and the *prix-fixe* menu *(drink, a salad or pizza or primi dish, a dessert, and coffee; €6.50)* is one of the cheapest in town.

Off V. XXVII Aprile. $ Pizza and soft drink €5, prix-fixe menu €6.50. Open daily noon-11 pm.

VIN OLIO — RISTORANTE 2

V. San Zanobi 126r ☎055 48 99 57 www.vinolio.com

Vin Olio is a quiet, grown-up sort of joint, with subdued art and fans slowly whirring under the high, beamed ceilings. The front room has a small bar, featuring mixed drinks *(€3)* and grappa *(€1.80).* Try the penne with duck meat.

From P. dell'Indipendenza, take V. XXVII Aprile to V. San Zanobi. $ Antipasti €5-9; primi €8-9. Grappo €1.80. Mixed drinks €3. Open daily 11am-midnight.

DIONISO — GREEK 2

V. San Gallo 16r ☎055 21 78 82

Sick of typical Tuscan cuisine? Have a little baklava! It's your predictable Greek joint, in that predictable shade of blue that seems to be international code for "here be filo dough." The menu's in Italian and Greek only, but we are confident you can recognize the Greek for "souvlaki."

Just to the west of San Marco. $ Baklava €3.50. Souvlaki and gyro plates €11. Ouzo €3. Open M-Sa noon-3pm and 7:30pm-midnight, Su 7:30pm-midnight.

SANTA CROCE

Where there are students, there's cheap food. We've picked out some highlights for you, but student whimsy shifts quickly. Visiting the university area during lunchtime on a weekday and seeing where the crowds are may be a better strategy for discovering tasty places than relying upon our listings. You can count on finding an abundance of kebab joints, automats, and other sources of cheap drunkfood to fuel the student population.

👍 EBY'S BAR — 🎓♿🍸🌙 MEXICAN [1]

V. dell'Oriuolo 5r and Borgo Pinti 2r — ☎055 90 62 116

Heck yes, burrito joint! America has the leg up on Europe in a certain area—Mexican food just ain't a thing on the continent. Kebabs aren't super big stateside, though, so we guess it's sort of a fair trade. Nonetheless, not even the best kebab in Italy can quite fill a craving for a bean-and-cheese-stuffed tortilla doused in hot sauce. Imagine our joy, then, when we found a top-notch burrito joint right on the edge of Santa Croce's nightlife scene. Eby's is even good! Not quite SoCal good, but definitely New York good. This is a place that knows its purpose: a boasting sign on the door proudly announces the availability of "LATE NIGHT CHICKEN QUESADILLA." Order your €4 burrito on the corner of Borgo Pinti and Dell Orioulo, then cross to Eby's colorful bar and upstairs dining room. Or chill with a €12 pitcher of sangria at the tables in the covered Volta di San Pietro alleyway—shared by none other than a kebab shop! So many options to satisfy a case of the drunkies! Drunktions, one might say. Oh dear, we're on a lollercoaster! No, seriously, the food is so good that you can come here sober, too.

🚶 Head away from Santa Croce, west from P. de Salvamini. $ Nachos €3. Burrito €4. Sangria pitcher €12. ⏰ Open daily 10am-3am.

👍 GELATERIA DEI NERI — 🎓♿ GELATERIA [1]

V. Dei Neri 20/22r — ☎055 21 00 34

Our job description compels us to have our thrice-daily dose of gelato at a different gelateria each time to sample Florence's wide range of offerings. So why can't we stop eating at this one? It might have something to do with the mousse-like *semifreddo*—try the tiramisu—or the insanely spicy Mexican chocolate, which we found too intense to even finish. The €0.50 mini-cones are perfect for trying each of the 30+ flavors on tap. We wish there was nice seating close enough to reach before having eaten all of one's gelato—but we'll happily take it as all the more reason to go back for more.

🚶 On the right when heading to city center. $ Cups and cones from €1.50. ⏰ Open daily 9am-midnight.

👍 LA GHIOTTA — 🥡♿❄ CAFE [1]

V. Pietrapiana 7r — ☎055 24 12 37

Take a number at this student-y rotisserie with student-y prices—the line is out the door during lunchtime. Pick your meal from platters behind the counter or order one of 20 varieties of pizza *(all €5.50)* and cram into the seats in the back. You'll eat even cheaper if you take it to go—get half a rotisserie chicken for a couple euro, go for a giant slab of eggplant parmigiana, or try whatever else they happen to have when you visit.

🚶 From Borgo Alegri, take a right. $ Primi €5-6; secondi €5-7. Liter of wine €6. ⏰ Open daily noon-5pm and 7-10pm.

ALL' ANTICO VINAIO — 🎓♿🍸 CAFE [1]

V. De' Neri 65r — ☎055 23 82 723

Self-service wine! What an idea! Walk up to the counter on the street, plop down €2, pour yourself a small-ish glass of wine, and enjoy. It's actually not as good a deal as it seems, given how dirt-cheap wine by the bottle is in this town. But still, self-service wine! If you bother going inside the tiny storefront, there's a student special of sandwich and a drink for €4.

➡ 2 blocks behind Uffizi. 💲 Sandwich and a drink €4. Glass of wine €2. ⏰ Open daily 8am-9pm.

IL GIOVA 💳🚭⛱ RISTORANTE ❷

Borgo la Croce 73r ☎055 24 80 639 💻www.ilgiova.com

Settle down with a giant slice of watermelon on the mismatched chairs of this busy little lunch joint. At night, the outside tables fill the otherwise deserted intersection with couples and young people sipping wine. Menu changes daily.

➡ At the corner of V. della Mattonaia. 💲 Primi €5; secondi €7. ⏰ Open M-F noon-5pm and 7:30-11pm, Sa 12:30-4:30pm and 7:30-11pm.

CIBREO CAFFE 💳♿🍸❄⛱ CAFE ❷

V. Andrea del Verrocchio 5r ☎055 23 45 853

If you want to experience the classiness of the Cibreo scene minus the wallet drain, try visiting this cafe for a not-quite-budget lunch or, if you're really cheap, a coffee. The dark wood of the inside seating will make you feel like you are crashing a university's faculty club, sipping old-fashioned cocktails (like the Sidecar and, well, the Old Fashioned) with patch-elbowed professor types.

➡ Facing the main Cibreo theater, it's behind you on your left. 💲 Primi €8; secondi €15. ⏰ Open Tu-Sa 8am-1am.

RUTH'S KOSHER VEGETARIAN FOOD 💳🚭❄ KOSHER ❷

V. L.C. Farini 2/A ☎055 24 80 888 💻www.kosheruth.com

There are probably some visitors to Florence who are stuck eating every meal here, and that must get old. For the carnivorous Christian getting sick of all that *bistecca alla fiorentina* or the nostalgic New Yorker who misses the Lower East Side, however, Ruth's provides some nice variety. Have a falafel while surrounded by Israelite kitsch like Hebrew calendars, maps of Israel, and photos of bearded old Jews. If you look Jewish, the locals may stop by your table to say hi.

➡ On the right of synagogue. ℹ Kosher. 💲 Falafel platter €9. Entrees €9-12. ⏰ Open M-Th 12:30-2:30pm and 7:30-10pm, F 12:30-2:30pm, Sa 7:30-10pm, Su 12:30-2:30pm and 7:30-10pm.

KOCCO 💳♿🍸⛱ RISTORANTE ❷

V. Farini 1/2 ☎055 23 44 020

This is the neighborhood for a rare dose of religious diversity—across the street is the **Synagogue** and inside Kocco there is a giant gold Buddha. The table service is expensive, but the unshaded outdoor seating is unpleasant at midday anyway. Go for the light lunch special: *primo*, bottled water, and coffee for €7 or the same with a *secondo* for €8. Come back at 6:30pm for the €4 *aperitivo* buffet.

➡ At the corner of Pilastri, across from the Synagogue. 💲 Lunch specials €7-8. ⏰ Open daily noon-11pm.

LA SEMOLINA 💳♿🍸⛱ RISTORANTE ❷

P. Ghiberti 87r ☎055 23 47 584

Semolina's exterior is a bit run down, but come in the evening to sit under the umbrellas and enjoy large portions of pasta and some excellent risotto. During the day, regulars hang out on the patio and chat with passersby. It's priced a little higher than equivalent options and may refuse to serve tap water, but the food is good.

➡ On the far corner of P. Ghiberti; it's the one with the plants and tents. 💲 Cover €2. Pizzas €5-7. Pasta €6-11. ⏰ Open daily noon-midnight.

S. CROCE 🍴♿🍸❄☁ RISTORANTE [2]

P. Santa Croce 11r ☎055 24 79 896

S. Croce is slightly pricier than it should be but good for being on a major *piazza*. The menu offers a nice range of salads in addition to the usual options, and even the side salad is surprisingly substantial *(€4.50)*.

*To the left of the Basilica di Santa Croce.* [$] *Cover €1.50, but when they're not busy a sign will announce that there's no cover. Pizza €5.50-8. Pasta €8.50. Salads €8.50.* ⏰ *Open daily 11am-11pm.*

WEST OLTRARNO

A lot of West Oltrarno's restaurants are quirkier than their counterparts on the other side of the river. Unfortunately, they're also a little bit more expensive and more likely to have a cover. Still, the locals who frequent these joints must know something we don't.

✓ **DANTE** 🍴♿🍸 RISTORANTE [2]

P. Nazario Sauro 12r ☎055 21 92 19 💻www.trattoria-dante.net

An excellent choice for students—with any meal, students get a free bottle of wine. No joke. The pizza is the same as anywhere, but dude, **[F]free wine.** Also hosts lots of images of Dante on the wall, as you'd expect. Free wine!

*A block south of Ponte alla Carraia, on the right.* [$] *Cover €2.50. Pizzas €6-9. Pastas €8-10.* ⏰ *Open daily noon-11pm.*

OSTERIA SANTO SPIRITO 🍴♿🍸☁ RISTORANTE [2]

P. Santo Spirito, 16r ☎055 23 82 383

Delightful wooden tables behind bamboo screens line the street in front of this osteria, while inside large round tables are suffused with a flickering red light. Linger after your pasta for the *crème brulée (€6)* and other posh desserts.

*Far end of the piazza from the church, on the right.* [$] *Pizza €6-9. Primi €7-12. Wine by the bottle from €12.* ⏰ *Open daily noon-11:30pm.*

NAPO LEONE 🍴♿🍸☁ RISTORANTE [3]

P. del Carmine, 24 ☎055 28 10 15

The most famous rule of naming your restaurant Napo Leone is to never get involved in a land war in Asia, but only slightly less well-known is this: never have dinner in a parking lot when romance is on the line. Thankfully, Napo Leone is compensating quite well, thank you, creating a romantic atmosphere despite the location, with stained-glass lanterns and curlicue chairs. The menu features inconceivable appetizer platters like the spread of prosciutto, salami, artichokes, baked tomatoes, olives, peccorino cheese with jam, liver pate, *mozzarella di bufala*, and fried dough for €12.

*Against the wall in the back of the piazza.* [$] *Cover €3. Pastas €8-10. Meat entrees €10-24.* ⏰ *Open daily 7pm-1am.*

GELATERIA LA CARRAIA 🍴♿ GELATERIA [1]

P. Nazario Sauro 25r ☎055 28 06 95 💻www.lacarraiagroup.eu

An excellent gelato option right across the river, with cones starting at €1. Try the After Eight. Not much ambience in the shop itself, but go stand by the river—it's right outside.

*Right over the Ponte alla Carraia.* [$] *Gelato from €1.* ⏰ *Open daily 11am-11pm.*

PIZZERIA IL TIRATOIO 🍴♿🍸❄☁ PIZZERIA [2]

P. de Nerli 1r ☎055 28 96 13

This pizzeria offers simple outdoor seating on a *piazza* that's mostly a parking lot, but it's got a small knot of locals hanging out at any hour of the day, nabbing the specials scrawled on a white erase board in the street.

*From Borgo San Frediano, turn right.* [$] *Cover €1.50. Pizza €5-7. Primi €7.50-10. Bottled beer*

€5. Bottle of wine €8. ⏰ *Open M-Tu 5pm-1am, Th-F 5pm-1am. Open for lunch on weekends; call ahead for specific times.*

RISTORANTE RICCHI 💳♿🍸☁ RISTORANTE ❷

P. Santo Spirito 8r ☎055 28 08 30

Ricchi's menu includes fascinating dish concepts like "fried flowers stuffed with squid and ricotta," which sounds almost like someone was playing darts with an ingredients list. Slightly more formal outdoor seating—i.e., the tables are raised on a little platform instead of directly on the ground—makes for a slightly older clientele than that of the rest of the *piazza*. All the fish is fresh.

🧭 *To the right of the church.* $ *Cover €2. Appetizers €8-10; primi €9-12.* ⏰ *Open daily 11am-2-pm and 4pm-1am.*

IL CANTINONE 💳🚭🍸❄ RISTORANTE, ENOTECA ❸

V. Santo Spirito 6r ☎055 21 88 98 💻www.ilcantinoedifirenze.it

This intriguing basement *enoteca* is down a flight of stairs from the main drag. Given the interior akin to a wine cellar or some sort of underground cavern, all wood and cork and candlelight, Il Cantinone's menu focused on the cuisine (and wine) of the Chianti region makes perfect sense.

🧭 *Down a flight of stairs right at the door.* $ *Cover €2. Primi €6-9; secondi €8-18.* ⏰ *Open Tu-Su 7pm-1am.*

SANT'AGOSTINO 23 💳♿🍸☁ RISTORANTE ❸

V. Sant'Agostino 23r ☎055 21 02 08 💻www.sa23.it

The atmosphere here is simple considering the prices, but this restaurant is often packed with locals hanging out until late. And they must know something. A few tables on the side street have more ambience, with a high-climbing vine and old-timey street lamps.

🧭 *From Santo Spirito, on the left.* $ *Cover €2.50. Salads €10-12. Primi €10-14.* ⏰ *Open daily 7pm-2am.*

EAST OLTRARNO

The actually eastern part of East Oltrarno is rather far from most attractions, but if you venture out here, you'll find dinner joints frequented by locals and a whole lot less English on the menus. Our choices are right off the Ponte Vecchio, which is the area most likely to be frequented by our readers.

BIBO 💳♿🍸❄☁ RISTORANTE ❷

P. di Santa Felicita 6r ☎055 23 98 554

A quiet restaurant right past the Ponte Vecchio, Bibo is kinda on the tacky side of niceness, with electric candles on pink tablecloths, but it works.

🧭 *Bear left after crossing Ponte Vecchio.* $ *Pastas €9-10.* ⏰ *Open daily noon-11pm.*

RISTORANTE CELESTINO 💳♿🍸❄☁ RISTORANTE ❷

P. di Santa Felicita 4r ☎055 23 96 574 💻www.ristorantecelestino.it

Slightly nicer than its neighboring trattoria, Celestino has a grotto feel, with climby vines winding about the outdoor seating. The site was once a monastery, but now, it is full of mostly Tuscan wines. The €15 *prix-fixe* menu of chef's specials is a good deal, especially if you like the chef's specials.

🧭 *Turn left after Ponte Vecchio.* $ *Soups €6-8. Pastas €8-10.* ⏰ *Open daily noon-3pm and 7-11pm.*

SNACK LE DELIZIE 💳♿🍸☁ CAFE ❶

P. di Santa Felicita 2/3 ☎055 29 53 33

This is a simpler option in a *piazza* crowded with restaurants. Five euro here can get you a pizza *margherita* with olives. If you ever wondered what kind of Margarita takes an olive garnish, here's your answer: a pizza one.

🧭 *Turn left after Ponte Vecchio.* $ *Pizzas €5-7.* ⏰ *Open 24hr.*

nightlife

People don't come to Florence to party. They come to Florence to stare at pretty things. During peak season, major sporting events, and other cultural happenings, the streets will fill with young people clutching wine bottles. At other times, you will be better off simply hanging out with the people in your hostel. For more hopping after-hours entertainment, head to Santa Croce or deal with one of the bazillion American or Irish pubs that litter the city.

top 5 smooch spots

Florence is undeniably romantic, with movie-set side streets and constant streams of wine. If you're inspired to indulge in a Florentine romance, here are some options preferable to hostel bunk beds.

- **PONTE VECCHIO.** It's as cliché as the Eiffel Tower and not remotely private, but no one bats an eye at some smooching along the most famous bridge in town. Hope the constant stream of wedding parties isn't a turn-off, though.
- **PONTE SANTA TRINITA.** Keeping along the Arno, score a little more isolation and an even better view on one of the broad stone triangles over the edge of this less trafficked bridge. Come early (or very late) to find one unoccupied, though—this is prime canoodling real estate.
- **THE DUOMO.** Want to tick blasphemous make-out session off your "Never Have I Ever" list? The steps in front of Florence's most recognizable church are scenic and quiet after midnight, but more daring couples could try climbing the dome or tower. Right before closing, the 300+ steps of winding stairwells will be mostly deserted, and your hearts will already be racing from the climb. If you make it to the top, the view ain't too shabby either.
- **PIAZZALE MICHELANGELO.** It might seem like an obvious choice, but it's a bit too parking lot to really set the mood. Try a corner along the hike up to the more secluded piazzale or keep going up the hill to find a small park that's far darker, deserted, and every bit as scenic.
- **LEAVE THE CITY.** Take your romance out under the Tuscan sun and head to the hills. Hostels in adjacent towns let you escape the crowds and perhaps snag a private room while staying within a backpacker's budget.

THE DUOMO

This isn't exactly a traditional nightlife area. You'll find a couple of bars right by the Duomo, but mostly, you're going to be pushing into the edges of other neighborhoods. When the weather is beautiful and the town is particularly crowded, people hang out on the Duomo steps all evening.

SHOT CAFE

♿ 📶 🍸 BAR

V. dei Pucci 5 ☎055 28 20 93

At least it looks different from the other American bars? This aggressively quirky little bar is covered in inner tubes and stuffed fish because, well, why not? The music is American "oldies," if you define oldies as anything recorded between 1920 and 2005. The TV is usually tuned to MTV—now that's retro.

 # A block north of the Duomo. i Happy hour 1st drink €3.50, 2nd €3, 3rd €2.50. Free Wi-Fi. [$]

Shots €2.50. Pitchers €9. ⏰ Open daily 5pm-3am. Happy hour until 9pm.

ASTOR CAFE
🎟♿🍸 BAR

P. Duomo 20r ☎055 23 99 318

A contemporary cafe for all times of the day. Lunch specials draw people during the day, with *antipasti*, *primi*, water, and beer or wine for just €10. Sleek black furniture shifts the focus to nightlife, when the big projection screen is lit with sporting events. On non-sporty weekend nights, live music livens up the scene. Outdoor seating looks up at the Duomo.

➡ NE side of the piazza. $. Bottled beer €5. 1L of what's on tap €10. ⏰ Open daily 8am-3am.

PIAZZA DELLA SIGNORIA

The nightlife scene here is mostly of a DIY variety. The **Loggia, Piazza Della Repubblica,** and **Ponte Vecchio** are all excellent places to hang out with a ☐**beer,** so get one to go from Old Stove or a watering hole in a pubbier part of town. It should also be noted that the Ponte Vecchio is a fine place for a snog and that *Let's Go* does not condone drunk-riding the P. della Repubblica carousel.

NOIR
🎟♿🍸❄ BAR

Lungarno Corsini 12/14r ☎055 21 07 51

This super-classy watering hole spills over to the other side of the street, where patrons balancing cocktails and munchies lean against the wall of the Arno. Inside is dark, trendy, and loud, with low, cushioned benches lining the walls. Fill your plate from the extensive *aperitivo* buffet and go watch the sunset over the river.

➡ Facing Ponte Vecchio, it's on your right. $ Bottled beer €5. Cocktails €6-7. ⏰ Open daily noon-3am.

OLD STOVE
🎟♿🍸⛅ IRISH PUB

P. della Signoria 30r ☎055 29 52 32 💻www.theoldstovepub.com

Hey look, it's another Irish pub! Which, of course, actually means American because Irish people know better than to go to Florence for drinking. The dive-bar inside pales in comparison to the social and open outdoor seating. Wednesdays are Dollar Days—pay in US$ all day long. Other branches by the Duomo and *Il Porcellino*.

➡ Walk to the side of P. della Repubblica that doesn't have the carousel, and look down the street to the left. There it is. ℹ Happy hour pints €4. $ Pints €6. Mixed drinks €7. ⏰ Open M-Th noon-2am, F-Sa noon-3am, Su noon-2am. Happy hour M-Th 5-9pm.

TWICE
🎟♿🍸 CLUB

V. Giuseppe Verdi 57r ☎055 24 76 356

Twice is the sort of place for clubbing when you don't feel like making a big production out of it. No cover means a bit of a mixed bag crowd in terms of both age and attire, but, as is the case for many places in the Florentine nightlife scene, Italian men and American women dominate the clientele. The weird mix of music should have you giggling every time some forgotten hit from 8th grade starts to play. Epileptics take heed: Twice loves the strobe light.

➡ From Duomo, head east on V. Oriuolo, then right onto V. Giuseppe Verdi. $ Beer €6. Mixed drinks €8. ⏰ Open daily 9pm-4am.

SLOWLY
🎟♿🍸 BAR

V. Porta Rossa 63r ☎055 26 45 354 💻www.slowlycafe.com

Slowly will drain your bank account quickly. The trendier-than-thou atmosphere is made slightly more playful by glowing ball things on the tables, but the €10 mixed drinks will make Manhattan-ites feel at home. This is the kind of place that makes you wish you had money.

➡ Just off P. Davanzati. $ Mixed drinks start at €10. ⏰ Open daily 7pm-2:30am.

CAFFE BIGALLO

♨♿☕ BAR

V. del Proconsolo 73   ☎055 29 14 03 🖳www.caffebigallo.com

Caffe Bigallo's popularity with the young student crowd seems mysterious considering its plain, restaurant-like interior, but weekend nights still see the otherwise shuttered street crowded with the bar's drunken spillover. We'll shelve our curiosity for now and simply settle for joining in on the fun.

⚐ *South of the Duomo.* Ⓢ *Beer €5.* ⏰ *Open daily 2pm-1am.*

SANTA MARIA NOVELLA

There are a number of options in this area, but they are spread out, making bar-hopping difficult. If you are on the river side of the area, it's best to cross over to West Oltrano. If you are near the train station, well, you're screwed.

SPACE CLUB ELECTRONIC

♨♿☕ CLUB

V. Palazzuolo 37   ☎055 29 30 82 🖳www.spaceelectronic.net

Do you wish you could go clubbing in Epcot? Then this utterly ridiculous club is the place for you. Descend into the depths of its space-age neon dance hall for a taste of the European clubbing scene, or as close as you'll get to that in central Florence. If the bouncer waves you in, don't be fooled into thinking you got a free entrance—you pay the steep cover *(€16)* when you leave. And hold tight to your drink ticket when crowding around the aquarium bar, because the fine for losing it is sky high. Special events like guest bands and foam parties are extensively advertised on posters around town, so keep an eye out. The club's location means it's one of the few in the area from which you'll likely be able to return home without hailing a cab.

⚐ *From river, take V. Melegnano to V. Palazzuolo, then turn right.* Ⓢ *Cover €16 and it only goes up from there.* ⏰ *Open daily 10pm-4am.*

JOSHUA TREE

♨♿☕❄ BAR

V. della Scala 37r   🖳www.thejoshuatreepub.com

The dark, bold colors of this Irish-style pub may remind you of the nicer of your college haunts. It is smaller than similar places in town which means it doesn't feel deserted in the early hours of the evening. Good place to start your adventures, or to just hang out on a weeknight.

⚐ *At corner of V. Benedetta.* Ⓢ *Pints €5.* ⏰ *Open daily 4pm-2am. Happy hour 4-9:30pm.*

PUBLIC HOUSE 27

♨⊗☕ BAR

V. Palazzuolo 27/r   ☎339 30 22 330 🖳www.publichouse27.com

Public House 27 has a slightly more punk feel than the other bars in the area. It gets busy early, and with a €3 pint, the price is right.

⚐ *At the corner of Porcellana.* Ⓢ *Pints €3.* ⏰ *Open M-Sa 5pm-2am, Su 2:30pm-2am.*

CENTRAL PARK

♨♿☕❄☁ CLUB

V. del Fosso Macinate 2   ☎055 35 99 42 🖳www.centralfirenze.it

If you have money to burn and are willing to take a cab home, try trekking out to this enormous club in the middle of Parco delle Cascine. You'll be greeted by four outdoor dance floors with four different musical themes—hip hop, house, mainstream, and '70s/'80s. Be sure to pregame because the drinks are all €10. And hope Daddy's paying for your trip—the cover is an absurd €20.

⚐ *From the river, go to Ponte della Vittoria, the westernmost bridge of the city center. Follow Vle. Rosselli north (careful, it's busy), then turn left onto V. Fosso Macinante.* Ⓢ *Cover €20. All drinks €10.* ⏰ *Open daily 10pm-4am.*

SAN LORENZO

The headquarters of drunk backpackers from North America and down under.

MOSTODOLCE
💳♿🍸❄ BAR

V. Nazionale 114r ☎055 23 02 928 💻www.mostodolce.it

The one pub in the area likely to have one or two Italians present. Large and comfortable, with big crowds for sporting events and artisanal beers brewed in Prato. If you're around for a while (or drink fast) there's a "10th beer free" punch-card.

➜ On the corner of V. Guelfa. $ Pints from €6. ⏰ Open daily 5pm-2am.

DUBLIN PUB
💳♿🍸⛅ BAR

V. Faenza 27r ☎055 27 41 571 💻www.dublinpub.it

Dartboards, beer ads, drunk Americans—the works. There are a few tables outside, but beware the splash of street-cleaning zambonis after midnight. Across the street is a fine gelateria for when you want to wash down the beer with something sweet.

➜ The far end of V. Faenza. $ Pint of cider €4.40. Pint of Guinness €6. Pizza €5. ⏰ Open daily 5pm-2am.

KITSCH THE PUB
💳♿🍸 BAR

V. San Gallo 22r ☎328 90 39 289 💻www.kitsch-pub.com

What do you expect from a place that has "kitsch" as its name? Tarot readers, that's what. Also red velvet, stained glass, and a surprisingly late happy hour with mixed drinks *(€5)* and beer from 11pm to 1am.

➜ Off V. Cavour. $ Shots €3.50-4.50. Mixed drinks €5-6. ⏰ Open daily 5pm-3am. Aperitivo 6-9:30pm.

THE FISH PUB
💳♿🍸⛅ BAR

P. del Mercato Cenrale 44r ☎055 26 82 90 💻www.thefishpub.com

The "free crazy party!" announced on the promoter's fliers doesn't usually materialize, but at least the flier gets you a free shot. It's mostly orange juice but, hey, refreshing! And you can get five more of them for €5. On the plus side, come any time before midnight with your friends and you can totally take over the joint.

➜ Right off Mercato Centrale. $ 5 shots for €5. Mixed drinks €7. ⏰ Open daily 3pm until "late night." Happy hour 3-9pm.

SAN MARCO

The intersection directly to the west of San Marco is pretty lively, but other than that, you'll want to avoid this area if you're looking for proper nightlife. The area north of San Marco is particularly deserted, especially after the buses stop running.

THE CLUBHOUSE
💳♿🍸⛅ BAR

V. de' Ginori 6r ☎333.26 95 434 💻www.theclubhouse.it

An American sports bar that, with its white tiles and blue-tinged lighting, might be best suited for watching swimming. Plasma TVs and martinis are at your disposal all day, and at night, the pints are €5.50. Excellent weekday lunch specials *(pizza, water, and espresso €5; with primo or secondo instead of pizza €6-7).*

➜ Off V. dei Pucci. $ Shots €3. Beer €5.50. ⏰ Open daily noon-2am. Kitchen open until 11pm.

FINNEGAN IRISH PUB
💳♿🍸⛅ IRISH PUB

V. San Gallo 123r ☎055 49 07 94 💻www.finneganpub.com

Another ☘**Irish pub!** This one has outdoor seating, dedicated screenings of football and rugby games, dart boards, those usual pub booths, and rugby paraphernalia on the walls. You know the drill. Good place for casually watching the game, whatever the game may be, and hanging with the regulars.

➜ North of San Marco. $ Beer €5. ⏰ Open M-Th 1pm-12:30am, F-Sa 1pm-1am, Su 1pm-12:30am.

WINE BAR NABUCCO 💳♿📶🍸❄ BAR

V. 27 Aprile 28r ☎055 47 50 87 💻www.nabuccowine.com

This sunny, citrus-colored bar has you covered from dawn to dusk. Start your day with the international breakfast menu *(€1-4.20)*, then take advantage of the free Wi-Fi and coffee bar *(coffee €1, latte €1.10)* until lunch is served. Then it's just a few hours until you can enjoy the *aperitivo* buffet as a pregame for when Wine Bar Nabucco begins living up to its name. Try the frozen Bailey's *(€4)*.

➡ Corner of V. Santa Reparata. ℹ Free Wi-Fi. $ Breakfast items €1-4.20. Nutella coffee €2. Frozen Bailey's €4. ⏰ Open daily 8am-midnight. Aperitivo bar 6:30-9:30pm.

SANTA CROCE

This is the place to go for Florentine nightlife. On nice evenings, **Piazza Sant'Ambrogio** and **Piazza Ghiberti** are swarmed with young people carrying drinks from the few area bars. Venture too far from the main drag, however, and Santa Croce is as dead as the rest of the city.

glbt nightlife

A number of bars and clubs in this area cater to a ▼**GLBT** clientele—however, they would prefer not to be listed in guidebooks. Many of these establishments are unmarked or tucked down alleys. If you can get yourself in the correct general vicinity, the staff at neighboring bars can usually direct you the rest of the way. For a list of gay-friendly nightlife options, contact the organization Arcigay *(💻www.arcigay.it)*.

👍 **LAS PALMAS** 💳♿🍸☀ BAR

Largo Annigoni ☎347 27 60 033 💻www.laspalmasfirenze.it

Hundreds of locals pack this stretch of blacktop, transforming what may or may not qualify as a *piazza* by day into a rowdy block party by night. There's a lovely neighborhood feel here, with groups of students, families, and older folk crammed into the scores of tables covered by piles of food from the generous *aperitivo* buffet and children entertaining themselves at the foosball and table tennis games off to the side. A big stage bordering the space features performances and movies all summer as well as live screenings of sporting events.

➡ Off of P. Ghiberti, in front of the La Nazione building. ℹ Check website for full-season performance and screening schedule. $ Beer €5. Pizza €5-8. Primi €7-10. ⏰ Open daily May-Sept, hours vary.

👍 **CIBRÉO TEATRO DEL SALE** 💳♿🍸❄ CLUB, PERFORMANCE VENUE

V. De' Macci 111r ☎055 20 01 492 💻www.cibreo.fi

"Happiness is an obligation" begins the multilingual list of rules in the foyer of this members-only cultural venue—other entries include "with the welcoming spirit of the club, members are permitted to bring cats and dogs" and "reflective silence will be greatly appreciated." Members come to Cibreo for dinner, but the club considers itself a primarily cultural institution and puts the main focus on each evening's performance. For a flat €30 fee, enjoy a self-service open wine bar, a buffet dinner with each dish announced by the chef in a resonant town-crier voice, and a live performance—musical acts, dance performances, film screenings, and lectures are all frequently on rotation. Membership may be private, but it's not exclusive—a one-year membership costs just €5 if you are foreign or under 26.

➡ Just west of P. Sant'Ambrogio. ℹ There's no stated dress code, but try not to look like a backpacker. $ All-you-can-eat and drink €30. ⏰ Dinner served promptly at 7:30pm. Performances begin around 9pm.

👍 SANT'AMBROGIO
💳♿🍸⛅ BAR

P. Sant'Ambrogio 7r ☎055 24 10 35

This bar seems to single-handedly service the entire P. Sant'Ambrogio scene. And since this *piazza* is responsible for about 40% of Florentine nightlife overall, that's saying something. The plentiful outdoor seating located across the *piazza* from the bar itself spills over onto the steps of the church, creating a pleasant evening bustle. By nightfall, the whole area is full of young people sipping drinks from Sant'Ambrogio.

➡ The piazza is at the end of V. Pietrapiana. $ Wine €4-7. Hard liquors €6-7. ⏰ Open M-Sa 8:30am-2am. Aperitivo happy hour 6-9pm.

PLAZ
💳♿📶🍸⛅ CAFE, BAR

V. Pietrapiana 36r ☎055 24 20 81

Sit under a tent on this busy little *piazza* and do some quality web surfing (courtesy of free Wi-Fi) while attacking an enormous salad *(€8)* or sweet crepe *(€5)*. At night the scene shifts, and you'll begin to see drunk university students stumble past as you sip an aromatic *(€9-10)*.

➡ On P. die Ciompli. $ Cover €1.50. Aperitivo buffet from €8. ⏰ Open daily 8am-3am.

KITSCH BAR
💳♿🍸⛅ BAR, CONCERT VENUE

Vle. Gramsci 1r ☎055 23 43 890

If a summer evening's booze-fueled wanderings take you straying to the edge of the historic city center, a small outdoor stage featuring local musicians will probably attract you to Kitsch. On evenings that don't feature live music, you can still find a bar that, bedecked with a giant Buddha, knock-off Klimt, and patio with glowing floors, certainly lives up to the place's name. Kitsch's proximity to parking and the edge of the city center must attract a lot of locals driving from the parts of Florence they didn't include on your tourist map, because Kitsch also offers an extremely classy coin-operated breathalyzer.

➡ The traffic circle on the far right edge of your map, just above the river. $ Aperitivo buffet €8. Happy hour beer and mixed drinks €5. ⏰ Open daily 6:30pm-2am. Aperitivo buffet 6:30-10:30pm. Happy hour 10pm-1am.

BEBOP MUSIC CLUB
💳🚫🍸❄ CLUB, CONCERT VENUE

V. Dei Servi ☎055 26 45 756 💻www.bebopclub.info

Hey you! Do you like air-conditioning? Well, if you like air-conditioning, then have we got the air-conditioned place for you! The live band in this basement club will tell you about the air-conditioning from the stage! The postcards announce the air-conditioning with that super-rad **👍icicle** font! The promoter on the street leads his spiel with the gospel of air-conditioning! And while you enjoy their air-conditioning, they even provide live music with no cover charge! Oh, and just in case you were wondering, it's **❄air-conditioned.**

➡ Although the postcards hilariously provide a map all the way from the train station (clear on the other side of town), just walk up dei Servi from the Duomo and look for the A/C. ℹ Air-conditioned. $ Beer €6. Cocktails €6-7. ⏰ Open daily 11am-2am. Concerts start at 9pm.

I VISACCI
💳♿🍸 BAR

V. Borgo degli Albizi 80/82r ☎055 26 39 443

Five shots for €5 is a deal offered at a few places in town, but it's good to know which they are. This is an excellent joint for a pre-game—if you ever make it out the door after the €5 mixed drinks and three beers for €10.

➡ Coming from Duomo, take a left off Proconsolo. $ 5 shots for €5. 3 beers for €10. Mixed drinks €5. ⏰ Open daily 10am "till late."

GRAN TINTORI
💳♿🍸 BAR, CONCERT VENUE

C. dei Tintori 34r ☎055 24 09 81 💻www.sauro.biz/grantintori

This trendy, T-shaped bar has a large airy space for dancing, a piano, and frequent though irregularly scheduled live music. If you get lost, look for the maps of Florence projected on the wall.

✢ On the right if you're heading to city center. Ⓢ Glass of wine from €4. Mixed drinks €6. ⏰ Open M-F 11am-3pm and 7pm-late, Sa-Su 7pm-late.

THE WILLIAM
◆♿♀♺ BAR, CONCERT VENUE
V. Magliabecchi 7/9/11r
☎055 26 38 357

The enormous railroad car of an English pub, The William features live music many nights and reasonably priced pub food of the burger variety. It's also got a full dinner menu—check out the octopus salad, whatever that is—and the requisite pints. Belying the customer base, international flags line the comfy side room to the left of the bar.

✢ To the right of the Basilica di Santa Croce. Ⓢ Pints from €5. ⏰ Open M-Th 11:30am-2am, F-Sa 11:30am-3am, Su 11:30am-2am.

WEST OLTRARNO

▨ VOLUME
◆♿♀♺ BAR
P. di Santo Spirito 5r
☎055 23 81 460

There's a great quirky atmosphere in this "museo libreria caffe." Cluttered and busy, Volume sports mismatched chairs low to the ground and stacks of books, a juke box (€0.50 per play) and a giant old printing press for good measure. The place is just as much about gelato and sweets as it is about cocktails, but the gelato is fancy, starting at €2.50. Don't drunkenly nibble on the cones in the display case—they're coated with something icky to keep the flies away.

✢ Right of the church, sandwiched between 2 larger establishments. Ⓢ Cocktails €7. Crepes €4-7. ⏰ Open daily 11am-3am.

POP CAFE
◆♿♀♺ BAR
P. di Santo Spirito 18a
☎055 21 38 52 ▢www.popcafe.it

This simple setup on a lively piazza is enlivened by a DJ and cheap drinks. Beer, shots, and prosecco are all €3 at the bar, €4 at the outside tables. Non-carnivores take heed—the aperitivo buffet is vegetarian, as is the weekday lunch menu. Stumble back in the morning, because they proudly offer bagel sandwiches.

✢ To the left of the church. Ⓢ Beer, shots, and prosecco €3-4. Bagel sandwiches €5. ⏰ Open daily 11:30am-2am.

CABIRIA
◆♿♀♺ BAR
P. di Santo Spirito 4
☎055 66 26 18

If you penny-pinch by always ordering the menu's cheapest item, you're in luck— all the primi, salads, and pizzas here are €6. Options! The aperitivo buffet is also a good choice. At night, the DJ blasts legit oldies, and if it gets a bit intense, the outdoor seating is plentiful but crowded.

✢ To the right of the church. Ⓢ 0.5L of wine €6. Primi, salads, and pizza €6. ⏰ Open daily noon-3pm and 7pm-3am. Aperitivo 7-9pm. Kitchen closes 10pm.

HEMINGWAY
◆♿(ʷ)♀ CAFE
P. Piattellina 9
☎055 28 47 81 ▢www.hemingway.fi.it

Cozy and popular, Hemingway is worth the bit of pricey-ness to sample its fancy gelato, chocolates, tea, and cocktails while surrounded by bookshelves and armchairs. Have a Turkish coffee or a truffle-based cocktail—in the winter, try the chocolate soup with hot pepper or pistachio.

✢ From P. di Santo Spirito, walk down V. Sant'Agostino, which becomes V. Santa Monaca. 𝑖 Free Wi-Fi M-F until 9pm. Ⓢ Cocktails from €7. Fancy coffees from €4. Cakes from €5. ⏰ Open M-Th 4:30pm-1am, F-Sa 4:30pm-2am, Su 2pm-1am.

EAST OLTRARNO

Far east of any part of the city you're likely to visit, East Oltrarno is where the locals go to party. Since they're real people with real jobs, things are only happening here on weekends. Investigate **Piazza Poggi,** at the base of Piazzale Michelangelo, and the area just over the **Ponte San Niccolo** to get your game on. In late summer, bars along the southern banks of the Arno enliven the entire scene.

JAMES JOYCE PUB

BAR

Lungarno b. Cellini 1r ☎055 65 80 856

This enormous, popular bar is lively with students, particularly on nice weekend evenings. You don't even have to step inside to order another round of drinks—a window in the bar opens onto the patio. There's foosball and literary kitsch on the walls, and a generally local, fun vibe.

On the right, following the perilous traffic circle after the Ponte San Niccolo. $ Shots €3-4. Wine from €4.50. Bottled beer €5. ⏰ Open daily until 3am.

NEGRONI

BAR

V. de' Renai 17r ☎055 24 36 47 www.negronibar.com

This is the principal bar of the lovely P. Poggi, where patrons spill out of the official outdoor seating to populate the small green square and the banks of the Arno. The petite interior is hopping when the DJ's there or the weather's bad.

On P. Poggi. $ Grappo €4. Beer €5.50. Apertivo €7-11. ⏰ Open M-Sa 8am-2am, Su 6:30pm-2am. Aperitivo 7-11pm.

FLO

BAR

Piazzale Michelangelo 84 ☎055 65 07 91 www.flofirenze.com

If the climb to the Piazzale at night leaves you needing a drink to recover, check out Flo. The scene is noisy and crowded, but the view is divine. If you're staying at the camping hostel next door, then the music from Flo is likely to keep you up. Might as well join the party.

To the left of the Piazzale, or take the #12 or 13 bus. $ Beer €6. Cocktails €8. ⏰ Open daily 7pm-3am.

CHECK POINT (IL CHIOSCO)

BAR

P. Ferrucci ☎339 61 95 125

This bar serves as more of a snack bar in the middle of a traffic circle, except it sells alcohol and seems to be a favorite local hangout. Try not to go stumbling into the oncoming traffic after too much *grappa.*

On the piazza right over Ponte San Niccolo. $ Grappa €3. Bottled beer €4. ⏰ Open daily 7pm-3am. Aperitivo 7-10:30pm.

arts and culture

You may have heard there was this Renaissance thing here once. As you might guess, this is very much a visual arts town. To read about Florence's prodigious collection of art, see **Sights**.

THEATER AND MUSIC

There's not much of a scene for original theater in Florence, but when something comes to town you'll know about it—the city is emblazoned with posters for theatrical events up to a month away. **Teatro Verdi** is mainly a concert hall, so check its website or box office if you're looking for live music. The box office here also functions as the ticket office for theatrical, cultural, and sporting events all over the city, so the website is a good resource for finding out what's coming up. If you're here during peak tourist times, you're out of luck—the theaters go dark from June to September. In the summer, site-specific productions are sometimes held in the courtyard of the Bargello, and temporary stages in the Piazza Della Signoria host musical and dance acts. The classy cabaret at **Cibreo** frequently includes theatrical work in its repertoire.

CHIESA DI SANTA MARIA DE' RICCI ♿ DUOMO
V. del Corso ☎055 21 50 44
An unassuming little church with a loud voice, this *chiesa* boasts a pretty spectacular pipe organ. Fortunately for the music-starved traveler, it likes to show it off. Organ vespers are played every evening at 7pm, followed by a recital of organ music from 8-10 pm. The programs are crowd pleasers—of the vast literature for organ you probably only know Bach's *Toccata & Fugue*, and the odds of hearing it here are in your favor. The performances are not exactly masterful, but they're free and very, very loud.
#From the Duomo, take V. dei Calzaioli south and turn left onto del V. del Corso. $ Free. ⏰ Daily vespers 7pm, recital 8pm.

TEATRO VERDI 💳♿ SANTA CROCE
V. Ghibbellina 99r ☎055 21 23 20 💻www.teatroverdionline.it
This grand concert hall lined with box seats is home to orchestra concerts and other live music events.
#From P. Santa Croce, walk up V. Giovanni da Verazzano. ℹ Credit card required for phone or online reservations. ⏰ Box office open daily 4-7pm during the theater season. Alternative box office at V. Alammani 39 (near the train station) open M-F 9:30am-7pm, Sa 9:30am-2pm.

CINEMA

Check listings for v.o. (or *versione originale*) to find films that have not been dubbed into Italian. The **Cinema Teatro Odeon** is a classic golden-age hall, so if for some reason you're going to the movies while traveling, make it your destination. *Schermo del arte* films follow a new trend in the cinema of focusing on contemporary, traditional, and classical art. These aim to be entertaining and tend to be screened in proper theaters.

CINEMA TEATRO ODEON 💳♿🍸❄ PIAZZA DELLA SIGNORIA
P. degli Strozzi ☎055 21 40 68 💻www.odeon.intoscana.it
Check the poster outside the box office for the month's schedule of English-language features at this beautiful classic movie hall, which generally runs three screenings per evening for new releases.
#From P. della Repubblica, walk up V. degli Strozzi. ⏰ Screenings begin in early evening.

SPECTATOR SPORTS

STADIO ARTEMIO FRANCHI 💳♿ OUTSKIRTS
Vle. Manfredo Fanti 4/6 ☎055 58 78 58 💻www.fiorentina.it
As is true for most Italian cities, Florence has a soccer team, and that soccer team is one of the primary obsessions of the city's residents. Purple-clad Fiorentina waver on the brink of success but never quite seem to achieve it, making them a great team to support if you're more into roller-coaster rides than easy victories. Catch a game here on Sundays throughout most of the year. The stadium is mostly uncovered, though, so pick a day when it's not raining.
#Take bus #7, 17, or 20 or train from Santa Maria Novella to Firenze Campo Marte. The bus takes you directly to the stadium; it's a short walk from the train. ℹ Call ahead for wheelchair-accessible seats. ⏰ Ticket office open M-F 9:30am-12:30pm and 2:30-6:30pm. Most matches Su afternoons Sept-May.

CALCIO STORICO ♿ SANTA CROCE
P. Santa Croce
Europeans love really rough sports. As if the English with their rugby weren't

enough, the Florentines play this bizarre game with Renaissance origins. Legal moves include head-butting and choking. To figure out what on earth is going on here, head to P. Santa Croce for the three annual matches held in the third week of June. If you think you've walked into a riot, you're in the right place.

➤ In P. Santa Croce. ℹ Check with newspapers of a tourist office for exact times. ⏰ 3rd week in June.

shopping

Florentines cook up some of the snazziest window displays you'll ever see—you'll be tempted to stop in nearly every store you pass. If you're going to be in the city for a while, wait for the sales. The best months for shopping are January and July. As retailers prepare for the August slump, when the locals desert the city for the seashore, they chop prices drastically. Mid-July is also the season of scorching temperatures, so you'll have more than one reason to stay inside the air-conditioned stores.

OPEN-AIR MARKETS

👍 MERCATO CENTRALE — 💳♿ SAN LORENZO

P. Mercato Centrale

It's best to come here to eat, but you can come to sightsee too. Watch real Florentines (and clever tourists) peer at tomatoes and squeeze melons in the vast produce market. On the main floor, stalls hawk dried fruit, fresh fish, divine *mozzarella di bufala*, logs of salami, and all the other raw materials of Italian food. You don't have to just buy groceries—along the edges, counter cafes and cafeterias sell panini and lunch dishes. 👍**Negrone** is the best bet.

➤ It's the huge green-and-red building in the middle of all those sidewalk vendors. ℹ Some stalls accept credit cards, others don't. $ Market rate. ⏰ Open M-F 7am-2:30pm, Sa 7am-5pm.

👍 SAN LORENZO — 💳♿ SAN LORENZO

San Lorenzo

Unless you're very serious about going off the beaten path, this is where you'll come for souvenir and knockoff shopping. You'll find leather bags, jackets, belts, journals, and gloves, as well as stationery, hats, tapestries, pashminas, doodads, and tourist schlock. The merchandise is sometimes repetitive from stall to stall, but the good news is that means you can check four places to find the best price on a particular handbag style. The vendors know their stuff and aren't lacking for chump tourists, so don't expect to shave more than a few euro off the prices except through hard-line bargaining. Leather journals run €7-15 for standard paperback size, and you should be able to find nice pashminas for €4-5. For most other things, prices will vary widely.

➤ The area around San Lorenzo and Mercato Centrale ℹ Some are cash only, some take credit cards. ⏰ Open daily 9am-7pm.

MERCATO NUOVO (MERCATO DEL PORCELLINO) — 💳♿ PIAZZA DELLA SIGNORIA

P. di Mercato Nuovo

A similar selection to the San Lorenzo market can be found here, but the posher location means higher prices in this ancient marketplace. Then again, there are instances of the real deal mixed in with the knock-offs, so this is a good spot if you know enough to judge the quality of what you're looking at. Also check out the bronze boar *(il Porcellino)* and pop a coin in his drooling fountain mouth for good luck.

➤ From Ponte Vecchio, take V. Santa Maria north. ℹ Most, but not all, take credit cards. ⏰ Open daily 9am-7pm.

SANTO SPIRITO

P. di Santo Spirito

This *piazza* across the Arno offers a smaller and less souvenir-oriented flea market. New but disheveled clothing is piled on to folding tables—paw through the selections and then compare the tag to a posted price chart to see what you've got. Other stands offer shoes, linens, and other day-to-day items. On Saturdays, the flea market is larger and includes more food vendors.

⧻ *From Ponte Santa Trinita, walk a little past the bridge, go right onto V. di Santo Spirito, then left onto V. del Presto di San Martino. It's in the piazza at the end of the street.* ⓘ *Most stalls don't take credit cards.* ⌚ *Open M-Sa 8am-1pm.*

PIAZZA DEI CIOMPI

P. dei Ciompi

There's nothing particularly Florentine about the goods here—it's more an eclectic jumble of furniture, gladiator helmets, records, light fixtures, model sailboats, lira coins, and gadgets and gizmos aplenty. On the last Sunday of the month, the daily market is expanded into a legit antiques fair.

⧻ *From the basilica, walk north on Borgo Allegri until you see the arches.* ⓘ *Most stalls take credit cards, but it varies.* ⌚ *Semi-permanent stalls open M-Sa roughly 9am-1pm and 4-7pm. Open last Su of each month.*

---

are those fake?

The streets of Florence are lined with vendors ready to trick tourists into buying imitation designer bags, belts, and wallets. Buyers beware: purchasing fake designer merchandise is a crime and can result in a fine so monstrous that the full-price version will seem like a bargain. Here are a few pointers on how to be a smart shopper.

1) If your Gucci is lying on the ground, it's too good to be true. You're intelligent enough to realize that designer goods sold on a blanket on the street are most likely fake.

2) Street vendors in Florence are more easily riled than a feminist at a beauty pageant. If they catch you looking at their wares, they're likely to yell, follow you, and pressure you into buying something. Our advice: don't make eye contact.

3) If you are incapable of controlling yourself and do meander over to a pile of cheap merch, keep your eyes peeled for *polizia*. Most street vendors will yank up their blankets and run at the popo's approach. If police catch you with merchandise in your hands, you can get in trouble too. So, just as in Florence's many museums, look but don't touch.

CLOTHING

Many department stores dot the area around P. della Signoria and Santa Maria Novella. Here are some good picks for filling out a travel wardrobe with more European styles.

PROMOD

V. dei Cerretani 46-48r   ☎055 21 78 44 🖳www.promod.eu

Akin to H and M or Forever 21, Promod sells bargain-priced, relatively disposable current fashions. Stocks mostly women's clothing

⧻ *Take V. Cerretani west from the Duomo.* ⌚ *Open daily 10am-8pm.*

GOLDENPOINT 💳♿ SAN LORENZO

V. dei Cerretani 40r ☎055 28 42 19 💻www.goldenpointonline.com

Goldenpoint deals in women's swimsuits and lingerie. It offers no bargains, but there's a bigger selection of swimsuit sizes and styles than elsewhere. Curvy women take note: Italian swimsuits offer far better support than American styles. Other locations at V. Panzani 33 *(☎055 21 42 96)* and V. dei Calzaioli 6 *(☎055 27 76 224).*

➜ Take V. Cerretani west from the Duomo. ⏰ Open daily 10am-7pm.

LA RINASCENTE 💳♿ PIAZZA DELLA SIGNORIA

P. della Repubblica ☎055 21 91 13 💻www.rinascente.it

A more upscale department store, like Macy's, La Rinascente is much smaller. Men's, women's—you name it, they've got it.

➜ The southeast face of P. della Repubblica. ⏰ Open M-Sa 9am-9pm, Su 10:30am-8pm.

PAPER GOODS AND JOURNALS

Florentine stationery is a big deal, whether we're talking leather-bound journals, marbleized paper, or that colorful notepaper reminiscent of illuminated manuscripts. The journal styles are similar to what you'd find in a Barnes and Noble in the US, and in San Lorenzo, the prices are about the same too. The Florentine selection, however, is across the board far greater. For really luxe versions, follow our lead. Perhaps you too will coo at the gorgeous leather journals—then cry when you realize they go for upwards of €60.

IL PAPIR 💳♿ SAN MARCO

V. Cavour 49r ☎055 21 52 62 💻ilpapirofirenze.it

Il Papir sells beautiful leather-bound and marbleized journals that are three times the prices of similar products in the San Lorenzo market but also three times the quality.

➜ South of P. San Marco, off V. Guelfa. i Other locations in P. del Duomo 24r, P. Rucellai 8r, V. de Tavolini 13r, V. Porta Rossa 76r. $ Leather journals from €50. ⏰ Open daily 10am-1pm and 2-7pm.

MADE IN TUSCANY 💳♿ SAN MARCO

V. Degli Alfani 120r

This is the budget way to have the artisan experience. Journals and sketchbooks are custom-made based on your selection of leather color and cover stamp.

➜ Just south of the Accademia, off V. Ricasoli. $ Prices vary widely. ⏰ Open M 2:30-7pm, Tu-Su 9:30am-2pm and 2:30-7pm.

MASKS

The *commedia dell'arte* tradition is alive and well in Italian mask-making, and though you'll find masks to be more of a big deal in Venice, this shop is worth a visit. Chintzier options are easy to find in San Lorenzo and standard souvenir stores.

👍 **ALICE'S MASKS ART STUDIO** 💳⊗ SAN LORENZO

V. Faenza 72r ☎055 28 73 70 💻www.alicemasks.com

Even if you have no interest in buying a mask, stop by this tiny cluttered shop to ooh and ahh at the gorgeous, handmade masks for theater, panto, and Carnival. Professor Agostino Dessi and his daughter Alice have been supplying masks to major exhibitions, films, and performances since the '70s. Mask-making workshops take place the last week of every month. Email agostinodessi@tiscalinet.it for rates.

➜ Between the railway station and the Medici Chapel. $ Masks from €50. 5-lesson course €500. ⏰ Open daily 9am-1pm and 3:30-7:30pm.

GOLD

You should probably do some research on how to judge the quality of gold before doing any major jewelry shopping, whether in Florence or anywhere in the world. If you think you know what you're looking at, then the Ponte Vecchio, lined with numerous goldsmiths and jewelers as well as shady street sellers, is the place for you. There are also a smattering of stores around the city, including the following.

THE GOLD CORNER

💳♿ SANTA CROCE

P. Santa Croce 15r ☎055 24 19 71 💻www.goldcorner.it

The Gold Corner's helpful, English-speaking staff await to talk you into frivolous purchases. Many designer brands are available at this fairly busy store where you can actually get a chance to browse for a minute before being attacked by a salesperson. Only a minute, though.

🧭 Facing the basilica, it's on your right. ⏰ Open daily 10am-7pm.

LEATHER

Florence is famous for its soft, quality leather, but as with any luxury good, you need some amount of background knowledge before making any big purchase. If you really want to learn about leatherworking, try visiting the **Scuola del Cuoio** within the basilica of Santa Croce. Founded by the Franciscan friars in the 1930s, this leather school continues to offer courses lasting from one day to six months to anyone interested in learning the craft of leatherworking. They don't come cheap, though. Visit 💻www.scuoladelcucio.com for information, or enter their storefront in the basilica via the apse entrance at V. San Giuseppe 5r.

TORNABUONI

💳♿ DUOMO

P. Duomo 21/22r ☎055 28 01 98 💻www.tornabuonionline.com

This large leather-goods shop stocks a huge selection of purses. Prices start at several hundred euro, but they start offering discounts as soon as you walk in the door. Ask if you're contemplating a purchase.

🧭 North side of P. Duomo. $ Handbags starting around €200. ⏰ Open daily 10am-7pm.

GALLERIA MICHELANGELO

💳♿ SANTA CROCE

P. Santa Croce 8 ☎055 24 16 21 💻www.leatherguild.it

This vast, Japanese-run leather emporium is a frequent stop for cruise-ship shore excursions. We're not entirely sure what that says about it (lots of bargains available? tourist rip-offs?), but there's a helluva lot of people here.

🧭 The left side of the piazza, facing the cathedral. $ Bags from €80. ⏰ Open daily 9am-2pm and 2:30-8pm.

ARTISAN GOODS

If you want the fancy handmade goods, you're going to have to pay through the nose.

👍 FARMACEUTICA DI SANTA MARIA NOVELLA

💳♿ SANTA MARIA NOVELLA

V. Della Scala 16 ☎055 21 62 76 💻www.smnovella.com

You can smell the talcum and perfume before setting foot in this time capsule of a perfumery. The Santa Maria Novella monks have been bottling medicines since the 13th century, but this "modern" pharmacy is straight from the Victorian age. Elixirs, perfumes, juleps, salts, spirits, waters, and protective oils are all available here, displayed on shelving and sold in packaging that has been updated little over the course of the past century. The current *farmaceutica* is still run by descendents of the 19th-century owners. Imagine yourself to be a visiting European aristocrat, shopping for essence of myrrh under a chandelier and a fresco of American Indians and African tribal leaders. Be sure to grab one of the fantastic product lists, printed in tiny type on thick paper and listing the various candles *(€10-50)*, liqueurs *(500 ml for €49.50)*, and dog collars *(€30 and up)* available for the sophisticated shopper.

⇆ At the corner of V. della Porcellana. Coming from P. Santa Maria Novella, take a right onto V. della Scala. $ Free to browse. ⏰ Open daily 10:30am-7:30pm. In Aug, closes Sa at 1pm.

essentials

PRACTICALITIES

- **TOURIST OFFICES:** Tourist Information Offices, or **Uffici Informazione Turistica,** are staffed by qualified, multilingual personnel who can provide general information about visiting Florence and city services in addition to specifics about events, exhibitions, accommodations, and tours. There are numerous locations around the city, but one of the most useful is at **Piazza Stazione 4** *(☎055 21 22 45 ⏰ Open M-Sa 8:30am-7pm, Su 8:30am-2pm.)*
- **CONSULATES: UK** *(Lungarno Corsini 2 ☎055 28 41 33).* **USA.** *(Lungarno Vespucci 38 ☎055 26 69 51).*
- **LUGGAGE STORAGE:** At Stazione di Santa Maria Novella, by platform 16. *(i Cash only. $ 1st 4hr. €4, 6th-12th hr. €0.60 per hr., then €0.20 per hr. thereafter. ⏰ Open 6am-11:50pm.)*
- **INTERNET: Internet Train** can be found all over the city. For a central location, try V. de' Benci 36r. *(☎055 26 38 555 💻www.internettrain.it ⇆ From P. Santa Croce, go left onto V. de' Benci. $ Wi-Fi €2.50-3 per hr. Internet €3-4.50 per hr. ⏰ Open daily 10am-10:30pm.)*
- **POST OFFICES:** *(V. Pellicceria 3 ☎055 27 36 481 ⇆ South of P. della Repubblica. ⏰ Open M-F 8:15am-7pm, Sa 8:15am-12:30pm.)*
- **POSTAL CODE:** 50100.

EMERGENCY!

- **POLICE: Polizia Municipale** *(☎055 32 85).* 24hr. non-emergency helpline *(☎055 32 83 333).* Help is also available for tourists at the mobile police units parked at V. de' Calzaioli near P. della Signoria and Borgo S. Jacopo in the Oltrarno near the Ponte Vecchio.
- **LATE-NIGHT PHARMACIES: Farmacia Comunale** is in Stazione Santa Maria Novella and is open 24hr. *(☎055 21 67 61).* Other 24hr. pharmacies include **Farmacia Molteni** *(V. Calzaioli 7r ☎055 21 54 72 ⇆ Just north of P. della Signoria.)* and **Farmacia All'Insegna del Moro.** *(P. San Giovanni 20r ☎055 21 13 43 ⇆ A little east of the Duomo.)*
- **HOSPITALS/MEDICAL SERVICES: Ospedale Santa Maria Nuova** near the Duomo has a 24hr. emergency room *(P. Santa Maria Nuova 1 ☎055 27 581).* Tourist medical services can be found at V. Lorenzo Il Magnifico 59. *(☎055 47 54 11 ⇆ In the north of the city, near P. Liberta.)*

GETTING THERE

By Plane

Aeroporto Amerigo Vespucci. *(V. del Termine 11 ☎055 30 615 main line; 055 30 61 700 for 24hr. automated service 💻www.aeroporto.firenze.it i For lost baggage, call ☎055 3061302.)* From the airport, the city can be reached via the **VolainBus shuttle.** Pick up the shuttle from the Departures side—exit the airport and look to the right. Drop off is at Santa Maria Novella station. *($ €5. ⏰ 25min., every 30min. 5:30am-11:30pm.)*

By Train

Stazione Santa Maria Novella will likely be both your entry point to and exit point from the city. The ticket station is open daily 6am-9pm. Self-service kiosks are available 24hr. The Information Ofice is next to track 5. (🕐 *Open daily 7am-9pm.*) Luggage storage is by platform 16. Trains run to and from **Bologna** (💲 *€42.* 🕐 *37min., 2 per hr. 7am-10:35pm.*), **Milan** (💲 *€52.* 🕐 *1¾hr., 1 per hr. 7am-9pm.*), **Rome** (💲 *€44.* 🕐 *95min., 2 per hr. 7am-10:45pm.*), **Siena** (💲 *€6.20.* 🕐 *90min., 6 per hr. 8:10am-8:10pm.*), **Venice** (💲 *€42.* 🕐 *2hr., 2 per hr. 8:30am-8:30pm.*), and numerous local destinations.

By Bus

Three major intercity bus companies run out of Florence. **SITA** (*V. Santa Caterina da Siena 17* ☎*800 37 37 60* 🖥*www.sita-on-line.it*) runs buses from **Siena, San Gimignano,** and other Tuscan destinations. **LAZZI** (*P. Stazione 4/6r* ☎*055 215155; for timetable info* ☎*055 35 10 61* 🖥*www.lazzi.it*) buses depart from P. Adua, just east of the train station. Routes connect to **Lucca, Pisa,** and many other local towns. **CAP-COPIT** (*Largo Fratelli Alinari 10* ☎*055 21 46 37* 🖥*www.capautolinee.it*) runs to local towns. Timetables for all three companies change regularly, so call ahead or check online before traveling.

GETTING AROUND

By Bus

Since buses are the only public transportation in Florence, they are surprisingly clean, reliable, and easy to manage. Not to mention adorably orange and tiny! They are operated by **ATAF** and **LHNEA.** Buy a ticket before boarding from most newsstands and tabacconists, from a ticket vending machine, or from the ATAF kiosk in P. Stazione (☎*800 42 45 00* 💲 *90min. ticket €1.20, €2 if purchased on board; 24hr. €5; 3-day €12.*) Time-stamp your ticket when you board the bus—there are sporadic ticket checks, and if you forget, are caught without a stamped ticket, or can't successfully play the "confused foreigner" card, it's a €50 fine. You're unlikely to need to use the buses unless you're leaving the city center. The network is extensive, with several night-owl buses taking over for the regular routes in the late evenings, so if you are venturing out of town, pick up a schematic bus map from the ATAF kiosk or use the trip planner at 🖥www.ataf.net.

Unlike most city bus systems, Florence's is organized well enough that you can plan on the fly. Every bus stop is named, as in a metro system, and the name is posted clearly on top of the bus stop, making it possible to identify your stop even if you don't know what it looks like. At each bus stop, the entire schedule for every line that stops there is posted on the pole. The top of the schedule tells you what direction the bus is going when it stops there (San Marco to La Fonte is outbound, La Fonte to San Marco is inbound). Then there is a list of every stop, in order, so you can identify whether this particular bus is going where you need to be. A simple 24hr. diagram tells you at what minutes in each hour the bus will stop. Most buses originate at either P. Stazione or P. San Marco. #12 and #13 run to the Piazzale Michelangelo. #7 runs to Fiesole.

By Taxi

To call a cab, try calling ☎055 4390, 055 4499, 055 4242, or 055 4798. Tell the operator your location and when you want the cab, and the nearest available car will be sent to you. Each cab has a rate card in full view, and the meter displays running fare based on distance traveled as well as any supplements charged, but if you're going far or are nervous, it never hurts to ask for an estimate before boarding. There are surcharges for Sundays, holidays, luggage, late nights, etc. Unless you have a lot of baggage, you probably won't want to use a taxi during the day, when traffic will make the meter tick up mercilessly. At lunchtime, a 5min. ride from the Duomo to the Oltrarno will cost €7. Nevertheless, cabs are a manageable late-night option if you're outside the city and especially if you're in a group (for instance, when returning from out-of-town clubbing). Bagno a Ripoli to Santa Maria Novella (8km) at midnight will cost around €30. Designated cab stands can be found at P. Stazione, Fortezza da Basso, and P. della Repubblica. Cabs between fares can also often be found at Santa Maria Novella.

By Bike

It takes some confidence to bike in the crowded parts of central Florence, but cycling is a great way to check out a longer stretch of the Arno's banks or to cover a lot of territory in a fast-paced day. **Mille E Una Bici** (☎055 65 05 295) rents out 200 bikes in four locations, and they can be picked up and returned at any of four locations: P. Stazione, P. Santa Croce, P. Ghiberti, and Stazione F.S. Campo Di Marte. **Florence By Bike** (V. San Zanobi 91r and 120-122r ☎055 48 89 92 🖳www.florencebybike.it) is another good resource. Staff will help renters plan routes, whether for an afternoon or for a multi-day trip outside of town.

ESSENTIALS

You don't have to be a rocket scientist to plan a good trip. (It might help, but it's not required.) You do, however, need to be well prepared, and that's where we come in. Essentials is the chapter that gives you all the nitty-gritty you need to know for your trip: the hard information gleaned from 50 years of collective wisdom (and that phone call to Florence the other day that put us on hold for an hour). Planning your trip? Check. Staying safe and healthy? Check. The dirt on transportation? Check. We've also thrown in communications info, meteorological charts, and a 📖phrasebook, just for good measure. Plus, for overall trip-planning advice from what to pack (money and as little underwear as possible) to how to take a good passport photo (it's physically impossible; consider airbrushing), you can also check out the Essentials section of 🖥www.letsgo.com.

We're not going to lie—this chapter is tough for us to write, and you might not find it as fun a read as 101 or Discover. But please, for the love of all that is good, read it! It's super helpful and, most importantly, it means we didn't compile all this technical info and put it in one place for you (yes YOU) for nothing.

greatest hits

- **PASSPORT: YES, VISA: NO.** Remember to take your passport! But if you're spending less than 90 days in Europe (note: Europe, not just Italy), no visa is required (p. 242).

- **RAIN, RAIN, GO AWAY.** See our climate table (p. 252) to get an idea of what the weather might be like during your trip. Yes, that word was "might."

- **DON'T PANIC!** We list information inside for all major consulates of English-speaking countries in Rome, Venice, and Florence. In an emergency, they'll be your first resort (p. 243).

- **ACCESSIBLE TRAVEL.** Navigating these cities can be seriously tricky for travelers with wheelchairs. Read inside to learn how it can be done, even through the canals and stairways of Venice (p. 246).

planning your trip

- **PASSPORT:** Required of any citizen, of anywhere.
- **VISA:** Required of non-EU citizens staying longer than 90 days.
- **WORK PERMIT:** Required of all non-EU citizens planning to work in Italy.

DOCUMENTS AND FORMALITIES

You've got your visa and your work permit (if necessary), just like Let's Go told you to, and then you realize you've forgotten the most important thing: your passport. Well, we're not going to let that happen. **Don't forget your passport!**

Visas

Those lucky enough to be citizens of the European Union do not need a visa to travel to Italy. You citizens of Australia, Canada, New Zealand, the US, and other non-EU countries do not need a visa for short trips to Italy, but if your trip lasts more than 90 days, you will need one. Take note that this 90-day period begins when you enter the EU's **freedom of movement** zone, so ask yourself if you really want to spend 89 days in Slovakia and apportion your time wisely. If you really can't pull yourself away from the wonders of Bratislava, visas can be acquired at your neighborhood Italian consulate or embassy. With this visa safely tucked away in your backpack, you'll be free to stay between 90 and 365 additional days in Italy.

Double-check entrance requirements at the nearest embassy or consulate of Italy for up-to-date information before departure. US citizens can also consult ✈travel. state.gov.

Entering Italy to study requires a special visa. For more information, see the **Beyond Tourism** chapter.

one europe

The EU's policy of freedom of movement means that most border controls have been abolished and visa policies harmonized. Under this treaty, formally known as the Schengen Agreement, you're still required to carry a passport (or government-issued ID card for EU citizens) when crossing an internal border, but, once you've been admitted into one country, you're free to travel to other participating states. Most EU states are already members of Schengen (excluding Cyprus), as are Iceland and Norway.

Work Permits

Admittance to Italy as a non-EU traveler does not include the right to work, which is authorized only by a work permit. For more information, see the **Beyond Tourism** chapter.

essentials

- **ITALIAN EMBASSY IN AUSTRALIA:** *(12 Grey St., Deakin, Canberra ACT 2600* ☎*02 6273 3333* ▣*www.ambcanberra.esteri.it* ☼ *Open M-F 9am-noon.)*

- **ITALIAN EMBASSY IN CANADA:** *(275 Slater St., 21st fl., Ottawa, ON K1P 5H9* ☎*613-232-2401* ▣*www.ambottawa.esteri.it* ☼ *Open M-Tu 9am-noon, W 9am-noon and 2-4pm, Th-F 9am-noon.)*

- **ITALIAN EMBASSY IN IRELAND:** *(63/65 Northumberland Rd., Dublin 4* ☎*01 660 1744* ▣*www.ambdublino.esteri.it* ☼ *Open M-W 10am-noon, Th 1:30-3:30pm, F 10am-noon.)*

- **ITALIAN EMBASSY IN NEW ZEALAND:** *(34-38 Grant Rd., PO Box 463, Thorndon, Wellington* ☎*04 4735 339* ▣*www.ambwellington.esteri.it* ☼ *Open M-Tu 9am-1pm, W 9am-1pm and 3-4:45pm, Th-F 9am-1pm.)*

- **ITALIAN CONSULATE GENERAL IN UK:** *(38 Eaton Pl., London SW1X 8AN* ☎*020 7235 9371* ▣*www.conslondra.esteri.it* ☼ *Open M-F 9am-noon.)*

- **ITALIAN EMBASSY IN USA:** *(3000 Whitehaven St. NW, Washington, DC 20008* ☎*202-612-4400* ▣*www.ambwashingtondc.esteri.it* ☼ *Open M 10am-12:30pm, W 10am-12:30pm, F 10am-12:30pm.)*

- **AUSTRALIAN CONSULAR SERVICES IN ITALY: Embassy.** *(V. Antonio Bosio 5, Rome* ☎*06 85 27 21; emergency* ☎*800 87 77 90* ▣*www.italy.embassy. gov.au* ☼ *Open M-F 9am-5pm.)*

- **CANADIAN CONSULAR SERVICES IN ITALY: Embassy.** *(V. Zara 30, Rome* ☎*06 85 444* ▣*www.canada.it* ☼ *General Services available by appointment M-F 9am-noon; emergency services available M-F 9am-4pm.)* **Consulate.** *(25 Riviera Ruzzante, 35123 Padua* ☎*049 876 4833* ☼ *Open M-F 9:30am-1pm.)*

- **IRISH CONSULAR SERVICES IN ITALY: Embassy.** *(P. di Campitelli 3, Rome* ☎*06 69 79 121* ▣*www.ambasciata-irlanda.it* ☼ *Open M-F 10am-12:30pm and 3-4:30pm.)*

- **NEW ZEALAND CONSULAR SERVICES IN ITALY: Embassy.** *(V. Clitunno 44, Rome* ☎*06 85 37 501* ▣*www.nzembassy.com/italy* ☼ *Open M-F 8:30am-12:45pm and 1:45-5pm.)*

- **BRITISH CONSULAR SERVICES IN ITALY: Embassy.** *(V. XX Settembre 80a, Rome* ☎*06 42 20 00 01* ▣*www.britain.it* ☼ *Open M-F 9:15am-1:30pm.)* **Consulate.** *(Piazzale Donatori di Sangue 2/5, Venice* ☎*041 505 5990* ☼ *Open M-F 10am-1pm.)* **Consulate.** *(Lungarno Corsini 2, Florence* ☎*055 28 41 33* ☼ *Open M-F 9am-1pm and 2-5pm.)*

- **AMERICAN CONSULAR SERVICES IN ITALY: Embassy.** *(V. Vittorio Veneto 121, Rome* ☎*06 46 741* ▣*rome.usembassy.gov* ☼ *Open M-F 8:30am-12:30pm.)* **Consulate General.** *(Lungarno Vespucci 38, Florence* ☎*055 26 69 51* ▣*florence.usconsulate.gov* ☼ *Open M-F 8:30am-12:30pm.)*

planning your trip · time differences

TIME DIFFERENCES

Rome, Venice, and Florence are all 1hr. ahead of Greenwich Mean Time (GMT) and all observe Daylight Saving Time. This means that they are 6hr. ahead of New York City, 9hr. ahead of Los Angeles, 1hr. ahead of the British Isles, 8hr. in Northern Hemisphere summer and 10hr. in Northern Hemisphere winter behind Sydney, and, in the same fashion, 10hr./12hr. behind New Zealand. Don't get confused and call your parents while it's actually 4am their time! Note that Italy changes to Daylight Savings Time on different dates from some other countries, so sometimes, though not often, the difference will be one hour different from what is stated here.

money

GETTING MONEY FROM HOME

Stuff happens. When stuff happens, you might need some money. When you need some money, the easiest and cheapest solution is to have someone back home make a deposit to your bank account. Otherwise, consider one of the following options.

> ## the euro
>
> Despite what many dollar-possessing Americans might want to hear, the official currency of 16 members of the European Union—Austria, Belgium, Cyprus, Finland, France, Germany, Greece, Ireland, Italy, Luxembourg, Malta, the Netherlands, Portugal, Slovakia, Slovenia, and Spain—is the euro.
>
> Still, the currency has some important—and positive—consequences for travelers hitting more than one eurozone country. For one thing, money-changers across the eurozone are obliged to exchange money at the official, fixed rate (below) and at no commission (though they may still charge a small service fee). Second, euro-denominated traveler's checks allow you to pay for goods and services across the eurozone, again at the official rate and commission-free. For more info, check a currency converter (such as ■www.xe.com) or ■www.europa.eu.int.

Wiring Money

Arranging a **bank money transfer** means asking a bank back home to wire money to a bank in Italy. This is the cheapest way to transfer cash, but it's also the slowest and most agonizing, usually taking several days or more. Note that some banks may only release your funds in local currency, potentially sticking you with a poor exchange rate; inquire about this in advance. Money transfer services like **Western Union** are faster and more convenient than bank transfers—but also much pricier. Western Union has many locations worldwide. To find one, visit ■www.westernunion.com or call the appropriate number: in Italy ☎800 788 935,in Australia ☎1800 173 833, in Canada ☎800-235-0000, in the US ☎800-325-6000, and in the UK ☎0800 731 1815. Money transfer services are also available to **American Express** cardholders and at selected **Thomas Cook** offices.

US State Department (US Citizens only)

In serious emergencies only, the US State Department will forward money within hours to the nearest consular office, which will then disburse it according to instructions for a US$30 fee. If you wish to use this service, you must contact the Overseas Citizens Services division of the US State Department (☎+1-202-501-4444, from US 888-407-4747) .

essentials

pins and atms

To use a debit or credit card to withdraw money from a cash machine (ATM) in Europe, you must have a four-digit Personal Identification Number (PIN). If your PIN is longer than four digits, ask your bank whether you can just use the first four or whether you'll need a new one. Credit cards don't usually come with PINs, so if you intend to hit up ATMs in Europe with a credit card to get cash advances, call your credit card company before leaving to request one.

Travelers with alphabetic rather than numeric PINs may also be thrown off by the absence of letters on European cash machines. Here are the corresponding numbers to use: 1 = QZ; 2 = ABC; 3 = DEF; 4 = GHI; 5 = JKL; 6 = MNO; 7 = PRS; 8 = TUV; 9 = WXY. Note that if you mistakenly punch the wrong code into the machine multiple (often three) times, it can swallow (gulp!) your card for good.

TAXES

The **Value Added Tax** (**VAT**; *imposto sul valore aggiunta*, or IVA) is a sales tax levied in EU countries. Foreigners making any purchase over €155 are entitled to an additional 20% VAT refund. Some stores take off 20% on site. Others require that you fill out forms at the customs desk upon leaving the EU and send receipts from home within six months. Not all storefront "Tax-Free" stickers imply an immediate, on-site refund, so ask before making a purchase.

TIPPING AND BARGAINING

In Italy, as in the rest of Europe, tips of 5-10% are customary, particularly in restaurants. Italian waiters won't cry if you don't leave a tip; just get ready to ignore the pangs of your conscience later on. Taxi drivers expect the same kind of tip, but lucky for you alcoholics, it is unusual to tip in bars. Bargaining is appropriate in markets and other more informal settings, though in regular shops it is inappropriate. Hotels will often offer lower prices to people who arrive looking for a room that night, so you will often be able to find a bed cheaper than what is officially quoted.

safety and health

GENERAL ADVICE

In any type of crisis, the most important thing to do is **stay calm.** Your country's embassy abroad is usually your best resource in an emergency; registering with that embassy upon arrival in the country is a good idea. The government offices listed in the **Travel Advisories** feature at the end of this section can provide information on the services they offer their citizens in case of emergencies abroad.

Local Laws And Police

In Italy, you will mainly encounter two types of boys in blue: the *polizia* (☎113) and the *carabinieri* (☎112). The *polizia* are a civil force under the command of the Ministry of the Interior, whereas the *carabinieri* fall under the auspices of the Ministry of Defense and are considered a military force. Both, however, generally serve the same purpose—to maintain security and order in the country. In the case of attack or robbery, both will respond to inquiries or desperate pleas for help.

Drugs And Alcohol

Needless to say, **illegal drugs** are best avoided altogether, particularly when traveling in a foreign country. In Italy, just like almost everywhere else in the world, drugs including marijuana, cocaine, and heroin are illegal, and possession or other drug-related offenses will be harshly punished.

If you carry **prescription drugs**, bring copies of the prescriptions as well as a note from your doctor, and have them accessible at international borders.

The legal drinking age in Italy is (drumroll please) 16. Remember to drink responsibly and to **never drink and drive**. Doing so is illegal and can result in a prison sentence, not to mention early death. The legal blood alcohol content (BAC) for driving in Italy is under 0.05%, significantly lower than the US limit of 0.08%.

travel advisories

The following government offices provide travel information and advisories by telephone, by fax, or via the web:

- **AUSTRALIA: Department of Foreign Affairs and Trade** (☎+61 2 6261 1111 📺www.dfat.gov.au)

- **CANADA: Department of Foreign Affairs and International Trade (DFAIT).** Call or visit the website for the free booklet *Bon Voyage...But* (☎+1-800-267-8376 📺www.dfait-maeci.gc.ca)

- **NEW ZEALAND: Ministry of Foreign Affairs** (☎+64 4 439 8000 📺www.mfat.govt.nz)

- **UK: Foreign and Commonwealth Office** (☎+44 20 7008 1500 📺www.fco.gov.uk)

- **US: Department of State** (☎888-407-4747 *from the US*, +1-202-501-4444 *elsewhere* 📺travel.state.gov)

SPECIFIC CONCERNS

Travelers with Disabilities

Those in wheelchairs should be aware that travel in Italy will sometimes be extremely difficult. Many cities predate the wheelchair—and sometimes it seems even the wheel—by several centuries and thus pose unique challenges to disabled travelers. Venice is particularly difficult to navigate in a wheelchair given its narrow streets and numerous bridges (many with steps). Be aware that while an establishment itself may be wheelchair-accessible, getting to the front door in a wheelchair might be virtually impossible. **Accessible Italy** (☎+378 941 111📺www.accessibleitaly.com)is an organization that offers advice to tourists of limited mobility heading to Italy, with tips offered on subjects ranging from finding accessible accommodations to organizing wheelchair rental.

Pre-Departure Health

Matching a prescription to a foreign equivalent is not always easy, safe, or possible, so if you take **prescription drugs,** carry up-to-date prescriptions or a statement from your doctor stating the medications' trade names, manufacturers, chemical names, and dosages. During flights, be sure to keep all medication with you in your carry-on luggage.

All basic drugs can be bought at Italian pharmacies, and sometimes supermarkets. Pharmacies are incredibly wide-spread but generally quite small, so you often have to ask the pharmacists to receive what you're looking for. Most pharmacists tend to speak at least a little English, and will often be able to guide you towards the purchase you need.

Immunizations And Precautions

Travelers over two years old should make sure that the following vaccines are up to date: MMR (for measles, mumps, and rubella); DTaP or Td (for diphtheria, tetanus, and pertussis); IPV (for polio); Hib (for *Haemophilus influenzae* B); and HepB (for Hepatitis B). For recommendations on immunizations and prophylaxis, check with a doctor and consult the **Centers for Disease Control and Prevention (CDC)** in the US or the equivalent in your home country. (☎+1-800-CDC-INFO/232-4636 ▣www.cdc.gov/travel)

getting around

For information on how to get to Italy and save a bundle while doing so, check out the Essentials section of ▣**www.letsgo.com.** (In case you can't tell, we think our website's the bomb.)

budget airlines

The recent emergence of no-frills airlines has made hopscotching around Europe by air increasingly affordable. Though these flights often feature inconvenient hours or serve less popular regional airports, with ticket prices often dipping into single digits, it's never been faster or easier to jet across the continent. The following resources will be useful not only for crisscrossing Italy but also for those ever-popular weekend trips to nearby international destinations. Be warned—calling some of the phone numbers listed below will cost as much as €1 per minute, so it may be best to use their websites.

- **BMIBABY:** Departures from East Midlands in the UK to Venice. (☎0871 224 0224 for the UK, +44 870 126 6726 elsewhere ▣www.bmibaby.com)
- **EASYJET:** Flies from multiple European locations to Rome, Venice, and Pisa. (☎+44 871 244 2366 ▣www.easyjet.com Ⓢ UK£50-150.)
- **RYANAIR:** From numerous European airports to Rome, Venice, and Pisa. (☎899 018 880 in Italy (Italian-speaking), 0871 246 0000 in the UK ▣www.ryanair.com)
- **STERLING:** Flies from Denmark to Rome, Venice, and Florence. (☎70 10 84 84 for Denmark, 0870 787 8038 for the UK ▣www.sterling.dk)
- **TRANSAVIA:** Flies from the Netherlands and Denmark to Rome, Venice, and Pisa. (☎899 009 901 in Italy)▣www.transavia.com Ⓢ From €49 one-way.)
- **WIZZ AIR:** Flies from many Eastern European destinations to Rome, Venice, and Pisa. (☎899 018 874 in Italy ▣www.wizzair.com)

getting around

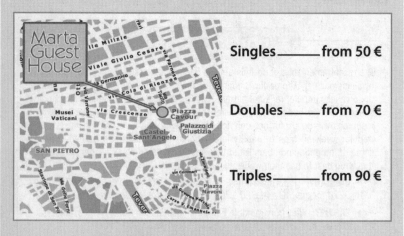

BY PLANE

Commercial Airlines

For small-scale travel on the continent, *Let's Go* suggests taking advantage of **budget airlines**. More traditional carriers have also made efforts to keep up with the low-price revolution, however. The **Star Alliance Europe Airpass** offers low economy-class fares for travel within Europe to 220 destinations in 45 countries. The pass is available to non-European passengers on Star Alliance carriers, including United, U.S. Airways, Continental, and Air Canada. *(💻www.staralliance.com)* **EuropebyAir's** snazzy FlightPass also allows you to hop between hundreds of cities in Europe and North Africa. *(☎+1-888-321-4737 💻www.europebyair.com. Most flights US$99.)*

In addition, a number of European airlines offer discount coupon packets. Most are only available as tack-ons for transatlantic passengers, but some are standalone offers. Most must be purchased before departure, so research in advance. For example, **oneworld,** a coalition of 10 major international airlines, offers deals and cheap connections all over the world, including within Europe *(💻www.oneworld.com).*

BY TRAIN

Trains in Italy are generally comfortable, convenient, and reasonably swift. Make sure you are on the correct car, as trains sometimes split at crossroads. Towns listed in parentheses on European train schedules require a train switch at the town listed immediately before the parentheses.

rail resources

- **WWW.RAILEUROPE.COM:** Info on rail travel and railpasses.
- **POINT-TO-POINT FARES AND SCHEDULES:** 💻www.raileurope.com/us/rail/fares_schedules/index.htm allows you to calculate whether buying a railpass would save you money.
- **WWW.RAILSAVER.COM:** Uses your itinerary to calculate the best railpass for your trip.
- **WWW.RAILFANEUROPE.NET:** Links to rail servers throughout Europe.
- **WWW.LETSGO.COM:** Check out the Essentials section for more details.

You can either buy a **railpass,** which allows you unlimited travel within a particular region for a given period of time, or rely on buying individual **point-to-point** tickets as you go. Almost all countries give students or youths (under 26, usually) direct discounts on regular domestic rail tickets, and many also sell a student or youth card that provides 20-50% off all fares for up to a year.

BY BUS

Though European trains and railpasses are extremely popular, in some cases buses prove a better option. Daytrips from these cities to certain smaller towns may necessitate bus travel, since not everywhere is serviced by a train line. For long range travel, buses are often cheaper than railpasses; **international bus passes** allow unlimited travel on a hop-on, hop-off basis between major European cities. **Busabout,** for instance, offers three interconnecting bus circuits covering 29 of Europe's best bus hubs. *(☎+44 8450 267 514 💻www.busabout.com $ 1 circuit in high season starts at US$579, students US$549.)* **Eurolines,** meanwhile, is the largest operator of Europe-wide coach services. We get misty-eyed just thinking about their unlimited 15- and 30-day passes to 41 major European cities. *(☎086 1199 1900💻www.eurolines.com $ High season 15-day*

pass €345, 30-day pass €455; under 26 €290/375. Mid-season €240/330; under 26 €205/270.
Low season €205/310; under 26 €175/240.)

BY BICYCLE

Renting a bike in Italy is generally quite easy and inexpensive. Many hostels will rent bikes for low prices. For information on bike rentals in individual cities, check the **Getting Around** sections found in this book's different chapters.

Ciclismo Classico, 30 Marathon St., Arlington, MA 02474, USA (☎+1-800-866-7314; ▧www.ciclismoclassico.com), offers numerous beginner to advanced level trips across Italy, including trips through Tuscany, the Amalfi Coast, Venice to Bologna, and the route of the Giro d'Italia.

keeping in touch

BY EMAIL AND INTERNET

Hello and welcome to the 21st century, where you can check your email in most major European cities, though sometimes you'll have to pay a few bucks or buy a drink for internet access. **Internet cafes** and the occasional free internet terminal at a public library or university are listed in the **Practicalities** sections of cities that we cover. For lists of additional cybercafes in Italy, check out ▧cafe.ecs.net.

Wireless hot spots make internet access possible in public and remote places. Unfortunately, they also pose security risks. Hot spots are public, open networks that use unencrypted, unsecured connections. They are susceptible to hacks and "packet sniffing"—the theft of passwords and other private information. To prevent problems, disable "ad hoc" mode, turn off file sharing and network discovery, encrypt your email, turn on your firewall, beware of phony networks, and watch for over-the-shoulder creeps.

BY TELEPHONE

Calling Home From Italy

Without a doubt, the cheapest, easiest, and downright coolest way to call home is ▧**Skype** (▧www.skype.com). You can even videochat if you have one of those new-fangled webcams. Calls to other Skype users are free; calls to landlines and mobiles

international calls

To call Italy from home or to call home from Italy, dial:

- **1. THE INTERNATIONAL DIALING PREFIX.** To call from Australia, dial ☎0011; Canada or the US, ☎011; Ireland, New Zealand, the UK, or Italy ☎00.

- **2. THE COUNTRY CODE OF THE COUNTRY YOU WANT TO CALL.** To call Australia, dial ☎61; Canada or the US, ☎1; Ireland, ☎353; New Zealand, ☎64; the UK, ☎44; Italy ☎39.

- **3. THE CITY/AREA CODE.** *Let's Go* lists the city/area codes for cities and towns in Italy opposite the city or town name or on the chapter opening page, next to a ☎, as well as in every phone number. If the first digit is a zero (e.g., ☎041 for Venice), omit the zero when calling from abroad (e.g., dial ☎41 from Canada to reach Venice).

- **4. THE LOCAL NUMBER.**

essentials

worldwide start at US$0.021 per minute, depending on where you're calling. Skype's only drawback is that it requires an active internet connection.

For those who can't find Wi-Fi or prefer to pretend that it's still the 20th century, **prepaid phone cards** are a common and relatively inexpensive means of calling abroad. Each one comes with a Personal Identification Number (PIN) and a toll-free access number. You call the access number and then follow the directions for dialing your PIN. To purchase prepaid phone cards, check online for the best rates; ■www.call-ingcards.com is a good place to start. Online providers generally send your access number and PIN via email, with no actual "card" involved. You can also call home with prepaid phone cards purchased in Italy.

Another option is a **calling card,** linked to a major national telecommunications service in your home country. Calls are billed collect or to your account. Cards generally come with instructions for dialing both domestically and internationally.

Placing a collect call through an international operator can be expensive but may be necessary in case of an emergency. You can frequently call collect without even possessing a company's calling card just by calling its access number and following the instructions.

Cellular Phones

Sadly, the world refuses to be a simple place, and cell phones bought abroad, particularly in the US, are unlikely to work in Italy. Fortunately, it is quite easy to purchase a reasonably-priced phone in Italy. Plus, you won't necessarily have to deal with cell phone plans and bills; prepaid minutes are widely available, and phones can be purchased cheaply or even rented, avoiding the hassle of pay phones and phone cards.

The international standard for cell phones is **Global System for Mobile Communication (GSM).** To make and receive calls in Italy,you will need a GSM-compatible phone and a **SIM (Subscriber Identity Module) card,** a country-specific, thumbnail-size chip that gives you a local phone number and plugs you into the local network.Many SIM cards are prepaid, and incoming calls are frequently free. You can buy additional cards or vouchers (usually available at convenience stores) to "top up" your phone. For more information on GSM phones, check out ■www.telestial.com. Companies like **Cellular Abroad**(■www.cellularabroad.com) and **OneSimCard**(■www.onesimcard.com) rent cell phones and SIM cards that work in a variety of destinations around the world.

BY SNAIL MAIL

Sending Mail Home From Italy

Airmail is the best way to send mail home from Italy. **Aerogrammes,** printed sheets that fold into envelopes and travel via airmail, are available at post offices. Write "airmail," or *"per posta aerea,"* on the front. Most post offices will charge exorbitant fees or simply refuse to send aerogrammes with enclosures. Surface mail is by far the cheapest but also slowest way to send mail. It takes one to two months to cross the Atlantic—good for heavy items you won't need for a while, like souvenirs that you've acquired along the way, or gifts you're obligated to send home but don't actually care about people receiving promptly.

Sending Mail To Italy

Federal Express offers express mail services from most countries toItaly *(☎+1-800-463-3339 ■www.fedex.com).*

To arrange pickup of letters sent to you while you are abroad. Mail can be sent via **Poste Restante** (General Delivery; **Fermo Posta** in Italian) to almost any city or town in Italy with a post office, and it is generally reliable (though in Italy it's not a surprise for things to be a little untimely). Address Poste Restanteletters like so:

Leonardo DA VINCI
c/o Ufficio Postale Centrale

FERMO POSTA
48100 Ravenna
Italy

The mail will (in theory) be sent to the post office you specify, or if you simply specify the city, it will be held at a special desk in the central post office. It's best to use the largest post office, since mail may be sent there regardless. It is usually safer and quicker, though more expensive, to send mail express or registered. Bring your passport (or other photo ID) for pickup; there may be a small fee. If the clerks insist that there is nothing for you, ask them to check under your first name as well. *Let's Go* lists post offices in the **Practicalities** section for each city.

American Express has travel offices throughout the world that offer a free **Client Letter Service** (mail held up to 30 days and forwarded upon request) for cardholders who contact them in advance. Some offices provide these services to non-cardholders (especially AmEx Travelers Cheque holders), but call ahead to make sure. For a complete list of AmEx locations, call ☎+1-800-528-4800 or visit ▦www.americanexpress.com/travel.

climate

You'd think that Italy was balmy and beautiful, bordering the Mediterranean as it does. And you'd be right—for some places, some of the time. Actually, the country is pretty diverse, climate-wise. Italy definitely has seasons; if you're in Venice in January, you need a coat. A thick one. If you're in Rome in July, you'll probably be asking if it's really necessary to wear more than a bikini to the Sistine Chapel (the answer is unfortunately yes). In general, summertime is hot, sometimes extremely so. Heatwaves are not uncommon, so be prepared to hydrate heavily. Venice tends to be cooler than Florence or Rome due to the pleasant breezes that blow in over the Adriatic, but it's certainly not immune to sweltering summers. Rome tends to be the driest of the three cities and also the hottest in summer. Florence comes somewhere in the middle, with chilly winters, hot summers, and intermittent rain. Long story short, we at *Let's Go* can't really tell you what the weather is going to be like on your trip, so check the forecast before you go. And then don't trust it, because it's probably wrong anyway.

AVG. TEMP. (LOW/HIGH), PRECIP.	JANUARY			APRIL			JULY			OCTOBER		
	°C	°F	mm	°C	°F	mm	°C	°F	mm	°C	°F	mm
Rome	5/11	41/52	71	10/19	50/66	51	20/30	68/86	15	13/22	55/72	99
Venice	1/6	34/43	37	10/17	50/63	78	19/27	66/81	52	11/19	52/66	77
Florence	1/10	34/50	73	8/19	46/66	78	17/31	63/88	40	10/21	50/70	88

To convert from degrees Fahrenheit to degrees Celsius, subtract 32 and multiply by 5/9. To convert from Celsius to Fahrenheit, multiply by 9/5 and add 32. If thinking about that makes your brain hurt, just use this handy chart.

°CELSIUS	-5	0	5	10	15	20	25	30	35	40
°FAHRENHEIT	23	32	41	50	59	68	77	86	95	104

measurements

Like the rest of the rational world, Italy uses the metric system. The basic unit of length is the meter (m), which is divided into 100 centimeters (cm) or 1000 millimeters (mm). One thousand meters make up one kilometer (km). Fluids are measured in liters (L), each divided into 1000 milliliters (mL). A liter of pure water weighs one kilogram (kg), the unit of mass that is divided into 1000 grams (g). Italian food stores will sometimes measure by *ettos*, which are equal to 100g. One metric ton is 1000kg. Again, you should probably just use the chart:

MEASUREMENT CONVERSIONS	
1 inch (in.) = 25.4mm	1 millimeter (mm) = 0.039 in.
1 foot (ft.) = 0.305m	1 meter (m) = 3.28 ft.
1 yard (yd.) = 0.914m	1 meter (m) = 1.094 yd.
1 mile (mi.) = 1.609km	1 kilometer (km) = 0.621 mi.
1 ounce (oz.) = 28.35g	1 gram (g) = 0.035 oz.
1 pound (lb.) = 0.454kg	1 kilogram (kg) = 2.205 lb.
1 fluid ounce (fl. oz.) = 29.57mL	1 milliliter (mL) = 0.034 fl. oz.
1 gallon (gal.) = 3.785L	1 liter (L) = 0.264 gal.

language

It is (hopefully) not necessary to inform you that the primary language spoken in Italy is Italian. Prevalence of English-speaking varies wildly. Rome, Venice, and Florence are all heavily touristed cities (get ready to join the crowds!), and the locals are intelligent enough to figure out that speaking English is a seriously useful skill. It will generally not be necessary to speak Italian at major sights or large hotels. Once you venture to more out-of-the-way hostels or cozy trattorias, however, don't take it for granted that you'll find someone speaking English. You probably won't. That means it's time to dip into *Let's Go*'s ⬛Phrasebook and try to adapt your high school knowledge of French and Spanish into passable Italian. And don't discount pointing and hand signals, the source of endless hilarity, numerous misunderstandings, and occasional epiphanies. Read through the pronunciation tips below if you're planning to try to fit in like a local, although you should probably come to terms with the fact that most people will smell your English-speaking blood from miles away, no matter how much effort you put into saying *"Ciao"* with just the right degree of aloof coolness.

PRONUNCIATION

Vowels

There are seven vowel sounds in standard Italian. **A, i,** and **u** each have one pronunciation. **E** and **o** each have two slightly different pronunciations, one open and one closed, depending on the vowel's placement in the word, the stress placed on it, and the regional accent in which it is spoken. Below are approximate pronunciations.

PHONETIC UNIT	PRONUNCIATION	PHONETIC UNIT	PRONUNCIATION
a	"a" as in "father" (*casa*)	o (closed)	"o" as in "bone" (*sono*)
e (closed)	"ay" as in "gray" (*sera*)	o (open)	"aw" as in "ought" (*bocca*)
e (open)	"eh" as in "wet" (*sette*)	u	"oo" as in "moon" (*gusto*)
i	"ee" as in "cheese" (*vino*)		

Consonants

C and G Before a, o, or u, **c** and **g** are hard, as in *candy* and *goose* or as in the Italian *colore* (koh-LOHR-eh; color) and *gatto* (GAHT-toh; cat). Italians soften c and g into **ch** and **j** sounds, respectively, when followed by i or e, as in *cheese* and *jeep* or the Italian *cibo* (CHEE-boh; food) and *gelato* (jeh-LAH-toh; ice cream).

Ch and Gh H returns **c** and **g** to their "hard" sounds in front of i or e (see above): *chianti* (ky-AHN-tee), the Tuscan wine, and *spaghetti* (spah-GEHT-tee), the pasta.

Gn and Gli: Pronounce **gn** like the **ni** in *onion*, or as in the Italian *bagno* (BAHN-yoh; bath). **Gli** is pronounced like the **lli** in *million*, or as in the Italian *sbagliato* (zbal-YAH-toh; wrong).

Sc and Sch When followed by **a, o,** or **u,** sc is pronounced as **sk.** *Scusi* (excuse me) yields "SKOO-zee." When followed by an **e** or **i,** sc is pronounced **sh** as in *sciopero* (SHOH-pair-oh; strike). The addition of the letter **h** returns **c** to its hard sound (sk) before **i** or **e,** as in *pesche* (PEHS-keh; peaches).

Double consonants When you see a double consonant, stress the preceding vowel; failure to do so can lead to confusion. For example, *penne all'arrabbiata* is "short pasta in a spicy, red sauce," whereas *pene all'arrabbiata* means "penis in a spicy, red sauce."

PHRASEBOOK

ENGLISH	ITALIAN	ENGLISH	ITALIAN
Yes	Sì	Is there a bed available tonight?	C'è un posto libero stasera?
No	No	With bath/shower	Con bagno/doccia
Stop	Ferma	With hot bath/shower	Con bagno/doccia caldo/a
Go	Va'	Is there air conditioning?	C'è aria condizionata?
Goodbye	Arrivederci	Does it work?	Funziona?
Hello	Buongiorno	Do you think I'm stupid?	Pensi che io sono stupido?
High	Alto	I would like to buy a ticket / pass	Vorrei comprare un biglietto / una tessera
Low	Basso	One-way	Solo andata
Why?	Perché?	Round-trip	Andata e ritorno
I don't know	Non lo so	I got on the wrong train	Sono salito sul treno sbagliato
Thank you	Grazie	The middle of nowhere	Nel mezzo del nulla
How are you?	Come stai?	Help!	Aiuto!
I am from the US	Sono degli Stati Uniti	I lost my passport/wallet	Ho perso il passaporto/ portafoglio
I have a visa/ID	Ho un visto/ carta d'identità	I've been robbed	Sono stato derubato/a
I have nothing to declare (but my genius)	Non ho nulla da dichiarare (ma il mio genio)	Leave me alone!	Lasciami stare!/Mollami!
I will be here for less than three months	Lo sarò qui per meno di tré mesi	I'm calling the police!	Telefono alla polizia!
No, I swear, I'm not smuggling anything	No giuro, io non ho nulla di contrabbando	You're going to jail	Si sta andando in prigione
Please release me from jail	Vi prego di liberare dal carcere	Go away, moron!	Vattene, cretino!
Could you repeat that?	Potrebbe ripetere?	And now for something completely different	E ora qualcosa di completamente diverso
I don't understand	Non capisco	You're cute	Sei carino/a (bello/a)
Help!	Aiuto!	Nice dress, it'd look good on my bedroom floor	Bel vestito, sarebbe guardare bene sul pavimento della mia camera da letto
Leave me alone!	Lasciami stare!/Mollami!	I've lost my telephone number, could I borrow yours?	Ho perso il mio numero di telefono, potrebbe prestarmi il suo?
I don't want to buy your souvenirs	Non voglio acquistare il souvenir	I love you, I swear	Ti amo, te lo giuro

essentials

Hotel/hostel	Albergo/ostello	I only have safe sex	Pratico solo sesso sicuro
I have a reservation	Ho una prenotazione	The profound mystery of what you just said sets my soul on fire	Il profondo mistero di ciò che stai dicendo mi infuoca il cuore
Could I reserve a single room/double room?	Potrei prenotare una camera singola/doppia?	Not if you're the last man on earth	Neanche se lei fossi l'unico uomo sulla terra

let's go online

Plan your next trip on our spiffy website, ◼www.letsgo.com. It features full book content, the latest travel info on your favorite destinations, and tons of interactive features: make your own itinerary, read blogs from our trusty Researcher-Writers, browse our photo library, watch exclusive videos, check out our newsletter, find travel deals, follow us on Facebook, and buy new guides. Plus, if this Essentials wasn't enough for you, we've got even more online. We're always updating and adding new features, so check back often!

language · phrasebook

HOTEL NAVONA

Via dei Sediari,
8 00186 Roma
Tel. +39 06 6864203
www.hotelnavona.com

Hotel Navona is situated in the historical center of
Rome, only a few steps away from the splendid Piazza
Navona, an ancient palace of the 1400s where you can
see Roman ruins.

Our convenient location also allows you to reach the
beautiful squares and famous monuments of Rome in just
a few minutes. The Pantheon, the Trevi Fountain, Piazza
di Spagna, St. Peter's and the Colosseum are all easily
accessible and just a stone's throw from Hotel Navona.

Elegantly restructured with care given to every detail,
Hotel Navona offers spacious rooms designed with
ancient caisson ceilings and delicate frescoes and
equipped with every modern amenity—satellite TV, air
conditioning, safes, hair dryers and telephones.

Singles: 90-120 €
Doubles: 120-150 €
Triples: 170-190 €

Benvenuto!

Residenza Zanardelli is an intimate, family-run, 4 star hotel located in the
historical center of Rome. Many well-known sites and monuments,
including St. Peter's Basilica, the Pantheon, the Trevi Fountain, and the
Spanish Steps, are within walking distance.

The hotel is a palazzo constructed in the "Barocchetto Romano" style, one
of the architectural designs most characteristic of the late 19th century in
Rome.

Newly renovated and beautifully furnished rooms await our guests. Each
room has its own private bathroom, satellite plasma TV, telephone and air
conditioning.

Several of the rooms have a direct view of the Palazzo Altemps, which has a
wonderful collection of ancient sculpture.

Residenza Zanardelli

ROME, VENICE, AND FLORENCE 101

Somewhere between the Roman Empire, the Venetian Republic, and the Italian Renaissance, a lot of *stuff* ended up in Italy. Roman-style sculptures, unimaginably ornate *palazzi*, more Roman-style sculptures, and dramatic oil paintings stuff the cities of Rome, Venice, and Florence, and they're all on view for you to enjoy. However, wherever there's a lot to see, there's also a lot to know—from who painted the Sistine Chapel to what the heck a *doge* is and why it had such a nice house. To save you from looking like a tool when you can't tell if something's a Botticelli or a Bernini, we've written up some summaries of the art, architecture, and history of this tricked-out triumvirate. Think of it as Art History 101, but with fewer lectures and more penis jokes. There are also tips on how to avoid offending the Florentines, Venetians, and Romans who *aren't* dead. These are some seriously amazing cities with some seriously incredible collections of artistic and historical goods, so read up to make the most of your time here. What else are you going to do on the plane ride, anyway?

facts and figures

- **ROME POPULATION** 2,731,996.
- **VENICE POPULATION** 270,660.
- **FLORENCE POPULATION** 368,362.
- **COINS THROWN INTO THE TREVI FOUNTAIN** About €3000 daily.
- **NUMBER OF BRIDGES IN VENICE** About 400.
- **NUMBER OF BRIDGES IN FLORENCE** A lot less than 400.

history

YES WE (ETRUS)CAN! (BEGINNING OF TIME-753 BCE)

The first evidence of human life in what is now Italy dates back around 50,000 years. However, the most famous Italian remains are somewhat newer: **Ötzi the Iceman,** a naturally formed mummy and archaeological superstar, was found in the frosty Dolomites and dated to 3000 BCE. After Ötzi's tribe, several primitive peoples cycled through the area before **the Etruscans** settled down for good (800 BCE). A relatively advanced society with its own state system (as opposed to a whole lot of chieftains), the Etruscan civilization was only rivaled by the presence of Magna Graecia along the Mediterranean coast. However, it was not long before the **Roman Empire,** that famous kudzu of cultures, overtook both of these early societies.

LITERALLY ANCIENT HISTORY

Kingdom (753-509 BCE)

There are many tales about the founding of Rome, but by far the best known involves two sons of the god Mars, **Romulus** and **Remus.** Given that their mother was one of the sacred Vestal Virgins, the birth of the twins caused a bit of a scandal—in fact, a concerned royal uncle ordered that they be killed immediately. However, the man ordered to do so pitied the helpless infants and instead left them in a basket by the Tiber River. Various accounts exist for what happened next, the most common being that an oddly compassionate **she-wolf** (as in a female wolf, not the Shakira kind) rescued and suckled the twins, caring for them into adulthood. She seems to have raised some ambitious young men, for the brothers founded Rome together in 753 BCE. Fraternal rivalry soon brought this partnership to an end when Romulus, understandably offended when Remus dared to jump over a wall he had built, did what any upstanding man-raised-by-she-wolves would do and killed his brother, thereby ensuring their newly established kingdom would bear his name. Rome remained a kingdom for a couple hundred years, with the Etruscans making their way back into power for a while in the form of the **Tarquin Dynasty** (616 BCE). However, after another big **sex scandal,** a man named Lucius Brutus got the gumption to overpower the Tarquins and establish a Republic.

To the Republic (509-27 BCE)

Contrary to the teachings of your eighth grade history teacher, functional republican government did exist before the United States. Indeed, the Roman Republic had a lot of the staples of a good Republic down—checks and balances, separation of powers, the whole shebang. What it didn't master so well was equality; contention raged between the **aristocracy,** the **patricians,** and the lowest class, the **plebeians.** Despite these tensions, the Roman dominion began to expand way beyond modern day Italy, northward to what is now England and all the way to Iran in the East. This expansion only further weakened the rule of the aristocracy and led to an uprising of slaves, led by ex-gladiator and historical VIP **Spartacus** (73 BCE). When Spartacus was finally stopped by Pompey the Great and Marcus Cressus, another big name decided to throw himself into the mix and quickly overtook these "allies." That's right, **Julius Caesar** emerged as self-declared Dictator for Life in 45 BCE However, we all know that "Life" was not so long—his dear friend **Marcus Brutus** led his assassination on March 15th, 44 BCE After another struggle for power, Caesar's adopted nephew Octavian came out on top and was granted the honorific title Caesar Augustus in 27 BCE.

Age of Empire (27 BCE-476 CE)

Roman civilization reached its largest size during this Empire period, so called after Caesar Augustus took the title of Emperor. Containing 6,500,000km of land at its peak, the Empire asserted its influence over a whole lot of cultures, and this influence is still felt today (see Romance languages, republican governments, etc.). In fact, the Empire was so vast that a third-century Roman Emperor named **Diocletian,** known for his hatred and persecution of Christians, saw fit to divide the authority up among four co-emperors. This worked just fine until Diocletian died and passed the severed empire to his less capable (but more tolerant) successor, **Constantine.** Constantine moved the capital to Byzantium, narcissistically renamed it **Constantinople,** and set the stage for one of the most annoying songs of all time. This reshuffling broke up the already divided empire permanently, leaving a large, successful Byzantine Empire in the East and a relatively puny Roman Empire in modern day Italy. It was all pretty much downhill from there, with Rome's final blow being dealt when a German chief, **Odoacer,** crowned himself king and put the last Roman Emperor, ironically named Romulus, under house arrest.

MEDIEVAL TIMES (476-1375)

Often called the **Dark Ages,** this time period in Italy is probably best defined by religious contention: with the Roman Empire out, the Roman Catholic papacy saw an opportunity to extend its power and began to take action without the emperor's blessing. Case in point: Pope Gregory I independently decided to add Italy to the Holy Roman Empire with the help of a barbarian chieftain named **Charlemagne.** This famous crusader went on to have an illustrious career as Holy Roman Emperor. His disappointing descendants did not—Italy was subject to small but numerous wars for centuries to come. This led to Italy's division into rival city-states, causing cultural and mental divisions that are obvious even today. Division seems to be a theme of the period, in fact, because the Middle Ages simply wouldn't be the Middle Ages without the next big event: **The Western Schism** (1378-1417). It all started when a rebellious Emperor, Henry IV, started a name-calling war with the then-pope, Gregory VII. The conflict escalated until the papacy huffily moved from Rome to Avignon, France, ushering in a period known as the **Babylonian Captivity** (1309-77). To top off all the confusion, three popes simultaneously claimed holiness—sometimes, not even a tall, pointy hat can get you the respect you deserve, it seems. As if this papal politicking weren't enough, the tragedy that was the **Bubonic Plague** swept through Europe, killing a third of the total population.

RINASCIMENTO (1375-1540)

The more secular humanism of the Italian Renaissance can be, in part, attributed to the political shifts that accompanied it. A number of ancient Italian families who exercised a positively papal power over their respective city-states gradually grew to rival the Holy Roman Emperor. The most famous of these families, the **Medici** of Florence, set the standard for Renaissance rule, shifting their focus from banking and stabbing people to patronizing the arts. They even fought with the pope himself (Julius II) to bring the artist **Michelangelo** to Florence. However, just as humanitarianism was beginning to flourish, a wet blanket of a friar named **Girolamo Savonarola** stepped up and fought ferociously against what he considered "excesses of the church." In 1497, he and his followers burned thousands of "blasphemous" books, works of art, musical instruments, and other tools of sin in what became known as **The Bonfire of the Vanities.** Boticelli even got in on the action, apparently realizing the error of his myth-painting ways. Savonarola was a controversial hero until the Pope realized what a threat he had become and excommunicated him. In the end, Savonarola found himself rejected on all sides, as he was eventually executed by the very same Florentines who had previously been his partners in arson. Meanwhile, the feuding Italian princes left the country open to more petty wars, and Spanish armies quickly jumped at the opportunity to invade. By 1540, Spain controlled all Italian cities except Venice.

DIVIDED AND CONQUERED (1540-1815)

Divided and under the rule of the Spanish Habsburgs, Italy had fallen a long way from its powerful beginnings. When the last Habsburg ruler, Charles II, died in 1700, the country was so weak that the game of **tug-of-war** that ensued as Austria, France, and Spain all vied for possession of the decentralized peninsula was inevitable. After a hundred years of this back and forth, a Frenchman named **Napoleon Bonaparte** came along and settled things pretty quickly: he took Italy for himself. By uniting many of the cities into the **Kingdom of Italy** in 1804 he brought unity back to the broken country and positioned himself as its monarch. After his final defeat at **Waterloo** in 1815, however, the Congress of Vienna re-divided poor Italy and gave much of the power, unsurprisingly, to Austria.

FORZA ITALIA (1815-PRESENT)

With newfound national spirit, the Italians revolted against this latest injustice: the Risorgimiento, a nationalist movement, was born. Superstars of this rebellion included **Giuseppe Mazzini**, **Giuseppe Garibaldi**, and **Camillo Cavour**, whose efforts culminated with the political unification of Italy in 1860. Despite persistent intra-country conflicts, Italy remained unified throughout the centuries to come, with World War I only adding to the country's nationalistic spirit. A gifted orator named **Benito Mussolini** piggybacked on such patriotic fervor, promising Italians order and stability as well as the rise of a "Third Rome." Unfortunately, his idea of order and stability included the establishment of the world's first fascist regime in 1922. Not all Italians were thrilled with this development—sentiment towards Mussolini ran the gamut from total devotion to fierce opposition. Debate over Mussolini became a moot point, however, as Italy entered the World War II on the side of the Axis, and **Nazi occupation** redefined Italy's political reality.

In 1945 the occupation ended, ushering in the modern era of Italian politics. The current constitution, instituted in 1948, allows for a democratic republic, with a president, a prime minister, a bicameral parliament, and an independent judiciary. Though the government has changed nearly 60 times since, one element remains consistent: powerful, bold leaders. Self-made tycoon **Silvio Berlusconi** is the latest in this colorful lineup, elected as prime minister in 1999...and 2001...and 2008, with plenty of corruption scandals as well as two resignations in between. Berlusconi's middle-right stance aligned him with American President George Bush and the Iraq war. Though the unpopularity of this decision opened the doors for the more liberal Romano Prodi to move into power, Italians have proven themselves to be more forgiving than the oft-divorced Berlusconi's ex- and estranged wives, as this philanderer now once again serves as Prime Minister of Italy.

customs and etiquette

Undeniably a friendly bunch, Italians do have their own ways of doing things, and if you want to fit in, you might need a small course in Italian etiquette. Chances are, with 4,000,000 visitors each year, they'll still know you're a tourist, but at least they'll think you're a polite one.

AT THE CLUB

Italians place a lot of emphasis on first impressions, so don't get yourself into a *mi scusi* situation. When meeting someone for the first time, a handshake is the way to go—**air kissing** (left side first!) generally comes with a little more familiarity. The Italian people are known to stand pretty close, so get ready to readjust your personal space boundaries. When it comes to clothing, Italians find having *bella figura*, or a good image, very important and tend to value quality over quantity. They dress formally more frequently than Americans. Women should be warned that short skirts and shorts are considered slightly more risqué in Italy than America, though revealing tops are a little less so.

AT THE TABLE

Italian mealtime etiquette is not so very different from American—at home, courses are served one by one and passed around the table, and at restaurants, the waiter should bring all dishes at once. What you may not be used to are the meal*times:* lunch is usually served anywhere from 1-3pm, and dinner can be as late as 10pm. As for formal table manners, if you're concerned about looking like a foreigner, then remember to keep your fork in your left hand and your knife in your right hand at all times, **Continental-style.** It isn't offensive to switch the fork hand, but it is conspicuous. Finger food is rare—even fruit is generally eaten with a fork and knife at the table. Finally, be sure to ask for seconds when they're available. Not only will you most likely want them, you'll also win brownie points for your *buone maniere.*

art and architecture

ROME

Roman Republic

The earliest Romans left few traces of their Etruscan influence—the remains of simple **dome houses** and **tombs** commemorate a young city better known for fending off barbarians than for intricate arts and crafts. As Rome grew, practical concerns of safety and sanitation were addressed with new city walls and Rome's first major **aqueducts**. Fed up with horse-and-carriage gridlock, Romans began construction of their first superhighway, the **Via Appia,** in 312 BCE, finishing 132 mi. of road during the first year of work. Republican portrait sculpture, all the rage in this period, emphasized realism: sculptors had no qualms about featuring their patrons' physical imperfections—warts, scars, and all.

Roman Empire

While earlier sculptors and painters idolized (and plagiarized) Greek tradition, the Imperial Period brought fresh innovation. Rome's increasingly wealthy upper class developed a taste for luxury, from decorative frescoes to intricate wall-sized mosaics, on subjects ranging from **octopi** and **mythical beasts** to the famous **Bikini Girls** (300 CE). Sculpture blended art and propaganda—emperors, tired of the brutal honesty of Republican portraiture, commissioned idealized self-portraits that likened them to the gods. For a classic example, see the impressive **Augustus of Prima Porta** (20 BCE). Architecture evolved into the arch-crazy, column-obsessed style of the **Colosseum.** Constructed in the first century CE, the Colosseum could accommodate an audience of 50,000 to view elaborate shows featuring gladiatorial combat; hunts of hippos, giraffes, and lions; and even staged naval battles. The **Pantheon,** complete with a concrete dome weighing 4,500,000kg, and the **Baths of Caracalla,** a 33-acre complex with heated swimming pools and even a public library, are other examples of Imperial architecture's epic scale.

Early Christian and Byzantine

After the **Edict of Thessalonica** in 380 CE, Christian themes began to dominate Roman art. No painting or mosaic was complete without one or more haloed figures, and some individuals were even featured with fashionable **square** or **triangular halos**. New monuments, from the Old St. Peter's Basilica (330 CE) to the magnificent Arch of Constantine (315 CE), glorified the city's two most important figures: God and the emperor (which of the two was most important was up for debate). Romans were hard at work beneath the city as well, creating an extensive network of tunnels, including the 15km **Catacombs of Domitilla**, which feature an elaborate fresco of the Last Supper.

Romanesque and Gothic

The Romanesque Period, as the name oh-so-subtly hints, drew its inspiration from the arches and columns of ancient Rome. Churches were modeled on ancient legal courts, complete with broad aisles and extensive seating to accommodate the pious masses. By the end of the 12th century, stuffy, small-windowed Romanesque churches had started to bore churchgoers, allowing the Gothic style of **soaring ceilings** and **large windows** to rise in popularity. Gothic artist **Giotto** (1266-1337) left his mark on Rome with the *Stefaneschi Triptych* (1320), which stood on the altar of the Old St. Peter's Basilica.

Renaissance

The Renaissance lived up to its name: art broke free from static tradition and was reborn with the greatest degree of expressiveness seen in centuries. Under the brush-strokes of masters like **Raphael** (1483-1520) and **Michelangelo** (1475-1564), stiff portraits of saints gave way to natural-looking figures. Only 37 years old when he died (allegedly after a night of excessive exertion with his mistress), Raphael left an impressive volume of work and an enduring legacy. His heavenly *Transfiguration* (1520) and his Vatican fresco *The School of Athens* (1511) are among the finest examples of his work. Michelangelo was similarly prolific both as a sculptor and painter, crafting his masterpiece *La Pietà* (1499) at the age of 25 before painting the frescoes of the **Sistine Chapel** (1508-12) and *The Last Judgment* (1541). Michelangelo's work was not without controversy, however—the Church accused him of obscenity for painting so many **naked figures** in the holiest of churches and hired painter Daniele da Volterra, nicknamed *Il Braghettone* ("the breeches maker"), to cover up the figures. Architecture also flourished during the Renaissance. **Donato Bramante** (1444-1514), who created the original designs for **St. Peter's Basilica** and planned the *Tempietto* (1502), a picture-perfect example of Renaissance style, led the movement.

Baroque and Rococo

Baroque art drew much of its inspiration from past masters but favored **super-realism,** achieved through the use of bright colors and **chiaroscuro,** dramatic contrasts between light and dark. The master of Baroque painting was **Caravaggio** (1573-1610), whose striking use of light and intensely emotional works brought him renown. Yet Caravaggio was as notorious as he was famous—he regularly engaged in **deadly brawls** and allegedly decided that a well-known prostitute was the perfect model for his church-funded painting of the Virgin Mary. Baroque sculptor **Bernini**, obsessed with fusing architecture and art into a unified whole, designed the colonnade of St. Peter's Piazza and crafted masterpieces like *The Rape of Proserpina* (1622) and *Apollo and Daphne* (1625). Eventually fed up with harsh contrast and often-violent scenes, Rome made a 180-degree turn away from Baroque drama towards frou-frou Rococo. Rococo decorations—think ornate seashells, vines, and flowers—adorned works like the famous **Trevi Fountain** (1762).

Neoclassical to Modern

After the frilly designs of Rococo, Rome was ready for a return to simplicity and ancient influence in the form of **Neoclassicism.** Antonio Canova (1757-1822) became Italy's foremost Neoclassical sculptor and was even hired to sculpt the siblings Bonaparte in the nude. The 20th century witnessed the rise of **Futurism,** a uniquely Italian movement that elevated violence, technology, speed, and the modern city in lieu of classical tradition. Artists like **Giorgio de Chirico** (1888-1978) favored bizarre, often disturbing juxtapositions and strange perspective, foreshadowing the birth of surrealism. Fascist architecture dominated the early 20th century, with the construction of the

Esposizione Universale Roma (EUR), a large business complex that includes an angular interpretation of Rome's Colosseum, the aptly named **Colosseo Quadrato** ("Square Colosseum"). The 20th century also brought skyscrapers, leaving Rome an eclectic jumble of architectural styles spanning more than two millennia.

VENICE

Two for the Money

Venice is defined by dualities: isolation from the mainland and integration into a global trading network; competing influences of the East and the West; the unadulterated awesomeness of the fact that the city was built on more than 100 tiny **islands,** and the fact that this makes getting anywhere a complete nightmare. Most visitors to Venice, however, reconcile themselves to this final duality, finding that the canals' romantic nature trumps their inconvenience and embracing the meandering routes they demand. The unique layout of the city and a millennium of self-governance (from the fall of Rome until 1797) have lent Venice a strong sense of identity, though, like most centers of international trade, it owes many aspects of its culture to external influences.

Eastward Ho!

Ever since the Roman Empire split in two, and the province of Venetia was given to the Eastern Empire, Venice's attentions have lain to the east. This oriental focus only intensified when the knights of the Fourth Crusade sacked Constantinople for the umpteenth time in 1204—a very profitable move for Venice, and one that solidified its dominant role in the eastern Mediterranean. The **blend of eastern and western influences** can be seen on the facades of the palaces lining the Grand Canal, the exterior of the Doge's Palace, and the walls of countless other buildings hiding in the corners of the city's watery labyrinth. Gothic elements mix with Islamic and Byzantine motifs to create a uniquely Venetian architectural style. This fusion is obvious in the **Basilica di San Marco**, one of Venice's most recognizable landmarks. Some of the arches look traditionally Italian, while others appear distinctly Moorish. The mosaics on the facade, although an Islamic tradition, are in the Byzantine style, and the tall domes are meant to imitate contemporary Egyptian ones.

Looking back today, we generally view Florence and Rome as the chief centers of the Renaissance. But 16th-century Venetians—as is the wont of northern, east-coast city-dwellers—viewed themselves as superiors rather than rivals of their Florentine and Roman brethren: too wealthy, too powerful, and too busy fighting the Muslim Turkish empire to the east, Venice wasn't about to get caught up in petty skirmishes between city-states.

Paint the Town

In painting as well, Venice was ahead of the game, making the transition from frescoes to large oil paintings on canvas before any other city-state. **Giorgione,** whose works date from around the turn of the 16th century, was one of the first Venetians to switch to the medium of oil on canvas. Like so many great artists after him, Giorgione died young, though the cause of his death was more likely **the plague** than a drug overdose. He introduced to Venetian painting new pastoral themes inspired by ancient poetry as well as an appreciation for the natural landscape that remained a characteristic of Venetian painting for generations to come. Giorgione's paintings have a sort of hazy quality, most likely due to the thicker air that hangs over Venice and its lagoon and through which Giorgione and his successors would have seen the world. From Giorgione to **Titian** (stop giggling—it's pronounced "TISH-un") to **Veronese** and **Tintoretto,** this haziness evolved into heavier brushstrokes and a more dramatic use of light and shadow. This style's influence is also seen in the works of Domenikos Theotokopoulos, better known by his much more marketable nickname, **El Greco.** Though born in Crete, El Greco lived and studied in Venice, where he became a devoted disciple of the aforementioned artists before moving on to bigger and better things in Spain.

FLORENCE

Show me the Money

Although founded in the first century BCE, Florence did not attain its prominence as one of Europe's most important cities until the very end of the Middle Ages, when it began to consolidate its military power in Tuscany and its financial power throughout Europe. The exorbitantly wealthy **⬜Medici** family, leaders of an international finance empire, used their money and clout to become de facto rulers of their city—basically the Mike Bloombergs of the 15th century. Based in Florence but with banks all over Europe, the Medici held the purse strings not only of their city but of the entire continent. Fortunately for the artists of the 15th century (and for the Italian tourism board of the 21st), the Medici were avid **patrons of the arts,** as were the other wealthy Florentine families whose fortunes rose with the city's. Artists also found a patron in the **Catholic Church,** whose ever-influential combination of wealth and spiritual succor made it the inspiration and setting for much of the era's surging artistic expression.

The Works

Florence's most impressive architectural work is **Filippo Brunelleschi's** *cupola* of the city's Duomo (completed in 1436). This egg-shaped dome towers over the city with its stunning combination of sheer mass and geometrical perfection. At the time of the Duomo's construction, it was thought impossible to build a dome so enormous, but the ingenious engineer Brunelleschi solved the problem by using temporary wooden supports. The facade, however, was not added until the 19th century, which, by Florentine standards, is so recent that it still has that new cathedral-facade smell.

In the world of painting, **Giotto** kicked off the 14th century in style, shying away from the flat look of medieval art and developing the more realistic spaces and individualized figures that defined Renaissance painting. This was a crucial stepping-stone in humankind's quest to recreate the world as accurately as possible, an endeavor that has recently reached its peak (or valley?) with the advent of 3D movies. About a hundred years later, **Masaccio** built on Giotto's treatment of space, becoming an early master of the one-point **perspective** that so fascinated Renaissance painters. His major works include *The Trinity*, in the Basilica di Santa Maria Novella and the Brancacci Chapel, where one can find the *Expulsion from Paradise*, along with frescoes of St. Peter performing magic tricks known as "miracles."

In the 1480s, **Sandro Botticelli** painted some of the Renaissance's most enduring images, including *Primavera* and *The Birth of Venus* (today housed in the Uffizi). *The Birth of Venus* is a neoplatonic allegory of divine love—in layman's terms, a really hot, naked chick with a bad haircut. A crisis of faith in his later career led Botticelli to burn much of his earlier work. Given that the very nude *Birth of Venus* survived his post-religious-awakening self-censorship, one can only imagine the kind of racy stuff that was to be found in his less mature work.

Moving from one master to the next, a guy by the name of **Leonardo da Vinci** was also born near Florence, in 1452. Though he apprenticed there for about 10 years, he spent much of his career elsewhere. A jack-of-all-trades and a master of, well, all, Leonardo is often pointed to as the archetypal **Renaissance Man.** Only two of his paintings, an *Annunciation* and an unfinished *Adoration of the Magi*, can be found in the Uffizi, but his influence can be seen in the works of his contemporaries and successors. Among Leonardo's followers was **Raphael,** who incorporated (read: stole) Leonardo's techniques of *chiaroscuro* and *sfumato* to enhance his own compositions.

Leonardo's rival, **Michelangelo,** grew up in Florence as well. As a teenager, he was accepted into the Medici household, where he rubbed elbows with the leading philosophers and artists of his day, including followers of the sculptor **Donatello** (all four Ninja Turtles—check). From 1500 to 1504, Michelangelo carved what are today considered two of the greatest sculptures of all time: the *Pietà* and the *David*. Though the former remains in Rome, the latter is housed in Michelangelo's hometown, in the Galleria dell'Accademia.

music

VENICE AND VIVALDI

Baroque music, which has for centuries fought unsuccessfully to break into the Billboard Top 100, began to take hold in Venice around 1600. As complex and ornate as the canals and the city itself, Baroque is Venice's most famous musical style. Baroque music developed in churches as accompaniment to services, and in orphanages, where children who needed to learn a trade were taught music. One such orphanage was the Ospedale della Pietà, where the composer **Antonio Vivaldi** taught from 1703-17. Vivaldi is best known for his incredibly descriptive *Four Seasons*, which is often considered the most popular piece of classical music ever written. Just don't tell those classical music buffs who roll their eyes every time they hear it played in the corner coffee shop.

Lovers of 🎭opera have Venice to thank, too, for it was here that the first opera house aimed at the general public opened in 1637. Although this theater was demolished in the early 19th century, today Venetians can get their opera fix at the appropriately named *Teatro La Fenice* ("The Phoenix"), a theater that has burnt down and been rebuilt twice, most recently reopening in 2003.

food and drink

ROME

Eating Like a Gladiator

A typical Roman meal begins with an appetizer like *bruschetta*, toasted bread topped with cheese, tomato, and garlic. If you've brought a breath mint, try *bruschetta ammazzavampiri* ("toast so full of garlic it would kill vampires"). After journeying though millennia of art and architecture, replenish your strength with a hearty pasta dish. For simpler fare, order *spaghetti alla carbonara*, pasta topped with a mixture of cheese, eggs, cured pork, and pepper. If you're feeling adventurous, seek out a traditional trattoria and try *rigatoni alla pajata*, pasta topped with the milk-filled intestines of an unweaned calf. For casual fare, look for *pizza al taglio* ("pizza by the slice"). Specialty meat dishes in Rome include *coda alla vaccinara*, savory stew made from veal tail, and *saltimbocca alla romana* (literally "jump in the mouth"), a delicious combination of veal, white wine, sage, and prosciutto. Rome's favorite side dish is *carciofi alla giudia* ("Jewish-style artichokes"), fried and seasoned with lemon and pepper.

Drink Up!

Wet your throat after a long day of trekking around the city with *grattachecca*, hand-shaved ice topped with fresh fruit and flavored syrup. To accompany your meal, Frascati, a chilled white wine produced locally for more than 2000 years, is a divinely inspired bet – Pope Gregory XVI said that it was his favorite wine. Caffeine addicts can get their fix by ordering a *caffè latte* (order a *latte*, and you'll be served a glass of milk). Cappuccino is another classic option, but take note: Italians only drink cappuccino early in the day. For something stronger, sip *Espressodoppio*, a double shot.

VENICE

Italy has some of the best food in the world, but Venetian cuisine is not particularly remarkable. It's hardly surprising that **seafood** forms a large part of the menu, given Venice's geography (its proximity to the sea, that is—the fish on your plate will not come from the *canali* outside). Watch out for the calamari, though, which are often not the fried appetizers found in American restaurants but rather squid cooked in their own ink. However, as is the case anywhere in Italy, you can't go wrong with **pasta.**

FLORENCE

Florentine food is marked by its **simplicity** and devotion to **tradition,** so don't expect to encounter a menu rife with neo-Tuscan po-mo fusion creations at the corner *ristorante*. As is the case with many culinary traditions, Florentine cuisine has been passed down for generations among the peasantry and laboring classes. Thus, the dishes are not elaborate but rely on fresh, high-quality ingredients and the generous use of certain herbs. Traditional first courses include *panzanella*, a bread-based salad, in summer, and *ribollita*, a bread-based soup, in winter. (Notice a pattern?) For a main course, the most famous dish is the Florentine T-bone steak, often simply referred to as the *"bistecca alla fiorentina"* or "really really delicious hunk of beef." And for the more adventurous eater, liver and tripe remain staples of Florentine cuisine.

As in all wine-producing countries, the locals will tell you that their wine is the world's greatest. Tuscany is best known for the **Chianti Classico,** a red wine distinguished by its firm tannins and high acidity—or the black rooster found labeled on every bottle's neck.

literature

VENICE

From the timeless plays of Shakespeare to the more recent Commissario Guido Brunetti mysteries, Venice has served as the setting for centuries' worth of literature. The city is chosen for its convenient location at the crossroads of different cultures, as in *The Merchant of Venice* and the beginning of *Othello*. It is also chosen for its intangible beauty, which in Italo Calvino's *Invisible Cities* can only be depicted through descriptions of dozens of fictional cities that are all—spoiler alert!—pieces of Venice. And it is chosen, perhaps most commonly, because if an author has to bum around somewhere while writing a novel, what better place than Venice? **Visiting Venice after reading a book that takes place there** can add another layer of meaning to one's experience of both the city and the words on the page.

FLORENCE

The Birthplace of "Italian"

Some of the greatest writers of the Western tradition have called Florence "home" (or, more likely, "Firenze"). In fact, when it became necessary to standardize the Italian language after national unification in 1861, it was the literary Tuscan dialect of Florence that became the basis of modern Italian.

Dante Alighieri is Florence's most celebrated author, though Florence can hardly claim credit for his most famous work. *The Divine Comedy* was written after Dante was exiled from Florence in 1302 on pain of death, a sentence finally repealed in 2008 by Florence's very bored or very literary city council. Other members of Florence's illustrious literary culture include the 14th century's **Giovanni Boccaccio,** best known for his satirical and entertaining *Decameron*, and the ruthlessly cynical 15th- and 16th-century **Niccolò Machiavelli,** whose political treatises inspire dishonesty in politicians and distrust among their constituents to this very day.

BEYOND TOURISM

If you are reading this, then you are a member of an elite group—and we don't mean "the literate." You're a student preparing for a semester abroad. You're taking a gap year to save the trees, the whales, or the dates. You're an 80-year-old woman who has devoted her life to egg-laying platypuses and figuring out what the hell is up with that. In short, you're a traveler, not a tourist; like any good spy, you don't observe your surroundings—you become an active part of them.

Your mission, should you choose to accept it, is to study, volunteer, or work in Italy as laid out in the dossier—er, chapter—below. More general wisdom, including international organizations with a presence in many destinations and tips on how to pick the right program, is also accessible by logging onto the Beyond Tourism section of ■www.letsgo.com. We leave the rest (when to go, whom to bring, and how many changes of underwear to pack) in your hands. This message will ■self-destruct in five seconds. Good luck.

greatest hits

- **BE INDIANA JONES, EXCEPT REAL.** Dig up artifacts dating from the first century with real-life archaeologists (p. 272).

- **PERFECT YOUR PIZZA-TOSSING SKILLS.** Apprentice with an Italian chef while studying at a culinary academy in Florence (p. 272).

- **BELLA ITALIANA.** Sure, you can learn how to speak Italian anywhere, but where could be better than in a 16th-century *palazzo* overlooking the Ponte Vecchio (p. 271)?

studying

The best cure for a quarter-life crisis (you know—that moment when, while sitting at your desk attempting to memorize your ten amino acids of the day, you start asking yourself what's the point of it all) is some time spent studying abroad. When going to class means walking by the Roman Colosseum, it's hard to become jaded, and being forced to reevaluate your habits and cultural norms in the full-on immersion experience of a homestay can help you find a refreshingly new worldview. Do your research before you go abroad, keeping in mind that different programs will be populated by different kinds of students (summer programs, especially, tend to be filled with lots of Americans likely to slip into English). Where and with whom you choose to live can have a major impact on your experience. If you are a college student, your local study abroad office is a great place to begin your investigation. Many American universities partner with universities abroad to set up great international opportunities, and some offer foreign campuses staffed by faculty of the home institution.

visa information

All non-EU citizens visiting Italy must obtain a visa for any stay **longer than three months**. You can apply for a student visa at your local Italian embassy or consulate. Make sure to bring a valid passport, visa application form, a passport photo, proof of residency, documentation of the course or program in which you are participating, proof of health insurance coverage, and (if you are under the age of 18) an affidavit of financial support from your parents as well as your parents' most recent bank statement. Within eight days of your arrival in Italy, you will need to obtain a **Permesso di Soggiorno** (residency permit) from your local police station.

UNIVERSITIES

Whether you choose to go through a study-abroad organization or enroll directly in to an Italian institution (possibly a cheaper option), numerous universities will be happy to welcome you to Rome, Venice, or Florence.

International Programs

INSTITUTE FOR THE INTERNATIONAL EDUCATION OF STUDENTS

33 N. LaSalle St., 15th fl., Chicago, IL ☎1-800-995-2300 🖥www.iesabroad.org

Semester, academic year, January term, and summer programs offered in Rome. Instruction given in both English and Italian. Opportunity for enrollment in courses at local universities, term-time and summer internships, "field study activities" (read: field trips), and language improvement. Homestays or apartment housing through the institute.

[i] 18+ for semester programs. College students 3.0 min. GPA, though graduate students welcomed for summer programs. $ Semester $17,615-18,760, depending on location; summer $6550-6698, depending on location; Jan term $3500. Does not include all meals or food costs. Semester price does not include fees for enrollment in local universities.

AMERICAN INSTITUTE FOR FOREIGN STUDY

College Division, River Plaza, 9 W. Broad St., Stamford, CT ☎800-727-2473 🖥www.aifs.com

Summer, semester, and academic-year programs in Florence and Rome. Programs are taught by faculty from Richmond, an American international university based in London. Internship program available in Florence. Courses available in English language instruction, but at least one Italian language course must be taken.

[i] College students; summer program also open to high school graduates. 2.5 min. GPA. $ Semester $15,995; summer $6495.

ARCADIA UNIVERSITY

450 S. Easton Rd., Glenside, PA ☎866-927-2234 🖳www.arcadia.edu/abroad

Semester and year-long programs offered in Florence and Rome. A special program in Rome has a business concentration. During the summer, Arcadia runs Italian language and culture programs as well as special design and intensive fashion design programs in Florence.

[i] 2.7-3.0 min. GPA depending on program. $ Semester $12,500-16,500; full year $21,500-28,850, depending on program; summer $2550-5500, depending on program location and length. Semester and full-year estimates do not include meal costs; summer estimate does not include room and board.

EXPERIENTIAL LEARNING INTERNATIONAL

1557 Ogden St., Denver, CO ☎303-321-8278 🖳www.eliabroad.org

A smaller study-abroad organization, ELI offers summer, semester, and academic-year programs in Florence. Take your pick of a Studio Art, Intensive Italian Language, or Liberal Arts program of study. You'll likely share an apartment about 20min. away from the main campus with a fellow student unless you arrange your own housing.

$ Semester $12,595-13,595 depending on program; summer $4195-5335, depending on program. Does not include meals.

CULTURAL EXPERIENCES ABROAD (CEA)

2005 W. 14th St., Ste. 113, Tempe, AZ ☎800-266-4441 🖳www.gowithcea.com

This company (yes, study abroad has become an industry) will set you up at its partner institutions in Florence and Rome to study for the summer, a semester, or the academic year. CEA's "GlobalCampus"es (GlobalCampi, anyone?) in both cities are accredited by the University of New Haven and offer instruction in both English and Italian; a program in studio art at the Santa Reparata International School of Art in Florence is also available and taught entirely in English.

[i] 18+. High school graduates (some courses require 1 year of college). 2.5-3.0 min. GPA, depending on program. $ Semester $13,495-15,995; full year $25,495-30,495; summer $4395-5795. All cost estimates depend on program and do not include meals.

WORLD ENDEAVORS

3015 E. Franklin Ave., Minneapolis, MN ☎866-802-9678 🖳www.worldendeavors.com

Founded by a dissatisfied IT project manager, this company runs summer, semester, and academic-year programs in Florence. The four-week summer program is an intense Italian immersion, while term-time options can accommodate complete novices to advanced scholars of the language. Housing in shared apartments.

[i] 18+. College students in good standing. $ Semester $12,985; full year $23,000; summer $4850. Does not include meals.

GLOBAL LEARNING SEMESTERS

14525 SW Millikan Way, #32004 Beaverto ☎877-300-7010 🖳www.globalsemesters.com

While you won't find an Italy-only program with this study abroad company, you will be able to choose from their plethora of multi-country summer and semester programs. Summers focus on the Mediterranean, with programs in art and photography, early Christianity, Greek heritage, international marketing, and music that all make stops in Rome. You can also do a semester across the Mediterranean or throughout Europe that will include stays in Rome, Venice, and Florence and may be thematically organized.

i College students with min. sophomore standing. 2.5 min. GPA. [$] Semester $12,950-16,950, depending on program and time of confirmation deposit; summer $6250-6500, depending on when confirmation deposit is made. Does not include meals, except breakfast at hotels during travel.

INTERNATIONAL PARTNERS FOR STUDY ABROAD

13832 N. 32nd St., Phoenix, AZ ☎602-743-9682 🖥www.studyabroadinternational.com

It may be more difficult to arrange credit transfers for classes taken through International Partners for Study Abroad (IPSA)'s programs, which enroll you directly in Italian institutions, but this direct enrollment also could make studying with IPSA in Florence or Rome quite the steal.

i 18+. [$] Semester €2000-6350; summer €900-2950; Jan term €900-1600. Cost depends on location and academic program. Does not include room and board.

LEXIA

6 The Courtyard, Hanover, NH ☎800-77-LEXIA 🖥www.lexiaintl.org

Summer and semester programs in Rome and Venice. Venice curriculum focuses on area and cultural studies; Rome program has options in classical or cultural studies. Housing is generally shared in either apartments or student residences.

i College students with minimum sophomore standing. 2.5 min. GPA in major. [$] Semester $15,750-16,750, depending on location; full year $31,550; summer $7650-7950, depending on location. Does not include meals.

CCIS STUDY ABROAD

2000 NW P St., Ste. 503, Washington, DC ☎800-453-6956 🖥www.ccisstudyabroad.org

Jet to Florence, Rome, or Venice for a summer or a semester, or take advantage of CCIS' three-city program (only available in semester length) and turn your study abroad into a regular sightseeing vacation. You can figure out your own housing or live in a student apartment.

i 18+. 2.5-2.6 min. GPA. [$] Semester $4685-8580, depending on program; academic year $14,800; summer $1640-5925, depending on program. Does not include room and board. Non-NY residents should contact the College of Staten Island for cost information.

INTERNATIONAL STUDIES ABROAD

1112 W. Ben White Blvd., Austin, TX ☎800-580-8826 🖥www.studiesabroad.com

Studying abroad during the summer, over a semester, or during an academic year in International Studies Abroad (ISA)'s Rome or Florence programs means you'll be in an international university filled largely with other Americans, but trips (included in the program fees) to places like Pompeii, Capri, Cinque Terre, and Orvieto may help you escape your English-speaking peers.

i 2.5-3.3 min. GPA, depending on program. [$] Semester $14,500-15,500, depending on program; full year $26,000-29,800, depending on program; summer $4100-8900, depending on program. Does not include meals.

Italian Programs

UNIVERSITÀ DEGLI STUDI DI ROMA SAPIENZA

Piazzale Aldo Moro 5, Rome 🖥www.uniroma1.it

As possibly made evident by the less-than-expert English version of Sapienza's website, those looking to study abroad here should probably make sure they are well-schooled in Italian, though higher-level courses taught in English are available. A summer school in Italian language and culture may be more appropriate for students less confident in their command of the language.

LANGUAGE SCHOOLS

As renowned novelist Gustave Flaubert once said, "Language is a cracked kettle on which we beat out tunes for bears to dance to." While we at *Let's Go* have absolutely no clue what he was talking about, we do know that the following are good resources for learning Italian.

EUROCENTRES

56 Eccleston Sq., London, UK   ☎+41 044 485 5040 💻www.eurocentres.com
Study Italian in a 16th-century *palazzo* near the Ponte Vecchio while following Eurocentres' basic general language or more intensive language and culture programs, both of which can be enriched with add-on packages of five one-on-one lessons.
i 16+. Ⓢ *Semester €3456-4272; full year €5184-8544. 20-week €378-1812; 25-week €450-2244. Cost depends on number of lessons per week and type of program. Does not include room and board.*

A2Z LANGUAGES

3219 E. Camelback Rd #806, Phoenix, AZ   ☎888-417-1533 💻www.a2zlanguages.com
Any of Rome, Venice, or Florence could be the place you master Italian if you study in one of A2Z's numerous programs which vary from one location to the other. All sites service everyone from the complete beginner to the student hoping to master the language.
Ⓢ *$890-5930, depending on program length (2-5 weeks), number of classes per week (20, 25, or 30), choice of accommodations (apartment or host family), and time of year (low or high season).*

AMERISPAN STUDY ABROAD

1334 Walnut St., 6th fl., Philadelphia, PA   ☎800-879-6640 💻www.amerispan.com
With a presence on Facebook, Twitter, YouTube, and Skype, Amerispan may be invading all the newfangled social mediums, but it actually provides helpful information about a bunch of Italian-language schools in Italy.
Ⓢ *$320-3135, depending on program location, length, and choice of accommodations; Switzerland can be considerably more expensive ($6835 more, to be exact). Typical.*

SPRACHCAFFE

Gartenstr. 6, Frankfurt, Germany   ☎+356 25 70 1000 💻www.sprachcaffe.com/english
While you'll be hitting the books in Sprachcaffe's standard 4-classes-a-day curriculum offered at their schools in Florence and Rome, their suggestively titled "Holiday Courses" in Florence cut the workload in half—perfect if your vacation isn't complete without a little homework.
Ⓢ *€210-6555, depending on program location, length (2-5 weeks), number of classes per day (2-6), group or private classes, and choice of accommodations.*

LANGUAGES IN ACTION

💻www.languagesinaction.com
This company that specializes in language schools has more than 20 picturesque locations where you can learn Italian. Classes can be tailored to your interests as well, so if you want to come away with a vocabulary consisting only of cooking terminology, be our guest and put Languages in Action's service to the test.
Ⓢ *€520-3180, depending on program location, number of weeks (2, 4, or 6), choice of accommodations, and type of instruction (group or private lessons, or a mix of the 2).*

FINE ARTS SCHOOLS

Home to the Ninja Turtles of the art world (Leonardo, Donatello, Raphael, and Michelangelo, to be precise), Italy is the place where you too can wield spiffy Japanese weaponry and wear colorful headbands...or, more appropriately, learn how to paint like the masters.

- **STUDIO ART CENTERS INTERNATIONAL, FLORENCE:** Advanced students of the arts can embark on a year of self-structured study in Florence with Studio Art Centers International (SACI)'s Post-Baccalaureate Certificate Program in Art, Art History, and Art Conservation, while more casual artists can take classes in the summer for no academic credit. See p. 272 for SACI's archaeological program. (☎+39 055 289948 🖳www.saci-florence.org)

CULINARY SCHOOLS

While you've probably pulled out your stock Italian accent to gesticulate wildly and cry, "that's a spicy meat-a-ball!" it might be a bit more rewarding to learn how to cook Italian food from people whose accent is of greater authenticity.

- **APICIUS INTERNATIONAL SCHOOL OF HOSPITALITY:** At Apicius' campus in Florence, aspiring chefs, sommeliers, bakers, or extreme foodies can study their hearts out, with one-, two-, and four-year professional programs. Amateurs can also indulge in less intense instruction that may include gastronomic walking tours or visits to local farms and markets. (☎+39 055 265 81.35 🖳www.apicius.it)

SCHOOLS FOR INDIANA JONES WANNABES

While you may not discover the Temple of Doom, you might just find something even cooler: real artifacts from ancient Etruscan and Roman civilizations.

- **ARCHAEOSPAIN:** Check out the "ancient pottery dump" of Monte Testaccio in Rome. If that doesn't sound super-appealing, maybe knowing that the artifacts you'll be digging up date from the first to third centuries will make the excavation more exciting. Anyone 18+ welcome, and academic credit is available. (☎866-932-0003 🖳www.archaeospain.com)

- **STUDIO ART CENTERS INTERNATIONAL, FLORENCE:** While offering a comprehensive arts program, SACI also hosts a two-course summer program on archaeology that includes field work at the school's excavation site in Tuscany as well as study of Etruscan art and civilization. (☎+39 055 289948 🖳www.saci-florence.org)

volunteering

If you're that glutton for punishment who can't help feeling a pang of guilt while on vacation (Must offset the carbon emissions of my plane flight! Think of the baby seals I could be saving if I wasn't wandering the halls of the Uffizi!), perhaps it's time to consider traveling in Rome, Venice, and Florence as a volunteer. There are loads of opportunities to enjoy the beautiful canals of Venice, the rich history of Rome, or the artistic brilliance of Florence as a summer or year-long volunteer. In the listings below, you'll find a mix of organizations, some of which you can contact directly and others that are umbrella organizations with sweet hook-ups to local projects. In some cases, you will pay a fee for this service, but consider what a less altruistic vacation would cost you and then evaluate volunteer prices in that light. When choosing an organization with which to volunteer, always make an effort to speak with past participants, investigate how your participation fee is spent, and check out the group's reputability in order to ensure that your efforts are serving the people, creatures, or issues you signed up to help in the first place. The International Volunteer Programs Association has a user-friendly website (🖳www.volunteerinternational.org) that should help you as you plan your volunteering vacation.

ARCHAEOLOGY AND HISTORICAL RESTORATION

- **ARCHEO VENEZIA:** Organizes archaeological summer camps in which participants work to preserve the historical artifacts in the northern part of Venice's lagoon. Recommended for those comfortable with Italian. (☎041 71 05 15 ■www.archeove. com)

COMMUNITY OUTREACH AND ACTIVISM

- **GLOBAL VOLUNTEERS:** Teach English to adorable *bambini* in southern Italy. (☎800-487-1074 ■www.globalvolunteers.org)
- **MANI TESE:** This organization, committed to the fight against world hunger and with a particular focus on inequities between the north and south of the world, organizes summer work camps throughout Italy that focus on sustainability and "food sovereignty." (■www.manitese.it)
- **UNITED PLANET:** This international non-profit organizes "volunteer quests" in partnership with local programs in need of volunteers. Several such projects are available in Italy for lengths of four weeks to three months and offer the opportunity to experience a high level of cultural immersion while assisting disabled people or the elderly. (☎800-292-2316 ■www.unitedplanet.org)

FOR THE UNDECIDED ALTRUIST

- **SERVICE CIVIL INTERNATIONAL (SCI):** SCI lists a select number of service opportunities (30-40 total in Italy) but includes a wide range of project types, with activities ranging from restoration of a historical agricultural building in Pavia to the staffing of an environmentally-friendly youth festival near Bologna. (☎434-336 3545 ■www.sci-ivs.org)
- **VOLUNTEERS FOR PEACE:** Lists more than 70 volunteer opportunities in Italy, ranging from prepping a puppetry festival in Pinerolo (just hope that none of those puppets turn into real boys) to working at a summer animation camp for Arabic-speaking immigrant children in Turin. (☎802-259-2759 ■www.vfp.org)

working

While it might seem strange to travel to another country to work, Italy offers many singular experiences that you just can't replicate elsewhere. You'll experience cultural immersion like no other and have unique stories to tell when you return home. Work visas are necessary for stays longer than three months, so make sure to determine your plans in advance if you intend to work for an extended period. As these pesky documents can be difficult to obtain (see "more visa information," below), short-term work is easier to come by, especially in agriculture, the service sector, and the tourism industry.

LONG-TERM WORK

If you're serious about finding a job in Italy, make the **Sezione Circoscrizionate per l'Impiego** (government employment agency) your friend and register with the nearest employment office *(ufficio di collocamento)*. Be persistent and creative in your job hunt and consider checking out the tips offered on the wealth of expat websites floating around the interwebs. Keep in mind, however, that Italy suffers from a relatively high level of unemployment. For the student working in Italy, an internship or au pair position are probably the most reliable long-term options.

Teaching English

If you are not an EU citizen, getting a job teaching English in Italy will likely be a daunting task. Use the sites listed below to conduct your own investigation into the possibilities available to you. In the end, a long-term position may not be in the cards. Instead, consider a summertime camp counselor gig or dabble in freelance tutoring.

beyond tourism

- **ASSOCIAZIONE CULTURALE LINGUISTA EDUCATIONAL (ACLE):** This non-profit brings English to Italian children through the use of games, songs, and drama. Employees can act as counselors for the organization's summer camps and, during the school year, as English tutors, language school staff members, actors in ACLE's traveling theater program, or office assistants. (☎+39 018 450 6070 🖳www.acle.org)

- **ASSOCIAZIONE ITALIANA SCUOLE DI LINGUE:** One of Italy's largest English-language education providers. Pays teachers by the hour and gives preference to EU nationals. (🖳www.aisli.com)

- **ESL BASE:** This site is a helpful resource for those investigating the possibility of traveling through Italy on the strength of their English. (🖳www.eslbase.com)

- **INLINGUA:** Another of Italy's major English-language schools has branches in Rome and Florence. EU nationals often preferred. (🖳www.inlingua.com)

- **OXFORD SEMINARS:** Provides a ton of helpful information, including detailed explanations of how to obtain work visas for citizens of all different countries hoping to teach in Italy. (🖳www.oxfordseminars.com)

- **TEACHING ENGLISH AS A FOREIGN LANGUAGE:** A great source for listings as well as lots of information about how to get started as an English-language teacher. (🖳www.tefl.com)

- **TRANSITIONS ABROAD:** This extensive website's section on teaching English in Italy contains a mother lode of tips on finding teaching positions in Italy, many of them the result of the writers' first-hand experiences. (🖳www.transitionsabroad.com/listings/work/esl/index.shtml)

- **WANTED IN ROME:** A Craigslist-style assortment of listings and adverts for Rome. Sometimes postings looking for English teachers or tutors pop up, and given the difficulty of securing a long-term English-teaching post in Italy, finding more informal positions on this kind of listing service may lead to more job offers. (🖳www.wantedinrome.com)

Au Pair Work

If you find a family that will take you on for three months or less, you should be free to Mary Poppins your heart out as an au pair in Italy. Non-EU citizens hoping to take a job longer than three months will have to apply for a Long-Stay Au Pair Visa, which requires enrollment in Italian-language courses while working as an au pair. A spoonful of sugar helps the medicine go down, so make sure to indulge in a lot of gelato if you choose this option.

- **AU PAIR.COM:** Families post listings directly to this site. (🖳www.aupair.com)

- **AUPAIRCONNECT:** Potential au pairs and families can sign up to this service that matches them up for free. (🖳www.aupairconnect.com)

- **AUPAIR WORLD:** Gives free access to au pair listings from around the world and includes information about au pair and host family responsibilities. (🖳www.aupairworld.net)

- **CHILDCARE INTERNATIONAL:** Lists au pair opportunities throughout Europe, including Italy. (🖳www.childint.co.uk)

- **GEOVISIONS:** Be an au pair in Italy for two months to one year in this company's program. The site also includes details about how to obtain the Long-Stay Au Pair Visa for jobs of more than three months. *(☎877-949-9998 🖳www.geovisions.org)*
- **GREAT AU PAIR:** American website with au pair listings by location and country in English. *(🖳www.greataupair.com)*
- **NEW AUPAIR.COM:** This site offers lots of free listings for prospective au pairs as well as information about visas and (out of date, as they will inform you) average au pair salary listings. *(🖳www.newaupair.com)*
- **ROMA AU PAIR:** Places young EU citizens as au pairs with families throughout Italy. *(🖳www.romaaupair.it)*

Internships

Why do one at home when you could pad your resumé in Italy?

- **CENTER FOR CULTURAL INTERCHANGE:** Offers internships in Florence to those 20 and older. Min. stay of 3 months, including 4 weeks of intensive language training in preparation for the internship. Positions available in areas such as architecture, finance, and international business. Interns have the option of living in a homestay that provides 2 meals a day. *(🖳www.cci-exchange.com/abroad/intern.shtml $ $3090-11,850, depending on length of internship and choice of accommodations.)*
- **GLOBAL EXPERIENCES:** Arranges internships with companies in Florence and Rome. Programs include intensive language training, accommodation, emergency medical travel insurance, and full-time on-site support. *(🖳www.globalexperiences.com $ $6890-8990, depending on location and length of internship.)*
- **INSTITUTE FOR THE INTERNATIONAL EDUCATION OF STUDENTS:** Internships for academic credit in Rome during the summer based on availability, background, skills, and language ability. Past assignments at the Museo Nazionale Romano, the Explora Children's Museum, Associated Press Italia, Italian NGO Ricerca e Cooperazione, and Italian think tank Istituto Affari Internazionali. Includes tuition for six credits, orientation, housing, and medical insurance. *(🖳www.iesabroad.org $ $6655.)*
- **PEGGY GUGGENHEIM COLLECTION:** Interns assist museum operations such as gallery preparation, tour guidance, workshops with children, and administrative matters for one to three months. Offers a stipend. Italian skills a plus. *(🖳www.guggenheim-venice.it/inglese/education/internship.html)*
- **WORLD ENDEAVORS:** Three- to six-month internships in Florence in a wide variety of fields, from handicraft apprenticeships to sports training positions with professional *calcio* (aka soccer) teams. Include intensive Italian training and various English-speaking support services. *(🖳www.worldendeavors.com $ $4655-7755, depending on length of internship.)*

Other Long-Term Work

- **BOLLETTINO DEL LAVORO:** A monthly publication available in employment offices and libraries, this Italian job bulletin may be useful to those comfortable with the language and looking for long-term jobs. *(🖳www.bollettinodellavoro.it)*
- **ENGLISH YELLOW PAGES:** Resource for English-speaking expats in Italy founded by an American who relocated to the country in 1984. Includes job listings, classifieds, photos, blogs, and more. *(🖳www.englishyellowpages.it)*
- **ESCAPE ARTIST:** This listings website allows employers to post right on its directory and allows you to search listings by location, employment type, and your work experience. Also posts many articles on living and working abroad. *(🖳www.escapeartist.com/Overseas_Jobs)*

- **EXPAT EXCHANGE:** Includes an Italy forum with articles by Italian expats on everything from having a baby in Italy to where to find the best pizza. Also includes international job listings. (*www.expatexchange.com*)

- **EXPATS IN ITALY:** The subtitle of this website, "for those who dream and those who live the dream," pretty much says it all. (*www.expatsinitaly.com*)

- **WORKAWAY:** Site lists opportunities for work exchange (you work, they provide room and board) that can be searched by region and type of work. Lots of options to turn your man- or woman-power into a "vacation" of sorts at bed and breakfasts and farms in Italy. (*www.workaway.info*)

SHORT-TERM WORK

more visa information

Any non-EU citizen traveling in Italy to work must possess a work visa, a *permesso di soggiorno per lavoro* (permission to stay for those with a work visa), and a work permit. Both the permission to stay and an interim work permit (good for 90 days) can be obtained at the police station of the town in which you are residing once you have received your work visa. While there are many types of work visas, it is quite difficult for most **non-EU citizens** to obtain one of any kind because, in order for the visa to be issued, prospective employers must initiate the process by providing evidence that their foreign employee is both an expert in the field and that his or her employment does not take a job away from an EU citizen. As you might imagine, this process involves lots of paperwork and takes time—basically, it's a bureaucratic nightmare. If you want to give it a shot, your best bet is to bring your passport, proof of residency, a letter explaining the purpose and nature of your trip, your round-trip ticket to Italy, proof of financial means in Italy, and the necessary information from your employer to your local Italian embassy or consulate...and grovel. Visit the Italian Ministry of Foreign Affairs website (*www.esteri. it*) or the US Embassy site (*italy.usembassy.gov*) for more information.

Illegal working is not necessarily frowned upon in Italy. Indeed, the **black economy** is said to thrive in the south of the country, with conservative estimates placing the amount of southern income withheld from Italian tax authorities at **50%**. Itinerant workers are most commonly employed as bartenders or restaurant staff, construction workers, farmhands, tour guides or souvenir vendors, domestics, or language tutors. However, it's definitely illegal for non-EU citizens to work in Italy without a work permit. If you do so, you are liable to a hefty fine as well as deportation. *Let's Go* never recommends working illegally. Foreign students can obtain an **autorizzazione di lavoro provvisoria** (temporary work permit) for part-time work during the summer and term-time. As much as we like a little rule-breaking every now and then, *Let's Go* encourages you to work legally.

- **ALPITOUR ITALIA:** This vacation resort company hires holiday representatives for summer and winter hotels and camps to shepherd guests back and forth from the airport, arrange ski passes and equipment rental, and otherwise take care of clueless tourists. Jobs are competitive, requiring good people skills and good spoken Italian (fluency in other languages a plus). (*www.alpitour.it*)

- **IDEALIST.ORG:** Compiles an international listing of volunteer opportunities and public interest jobs. Several opportunities in Italy that offer room and board in exchange for your work can be found on the site. (📧 *www.idealist.org)*

- **INFORMAGIOVANI:** A great resource for young people (who are fairly fluent in Italian) looking for part-time and temp work, these local information centers found in most towns and cities post opportunities for baby-sitting, tutoring, gardening, and domestic work and also provide information about how to find jobs in Italy. You can post your CV to their website. (📧 *www.informagiovani.it)*

- **SEASONWORKERS.COM:** Lots of different opportunities including jobs as aerobics instructors and ski resort employees. Site also includes information on work visas and permits. (📧 *www.seasonworkers.com)*

- **TRANSITIONS ABROAD:** Check out this website (recommended above for its info on teaching English in Italy) for tips on how and where to find short-term work while abroad. (📧 *www.transitionsabroad.com)*

- **WORLD WIDE OPPORTUNITIES ON ORGANIC FARMS:** As a WWOOFer (there's nothing canine about it, we promise), you'll exchange your time and energy working on an organic farm for room and board. You'll likely undergo a unique cultural immersion, enjoy scrumptious, farm-fresh produce, and have free time to explore the countryside. Two-week trip to Tuscany anyone? (📧 *www.wwoof.it)*

tell the world

If your friends are tired of hearing about that time you saved a baby orangutan in Indonesia, there's clearly only one thing to do: get new friends. Find them at our website, 📧 www.letsgo.com, where you can post your study-, volunteer-, or work-abroad stories for other, more appreciative community members to read. There's also a Beyond Tourism section that elaborates on non-destination-specific volunteering, studying, and working opportunities. If you liked this chapter, you'll love it; if you didn't like this chapter, maybe you'll find the website's more general Beyond Tourism tips more likeable, you non-likey person.

INDEX

index

MAP INDEX

ITALY

Overview IV-V

ROME

Ancient City 37
Central Rome 20-21
Rome Metro 106
Rome Neighborhoods 23
Rome Overview 18-19
Vatican City 48

VENICE

Around Piazza San Marco 129
Central Venice 112-113
Dorsoduro 141
Vaporetti 180
Venice Overview 110-111

FLORENCE

Central Florence 186-187
Florence Overview 184-185
Uffizi Gallery 198

map index

MAP LEGEND

■	Sight/Service	✝	Church	📚	Library	🎿	Skiing
✈	Airport	⚑	Consulate/Embassy	Ⓜ Ⓜ	Metro Station	✡	Synagogue
⊓	Arch/Gate	⚏	Convent/Monastery	⛰	Mountain	☎	Telephone Office
$	Bank	⚓	Ferry Landing	☪	Mosque	♉	Theater
⛱	Beach	☉	Gondola Station	🏛	Museum	ⓘ	Tourist Office
🚌	Bus Station	347	Highway Sign	℞	Pharmacy	⟊	Traghetto Stop
✪	Capital City	✚	Hospital	⛊	Police	🚂	Train Station
♜	Castle	💻	Internet Cafe	✉	Post Office	ⱴ	Vaporetto Stop

The Let's Go compass always points NORTH.

┄┄┄ Pedestrian Zone
▨▨▨ Stairs

Park   Water   Beach

LET'S GO!

THE STUDENT TRAVEL GUIDE

These Let's Go guidebooks are available at bookstores and through online retailers:

EUROPE
Let's Go Amsterdam & Brussels, 1st ed.
Let's Go Berlin, Prague & Budapest, 2nd ed.
Let's Go France, 32nd ed.
Let's Go Europe 2011, 51st ed.
Let's Go European Riviera, 1st ed.
Let's Go Germany, 16th ed.
Let's Go Great Britain with Belfast and Dublin, 33rd ed.
Let's Go Greece, 10th ed.
Let's Go Istanbul, Athens & the Greek Islands, 1st ed.
Let's Go Italy, 31st ed.
Let's Go London, Oxford, Cambridge & Edinburgh, 2nd ed.
Let's Go Madrid & Barcelona, 1st ed.
Let's Go Paris, 17th ed.
Let's Go Rome, Venice & Florence, 1st ed.
Let's Go Spain, Portugal & Morocco, 26th ed.
Let's Go Western Europe, 10th ed.

UNITED STATES
Let's Go Boston, 6th ed.
Let's Go New York City, 19th ed.
Let's Go Roadtripping USA, 4th ed.

MEXICO, CENTRAL & SOUTH AMERICA
Let's Go Buenos Aires, 2nd ed.
Let's Go Central America, 10th ed.
Let's Go Costa Rica, 5th ed.
Let's Go Costa Rica, Nicaragua & Panama, 1st ed.
Let's Go Guatemala & Belize, 1st ed.
Let's Go Yucatán Peninsula, 1st ed.

ASIA & THE MIDDLE EAST
Let's Go Israel, 5th ed.
Let's Go Thailand, 5th ed.

Exam and desk copies are available for study-abroad programs and resource centers.
Let's Go guidebooks are distributed to bookstores in the U.S. through Publishers Group West and through Publishers Group Canada in Canada.
For more information, email letsgo.info@perseusbooks.com.

ACKNOWLEDGMENTS

BRONWEN THANKS: Cheez-Its, 30 Rock, Bob Dylan, Diet Dr. Pepper, and Giants baseball for getting me through it. Conor, for keeping me caffeinated and making sure I wasn't dead on the road. *Grazie galore* to Momo and Migs for introducing me to Italy—you couldn't have picked a better place than The Eternal City. To my RWs: I hope this book lives up to your memories of these cities. You made wish I was eating at a trattoria in Trastevere, tanning on the beach at Lido, or traipsing through the Boboli Gardens. Props to Marykate, her ikon magic, and *Annunciation* incarnations. Also a big shout-out to Rossi and the Masthead team of P1ers who gave us your time. **Chris,** I'm not Thumbpicking you just because you already T-picked me, but because I feel so fortunate to have worked with you all summer. If there are any errors in this book, they're mine.

CHRIS THANKS: **Bronwen,** for being the hardest-working person at LGHQ and an awesome person at the same time. Marykate, for remarkable patience in the face of an avalanche of questions. My RWs, for each bringing their own style and personality to this book, for being great at their jobs, and for a whole load of amity. DChoi and all of Prod land, for coming to the rescue countless times. *Let's Go Italy 1982*, for being totally baller. Any product preceded by the letter G, for making everything so much easier. Kirkland House, for being so damn fine. Catan, for the settlers. Tanjore, for feeding me. No thanks to the Nepalese flag, the Social Security Administration, or any and all Florentine purse-snatchers. Finally, the most special thanks to Area 51, for three years of happiness; my family, for 22 years of the same; and PJ, for everything.

DIRECTOR OF PUBLISHING   Ashley R. Laporte
EXECUTIVE EDITOR   Nathaniel Rakich
PRODUCTION AND DESIGN DIRECTOR   Sara Plana
PUBLICITY AND MARKETING DIRECTOR   Joseph Molimock
MANAGING EDITORS   Charlotte Alter, Daniel Barbero, Marykate Jasper, Iya Megre
TECHNOLOGY PROJECT MANAGERS   Daniel J. Choi, C. Alexander Tremblay
PRODUCTION ASSOCIATES   Rebecca Cooper, Melissa Niu
FINANCIAL ASSOCIATE   Louis Caputo

DIRECTOR OF IT   Yasha Iravantchi
PRESIDENT   Meagan Hill
GENERAL MANAGER   Jim McKellar

LET'S GO
masthead

ABOUT LET'S GO

THE STUDENT TRAVEL GUIDE

Let's Go publishes the world's favorite student travel guides, written entirely by Harvard students. Armed with pens, notebooks, and a few changes of clothes stuffed into their backpacks, our student researchers go across continents, through time zones, and above expectations to seek out invaluable travel experiences for our readers. Because we are a completely student-run company, we have a unique perspective on how students travel, where they want to go, and what they're looking to do when they get there. If your dream is to grab a machete and forge through the jungles of Costa Rica, we can take you there. If you'd rather bask in the Riviera sun at a beachside cafe, we'll set you a table. In short, we write for readers who know that there's more to travel than tour buses. To keep up, visit our website, www.letsgo.com, where you can sign up to blog, post photos from your trips, and connect with the Let's Go community.

TRAVELING BEYOND TOURISM

We're on a mission to provide our readers with sharp, fresh coverage packed with socially responsible opportunities to go beyond tourism. Each guide's Beyond Tourism chapter shares ideas about responsible travel, study abroad, and how to give back to the places you visit while on the road. To help you gain a deeper connection with the places you travel, our fearless researchers scour the globe to give you the heads-up on both world-renowned and off-the-beaten-track opportunities. We've also opened our pages to respected writers and scholars to hear their takes on the countries and regions we cover, and asked travelers who have worked, studied, or volunteered abroad to contribute first-person accounts of their experiences.

FIFTY-ONE YEARS OF WISDOM

Let's Go has been on the road for 51 years and counting. We've grown a lot since publishing our first 20-page pamphlet to Europe in 1960, but five decades and 60 titles later, our witty, candid guides are still researched and written entirely by students on shoestring budgets who know that train strikes, stolen luggage, food poisoning, and marriage proposals are all part of a day's work. Meanwhile, we're still bringing readers fresh new features, such as a student-life section with advice on how and where to meet students from around the world; a revamped, user-friendly layout for our listings; and greater emphasis on the experiences that make travel abroad a rite of passage for readers of all ages. And, of course, this year's 16 titles—including five brand-new guides—are still brimming with editorial honesty, a commitment to students, and our irreverent style.

THE LET'S GO COMMUNITY

More than just a travel guide company, Let's Go is a community that reaches from our headquarters in Cambridge, MA all across the globe. Our small staff of dedicated student editors, writers, and tech nerds comes together because of our shared passion for travel and our desire to help other travelers get the most out of their experience. We love it when our readers become part of the Let's Go community as well—when you travel, drop us a postcard (67 Mt. Auburn St., Cambridge, MA 02138, USA), send us an e-mail (feedback@letsgo.com), or sign up on our website (www.letsgo.com) to tell us about your adventures and discoveries.

For more information, updated travel coverage, and news from our researcher team, visit us online at www.letsgo.com.

THANKS TO OUR SPONSORS

HELPING LET'S GO. If you want to share your discoveries, suggestions, or corrections, please drop us a line. We appreciate every piece of correspondence, whether a postcard, a 10-page email, or a coconut. Visit Let's Go at **www.letsgo.com** or send an email to:

feedback@letsgo.com, subject: "Let's Go Rome, Venice & Florence"

Address mail to:

Let's Go Rome, Venice & Florence, 67 Mount Auburn St., Cambridge, MA 02138, USA

In addition to the invaluable travel advice our readers share with us, many are kind enough to offer their services as researchers or editors. Unfortunately, our charter enables us to employ only currently enrolled Harvard students.

Maps © Let's Go and Avalon Travel.
Design Support by Jane Musser, Sarah Juckniess, Tim McGrath

Distributed by Publishers Group West.
Printed in Canada by Friesens Corp.

ISBN-13: 978-1-59880-713-4

First edition
10 9 8 7 6 5 4 3 2 1

Let's Go Rome, Venice & Florence is written by Let's Go Publications, 67 Mount Auburn St., Cambridge, MA 02138, USA.

Let's Go® and the LG logo are trademarks of Let's Go, Inc.

quick reference

YOUR GUIDE TO LET'S GO ICONS

☎	Phone numbers	⊗	Not wheelchair-accessible	❄	Has A/C
🖳	Websites	(ᵖ)	Has internet access	⇄	Directions
💳	Takes credit cards	☂	Has outdoor seating	*i*	Other hard info
🚫	Cash only	▼	Is GLBT or GLBT-friendly	Ⓢ	Prices
♿	Wheelchair-accessible	⚗	Serves alcohol	⏰	Hours

PRICE RANGES

Let's Go includes price ranges, marked by icons ❶ through ❺, in accommodations and food listings. For an expanded explanation, see the chart in How To Use This Book.

ITALY	❶	❷	❸	❹	❺
ACCOMMODATIONS	under €20	€20-30	€31-45	€46-65	over €65
FOOD	under €7	€7-15	€16-25	€26-33	over €33

IMPORTANT PHONE NUMBERS

EMERGENCY: POLICE ☎112, FIRE ☎113, AMBULANCE ☎118			
Australian Embassy	☎06 85 27 21	New Zealand Embassy	☎06 85 37 501
Canadian Embassy	☎06 85 444	British Embassy	☎06 42 20 00 01
Irish Embassy	☎06 69 79 121	US Embassy	☎06 46 741

USEFUL ITALIAN PHRASES

ENGLISH	ITALIAN	ENGLISH	ITALIAN
Hi/Bye (informal)	Ciao	Do you speak English?	Parla inglese?
Good day / Hello	Buongiorno	What do you call this in Italian?	Come si chiama questo in Italiano?
Please	Per favore	Is there a bed available tonight?	C'è un posto libero stasera?
Thank you	Grazie	I would like to buy a ticket / pass	Vorrei comprare un biglietto / una tessera

CURRENCY CONVERSIONS

These rates are current as we go to press.

AUS$1 = €0.70	€1 = AUS$1.42	UK£1 = €1.20	€1 = UK£0.83
CDN$1 = €0.76	€1 = CDN$1.30	US$1 = €0.79	€1 = US$1.25
NZ$1 = €0.56	€1 = NZ$1.77	EUR€1 = €1	WOAH!

TEMPERATURE CONVERSIONS

°CELSIUS	-5	0	5	10	15	20	25	30	35	40
°FAHRENHEIT	23	32	41	50	59	68	77	86	95	104

MEASUREMENT CONVERSIONS

1 inch (in.) = 25.4mm	1 millimeter (mm) = 0.039 in.
1 foot (ft.) = 0.305m	1 meter (m) = 3.28 ft.
1 mile (mi.) = 1.609km	1 kilometer (km) = 0.621 mi.
1 pound (lb.) = 0.454kg	1 kilogram (kg) = 2.205 lb.
1 gallon (gal.) = 3.785L	1 liter (L) = 0.264 gal.